Arbitration & the Law

1989–90

AAA GENERAL COUNSEL'S
ANNUAL REPORT

OFFICE OF
THE GENERAL COUNSEL
AMERICAN ARBITRATION ASSOCIATION

Library of Congress Catalog Card Number:
81-70413

ISBN 0-943001-24-2

ORDER FROM:
American Arbitration Association
140 West 51st Street
New York, NY 10020–1203
(212) 484-4011

CONTENTS

PREFACE

In this new edition of *Arbitration & the Law, 1989–90*, the Office of the General Counsel of the American Arbitration Association (AAA) again presents a year's compilation of the latest developments in arbitration and other forms of alternative dispute resolution (ADR). Included in this volume are digests of court decisions and information on legislation, new procedures, and other ADR developments, with expert commentary from both here and abroad.

The case law during the past year addressed a variety of novel arbitration issues, reaffirming strong judicial support of the process. Thus, the U.S. Supreme Court found that a federal statute authorizing a deduction from an Iran-U.S. Claims Tribunal award to reimburse the federal government for its arbitration costs was a reasonable "user fee" that was neither unconstitutional nor in violation of the Fifth Amendment.

There were several notable U.S. Circuit Court decisions this year as well. For example, the *Securities Industry Association v. Connolly*, which addressed the preemptive reach of the Federal Arbitration Act, has added significance in light of the recent enactments of state international arbitration laws, as well as of state efforts to regulate the formation of arbitration agreements in the securities industry. In *Gilmer v. Interstate/Johnson Lane Corporation*, the Fourth Circuit's enforcement of agreements to arbitrate old age claims is but one example of how courts grapple with the application of new arbitration rules to such remedial legislation as the Employee Retirement Income and Security Act and the Age Discrimination in Employment Act. The subject in *Raytheon Co. v. Automated Business Systems* was the broad remedial powers of arbitrators, particularly in cases concerned with the application of a broad range of statutory rights.

In other significant decisions, the courts ruled on the arbitrability of unfair labor practice claims, the enforcement of arbitration agreements between domestic insurers and foreign reinsurers, the appealability of interlocutory orders, and resort to AAA securities arbitration under the so-called AmEx Window of the American Stock Exchange.

There was also considerable activity in the international sphere. Hong Kong has adopted the UNCITRAL Model Law on International Commercial Arbitration. The People's Republic of China enacted patent dispute procedures for the Shanghai municipality. The Hungarian Chamber of Commerce revised its Rules of Procedure for its Court of Arbitration, and the revised Commercial Arbitration Rules of the Japan Commercial Arbitration Association became effective in May, 1989. The AAA signed new cooperative agreements with the British Columbia International Commercial Arbitration Centre, the Chamber of Foreign Trade of the German Democratic Republic, and the Austrian Federal Economic Chamber, reflecting the steady expansion of cooperation among arbitral institutions around the globe.

Domestically, the growing use of ADR techniques is exemplified by the recent statutory enactments. The Americans with Disabilities Act, for example, encourages the use of ADR in an area that is bound to generate a large number of disputes in future years; the federal Clean Air Act providing for the arbitration of automobile emissions disputes shows how some environmental disputes may be resolved outside the courts. Government awareness of the benefits of ADR in the public sector is described in Chapter 4 in the section on the Administrative Conference of the United States. Various states have also enacted legislation, ranging from a new international commercial arbitration statute in Maryland to the voluntary arbitration of workers' compensation claims, the arbitration of customer-broker/dealer disputes, and second-generation lemon law statutes.

We hope that the materials in this volume of *Arbitration & the Law* provide a valuable reference to the dispute resolution community. It should be equally useful to business people, educators, students, and anyone interested in dispute resolution.

MICHAEL F. HOELLERING
General Counsel
American Arbitration Association

1

Commercial Arbitration

A. GENERAL COMMERCIAL FIELDS

CASE DIGESTS

ARBITRATION AGREEMENT—PUNITIVE DAMAGES—AMERICAN ARBITRATION ASSOCIATION—COMMERCIAL RULE 43—ARBITRATOR AUTHORITY

The appellate court held that the lower court correctly ruled that the arbitrators were authorized to award punitive damages.

A subsidiary of Raytheon entered into an exclusive dealership contract with Automated for the distribution of word-processing equipment manufactured by the subsidiary. The contract, containing an arbitration clause, was extended twice. A new contract was tendered by Raytheon but was never executed by the parties, who continued their relationship under the terms of the original contract until Raytheon terminated their relationship. Automated filed a demand for arbitration, alleging, among other causes of action, that Raytheon had breached the parties' agreement, and seeking compensatory and consequential damages. Automated requested punitive damages.

An award including punitive damages was rendered in favor of Automated. Raytheon moved to vacate the award, contending that the panel had not been empowered to award punitive damages and that the award was facially invalid because it made reference to the unexecuted agreement instead of the original agreement under which Automated had brought its claim. The court amended the reference in the award to the unexecuted agreement and confirmed the award. Raytheon appealed.

The appellate court rejected Raytheon's contention that the award should be vacated because the arbitrators did not make any "findings of fact" in support of their award. It also rejected the argument that Raytheon was denied the opportunity to argue the merits of the punitive damages claims during the hearing because the arbitrators never notified Raytheon that they "intended to reach the issue of punitive damages." As to the central issue of whether the arbitrators had the authority to award punitive damages, the court found that the arbitration clause in the parties' contract empowered the panel to do so.

In addition, the court found that the arbitration clause was neither limited in scope nor optional in application. Because the clause required arbitration to be conducted under the American Arbitration Association's Commercial Arbitration Rules, which empower AAA arbitrators under section 43 to "grant any remedy or relief that the arbitrator deems just and equitable and within the scope of the agreement of the parties," the court had to determine whether the parties had intended to include in their arbitration agreement the power to award punitive damages. The court concluded that they had, relying in part on *Bonar v. Dean Witter Reynolds, Inc.*, 835 F.2d 1378 (11th Cir. 1988), wherein the court upheld a punitive damages award. ***Raytheon Co. v. Automated Business Systems,*** 882 F.2d 6 (1st Cir. 1989). [**Editor's note**: at the time of the decision, the AAA rule at issue was section 42. The rule has since been renumbered as section 43, and this digest reflects the updated rules change.]

GUARANTOR LIABILITY—ARBITRATION AGREEMENT—SCOPE OF ORDER COMPELLING ARBITRATION—ARBITRATOR AUTHORITY—ENTRY OF MONEY JUDGMENT

A guarantor to an agreement containing an arbitration clause was held to be bound by the arbitration award only insofar as the merits of the disputes could not be relitigated, and not because the guarantor had consented to arbitral resolution of its obligations as guarantor.

Two telecommunications companies agreed to buy and sell the right to use a certain telecommunications system. NPS Corporation (Corp) had guaranteed that NPS Communications (NPS), Corp's subsidiary, would perform its duties under the agreement with the Continental Group (CGI). The contract between NPS and CGI contained a broad arbitration clause. A disagreement between CGI and NPS arose and CGI demanded arbitration of the conflict with NPS and Corp. Corp immediately responded by requesting a declaratory judgment in state court that CGI had breached the contract before the disagreement arose and that the breach nullified the agreement, thereby extricating Corp from its obligation as guarantor. CGI moved for an order requiring Corp to arbitrate the dispute. The state court ordered arbitration to proceed and gave the arbitrators discretion to determine which issues were arbitrable. It also described Corp as having "implicitly agree[d], for purposes of later determining its liability, to be bound by the resolution reached in arbitration."

An arbitration was held, and an award was rendered against Corp and NPS. CGI moved to confirm the award in district court pursuant to the Federal Arbitration Act. Corp, however, protested the award's confirmation on the ground that the arbitrators lacked the authority to render a monetary judgment directly against it. The district court agreed with Corp's argument, stating that the previous court had found only that Corp must determine its obligations according to the award, and not that the award could hold it directly liable. The court refused to enter a money judgment against Corp. CGI appealed.

The appellate court found that the state court's order compelling arbitration bound Corp to the arbitration award in the sense that the merits of the disputes submitted to arbitration cannot be relitigated. The fact that Corp consented to arbitral resolution of its obligations as guarantor was of no consequence.

The appellate court observed that although the lower court had defined the parameters of the arbitration proceeding, the arbitrators had exceeded those parameters when they sought to render their award directly against Corp. Because the arbitrators had no authority to decide on the issue of Corp's obligations as guarantor to NPS, and because the district court had correctly construed the limited scope of the state court's order directing arbitration, the court affirmed the district court's judgment. ***Continental Group, Inc. v. NPS Communications, Inc.,*** 873 F.2d 613 (2d Cir. 1989).

TEXTILES—CUSTOM AND USE—ARBITRATION AGREEMENT

Because of the manufacturer's customary use of confirmation forms that included an arbitration clause and the distributor's customary acceptance of these forms, an agreement to arbitrate was deemed to exist between the manufacturer and the distributor.

Pervel is a manufacturer of fabrics and wallcoverings. TM Wallcovering distributes Pervel's fabrics. Over the years, the two established a practice whereby TM would place an order with Pervel, which would then return a confirmation order containing an arbitration clause. Many of these forms were signed by TM, which also returned many unsigned forms to Pervel.

A dispute arose, and TM instituted an action against Pervel in state court to recover damages for a monetary loss allegedly suffered because Pervel's goods were non-conforming. Pervel successfully obtained a federal court order staying the state court action and compelling TM to arbitrate the dispute. TM appealed the order.

The appellate court agreed with the district court finding that because Pervel had a well-established custom of sending purchase order confirming forms that included arbitration clauses, TM had agreed to arbitrate any dispute relating to each confirmation form. The court stated that the practice of binding parties to such arbitration provisions, whether or not the forms were signed, was "particularly true in industries such as fabrics and textiles where the specialized nature of the product has led to the widespread use of arbitration clauses. . . ."

Because the arbitration clause bound TM only if the dispute "related to the contract," a finding on the nature of TM's dispute with Pervel was necessary. The appellate court found that the dispute over lost profits directly related to the purchase order agreement. Consequently, Pervel was obligated to arbitrate the dispute, and the district court's order was affirmed. ***Pervel Industries, Inc. v. TM Wallcovering Inc.,*** 871 F.2d 7 (2d Cir. 1989).

AGE DISCRIMINATION IN EMPLOYMENT ACT—EMPLOYMENT DISCRIMINATION—ARBITRABILITY

The court held claims arising under the Age Discrimination in Employment Act (ADEA) arbitrable.

Roger D. Gilmer was hired by Interstate/Johnson Lane as a manager of financial services. He registered as a securities representative with the New York Stock Exchange. The registration contained an arbitration clause requiring the arbitration of disputes between himself and Interstate arising out of his employment or the termination of his employment. Gilmer's employment was later terminated and he filed suit against Interstate, alleging an ADEA violation. The district court ruled that the arbitration agreement was not enforceable. The ruling was reversed on appeal.

The appellate court found that the dispute was arbitrable, reasoning that there is "no congressional intent to preclude enforcement of arbitration agreements in the ADEA's text, its legislative history, or its underlying purposes." The court disagreed with the reasoning of the Third Circuit in *Nicholson v. CPC Int'l, Inc.*, 877 F.2d 221 (3d Cir. 1989), regarding the role of the Equal Employment Opportunity Commission in ADEA claims, and further stated that "[w]e are reluctant to conclude that the mere fact of administrative involvement in a statutory scheme of enforcement operates as an implicit exception to the presumption of arbitral availability under the F[ederal] A[rbitration] A[ct]."

In addition, the court found that the fact that "arbitrators may lack the full breadth of equitable discretion possessed by courts to go beyond the relief accorded individual victims does not deny the utility of this alternative means of resolving disputes.'' It concluded that there is ''no reason . . . why an arbitrator of an ADEA dispute cannot award liquidated damages should he or she find a willful violation of the statute.'' Moreover, as to the ability of arbitrators to decide such disputes, the court stated that

> [i]n ruling that antitrust and RICO claims were not beyond the ken of arbitrators, the Supreme Court brushed aside objections that such statutory claims were too complex for arbitrators to handle. ADEA disputes are, to put it mildly, no more generically complex than claims pressed under the Sherman Act and R[acketeer] I[nfluenced] and C[orrupt] O[rganizations Act].

Gilmer v. Interstate/Johnson Lane Corporation, 895 F.2d 195 (4th Cir. 1990).

WRIT OF MANDAMUS—VENUE—FORUM-SELECTION CLAUSE

The lower court erred in transferring an action without regard to the forum-selection clause in the parties' agreement and in transferring venue of a motion to confirm the award.

Sunshine Beauty Supplies entered into a contract to sell products to Armstrong-McCall. The contract contained an arbitration provision and a forum-selection clause indicating Los Angeles as the appropriate forum. Armstrong refused to pay for goods shipped and demanded that Sunshine take back the goods. Sunshine filed a demand for arbitration with the American Arbitration Association.

Armstrong refused to arbitrate, forcing Sunshine to seek an order compelling arbitration. The order was granted and an award was rendered in favor of Sunshine, which moved to confirm the award. At the same time, Armstrong moved for an order transferring the action to the Western District of Texas. The court granted the motion and ruled that the motion to confirm would be left for the transferee court to decide. Sunshine filed a writ of mandamus in the appellate court.

The appellate court noted at the outset that it has the power to review by mandamus an order transferring a case to the district court in another circuit. It also noted that mandamus relief was warranted in this case because, even though ''Sunshine could appeal after final judgment in the Western District of Texas, the prejudice that results from an erroneous transfer order is of a type not correctable on appeal.'' The court found that the district court erred in transferring the underlying action without giving consideration to the forum-selection clause in the parties' agreement.

The court also considered whether the transfer of venue as to the motion to confirm was in error. Finding that the motion was made pursuant to section 9 of the Federal Arbitration Act and that there was no distinction between sections 9 and 10 of the Act (section 10 limits jurisdiction to vacate an award to the district where the award was made), the court concluded that the lower court erroneously transferred venue of Sunshine's motion to confirm. In accordance with its findings, the court granted the writ of mandamus and directed the district court to vacate its order transferring the action and to render a decision on Sunshine's motion to confirm. ***Sunshine Beauty Supplies, Inc. v. United States District Court for the Central District of California,*** 872 F.2d 310 (9th Cir. 1989).

COPYRIGHT—JUDICIAL AUTHORITY—RECONVENTION OF ARBITRATION PANEL—NEW YORK CIVIL PRACTICE LAW & RULES § 7511(d)

In the absence of corruption, fraud, or misconduct, a court that has vacated an arbitration award should order a rehearing before the same panel of arbitrators. In addition, a New York statute vests courts with the authority to order that the same panel be convened.

Steve Karmen, a jingle writer and member of the American Society of Composers, Authors & Publishers (ASCAP), was involved in a dispute with ASCAP over the allocation of three percent of a "use credit" per performance to jingle writers. A grievance was filed, and an ASCAP board rejected Karmen's claim. On appeal, an arbitration panel affirmed the board's determination. Karmen then filed a court action to vacate the panel's decision on the ground that his due process rights were violated by ASCAP's method of dispute resolution. Karmen also argued that because the grievance procedures were mandated by a consent judgment, there was sufficient state action to warrant constitutional protection.

The court disagreed, holding that the court-sanctioned dispute resolution procedures of a governing organization did not constitute state action so as to allow one to claim constitutional protection of one's due process rights. Because a question arose over whether the arbitrators had acted with full knowledge of the extent of their authority, the court remanded the matter for further consideration (708 F. Supp. 95 (S.D.N.Y. 1989)).

A dispute subsequently arose over a footnote in the court's opinion stating that although efficiency would be best served by returning the matter to the original arbitrators, the matter may be completely reconsidered with a newly constituted panel. Karmen argued that the court only suggested, not required, that the original panel be constituted, while ASCAP argued that a new panel would be constituted only if it were not possible to reconvene the original panel.

The court clarified its footnote by stating in its opinion that its intent was to direct the American Arbitration Association to try to reconvene the original panel. It noted that any court that has vacated an arbitration award should order a rehearing before the same panel, provided the vacatur was not based on corruption, fraud, or misconduct. In addition, the court stated that section 7511(d) of the New York Civil Practice Law & Rules specifically vests courts with the authority to order an arbitration panel to reconvene. ***United States v. American Society of Composers, Authors & Publishers,*** 714 F. Supp. 697 (S.D.N.Y. 1989).

MINI-TRIAL—AGENCY—SCOPE OF AUTHORITY

The court declined to enforce an agreement to resolve a dispute through a mini-trial because there was no indication that the parties intended to bind themselves to the agreement through their attorneys without obtaining the signatures and approval of corporate officials.

Lightwave filed an antitrust action against Corning, which counterclaimed for patent infringement. Settlement negotiations were conducted and the parties, through their attorneys, entered into an agreement to attempt resolution of their dispute through a five-day mini-trial. Signatures and approval of the corporate principals were apparently not obtained. Alleging that Lightwave reneged on the agreement, Corning moved to enforce the agreement.

The court refused to enforce the proposed agreement, finding that Lightwave's attorney lacked the requisite authority to bind Lightwave to the negotiated agreement. In fact, the court determined that the attorney did not agree to bind Lightwave. Moreover, the court also stated that it was unwilling to enforce the agreement because of the ambiguities and misunderstandings between the parties. Finally, because Corning could not prove that the parties intended to bind themselves to the agreement without obtaining the signatures and approval of the corporate officials, the court denied Corning's motion. ***Lightwave Technologies, Inc. v. Corning Glass Works,*** 725 F. Supp. 198 (S.D.N.Y. 1989).

FEDERAL VERSUS STATE LAW—CONSOLIDATION—FEDERAL ARBITRATION ACT—FEDERAL RULES OF CIVIL PROCEDURE 42(a) AND 81(a)(3)

Although a clause in a contract provided for state law to govern, the validity and application of an arbitration clause in a diversity case is still subject to federal law. In addition, a court acting pursuant to the Federal

Arbitration Act (FAA) can compel a consolidated arbitration when the agreements to arbitrate are embodied in separate contracts—even though neither of the contracts provides for consolidated arbitration—because the contracts contain one common party and the language of the arbitration agreements is identical.

Probala entered into a sales representative agreement with Hoover to sell Hoover's products in Ohio. Hoover was also a party to a sales representative agreement with Container Services and Supplies. Both contracts contained identical arbitration agreements and commission schedules. A dispute between Probala and Hoover arose over Hoover's alleged breach of its obligation to pay commissions, and Probala filed a demand for arbitration against Hoover. Hoover, which had paid the commission claimed by Probala to Container, demanded arbitration against Container, seeking a declaration that Container was the party properly entitled to the commission. Because all three parties did not agree to consolidation, Hoover petitioned the court for an order compelling consolidation.

The court noted at the outset that courts do not agree on whether the FAA allows for consolidation of arbitration proceedings. It determined that even though the sales agreement contained a provision stating that Michigan law would govern, "the validity and application of an arbitration clause in a diversity case is subject to federal law." Because of this, rule 42(a) of the Federal Rules of Civil Procedure, which calls for consolidation in situations involving common questions of law or fact and is made applicable to the FAA under rule 81(a)(3), provides " 'ample legal basis' for compelling joint arbitration."

The court stated that the FAA was designed to effectuate the private agreement of the parties as well as promote the efficient resolution of disputes. Consolidation would serve those purposes in this case because the two proceedings presented common questions of law and fact and a danger of conflicting awards. Besides, the court reasoned, the language in the two sales agreements was identical, and all three parties "should reasonably have expected joint arbitration in the circumstances presented in this case . . . [because the agreements required arbitration for disputes or controversies] arising under *or relating to* the subject matter of this contract." Consequently, the court ordered consolidation of the two arbitrations. ***Hoover Group, Inc. v. Probala & Associates,*** 710 F. Supp. 677 (N.D. Ohio 1989).

PREEMPTION—SUPREMACY CLAUSE—FEDERAL ARBITRATION ACT—VIRGINIA MOTOR VEHICLE LICENSING ACT—SUBJECT-MATTER JURISDICTION—FEDERAL QUESTION JURISDICTION

A state law provision precluding mandatory arbitration clauses in franchise agreements between automobile manufacturers and dealers was held not preempted by the Federal Arbitration Act (FAA).

Saturn Distribution Corporation, a subsidiary of a subsidiary of General Motors Corporation, was created to design, manufacture, and market a new model of car. It developed an alternative dispute resolution system, which included binding arbitration, and made it a mandatory part of its dealer agreement. Pursuant to the state's Motor Vehicle Dealer Licensing Act (MVDLA), the agreement was submitted to the commissioner of motor vehicles for approval. The commissioner declined to grant approval, stating that approval would be granted if the agreement were modified so as to give dealers the option of deleting the exclusive arbitration clause. The purported agreement, to protect automobile dealers from the imbalances in their bargaining power with automobile manufacturers, is required under a separate provision of the MVDLA to contain language identical in effect to allow dealers access to the "procedures, forums, or remedies" available under state law. Saturn disagreed with the commissioner and filed an action against him, claiming that the Supremacy Clause of the U.S. Constitution warranted preemption of the MVDLA by the FAA.

The court, finding that it had subject-matter jurisdiction to rule on Supremacy Clause challenges to state laws under federal question jurisdiction, concluded that the provision precluding mandatory arbitration clauses as part of the franchise agreement between automobile manufacturers and dealers was not preempted by the FAA. The court stated that in order to prevail on its preemption argument, Saturn must show that the MVDLA "'stands as an obstacle to the accomplishment and execution of the full purpose and objectives' of the Federal Arbitration Act." It found that this burden was not met. The court also stated that "[a]rbitration, in order to be legitimate, must result from the acquiescence of both parties; it may not be imposed by one party upon the other," and reasoned that "[b]y ensuring consensual rather than forced arbitration, the Virginia statute is entirely in harmony with the Federal Arbitration Act." In addition, the court rejected the preemption claim because it found that the MVDLA provision did not single out arbitration agreements for special treatment and that the effect on arbitration agreements did not in any way block the "accomplishment and execution of the full purposes and objectives of Congress." ***Saturn Distribution Corporation v. Williams,*** 717 F. Supp. 1147 (E.D. Va. 1989). **[Editor's note:** The Fourth Circuit reversed, holding the state provision preempted because it "treats arbitration agreements more harshly than other contracts by disallowing their formation as mandatory provisions." *Saturn Distribution Corporation v. Williams*, No. 89-2773 (4th Cir. June 6, 1990)].

ARBITRATION AGREEMENT—INCORPORATION BY REFERENCE—CLASS ACTION—INCONSISTENT RESULTS—STAY OF ARBITRATION—CALIFORNIA

The trial court's invalidation of an arbitration clause was inconsistent with its findings. Although there was concern about inconsistent results between the arbitration proceeding and a pending class-action suit, the proper determination was an order compelling arbitration pursuant to the arbitration clause and an order staying arbitration pending resolution of the class-action suit.

Pioneer Take Out Corporation and Bhavsar entered into a franchise licensing agreement that included a broad arbitration clause. Bhavsar also subleased its business premises from Pioneer. Although the sublease agreement did not contain an arbitration clause, it did incorporate by reference the license agreement.

Later, Pioneer wrote to Bhavsar stating that it was terminating both the license and sublease agreements because of Bhavsar's failure to remedy his delinquency in rent, advertising, and royalty payments owed. Pioneer served Bhavsar a five-day notice to quit the premises, which Bhavsar refused to do. Subsequently, Pioneer filed an unlawful-detainer complaint. Pursuant to the license agreement, Bhavsar demanded arbitration as one of his affirmative defenses to the unlawful complaint.

The trial court found that the arbitration clause applied to the dispute because Pioneer's notice to quit "was based upon alleged breaches of the license agreement." The court also discovered that Pioneer and Bhavsar were parties to a pending class-action lawsuit. Apprehensive that arbitration between the two parties might result in a decision inconsistent with the pending court action, the trial court invalidated the arbitration clause. Bhavsar appealed.

The appellate court reversed the lower court's decision and compelled arbitration, but stayed the order to arbitrate. It agreed with the trial court's initial findings that Pioneer "attempted to litigate the [license] agreement under the guise of unlawful detainer," and that a possibility for inconsistent decisions existed because of the class-action suit. It disagreed, however, with the trial court's invalidation of the arbitration clause to avoid inconsistent decisions between arbitration and the court proceedings. The appellate court noted that inconsistent judgments were still possible because the trial court had allowed the unlawful-detainer action to continue, and that Pioneer would still use the unlawful-detainer action to litigate the franchise agreement since Bhavsar's reasons for the alleged breach of the sublease agreement stemmed from problems with the license agreement. Because the trial court's order invalidating the arbitration clause was erroneous, and in view of the concerns regarding inconsistent results, the court deemed that the proper ruling was an order staying arbitration pending resolution of the class-action suit. ***Pioneer Take Out Corp. v. Bhavsar,*** 257 Cal. Rptr. 749 (Cal. Ct. App. 1989).

DEPOSITION OF ARBITRATORS—REVIEW OF AWARD—COLORADO

The court held that a party seeking to vacate an arbitration award could not depose the arbitrators to inquire into their thought processes. In addition, an inquiry into the arbitrators' interpretation of the contract was an impermissible inquiry into the merits of the award.

Container and Gadsden submitted their contract dispute to arbitration. The arbitrators rendered an award in Gadsden's favor, and Container filed an application to set aside the award. Container, alleging that the arbitrators failed to follow the terms of the contract and seeking to inquire into the thought processes of the arbitrators, also sought to have the arbitrators deposed. The trial court refused and confirmed the award. Container appealed.

The appellate court noted at the outset that an arbitration award is not open to review on the merits and that the merits of an award include the arbitrators' interpretation of the contract. Citing *United Steelworkers of America v. American Manufacturing Company*, 363 U.S. 564 (1960), the court stated that because "[i]t is the arbitrator's construction of the contract which was bargained for . . . the courts have no business overruling him because their interpretation of the contract is different from his." The court thus declined to set aside the lower court's confirmation of the award, reasoning that an inquiry into the arbitrator's interpretation of the contract was an impermissible inquiry into the merits.

The court also ruled that Container could not depose the arbitrators for the purpose of inquiring into their thought processes. It found that the case law relied on by Container was distinguishable from the facts in the instant case because in those other cases the arbitrators were deposed for the purpose of reconstructing a record of arbitration proceedings held outside the presence of the parties. Since the parties did not dispute what had occurred during the arbitration, and such an inquiry bore no similarity to an inquiry into the arbitrators' thought processes, the court concluded that there was no need to depose the arbitrators. ***Container Technology Corp. v. J. Gadsden, Pty. Ltd.,*** 781 P.2d 119 (Colo. Ct. App. 1989).

DOMESTIC RELATIONS—INTENT TO ARBITRATE—AWARD—EVIDENT PARTIALITY—SCOPE OF ARBITRAL AUTHORITY—COLORADO

A party who voluntarily agreed in writing to participate in the arbitration process and objected to neither the selection of the arbitrator nor the process until after he verbally received a tentative award cannot claim that he was coerced into participating in the arbitration. In addition, applicable law does not permit review of the merits of the arbitration award by a court.

Richard and Catherine Gravend entered into an arbitration agreement to submit to arbitration issues in connection with the dissolution of their marriage. An award was rendered and confirmed. Richard Gravend appealed the trial court's denial of his motion to vacate, modify, or change the arbitration award.

The appellate court affirmed the trial court's denial of Richard Gravend's motion. It rejected his claim that he had been coerced into participating in the arbitration, finding that he had voluntarily agreed in writing to participate in the arbitration process and had objected neither to the arbitrator nor the process until after he verbally received a tentative award. The court also ruled that Richard Gravend could not unilaterally attempt to terminate the arbitration before entry of the award, via a letter terminating the arbitrator's services. It reasoned that "[o]nce a controversy is submitted to arbitration, it remains before the arbitrator until an award is rendered unless the parties *mutually agree* to withdraw it."

In addition, the court rejected the claim that the award contained sufficient miscalculations and omissions to warrant a vacatur, change, or modification of the award. It found no evident miscalculation or evident mistake and stated that Richard Gravend's attempt to seek review of the merits was impermissible under applicable statute. The court also disagreed with his assertion that the arbitrator was guilty of evident partiality, finding that the assertion was made to challenge the merits of the award merely because he disagreed with the arbitrator's findings and conclusion. ***In re Marriage of Gravend,*** 781 P.2d 161 (Colo. Ct. App. 1989).

FEDERAL ARBITRATION ACT—STATE LAW—CHOICE OF LAW—WAIVER—AMERICAN ARBITRATION ASSOCIATION RULE 10(C)— ILLINOIS

The court ruled that a party's actions constituted a waiver of its right to arbitrate and its right to have a particular state's law apply. In addition, the Federal Arbitration Act (FAA) does not apply where the parties have agreed

to arbitrate in accordance with state law, even though the transaction involves interstate commerce, except where the applicable state law would prevent the arbitration agreement from being enforced according to its terms.

Richard T. Yates, along with other entities, and Doctor's Associates entered into eight franchise agreements, all containing the same substantive terms. The agreements contained a provision for arbitration in accordance with the American Arbitration Association's Commercial Arbitration Rules and a choice-of-law clause providing for Connecticut law to govern. Doctor's and the entity it created to assist in the leasing aspects of the franchise agreements were incorporated in Connecticut. Five of the franchises were located in Illinois. A dispute arose over Yates' expansion plans in connection with the remaining three franchise agreements. Several court actions and motions were filed, including a removal action to federal court, a motion to compel arbitration under Illinois law, and five forcible entry and detainer actions for eviction. The motion to compel arbitration was denied and Doctor's brought an interlocutory appeal.

The court addressed the threshold issue of the applicable governing law regarding the franchise agreements. It disagreed with Doctor's contention that the FAA governed, finding that the issue was waived because the doctrine of federal preemption was not invoked at the trial level. The court went on to note that even if there were no waiver, the FAA still would not control under *Volt Information Sciences, Inc. v. Stanford University,* 489 U.S. ____, 109 S. Ct. 1248 (1989), even though the transaction involved interstate commerce. The only exception, the court stated, is where the applicable state law would prevent the parties' arbitration agreement from being enforced according to its terms. Because neither party had asserted during the course of litigation that Connecticut law governed and because the actions and motions were filed pursuant to Illinois law, the court ruled that the parties had also waived their right to have Connecticut law govern.

Finding that Illinois governed, the court stated that it had no difficulty in concluding that there was sufficient showing to support the trial court's refusal to compel arbitration. Because the initiation of the forcible entry and detainer actions was a submission of arbitrable issues for judicial determination, the court found that Doctor's had waived its right to arbitration. In addition, Doctor's argued that section 10(c) of the Commercial Arbitration Rules prevents any litigation brought by it from being construed as a waiver of its right to arbitrate. The court found that Doctor's arguments regarding section 10(c) were waived because the rules were not invoked in its arguments before the trial court. Because it found no error in the refusal to compel arbitration, the court affirmed the trial court's order. ***Yates v. Doctor's Associates, Inc.,*** 549 N.E.2d 1010 (Ill. Ct. App. 1990).

PARTNERSHIP—PUBLIC POLICY—ARBITRATION AGREEMENT—PARTIES' INTENT—ILLINOIS

Several issues could not be referred to arbitration because they failed to meet the criteria enunciated in the arbitration agreement. In addition, courts cannot change the expressed intention of the parties on the ground of public policy.

Northwest entered into a limited partnership agreement with United for the purpose of acquiring and operating two cable TV systems. The agreement contained an arbitration clause. A dispute arose over the distribution of accumulated profits. Northwest also claimed that tax credits were improperly allocated and that United's depositing of partnership funds in a non-interest-bearing bank account was a waste of partnership assets. Northwest demanded arbitration, and United sought a stay on the grounds that none of the disputes was arbitrable.

The trial court held that two out of the three issues were not arbitrable. Both parties appealed. The intermediate appellate court reversed, finding that the subject matter of the disputes was not arbitrable, because the criteria for submission of the disputes to arbitration were not met.

The court found that resolution of the arbitrability issues rested not on the scope of the arbitration agreement but on the definition of the limiting conditions in the agreement. It determined that the arbitration agreement was clearly limited in scope because it set forth three conditions or requirements that must be met for a dispute to be submitted to arbitration.

Relying on expressions of intention by the parties, the court rejected Northwest's argument that the language of the arbitration agreement should be broadly construed. The court stated that

> public policy favoring submission of disputes to arbitration does not allow us to do violence to the expressed intention of the parties or to ignore the fundamental that an agreement to submit a dispute to arbitration is contractual in nature. Courts have consistently held that one can be required to arbitrate only what one has agreed to arbitrate.

In addition, with the exception of the arbitration agreement, the court noted that the parties had used broad clauses throughout their partnership agreement. Consequently, the court concluded that the parties had specifically contracted to limit the application of the arbitration agreement to select issues. In accordance with its findings, the court affirmed the intermediate appellate court's ruling. ***United Cable Television Corp. v. Northwest Illinois Cable Corp.,*** 128 Ill. 2d 301, 538 N.E.2d 547 (1989).

ARBITRATION AGREEMENT—MEETING OF THE MINDS—LOUISIANA

The court held that a party was bound by the arbitration provision contained in a signed, written acknowledgment of goods.

Southern Tile entered into a sales contract with Collins for the purchase of carpet from Collins. The carpet that it received was defective, causing Southern to be unable to meet its contractual installation date with its general contractor, Commercial. Southern subsequently installed the carpet, but Commercial refused to pay for the installation, claiming that the amount was an offset against liquidated damages made necessary by the delay. Southern then filed suit against Collins for damages resulting from the defective carpeting.

Collins filed an exception of prematurity against Southern, claiming that Southern had agreed to submit any controversy arising from their sales contract to arbitration. An arbitration provision appeared on the "acknowledgment" of the order that was signed by the president of Southern. Southern, however, claimed that there was no meeting of the minds as to the issue of arbitration. The lower court sustained the exception and ordered arbitration, and Southern appealed.

The appellate court affirmed the lower court's decision. It found that the terms of the agreement signed by Southern's president were very clear insofar as the arbitration provision was concerned. Because of the state legislative policy favoring arbitration, the court ruled that Southern was bound by the arbitration provision. ***Southern Tile v. Commercial Construction Co.,*** 548 So. 2d 47 (La. Ct. App. 3rd Cir. 1989).

CONSUMER DISPUTES—ATTORNEY FEES—MASSACHUSETTS

An automobile buyer involved in a consumer dispute that was submitted to arbitration was held not entitled to recover attorney fees incurred in connection with the arbitration.

Roberta Schultz purchased a new automobile from an authorized Subaru dealer. After experiencing problems with the vehicle, which the dealer failed to correct, Schultz tendered the vehicle to Subaru. Subaru rejected the tender and arbitration was initiated. An award was rendered in Schultz's favor, which included tender of the vehicle to Subaru. Schultz then filed an action in state court to recover attorney's fees incurred in connection with the arbitration provision. The court ruled that the relief sought was not recoverable under state law and Schultz appealed.

The appellate court affirmed. It stated that attorney's fees are not recoverable in the Commonwealth of Massachusetts without statutory authorization. The applicable statute authorizes recovery of attorney's fees for actions commenced under a particular statutory section. Because the arbitration was not commenced in connection with that particular statutory section, the court agreed with and affirmed the lower court's ruling. ***Schultz v. Subaru of America, Inc.***, 407 Mass. 1004, 553 N.E. 2d 893 (1990).

PREEMPTION—SUPREMACY CLAUSE—ARBITRABILITY—FEDERAL ARBITRATION ACT—FRANCHISE—ARBITRATION AGREEMENT—FRAUD IN THE INDUCEMENT—MICHIGAN

Because a transaction involved interstate commerce, the court determined that the Federal Arbitration Act (FAA) governed. Under the Supremacy Clause of the U.S. Constitution, federal and state courts are bound to enforce the substantive provisions of the FAA; therefore, a claim of fraud in the inducement of a contract with an arbitration clause is an arbitrable issue under the FAA.

Carol Scanlon entered into a franchise agreement with P & J Enterprises. The agreement provided for the transfer of a business plan and the right to use in Michigan the registered trademarks—including methods, trade secrets, procedures, programs, and systems—of Fantastic Sam's International. Scanlon subsequently sued P & J, claiming violation of the Michigan Franchise Investment Law and seeking monetary damages and a rescission of the franchise agreement. The trial court denied P & J's motion to compel arbitration. It ruled that arbitration was not required and ordered the parties to proceed to an evidentiary hearing on Scanlon's claim of fraud in the inducement of the franchise contract. P & J appealed.

The appellate court disagreed. It found that although Scanlon claimed that there was fraud in the inducement of the franchise contracts, she "did not attack the validity of the agreement to arbitrate in and of itself." Consequently, the court stated, the issue was whether a claim of fraud in the inducement of a franchise contract is arbitrable. Because Fantastic Sam's is a Tennessee corporation, and the transfer of marketing expertise from Tennessee to Michigan "is a transaction in or affecting interstate commerce, the Federal Arbitration Act governs." Further, because the FAA preempts conflicting provisions of the Michigan Franchise Investment Law, and federal and state courts are bound to enforce the substantive provisions of the FAA under the Supremacy Clause of the Constitution, the court concluded that the "claim of fraud in the inducement of an entire contract containing an arbitration clause is to be referred to arbitration under the Federal Arbitration Act." Accordingly, the appellate court reversed the trial court's order. ***Scanlon v. P & J Enterprises, Inc.***, 451 N.W.2d 616 (Mich. Ct. App. 1990).

EMPLOYMENT AGREEMENT—SCOPE OF ARBITRATION AGREEMENT—UNIFORM ARBITRATION ACT—MONTANA

The appellate court reversed a lower court's order refusing enforcement of an arbitration agreement, finding that the arbitration clause in an annual review document was part of the employment agreement and that the claim was within the scope of that clause.

Jean Vukasin was employed by D.A. Davidson. About six years after she was hired, Davidson implemented annual performance reviews. Vukasin signed her performance reviews, which contained a statement, directly above the entire signature line, providing for arbitration of controversies between Vukasin and Davidson in connection with her employment. Vukasin subsequently filed a court complaint against Davidson, alleging that a fellow employee had assaulted her. She later terminated her employment at Davidson. Davidson moved to dismiss the court action for lack of jurisdiction or, in the alternative, to stay the proceedings and compel arbitration. The district court denied the motions and refused to enforce the arbitration agreement. Davidson appealed.

The appellate court, which found that the Uniform Arbitration Act (UAA) governed the dispute, stated that the controlling issue was whether the arbitration clause between Vukasin and Davidson was enforceable. Because the "arbitration clause [was] only a part of the agreement with regard to her employment," and the document she signed "[was] clearly a binding agreement with regard to employment between Ms. Vukasin and [Davidson]," the court rejected Vukasin's claim that she "did not 'knowingly' agree to arbitration."

As for the arbitration agreement's enforceability, the court found that section 4 of the UAA provides "one of the few times when a contract containing an arbitration clause can be addressed by a court. . . ." Vukasin disputed the validity of the arbitration clause in connection with the employment contract as a whole. Finding that the issue before the court was the same as that before the U.S. Supreme Court in *Prima Paint Corporation v. Flood & Conklin Manufacturing Company*, 388 U.S. 395, 87 S. Ct. 1801, 18 L. Ed. 2d. 1270 (1967), the court held that Vukasin's claim was arbitrable because it was within the scope of the arbitration clause. ***Vukasin v. D.A. Davidson & Co.,*** 785 P.2d 713 (Mont. 1990).

LANDLORD/TENANT—LESSOR/LESSEE—SUBJECT-MATTER JURISDICTION—ATTORNEY FEES—UNIFORM ARBITRATION ACT—NEVADA

The appellate court held that the trial court erred in awarding attorney fees and costs because the court lacked subject-matter jurisdiction to render such an award under the state's arbitration statute.

Donald and Nova Baldwin entered into an agreement to lease premises to New Shy Clown Casino, Inc., for the Shy Clown Casino. The lease contained an arbitration clause and a provision stating that the "successful party" in an arbitration shall be entitled to recover costs and expenses, including attorney fees. After the lease term expired, a dispute arose over the return of the security deposit. The matter was referred to arbitration. The arbitrators awarded the Baldwins the right to retain a portion of the security deposit and directed that the balance, with interest, be paid to Casino. They also specified that "each party shall be responsible for their own costs, attorney's fees, and expenses." Casino moved to confirm the award, and the Baldwins moved to vacate or, in the alternative, to modify the award to include attorney fees. As the prevailing party in the arbitration, Baldwin was granted its request for attorney fees and costs. Casino appealed.

The appellate court found that the trial court's power of review of an arbitration award is limited to the statutory grounds provided by the Uniform Arbitration Act (UAA). It determined that the award of attorney fees and costs was not within the scope of review provided for in the UAA under either the provision governing when a court may vacate an arbitration award or that governing when a court may modify or correct an award. Consequently, the court ruled that the trial court lacked the subject-matter jurisdiction necessary to make such an award. ***New Shy Clown Casino, Inc. v. Baldwin,*** 737 P.2d 524 (Nev. 1987).

ENVIRONMENTAL—HAZARDOUS WASTE REMOVAL—SPILL COMPENSATION AND CONTROL ACT—RIGHT TO ARBITRATION—SCOPE OF ARBITRATION—NEW JERSEY

Party held not entitled to a convening of a board of arbitrators because one of the conditions required for convention was not met. In addition, the issue of the dispute was not within the scope of arbitration under the applicable state statute.

The New Jersey Department of Environmental Protection (DEP) issued a directive to 28 corporations, including BP America, requiring them to remove hazardous substances from a Borne Chemical Company site. BP formally demanded that David Mack, as administrator of the state Spill

Fund (Fund), convene an arbitration board pursuant to the state's Spill Compensation and Control Act (Act) to challenge the cleanup and removal cost assessments by the DEP in its directive. The demand was denied. BP, along with Exxon, filed a complaint to compel Mack to convene a board.

The court denied BP's request, concluding that BP was not entitled to the convening of a board of arbitration. It found that three conditions must exist before arbitration can take place: (1) there must be a demand for arbitration; (2) there must be a claim presented to the Fund; and (3) someone must contest the validity or amount of the claim. The DEP had drawn an amount from the Fund for testing and securing estimates for the cost of cleanup of the Borne Site. The court declined to agree with BP's claim that the amount drawn from the Fund was the equivalent of a claim against the Fund. After reviewing the Act's legislative history, the court concluded that the "overall scheme of the Act implies that the [DEP] is authorized to spend money from the Fund without the expenditure being considered a claim presented to the Fund" and that the "language of various other provisions of the Act also suggest that claims against the Fund are those made by independent third parties." It also found that Mack, as administrator, did not constitute a third party claiming damages or costs from the Fund.

In addition, the court concluded that arbitration under the Act was not appropriate for determining the responsibility for cleanup and removal costs. It found that per the statutory language of the Act, the use of arbitration is for the purposes of contesting "the validity or amount of damage claims or cleanup and removal costs presented to the Fund for payment," not for determining the responsibility of such cleanup or removal. ***Exxon Corporation v. Mack***, 237 N.J. Super. 16, 566 A.2d 828 (App. Div. 1989).

LEMON LAW—AWARD—MOTION TO VACATE—GENERAL BUSINESS LAW—NEW YORK

The court held that the replacement value of a "comparable vehicle" is a vehicle of the same year, model, and mileage as the vehicle being replaced and does not include a brand new vehicle.

John DePaola purchased a 1985 Volvo 745 GLE station wagon. After experiencing problems with his car, which were not resolved satisfactorily, DePaola requested arbitration pursuant to subdivision k of General Business Law section 198-a. A hearing was conducted and the arbitrator awarded DePaola, as a "comparable vehicle," a 1987 Volvo 745 GLE. The award was upheld by the trial court, which found that it was neither irrational nor arbitrary. Volvo appealed.

The appellate court agreed that DePaola was entitled to relief. However, it disagreed with the lower court's determination, finding that the arbitrator had exceeded his power in awarding DePaola a brand new 1987 Volvo. The court stated that in its view, a comparable vehicle "means a vehicle of the same year and model and which has approximately the same mileage as the vehicle being replaced." Consequently, it concluded that DePaola was not entitled to a "new" vehicle. The court also stated that its conclusion was supported by the legislative history of the lemon law because if the Legislature had intended that the vehicle in question be replaced with a "new" vehicle, the statute would have so provided. In accordance with its opinion, the court remanded the matter to the arbitrator for an award not inconsistent with the court's opinion and to allow DePaola the opportunity to change his choice of available alternative remedies of equivalent value. ***Volvo North America Corp. v. DePaola,*** 554 N.Y.S.2d 835 (1st Dep't 1990).

RATIONALITY OF AWARD—VACATUR—SCOPE OF ARBITRATOR AUTHORITY—SERVICE—NEW YORK

Merely because an award is a compromise is not sufficient evidence to support a claim against the rationality of the award. In addition, an award will not be vacated absent a showing that the arbitrators either rewrote the parties' agreement or exceeded their scope of authority.

Weinberger made a series of diamond sales to Krieger. At one of these transactions, Siegmann was sent to receive a shipment of diamonds from Weinberger in Krieger's absence. The shipment was delivered to Krieger, but Weinberger never received payment. All three are members of the Diamond Dealers Club (DDC), and the dispute over payment was submitted to arbitration per DDC rules. Siegmann did not make any motion for a stay. An award was rendered, resulting in liability for the loss to be split equally among the three parties. The award was confirmed and Siegmann appealed.

Siegmann argued that the award should be vacated because it was irrational and challenged the propriety of service upon him in connection with the commencement of the action at bar. Specifically, Siegmann attacked the award on the basis that it was irrational because he was not a party to the transactions between Weinberger and Krieger. The court did not rule on the issue because it was an unreviewable factual determination. It noted, however, that Siegmann's argument was unsupportable because he had accepted the shipment that was the subject of the parties' dispute. In addition, the court rejected Siegmann's argument that the award, being a compromise, was not a rational resolution of the issues on the basis that Siegmann had failed to show that the arbitrators either rewrote the parties' agreement or exceeded their scope of authority. As for the service issue, the court determined that the facts warranted a finding of proper service pursuant to N.Y. Civ. Prac. L. & R. § 308(5). ***In re World Trade Diamond Corp.,*** 550 N.Y.S.2d 706 (1st Dep't 1990).

EVIDENCE—STENOGRAPHIC RECORD—WAIVER—NEW YORK

A party who participated in an arbitration with knowledge that no record was being kept was held to have waived any issue regarding the lack of such record.

John J. Broderick and the Suffolk County Bar Association were parties to an arbitration proceeding. An award was rendered and Broderick moved to vacate or modify the award. The trial court dismissed the proceeding, and Broderick appealed.

The appellate court affirmed the trial court's ruling. It found that Broderick had failed to demonstrate that the arbitrators had acted improperly during the course of the arbitration proceeding and that he could not rely on the fact that his inability to provide the necessary proof for his claims resulted from the lack of a record of the hearing. Specifically, the court ruled that Broderick had waived any issue regarding the lack of such record because he had participated in the arbitration with the knowledge that no record was being kept. ***Matter of Broderick,*** 550 N.Y.S.2d 378 (2d Dep't 1990).

FRAUD IN THE INDUCEMENT—WAIVER—NEW YORK

In an action to recover damages on the ground of invalidity of a contract, the action must be submitted to arbitration where there is no evidence of fraud in the inducement of either the contract itself or the arbitration clause. In addition, a party is not deemed to have waived its right to arbitration merely because it filed a motion in court to dismiss the action or to compel arbitration.

Carroll Stoianoff filed an action against New American Library (NAL) to recover damages on the ground that his contract with NAL was invalid. The contract contained a broad arbitration clause. NAL successfully obtained a stay of the court action and an order compelling arbitration. Stoianoff appealed.

The appellate court affirmed, stating that its role was limited to determining the validity of the arbitration clause, even though there was an allegation that the contract itself was invalid in its entirety. It agreed with the lower court's determination that the arbitration clause was valid because Stoianoff "offered no evidence of fraud in the inducement of the arbitration clause or that the entire contract including the arbitration provision [was] permeated with fraud."

In addition, the court agreed with the lower court's finding that NAL's participation in an earlier court proceeding brought by Stoianoff did not constitute a waiver of its right to arbitration. The court reasoned that NAL's participation—which was limited to moving to dismiss the action or, alternatively, for a stay to compel arbitration—cannot be said to constitute actions inconsistent with NAL's intent to arbitrate Stoianoff's claim. ***Stoianoff v. New American Library,*** 539 N.Y.S.2d 66 (2d Dep't 1989).

DOMESTIC RELATIONS—LACHES—AWARD—RELIGIOUS COURT—NEW YORK

A religious court's arbitration award is not enforceable by way of motion practice in a party's matrimonial action.

Israel and Faige Unger appeared before the Beth Din Rabbinical Court of Justice (a Jewish religious court) to resolve their marital disputes. A stipulation of settlement was entered into by the parties in 1984 and was executed before the Beth Din. One of the resolved issues was that of maintenance. An uncontested judgment of divorce dissolved the marriage in 1986. The judgment was silent on the issue of maintenance and, because neither party requested it, did not incorporate the 1984 stipulation. Because Israel Unger failed to make annual maintenance payments per the stipulation, the issue was resubmitted to the Beth Din in 1988, which rendered an award favoring Faige Unger. She then sought an entry of judgment regarding the arrears owed under the stipulation, incorporation of the stipulation in the divorce judgment *nunc pro tunc*, and confirmation of the 1988 Beth Din arbitration award.

The court ruled that the divorce judgment should not incorporate the stipulation because it appeared that the parties had consciously decided not to include the agreement and its clauses in the divorce judgment. The court also denied the request for incorporation *nunc pro tunc* on the basis of laches because Faige Unger had waited for over three years before asserting her right or claim to incorporation.

As for judgment on the arrears, the court found that it could not rule on the issue in the matrimonial action before it because of the omission of the stipulation and any of its clauses from the final divorce judgment. The court also found that the present proceeding was not the appropriate procedure for requesting confirmation of the arbitration award and directed Faige Unger to N.Y. Civ. Prac. L. & R. § 7502(a). ***Unger v. Unger,*** 547 N.Y.S.2d 529 (Sup. Ct. Kings Cty. 1989).

COMPULSORY ARBITRATION—APPEAL OF AWARD—APPELLATE PROCEDURE—PENNSYLVANIA

When a party attempts to circumvent the proper appellate procedure for vacating an arbitration award by moving to strike a compulsory arbitration award, the court of common pleas cannot stay the period prescribed for filing an appeal.

A dispute arising from an automobile collision between Kathryn Spring and the Loughs was arbitrated pursuant to Pennsylvania's compulsory arbitration statute. Ten days after the arbitrators rendered their award, the Loughs filed a motion in the court of common pleas to strike the award. Three days after the court received that motion, it ordered a stay of all proceedings. The court subsequently rejected the Loughs' motion to strike and noted that the Loughs had to file for a trial de novo if they still objected to the award. It also dissolved its stay on the proceedings.

One month later, the Loughs filed for a trial de novo. The court of common pleas denied the Loughs' request, ruling that the appeal was untimely. It found that a dissatisfied party has 30 days after the award to request a trial de novo. Because the Loughs waited 10 days after the award was rendered to file the motion to strike, and then waited 29 days after the court's ruling denying that motion before filing for a trial de novo, a total of 39 days had passed since the beginning of the appeal period. According to the court, the Loughs violated the time limit for an appeal and disqualified themselves from a trial de novo. The Loughs appealed.

The appellate court ruled against the Loughs, stating that their motion to strike was not a mere technical error, but a calculated attempt "to secure a second arbitration of the same matter, thereby avoiding the necessity of a trial de novo in the court of common pleas." In addition, the appellate court held that the court of common pleas did not have the authority to stay the appeals period while it considered the Loughs' motion to strike, thus defeating the Loughs' claim that the court of common pleas could stop the appeal time and then begin it anew after the court's decision on the motion. The appellate court explained that the authority to stay an appeals period depended on the court's jurisdiction. The statutory jurisdiction allotted was clear, and it allowed the court of common pleas to stay the appeal period only to correct an award's patent and formal errors that do not affect the award's substance. ***Lough v. Spring,*** 556 A.2d 441 (Pa. Super. Ct. 1989).

VACATUR OF ARBITRATION AWARD—PREJUDGMENT INTEREST—AUTHORITY OF ARBITRATOR—PUBLIC WORKS ARBITRATION ACT—RHODE ISLAND

The trial court properly denied a motion to vacate an arbitration award because there was no basis for overturning the award. In addition, even though the arbitrator had the authority to award prejudgment interest, he would not be compelled to do so.

Hart Engineering entered into a contract with the City of Pawtucket Water Supply Board. The parties submitted a dispute to arbitration. An award was rendered in favor of Hart. In this award, the arbitrator stated that although he had the authority to award prejudgment interest, he elected not to do so in this case. Pawtucket moved to vacate the award, and Hart sought the addition of prejudgment interest. The trial court denied both requests.

On appeal, the appellate court refused to vacate the award. It found that judicial authority to overturn an arbitrator's award is limited, and that an arbitrator has the "inherent power to fashion an appropriate remedy as long as the award draws its essence from the contract and is based upon a 'passably plausible' interpretation of the contract." In addition, the court stated that although an arbitrator has the authority to award prejudgment interest in awards made pursuant to the Public Works Arbitration Act as well as the state's general commercial arbitration statute, the arbitrator cannot be compelled to do so by the court. ***Hart Engineering Co. v. City of Pawtucket Water Supply Board,*** 560 A.2d 329 (R.I. 1989).

ARBITRAL AUTHORITY—SCOPE OF AWARD—TENNESSEE

Because the limitation-of-liability clause in a contract is a valid provision, the trial court correctly refused to confirm an arbitration award that exceeded the limitation clause in that contract.

International Talent Group (ITG), a booking agency for performing artists, entered into an agreement with Copyright Management, Inc. (CMI), a company that administers music publishing and mechanical royalties, for the design of a software package by a CMI subsidiary for ITG. Several problems arose, including delay in the delivery of the computer system and failure to deliver the software package. Pursuant to the parties' license agreement, the matter was submitted to arbitration. An award was rendered in favor of ITG, which moved to confirm. CMI opposed on the ground that the arbitrators had exceeded their powers. The trial court agreed with CMI and vacated the award. ITG appealed.

Noting that the terms of the parties' arbitration agreement determine the scope of arbitral authority and that the arbitrators may not award relief in excess of the limit agreed upon by the parties, the court affirmed the trial court's order refusing to confirm the award. In the parties' contract was a limitation-of-liability provision stating that CMI's liability would not exceed the total license fee paid by ITG. That fee total was $7,500. Because the record showed that the parties had entered into their agreement freely and knowingly, the limitation on recovery of damages was a valid provision. Consequently, not only did the award of $76,400 exceed the scope of liability, it did not draw its essence from the arbitration agreement.

In addition, the court found that the arbitrators were not required to make detailed written explanations for all their conclusions. In accordance with its findings, the court affirmed the lower court's order. ***International Talent Group, Inc. v. Copyright Management, Inc.,*** 769 S.W.2d 217 (Tenn. Ct. App. 1988).

BANKING—GUARDIANSHIP—MANDATORY ARBITRATION—SUPERIOR COURT MANDATORY ARBITRATION RULES—TRIAL DE NOVO—SUMMARY JUDGMENT—ATTORNEY FEES—WASHINGTON

A party's misdeeds precluded him from relying on the principle of equitable estoppel to bar recovery from him for money owed. In addition, the applicable Superior Court Mandatory Arbitration Rules do not distinguish between either a summary judgment proceeding or a trial de novo for purposes of awarding attorney fees.

Wayne C. Richardson established guardianship accounts for his daughter, a minor, with the Puget Sound Savings Bank in the form of a blocked passbook savings account and two blocked certificates of deposit. Although such accounts require a court order for withdrawal, Richardson withdrew accrued interest from one of the blocked CDs and used a portion of those funds to open a new unblocked account in his daughter's name. At Richardson's request, the bank automatically transferred interest from the blocked CD to the unblocked account. Richardson subsequently withdrew sums from the new account for his own use.

Richardson was later removed as guardian of his daughter's person and estate. When his daughter's aunt and uncle (the Millers) were named as successor guardians, they had the assets inventoried and discovered Richardson's unauthorized action. An action was filed against the bank, seeking recovery of the misappropriated funds. The bank agreed to reimburse Richardson's daughter for the missing funds, and in turn, was assigned her claims against Richardson.

The matter was settled by mandatory arbitration, with a ruling in the bank's favor. Richardson sought a trial de novo in superior court, resulting in summary judgment for the bank, which was also awarded costs and attorney fees. Richardson appealed, contending that the negligence of the bank in allowing him to make unauthorized withdrawals from the blocked accounts equitably estopped the bank from seeking recovery from him.

The appellate court held that Richardson's own misdeeds had precluded his reliance on equitable estoppel. As for Richardson's contention that the bank was also barred from seeking recovery from him because it had failed to notify him of its settlement with the Millers, the court rejected this argument as having no legal support.

The court also rejected Richardson's claim that the bank should not have been awarded attorney fees because the trial de novo was cut short by a summary judgment. The Court was unpersuaded by Richardson's attempt to distinguish a trial de novo from a summary judgment for purposes of awarding attorney fees under the Superior Court Mandatory Arbitration Rules. It found that there is no distinction between either proceeding, since a summary judgment proceeding and a trial de novo both involve a judicial examination of legal and factual issues. Consequently, the judgment of the lower court was affirmed. ***Puget Sound Savings Bank v. Richardson,*** 773 P.2d 429 (Wash. Ct. App. 1989).

COMMENTARY

When Federal Law Preempts the States'*

Michael F. Hoellering

To accommodate and advance the use of commercial arbitration, a growing number of states have recently added to their legislation new provisions dealing with various aspects of the arbitration process. While the majority of these enactments are designed to facilitate arbitration in a manner that is harmonious with existing federal arbitration law, questions regarding the preemptive effect of the Federal Arbitration Act[1] are bound to arise in the wake of these enactments. Three recent court decisions, addressing arbitration act preemption claims in the context of consolidation, contract formation, and pre-arbitral attachment, provide illustrations of present-day interaction between state and federal arbitration law.

 Michael F. Hoellering is General Counsel of the American Arbitration Association.

Consolidation

A recurring issue in arbitral proceedings is that of consolidating claims arising under separate agreements that involve common issues of law or fact. The arbitration act does not contain any legislative direction on this aspect of arbitration procedure. Absent a governing provision in the agreement of the parties or arbitration rules, this has often led to litigation.

To clarify this situation, some states, such as Massachusetts, have added provisions to their arbitration rules, allowing for consolidation. Massachusetts provides as follows:

> A party aggrieved by the failure or refusal of another to agree to consolidate one arbitration proceeding with another or others, for which the method of appointment of the arbitrator or arbitrators is the same, or to sever one arbitration proceeding from another or others, may apply to the superior court for an order for such consolidation or such severance. . . . No provision in any arbitration shall bar or prevent action by the court under this section.[2]

The operative effect of this provision in cases governed by the arbitration act was addressed by the First Circuit Court of Appeals in *New England Energy, Inc. v. Keystone Shipping Co.*[3] The facts indicate that New England Energy and Keystone Shipping were signatories to one of two maritime contracts. Each contract contained clauses providing for the arbitration of disputes in Boston "pursuant to the laws relating to arbitration in force."[4] One contract involved the creation of a joint venture for the purpose of owning and operating a coal carrying ship, and the other contract involved the chartering of the ship from the joint venture. Both clauses were silent on consolidation.

After separate arbitrations were filed pursuant to the two contracts, one of the parties filed a motion in state court seeking consolidation of the two arbitrations. The action was removed to federal court based on diversity jurisdiction.

The district court ruled that, although it found that the factual circumstances warranted consolidation, it could not order consolidation because it lacked the power to join the cases. An appeal was filed. The appellate court held that federal courts have the power to order consolidation of arbitrations when the agreement of the parties is silent on the issue of consolidation. It rejected Keystone's argument that ordering consolidation pursuant to a state statute constituted a modification of the arbitration agreement in violation of section 4 of the arbitration act when the arbitration agreement is silent as to the parties' consent to consolidation.

The court also noted that the arbitration act has never been construed to preempt all state law on arbitration, but only those laws "that would override the parties' choice to arbitrate rather than litigate in court, in direct conflict with the act's primary purpose of ensuring the enforcement of privately negotiated arbitration agreements.''[5] Given the act's silence on the issue of consolidation, the court concluded that the Massachusetts provision allowing consolidation of arbitrations was not in conflict with the federal act. The opinion also indicated that the outcome would have been different had the contract included a consolidation disclaimer, despite the contrary provision of Massachusetts law.

Special Requirements

The imposition by a state of special requirements governing the enforcement of arbitration agreements within the purview of the federal act was addressed by the district court of Massachusetts in *Securities Industry Association v. Connolly*.[6] The facts indicate that following the U.S. Supreme Court's decision in *Shearson/American Express v. McMahon*,[7] holding that Securities Act of 1934 claims are arbitrable, Massachusetts promulgated regulations governing securities brokers' use of pre-dispute arbitration agreements. Under the new regulations, broker-dealers registered in Massachusetts were prohibited from requiring Massachusetts customers to sign a mandatory pre-dispute arbitration agreement as a nonnegotiable condition to opening a brokerage account. The Securities Industry Association filed an action contesting that the regulations were preempted by the federal act. The main issue to be decided was ''whether Congress (expressly) did or (impliedly) meant to displace state law or state law concepts in enacting the federal scheme set up by Congress.''[8]

In making its decision, the court considered the First Circuit's ruling in *New England Energy*, wherein the court observed that ''the Supreme Court's decisions support a conclusion that all state laws seeking to *limit* the use of the arbitral process are superseded by federal law.''[9] The court focused on the concept of voluntariness as used by the state, which it found addressed the ''fundamental principles of contract formation upon which questions of validity, revocability, and enforceability of arbitration agreements turn.''[10]

Used in that way, the court deemed that the concept was ''not a matter subject to idiosyncratic rules or definitions,''[11] particularly when the regulations at issue developed a definition of voluntariness applicable only to arbitration agreements and not to other contracts generally. Because the regulations single out arbitration agreements and ''represent a radical departure from the treatment of contracts generally in the state's common law,''[12] the court held that they were preempted by the arbitration act. In reaching its conclusion, the court observed that

> [t]he regulations are not concerned with ''matters collateral to the agreement to arbitrate,'' such as the procedural issues relating to consolidation of arbitration proceedings dealt with [in *New England*

> *Energy*]. Rather, the defendants' regulations govern the validity and enforceability of arbitration agreements themselves by establishing standards which, if not met, render the arbitration agreements unenforceable and the unsuccessful makers of those agreements subject to sanction. It is difficult to imagine regulation more central to the arbitral decision. . . . Because the voluntariness concerns expressed in the unique Massachusetts securities arbitration regulations impose conditions on the formation and execution of arbitration agreements which are not part of the generally applicable contract law of Massachusetts, they cannot be given effect under the Federal Arbitration Act.[13]

Pre-Arbitral Attachment

Decisions on the availability of pre-arbitral attachment as a provisional remedy are often tempered by the applicability of the United Nations Convention on the Recognition and Enforcement of Foreign Arbitral Awards (Convention),[14] as implemented by Chapter 2 of the arbitration act. Although the convention does not directly address the issue, it has been interpreted by several federal courts, and the New York Court of Appeals in *Cooper v. Ateliers de la Motobecane*,[15] as proscribing attachment.

Sometime after *Cooper*, to ensure the availability of attachments and preliminary injunctions in appropriate cases, New York State added to its arbitration law section, C.P.L.R. § 7502(c), which provides:

> The supreme court . . . may entertain an application for an order of attachment or for a preliminary injunction in connection with an arbitrable controversy, but only upon the ground that the award to which the applicant may be entitled may be rendered ineffectual without such provisional relief.[16]

The effect of this provision on cases governed by the convention was addressed by the Appellate Division, First Department in *Drexel Burnham Lambert, Inc., v. Ruebsamen*.[17] The facts indicate that Heinz and Werner Reubsamen, West German citizens, opened an account to engage in option transactions with Drexel Burnham Lambert, a securities broker-dealer, at its Brussels office. A dispute arose over a margin call made by Werner that resulted in Drexel's liquidation of their account. A debit balance ensued, and Drexel brought an arbitration proceeding against the Ruebsamens.

Drexel petitioned for an order of attachment and obtained an ex parte restraining order attaching assets owned by the Ruebsamens in a separate brokerage account. The Ruebsamens moved to vacate the temporary restraining order. Finding that C.P.L.R. section 6201(3) limits the availability for attachments in aid of arbitration to those circumstances in which it is shown that "the prospective arbitration award might become ineffectual because of some act threatened,"[18] and noting that Drexel failed to make the requisite showing, the court denied the petition. Drexel appealed.

The appellate court found that the language of C.P.L.R. section 7502(c)

> neither limits an order of attachment in aid of arbitration to the narrow circumstances set forth in C.P.L.R. § 6201(3) nor requires that [Drexel] demonstrate any affirmative conduct on the part of the [Ruebsamens].[19]

Thus, the court noted, the fact that an arbitration award may be rendered ineffectual in the absence of an order of attachment is sufficient to support provisional relief. Nevertheless, the court affirmed the lower court's decision.

Because the Convention applied, the court, following the rationale enunciated in *Cooper* that prejudgment attachment is prohibited when the Convention is applicable because the intention of the Convention is that there be no significant judicial interventions until after an arbitration award is made, affirmed the lower court's decision and refused Drexel's petition for an attachment order.

Given the clear conflict between the New York provision and federal law on the availability of an attachment in aid of arbitration, the decision does not bode well for like provisions recently enacted as part of state international arbitration statutes.

Conclusion

As illustrated by the above and other decisions, the preemptive effect of the arbitration act will depend on the nature of the particular state law provision. Where the state statute does not derogate from, but in fact supplements, the federal act, it will be upheld. On the other hand, where a state enactment clearly conflicts or departs significantly from the policies and existing interpretations of the act, the Supremacy Clause of the United States Constitution requires that federal rather than state law determine the outcome.

Notes

1. 9 U.S.C. §1 *et seq.*
2. Mass. Ann. Laws Chap. 251, § 2A.
3. 855 F.2d 1 (1st Cir. 1988).
4. *Id.* at 3.
5. *Id.* at 4.
6. No. 88-2153-WD, slipop. (D. Mass. 1988).
7. 482 U.S. 220 (1987).
8. No. 88-2153-WD at 8.
9. *Id.* at 10 (citing to *New England Energy*, 855 F.2d at 4).
10. *Id.* at 13.
11. *Id.*

12. *Id.* at 15.
13. *Id.* at 16 and 17.
14. 21 U.S.T. 2517, T.I.A.S. No. 6997, 330 U.N.T.S. 4739; also known as the New York Convention. The U.S. implementing legislation is codified at 9 U.S.C. § 201 *et seq.*
15. 57 N.Y.2d 408, 442 N.E.2d 1239, 456 N.Y.S.2d 728 (1982).
16. N.Y. Civ. Prac. L. & R. § 7502(c).
17. *New York Law Journal*, July 28, 1988, at 17, col. 3 (App. Div. 1st Dept. July 21, 1988).
18. *Id.* at 19.
19. *Id.*

Choice of Law and the Federal Arbitration Act: The Shock of *Volt**

Joseph D. Becker

The U.S. Supreme Court's 1989 affirmation of a California court's stay of arbitration sent shockwaves through the arbitration community. The ruling in *Volt*—which upheld the finding that a choice-of-law clause in the parties' contract precluded the Federal Arbitration Act in favor of state law—led many to question whether parties can feel reasonably secure that their arbitration agreements will continue to receive broad federal protection.

This article attempts to put this concern into perspective. Noting that the California court failed to discern a number of questions underlying the choice-of-law issue, and that the U.S. Supreme Court chose to limit its review of the case to whether there was a conflict between state law and the FAA, the author argues that the Court's finding does not significantly threaten the FAA. The author does advise parties, however, to use care in drafting the choice-of-law clause to ensure that their intent to arbitrate under federal law will be carried out.

California is notable for its tremors. In March 1989, in *Volt Information Sciences, Inc. v. Board of Trustees of Leland Stanford Junior University*,[1] the U.S. Supreme Court affirmed a California decision that shook the solidly built structures of the conflict of laws and the Federal Arbitration Act (FAA).[2] While the quake scored lower on the judicial Richter scale than early reports predicted,[3] the jolt was palpable. Damage control is necessary.

---

* This article is reprinted from *Arbitration Journal* (June, 1990) 45(2): 32–37. Joseph D. Becker is a partner with the law firm of Becker Glynn & Melamed in New York City and an adjunct professor at New York University School of Law. The author wishes to thank Professor Andreas F. Lowenfeld and Michael Gruson, Esq., for their helpful comments.

Constitutional Superiority of Federal Law

Formulating propositions of the conflict of laws may be risky. It seems clear, however, that irrespective of whether the law of state A or state B is chosen by the forum to govern a contract, relevant *federal* law will apply perforce.

As a taxonomic matter, that proposition is perhaps one of constitutional law rather than the conflict of laws. That is, it flows logically from article VI, clause 2, of the U.S. Constitution, which binds "the Judges in every State" to apply federal law. Federal law, in relation to state law, is not "foreign in the international sense," as the Rhode Island Supreme Court once dared to suggest.[4] Rather, as the U.S. Supreme Court stated more than one hundred years ago, federal law is "as much a part of the law of every State as its own local laws and Constitution."[5] Like a slice of apple pie, the state law filling has a federal crust.

Parties negotiating a contract may wish to simplify the search for the proper law. They may do so by expressing their intention as to the governing law in a choice-of-law clause in the contract. Such a clause might state that the "validity, performance, interpretation, and other incidents of this Agreement shall be governed by the law of state A." If parties choose more or less reasonably and the choice is within the bounds of their permitted autonomy, it will be respected: the law of state A will be applied to the dispute.[6]

When parties express such a choice, the resulting impact of relevant federal law on the contract is unchanged: "[T]he incorporation of state law [in a deed of trust] does not signify the inapplicability of federal law. . . ."[7] As in the case of a contract lacking a choice-of-law clause, relevant federal law must be considered.

When concurrent federal and state laws are harmonious, both operate in accordance with their respective terms; but when the two bodies of law conflict—directly, potentially, or otherwise—resolution of the conflict becomes necessary.[8] If the U.S. Constitution did no more than oblige the "Judges in every State" to apply federal law, the conflict would remain unresolved: federal law would be a constituent of the governing law, but the relative standings of federal and state law would be uncertain. The Constitution, of course, does go further: it is fundamental to the constitutional plan, expressed in the same article VI, clause 2, that federal law be superior, preempting state law in cases of significant conflict. The "Judges in every State" must now apply federal law without regard for the conflicting state law.

In light of these elementary constitutional rules, the drafter of a choice-of-law clause need not specify that relevant federal law also applies, and that, in the event of a conflict between federal and state law, federal law will control. That would belabor the obvious. At least, the position was obvious until the Supreme Court affirmed the decisions of the California courts in the *Volt* case.

Construction Contract Provides for Arbitration

Volt and Stanford University, in a transaction involving interstate commerce, entered into a standard construction contract under which Volt was to do electrical work at the university. The contract contained a broad arbitration clause and a choice-of-law clause stating that the contract was to be "governed by the law of the place where the Project is located."

When a dispute developed over compensation for extra work, Volt made a formal demand for arbitration. Stanford responded by suing Volt for fraud and breach of contract in California Superior Court. In the same action, Stanford also sued two indemnitors who were instrumental in the design and management of the project; Stanford's contracts with the indemnitors did not have arbitration clauses. Volt then petitioned the same court to compel arbitration, but Stanford moved to stay. A state statute permitted such a stay pending resolution of related litigation between a party bound to an arbitration agreement and third parties not so bound. The Superior Court denied Volt's motion and stayed arbitration pending the outcome of Stanford's suit against Volt and the two indemnitors.[9]

The decision of the California Superior Court was surely surprising. The 1980s had witnessed an extraordinary strengthening of the FAA by the U.S. Supreme Court, effectively federalizing arbitration law.[10] At the time the Superior Court decided *Volt*, it seemed clear that arbitration clauses in contracts involving interstate commerce were governed by substantive federal law emanating from the FAA, and that a party seeking judicial resolution of a dispute covered by such a clause must be dispatched summarily to arbitration.[11]

California Court Interprets Choice-of-Law Clause

Nevertheless, the California Court of Appeal affirmed. The court conceded that the FAA governs agreements to arbitrate in interstate commerce and does not provide for stays of arbitration. It also said that "were the federal rules to apply, Volt's petition to compel arbitration would have to be granted."[12] The court interpreted the choice-of-law clause, however, to mean that California law governed the contract, and that California law (and therefore the contract) included the procedural statute permitting stays of arbitration.

While the appeals court recognized that the FAA preempts state law that obstructs the enforcement of arbitration agreements, it noted that "it does not follow that the federal law has preclusive effect in a case where the parties have chosen in their agreement to abide by state rules."[13] The California Supreme Court denied Volt's petition for discretionary review. On further appeal, the U.S. Supreme Court affirmed.

Ouster of Federal Law?

The Court of Appeal's assertion that the FAA does not have "preclusive effect in a case where the parties have chosen in their agreement to abide by state rules" is flawed. The proposition conflates several discrete questions:

(1) Does the contract express an intention to exclude federal law?
(2) If it does, can it succeed?
(3) If it cannot succeed—that is, if the contract cannot exclude mandatory federal law—does the state law conflict with the federal law? and
(4) If there is a conflict, does the severity of the conflict require the state law to yield to the federal law?

The majority of the California Court of Appeal held that the Volt contract did, and could, choose to exclude relevant federal law. As to the meaning of the contract (the first question), there is no reason to believe that the choice-of-law clause was intended to oust federal law. It was a standard clause of the contractor, there was no extrinsic evidence adduced as to its meaning, and professional expectations about such clauses are clearly to the contrary.

The second question is different from the first and the third. Whether the parties have the *power* to exclude federal law from the governance of their contract—assuming their intention to do so—is a question of party autonomy. On the other hand, whether federal law conflicts with state law (the third question) is a question of statutory interpretation. Although none of the courts in this case noticed the second question, it becomes relevant when parties purport to choose between the laws of different *states*: the forum may ignore the parties' choice of law of a state when it conflicts with the fundamental policy of a more interested state whose law would otherwise apply.[14] The autonomy of parties, however, to exclude mandatory *federal* law—with its superior constitutional force and national ubiquity—must be feeble indeed.

The third question—whether there is a conflict between federal and state law—depends on the prescriptive character and reach of the federal statute. A strongly prescriptive federal statute on the labeling of food, for example, might collide with a state statute imposing contradictory food labeling requirements.[15] Relatively speaking, the FAA is not such a statute. It is weakly prescriptive, intended chiefly to validate arbitration agreements involving interstate commerce. To be sure, it is a cardinal sin for a state statute to block such an agreement; the conflict would not be tolerated.[16] But even Supreme Court Justice William J. Brennan, Jr., dissenting in *Volt*, conceded that the FAA leaves parties free "to write an agreement to arbitrate outside the FAA [and to] permit a state rule, otherwise preempted by the FAA, to govern their arbitration."[17] In other words, the FAA would not conflict with a state arbitration rule incorporated into such an agreement.

The final question—whether the conflict is severe enough to require the preemption of state law by the federal statute—is answered by reference to a body of rules under which the degree of actual or potential conflict is measured.[18]

The California Court of Appeal believed that the case turned on the first two questions, which it answered affirmatively: the parties intended to, and had the power to, reject the FAA by choosing California law as the governing law of the contract. The damage done to established precepts of the conflict of laws was mitigated, however, by Chief Justice William H. Rehnquist's opinion on the appeal.

Supreme Court Refuses to Second-Guess California Interpretation of Contract

The Supreme Court, as a matter of its reviewing authority, would not reconsider the state court's interpretation of the contract. That may have been bad federal court law (for reasons given by Justice Brennan in dissent) but, happily, it cannot be said that the California view of the meaning and effect of the choice-of-law clause won the approval of the high court. The California courts' answer to the first question—whether the contract expresses an intention to exclude federal law—remains an unsanctified statement of California law, not a federal common law rule.

The Court affirmed the California decison by ignoring the question whether the parties had the power to exclude federal law and by answering negatively the third question: the Court held that the FAA did not conflict with the state statute that authorized the stay, because the FAA permits parties to arbitrate by state rules, *including a rule that might stay an arbitration*. To this Justice Brennan said in dissent, "the California procedural rule, which stays arbitration while litigation of the same issue goes forward, means simply that the parties' dispute will be litigated rather than arbitrated."[19] (The fourth question—whether the severity of a conflict between federal and state law requires that the latter yield to the former—was not reached by the Court.)

Whether the "same issue" (the mutual liabilities of Stanford and Volt for breach of contract) will be tried by the California Superior Court remains to be seen. That court's stay simply orders that Stanford's motion "to stay arbitration is granted and [Volt's] motion to compel arbitration is denied."[20] Even though the order does not make any effort to preserve the future arbitrability of the claims and issues in dispute between Stanford and Volt, the trial court could attempt to separate the Stanford–Volt dispute from the dispute between Stanford and the other defendants. Even if that were possible, modern res judicata theory, which permits defensive and offensive use of collateral estoppel against a "non-party" to a prior litigation (namely, Volt), may make the subsequent arbitration proceeding derisory.[21] If the effect of the stay is as predicted by Justice Brennan, there is a conflict between the FAA and the trial court's order that is direct and irreconcilable.

Preserving the Supremacy of Federal Law

What lessons can be drawn from *Volt* by drafters of choice-of-law clauses who are concerned to preserve the supremacy of federal arbitration law? If California or similar law is the chosen law, the problem of *Volt* is exigent. Even for contracts governed by other state law, the uncertain implications of *Volt* require that special provisions be made, at least until the tremors cease.

In a contract containing an arbitration clause, the mere addition to a standard choice-of-law clause of the phrase "including federal law" may not be sufficient to overcome a statute of the California type, given that the Court in *Volt* held that there was no conflict between the FAA and a contract deemed to incorporate the California statute. That is, both the federal and state statutes were seen to coexist harmoniously; but had there been an express assertion of the dominance of federal law in the Volt–Stanford contract, the case would have turned out differently.

The addition of the following proviso to the choice-of-law clause would probably have done the job: " . . . *provided that any dispute, controversy, question, or issue arising out of or relating directly or indirectly to paragraph [ ] (Arbitration) of this Agreement shall be governed exclusively by the United States Arbitration Act as then in force.*"

The use of the word "exclusively" in the proviso should be sufficient to displace even state laws such as California's that are deemed to be compatible with the FAA. The exclusivity of the proviso should not be interpreted to bar references to state or foreign law that the FAA may choose to make (as distinguished from state law operating of its own force, as in *Volt*).[22] There are numerous references to state law made in cases governed primarily by federal law,[23] including arbitration cases.[24] When a choice-of-law clause, conditioned by the proviso, prompts the application of federal law, the parties to the contract may be presumed to contemplate that the federal law may choose to make appropriate references to state law, for in such cases "in the last analysis [the court's] decision turns upon the law of the

United States, not that of any state."[25] Put another way, federal law, not state law, is the "source of the right."[26] In any event, party autonomy in the choice of law has its limits.[27]

Conclusion

The tremor of the California decision, at least relative to the interpretation of choice-of-law clauses, has been moderated by the Supreme Court's avoidance of the issue. The magnitude of the aftershock to the FAA, however, is yet to be measured.

By insisting that the result is an incidence of the parties' choice of law, Chief Justice Rehnquist reassures us that *Moses H. Cone*,[28] *Southland*,[29] and other landmark cases of the modern arbitration era are good law when California law is not chosen in the arbitration agreement. In most cases, the edifice of federal substantive law constructed on the foundation of the FAA still stands.

Notes

1. 109 S. Ct. 1248, 103 L. Ed. 2d 488, 57 U.S.L.W. 4295 (U.S. Mar. 6, 1989).
2. 9 U.S.C. § 1 *et seq.*
3. See Robert Coulson, "High Court Jolts Arbitration in California Construction Case," *Arbitration Journal* 44 (June, 1989): 47.
4. *Robinson v. Norato*, 43 A.2d 467, 468 (R.I. 1945); see, also, *Testa v. Katt*, 330 U.S. 386, 388 (1947).
5. *Hauenstein v. Lynham*, 100 U.S. 483, 490 (1880); and *Claflin v. Houseman*, 93 U.S. 130, 136 (1876).
6. U.C.C. § 1-105; Restatement (Second) of Conflict of Laws § 187 (1988 Revisions); see, also, Joseph D. Becker, "Choice-of-Law and Choice-of-Forum Clauses in New York," *International and Comparative Law Quarterly* 38 (1989): 167–171.
7. *Fidelity Federal Savings & Loan Ass'n v. De la Cuesta*, 458 U.S. 141, 157 (1982), at note 12 ("Paragraph 15 [of the Deed of Trust] provides that the deed is to be governed by the 'law of the jurisdiction' in which the property is located; but the 'law of the jurisdiction' includes federal as well as state law").
8. For a discussion of various forms of conflict, see Laurence H. Tribe, *American Constitutional Law*, 2d ed. (Westbury, NY: Foundation Press, 1988), at 479–511.
9. *Trustees of Leland Stanford Jr. University v. Volt Information Sciences, Inc.*, No. P48603, slip op. (Cal. Super. Ct. Nov. 21, 1986) ("Plaintiff's motion to stay arbitration is granted and Defendant's motion to compel arbitration is denied").
10. See *Moses H. Cone Memorial Hospital v. Mercury Construction Corp.*, 460 U.S. 1 (1983); *Southland Corp. v. Keating*, 465 U.S. 1 (1984); *Dean Witter Reynolds, Inc. v. Byrd*, 470 U.S. 213 (1985); and *Mitsubishi Motors Corp. v. Soler Chrysler-Plymouth, Inc.*, 473 U.S. 614 (1985).
11. *Moses H. Cone, supra* note 10; and *Dean Witter, supra* note 10. In at least one reported case, the arbitral tribunal stayed its own proceedings to await the adjudication by a court of certain relevant issues (*Pacific Star Corp. v. Metal Transport Corp. of New York*, Society of Maritime Arbitrators, Inc. (SMA), Award No. 2065 (Apr. 24, 1986), as cited in *Yearbook Commercial Arbitration*, vol. 12 (Deventer, the Netherlands: Kluwer, 1987), at 172).

12. *Board of Trustees of Leland Stanford Jr. University v. Volt Information Sciences, Inc.*, 195 Cal. App. 3d 349, 352, 240 Cal. Rptr. 558, 559 (1987).
13. 195 Cal. App. 3d at 355, 240 Cal. Rptr. at 561.
14. *Restatement, supra* note 6, at § 187(2)(b) (limiting choice when issue is not one that parties can resolve by explicit agreement).
15. *McDermott v. Wisconsin*, 228 U.S. 115 (1913); see, also, Tribe, *American Constitutional Law, supra* note 8, at § 6-26.
16. *Southland, supra* note 10.
17. *Volt*, 109 S. Ct. at 1259.
18. See Tribe, *American Constitutional Law, supra* note 8, at 479–511.
19. *Volt*, 109 S. Ct. at 1259–1260.
20. *Supra* note 9, at 1.
21. See *Parklane Hosiery Co. v. Shore*, 439 U.S. 322 (1979) (trial court granted discretion to determine when offensive collateral estoppel may be used in light of previously approved defensive use). The doctrine has been applied by courts to give preclusive effect to prior arbitral awards. See, *e.g.*, *Wellons, Inc. v. T.E. Ibberson Co.*, 869 F.2d 1166 (8th Cir. 1989); Restatement (Second) of Judgments § 84 (1982); and G. Richard Shell, "Res Judicata and Collateral Estoppel Effects of Commercial Arbitration," *UCLA Law Review* 35 (1988): 623. But see *Dean Witter Reynolds, Inc. v. Byrd*, 470 U.S. at 222–223 (arbitral award need not be given preclusive effect where necessary to protect federal policy).
22. See Martha A. Field, "Sources of Law: The Scope of Federal Common Law," *Harvard Law Review* 99 (1986): 881, 961–981 (discussing differences between state law that federal courts choose to apply and state law operating of its own force).
23. See Paul Bator, Daniel Meltzer, Paul Mishkin, and David Shapiro, *Hart and Wechsler's The Federal Courts and the Federal System*, 3d ed. (Westbury, NY: Foundation Press, 1988), at 857–877.
24. See *e.g.*, *Astor Chocolate Corp. v. Mikroverk, Ltd.*, 704 F. Supp. 30 (E.D.N.Y. 1989). The court held that the question whether an international exchange of an offer and a discrepant acceptance resulted in an arbitration agreement cognizable by the FAA and the United Nations Convention on the Recognition and Enforcement of Foreign Arbitral Awards is governed by New York Uniform Commercial Code § 2-207, the "battle of the forms" provision. Other courts have held that, in such cases, the Uniform Commercial Code does not operate *ex proprio vigore* but as "a source of the 'federal' law of sales" (*United States v. Wegematic Corp.*, 360 F.2d 674, 676 (2d Cir. 1966) (Friendly, C.J.)); and *Lea Tai Textile Co., Ltd. v. Manning Fabrics, Inc.*, 411 F. Supp. 1404 (S.D.N.Y. 1975).
25. *D'Oench, Duhme & Co. v. FDIC*, 315 U.S. 447, 471–472 (1942) (Jackson, J., concurring).
26. *Board of County Commissioners v. United States*, 308 U.S. 343, 351–352 (1939) (Frankfurter, J.).
27. See *Restatement, supra* note 6, at § 187(2)(b).
28. *Moses H. Cone, supra* note 10.
29. *Southland, supra* note 10.

Specific Performance Awards*

Rosemary S. Page

The author has received a number of recent telephone calls asking if arbitrators may award specific performance and if courts will confirm arbitration awards that direct specific performance of a contract.

The select group of cases noted below indicate that federal courts and New York State courts have confirmed arbitration awards directing specific performance. The subjects of these awards were diverse: employment re-instatement, construction of a building, buying and selling of fungible goods, and even the buying and selling of coal on an interim basis.

Because arbitration is a matter of contract, an arbitrator may only award specific performance when the parties have authorized this relief in their contract—either specifically or by incorporating into their contract rules of procedure that authorize this relief.[1]

For example, section 43 of the Commercial Arbitration Rules of the American Arbitration Association states that:

> The arbitrator may grant any remedy or relief which the arbitrator deems just and equitable and within the scope of the agreement of the parties, including, but not limited to, specific performance of a contract.

Interim Specific Performance Award

When parties agree to arbitrate in accordance with these AAA Rules, this specific performance language will authorize an arbitrator to grant even an interim award of specific performance.

In *Island Creek Coal Sales Co. v. City of Gainesville, Fla.*[2] Island Creek and the City of Gainesville entered into a long-term agreement for Gainesville to purchase coal from Island Creek for a designated price. When the price of coal fell, Gainesville sought to terminate the agreement and initiated arbitration before the AAA with hearings held in Kentucky. Gainesville asked the arbitrators to terminate the coal contract and contended that Island Creek had breached the contract. After all of the evidence had been submitted but before the arbitrators could enter their final award, Gainesville announced that it was terminating the agreement.

---

* Copyright 1989. The New York Law Publishing Co. Reprinted with permission of the *New York Law Journal* (September 14, 1989). Rosemary S. Page is Associate General Counsel of the American Arbitration Association.

Island Creek's counsel asked the arbitrators to compel Gainesville to preserve the status quo until the final award was rendered.

A telephone conference was then conducted involving counsel for the two parties and the three arbitrators. After this conference, the arbitrators handed down the interim ruling that, since Gainesville had previously submitted to arbitration the issue of its right to terminate, the arbitrators would now restrain Gainesville from canceling the agreement and would order Gainesville to continue accepting coal shipments in accordance with the terms of the agreement until further order of the arbitrators.

Gainesville disobeyed this interim order by refusing to accept and pay for the coal. Island Creek commenced an action in federal district court in Kentucky to confirm the interim arbitration order, and the court confirmed the award.

On appeal, Gainesville argued that the arbitrators exceeded their authority when they rendered an award granting interim equitable relief and that furthermore the interim award was not a final award as required by 9 U.S.C. § 10(c). Gainesville reasoned that the court had no authority to confirm an interim award in any event.

In affirming the district court's order of confirmation, the Sixth Circuit Court of Appeals noted that the parties had incorporated the AAA Commercial Arbitration Rules in their agreement. While the agreement itself was silent in regard to the possibility of equitable relief, the court noted that "[t]he authority for equitable relief arises from Rule 43 of the AAA Commercial Arbitration Rules which the Agreement incorporates by reference."[3]

The court further observed that "[u]nder this Rule an arbitrator can order specific performance to preserve the status quo under the contract unless the contract expressly prevents such relief."

In response to Gainesville's argument that the district court lacked authority to confirm a nonfinal order under section 10(d), the appellate court said that this argument overlooks the rule that "an 'interim' award that finally and definitely disposes of a separate independent claim may be confirmed 'notwithstanding the absence of an award that finally disposes of all the claims that were submitted to arbitration.'"[4] The district court judge had concluded that the "interim award disposes of one self-contained issue, namely, whether the City is required to perform the contract during the pendency of the arbitration proceedings. Th[is] issue is a separate, discrete, independent, severable issue."

The appellate court also observed that "We find nothing in the contract between the parties or in Kentucky law that prevents the arbitrators from ordering the interim injunctive relief awarded in this case."[5]

The *Island Creek* court cited the Second Circuit Court of Appeals' ruling in *Sperry International Trade Inc. v. Israel*.[6]

As in *Island Creek*, the *Sperry* court was asked to determine the arbitrators' authority to grant interim injunctive relief under the AAA Rules. The *Sperry* court upheld the arbitrators' power to prevent drawing down the proceeds of a letter of credit pending their final decision on the merits.

The case of *Taunton Municipal Light Plant Commission v. Paul L. Geiringer & Associates*[7] involved AAA Rules administered in Boston, Massachusetts.

Valid, Reasonable Condition

Taunton and Geiringer had contracted to expand Taunton's power plant using Geiringer's consulting engineering services. Their dispute was arbitrated at the completion of the project, and the portion of the award that Taunton asked the court to vacate concerned as-built drawings. As to this claim, the arbitrators denied monetary damages and awarded specific performance that Taunton should collect the as-built drawings from all the prime contractors, deliver them to Geiringer for assembly with Geiringer's as-built drawings in accordance with the contract, and then deliver these drawings to Taunton by a certain date. The court footnoted the fact that these drawings were indispensable for the operation of the power plant.[8] The Consulting Agreement provided that the as-built drawings were to become the property of Taunton.

Although the Consulting Agreement required only that Geiringer provide the as-built drawings to Taunton, the court said that,

> [T]he [specific performance award] directing Taunton to provide Geiringer with the prime contractors' as-built drawings is a valid and reasonable condition precedent to performance by Geiringer (re-delivery of as-built drawings to Taunton). The arbitrators' decision . . . was not an ultra vires act. Even if there were an error of law or fact, such error of law or fact would be legally insufficient to set aside the award.[9]

In *Marion Manufacturing Co. v. W.B. Long*,[10] the arbitrators had refused to clarify their specific performance award by determining the amount of money damages for the breach of the parties' agreement for the purchase and sale of cotton.

This arbitration was held before the Board of Appeals of the Cotton States Arbitration Board in Memphis, Tennessee. The award directed the seller to deliver the cotton necessary to fulfill the contracts. The court confirmed the award while stating that "specific performance of a contract for the purchase and sale of fungible goods is somewhat unusual."[11]

On appeal, the Sixth Circuit Court of Appeals said in a footnote that the district court "found that the Board's decision requiring specific performance of the contract might be the more equitable result in light of the fact that both parties abused the . . . standards of commercial dealing in spirit, if not in fact."[12]

In an earlier New York case, *Bradigan v. Bishop Homes, Inc.*,[13] the Appellate Division ruled that the trial court lacked jurisdiction "upon the facts herein to modify the award to substitute monetary relief for the performance directed by the award."[14] The award had directed specific performance of uncompleted work.

New York State courts blazed the trail in confirming arbitral awards for specific performance. *Grayson-Robinson Stores, Inc. v. Iris Construction Corp.*[15] upheld confirmation of an award to construct a building. This arbitration was conducted under AAA Rules. *Matter of Staklinski (Pyramid Electrical Co.)*[16] upheld confirmation of an award that reinstated an employee to his former position under an employment contract. This arbitration, too, had been conducted under AAA Rules.

Matter of Ruppert (Egelhofer)[17] upheld an award that enjoined a strike in a labor dispute. In discussing the *Ruppert* case, the *Staklinski* court said:

> A supposed "public policy" against such an injunction was urged on us in *Ruppert* since there we had a specific statute (Civil Practice Act, §867-a) which would have made it impossible for a court to grant that same injunction. However, we held in *Ruppert* that the parties had agreed not only to submit their controversies to arbitration but had validly authorized the arbitrators to issue an injunction. The same is true here. Whether a court of equity could issue a specific performance decree in a case like this . . . is beside the point.[18]

An arbitration award may order specific performance to fulfill a contractual obligation and courts will enforce awards directing specific performance when there is no applicable law prohibiting an arbitrator from granting this relief and the parties have provided in their agreement that such a remedy is within the authority of the arbitrator. The opinions indicate that the award of specific performance may be confirmed even when the court itself would not have granted this relief.

Notes

1. Domke Comm Arbitration § 30:01 (Rev. Ed., Wilner).
2. 729 F.2d 1046 (6th Cir. 1984).
3. *Id.* at 1049.
4. *Id.* at 1049 citing to *Eurolines Shipping Co. v. Metal Transport Corp,* 491 F. Supp. 590, 592 (S.D.N.Y. 1980), quoting *Puerto Rico Maritime Shipping Authority v. Star Lines Ltd.*, 454 F. Supp. 368, 372 (S.D.N.Y. 1978).
5. *Id.* at 1049.
6. 689 F. 2d 301 (2d Cir. 1982).
7. 560 F. Supp. 1249 (1983).
8. *Id.* at 1250.
9. *Id.* at 1253.
10. 588 F.2d 538 (6th Cir. 1978).

11. *Id.* at 541. There was no shortage of cotton nor was the cotton referred to in the contract unique. Traditionally the equitable remedy of specific performance, when granted by courts, was sparingly ordered when monetary damages were unsatisfactory or the subject matter of the contract was "unique." See discussion in Oleck, "Specific Performance of Contracts through Arbitration," *Arbitration Journal*, American Arbitration Association, Vol. 6, 1951, pp. 163-167, and Oleck, "Specific Performance of Builders Contracts," *Fordham Law Review*, Vol. 21, Issue 2, June, 1952, pp. 156-171.
12. *Id.* at p. 541.
13. 249 N.Y.S.2d 1018 (4th Dept. 1964).
14. *Id.* at 1019.
15. 8 N.Y.2d 133, 202 N.Y.S.2d 303 (1960).
16. 6 N.Y.2d 159, 188 N.Y.S.2d 541, 160 NE2d 78 (1959).
17. 3 N.Y.2d 576, 170 N.Y.S.2d 785 (1958).
18. 188 N.Y.S.2d at 543.

Waiver of Right to Explanations*

Rosemary S. Page

Unless the contract or a statute provides otherwise, arbitrators are not required to include explanations with their awards. In 1960, the United States Supreme Court said, "Arbitrators have no obligation to the court to give their reasons for an award."[1]

Explanations When Required

As noted above, an arbitrator may be required to provide an opinion[2] or findings, conclusions, or a reasoned award under the statute that controls the arbitration process,[3] or under the arbitration contract.[4] For example, the Securities Arbitration Rules of the American Arbitration Association, which become part of the parties' contract if so specified, state, at Rule 42, that the award "shall include a statement regarding the disposition of any statutory claims."

However, as a general rule, the validity of the arbitration award is unaffected by the absence of a recital of the reasons for the award.[5] The grounds for vacatur of the award are limited to those provided under the pertinent statute.[6]

The language quoted above from the Supreme Court reflects the fact that awards without opinions are an accepted feature of arbitration. The few

 Rosemary S. Page is Associate General Counsel of the American Arbitration Association.

court orders that seek arbitrators' explanations, despite this legal principle, are the subject of this article.

This article does not discuss the mere itemization of an award—something that arbitrators may provide upon request in an appropriate case. For example, the association's *A Guide for Commercial Arbitrators* says: "when so requested by a party, [the arbitrator] may include a breakdown of items awarded."

This article focuses only on instances when an arbitrator's testimony was sought in connection with the upholding or overturning of the unreasoned award itself because it allegedly contained an infirmity. Discussed are: (1) why arbitrators are not required to provide arbitral opinions, (2) reasons given by some parties for seeking an arbitrator's explanation for the award, and (3) the reactions of courts to requests for arbitrators' explanations for their awards.

Arbitration is hailed as a prompt and economical contractual method of resolving disputes without resort to the courts. Thus, when parties choose arbitration in preference to litigation, they must be conscious of the trade-offs found in arbitration but not found in litigation, such as (1) the privacy of the process, (2) the parties' selection of their own decision maker, (3) the absence of a jury trial, (4) the absence of a judicial appeal on the law since arbitrators are not bound by principles of substantive law absent a contractual or statutory provision to the contrary,[7] (5) the absence of broad discovery, (6) the relaxed application of the rules of evidence, (7) the payment of arbitration administration costs by the parties themselves instead of by taxpayers and (8) the absence of a written opinion with the award unless otherwise required.

Why No Opinions

A contract may require the arbitrator to explain the award, but most contracts do not. The Commercial and Construction Rules of the American Arbitration Association, for example, which become a part of the parties' agreement when so specified, have no such requirement. Arbitration statutes like the Federal Arbitration Act (Title 9 of the United States Code), the Uniform Arbitration Act, and New York's Article 75 of the Civil Practice Law & Rules have no requirement that awards contain explanations.

The Association's *A Guide for Commercial Arbitrators* provides:

> No Written Opinion Is Required
> Commercial arbitrators are not required to explain the reasons for their decisions. As a general rule, the award consists of a brief direction to the parties on a single sheet of paper. One reason for brevity is that written opinions might open avenues for attack on the award by the losing party.

Robert M. Rodman notes that:

> A requirement that arbitrators explain their reasoning in every case would help to uncover extreme failures to apply the law to a dispute, but such a rule would undermine the purpose of arbitration to provide a relatively quick, efficient and informal means of private dispute settlement. . . .[8]

Martin Domke said:

> Although written opinions accompanying commercial awards might serve as a guide for future business relations and thus discourage disputes on similar issues, the drawbacks decisively outweigh this advantage. A detailed opinion written by a layman might expose the award to challenge in the courts, jeopardizing both the speed and finality of arbitration. Arbitrators, who regard their civic duty to the business community, might be reluctant to devote the extra time and effort required to produce a written opinion and loathe to lay the basis of their decision open to criticism by the community and the courts.[9]

Because parties increasingly use arbitration, it is an alternative dispute resolving (ADR) mechanism that effectively relieves the courts of many claims that would otherwise further overcrowd the courts. One of arbitration's attractions is its speed, which is accomplished, in part, by dispensing with a reasoned award. Changing this form of ADR could have the effect of undermining arbitration's role in assisting the court.

Some reasons given by parties asking courts either to question arbitrators or to overturn the unreasoned award are that the arbitrators may have awarded consequential damages, and thus exceeded their powers,[10] that the award may be illegal,[11] that the award itself shows arbitrator bias,[12] that the arbitrators refused to consider or to appreciate particular arguments of evidence tendered to them,[13] that the arbitration award is unsupported by the evidence,[14] or that the lump-sum award includes items expressly excluded under the contract.[15]

Judicial Reaction

While most judges have dismissed such entreaties, a few judges have agreed to ask the arbitrator to explain the award under these circumstances.

In a recent Mississippi case, *Craig v. Barber*,[16] the losing party said that the award itself exhibited the evident partiality of the arbitrator, and the trial court ordered the arbitrator to explain and clarify the award.

The arbitrator sought intervenor status to challenge the trial court's order and appealed to the Mississippi Supreme Court. That court ruled that the arbitrator had standing to challenge such order of the trial court and, in granting the arbitrator's application for a writ prohibiting enforcement of the order, explained that:

> These matters go to the very heart of the arbitration process. When they agree to arbitration the parties contract for an award without a formal, reasoned opinion, and, more specifically, without findings of fact or conclusions of law. Absent contractual agreement to the contrary—and no such agreement was made here—the parties waive any right to an explanation or clarification.[17]

The court went on to say that:

> If [the arbitrator] complies with the [order to explain and clarify the award] and on appeal at the end of the case we reverse, there is no way the status quo may be restored. [The arbitrator] will have been required to do that which he was under no obligation to do, and Stewart will have obtained from [the arbitrator], something Stewart had no legal right to demand.[18]

Award Impeachment

In addition, the court noted:

> Of relevance further is our general rule that the testimony of an arbitrator is incompetent to impeach his award.[19]

In a New York case, *Guetta v. Raxon Fabrics Corp.*,[20] the court remanded the award to the arbitrator for a modification reflecting a determination of the statute of limitations issue. On appeal, the First Department reversed the trial court and confirmed the award, stating:

> Because the arbitrator is not required to give any reasons for his decision, his award cannot be attacked on the ground that he refused to consider or failed to appreciate particular arguments or evidence tendered to him.

In the New York case of *Willow Fabrics, Inc. v. Carolina Freight Carriers Corp.*,[21] one party urged the court to vacate the award or to seek an explanation for the award from the arbitrators because the award might possibly allow an illegal rebate.

In refusing to remand the award to the arbitrators for specific findings, the court said:

> Appellant's attack upon the award proceeds on the assumption that any award less than the amount it claimed to be due would be illegal as in contravention of federal law prohibiting the payment of anything less than the published rates for transportation. . . . The arbitrator's award can be justified on [a legal] basis without there being *a compulsory conclusion* that there was an illegal ground for the award. The validity of the award is unaffected by the absence of a recital of the reasons for the award. [citations omitted, emphasis added]

In *Chasser v. Prudential-Bache Securities*,[22] the losing party moved to vacate the award in Florida federal court, stating that the arbitrators were evidently partial and that they manifestly disregarded the law. The award said:

> And having heard and considered the proofs of the parties, [we] have decided and determined that in full and final settlement, the claim of the claimant be and hereby is dismissed in all respects.

The court noted that the arbitrators ''failed to explain their conclusions or give any justifications for the outcome reached.''[23]

The court said, ''Nonetheless, the Supreme Court has held that this kind of conduct on the part of arbitrators is entirely appropriate.''[24]

Accordingly, the court said:

> The burden is on Ms. Chasser to demonstrate that the panel manifestly disregarded the law or that it was evidently partial to Prudential-Bache. Since absolutely nothing but the bottom line is ''manifest'' or ''evident'' from the decision of the panel, the Court must evaluate Plaintiff's contentions with reference only to the record produced at the arbitration hearing.[25]

The court's evaluation indicated that any one of five possible rationales could support the arbitrators' dismissal of the entire suit and, finding no other grounds for vacatur, denied Plaintiff's motion to vacate the award.

The *Chasser* court like the *Willow Fabrics* court examined the record before it in the face of allegations of ''manifest disregard of the law'' in *Chasser* and possible illegality in *Willow Fabrics*.

One Florida court[26] rejected the losing party's request that the award either be referred back to the arbitrator or be vacated because the award allegedly bore no rational relationship to the evidence presented on the issue of damages. The court affirmed the lower court's order confirming the award, saying that ''arbitrators are not required to disclose the precise mathematical basis upon which they arrived at a damages award.''

In other cases, courts have also refused to vacate awards or to question arbitrators whose awards contained no reasons. New York's Court of Appeals said, in *Silverman v. Benmore Coats, Inc.*[27] that:

> [The arbitrator's award] will not be vacated even though the court concludes that his interpretation of the agreement misconstrues or disregards its plain meaning or misapplies substantive rules of law, unless it is violative of a strong public policy or is totally irrational, or exceeds a specifically enumerated limitation on his power [citations omitted]. Nor will an arbitration award be vacated on ''the here possibility'' that it violates an express limitation on the arbitrator's power [citation omitted].

Absent a contrary requirement in the contract or a statute, parties who agree to arbitrate waive their right to an award with findings of fact, conclusions of law, or other explanation of the award.

Further, arbitrators are immune from giving testimony for the purpose of impeaching their award.

The sampling of cases above demonstrates judicial encouragement to parties to honor their agreements to arbitrate, and, in so doing, to adhere to the principles of arbitration. In this way arbitration can best fulfill its role as an aid in reducing court congestion.

Notes

1. *United Steelworkers of America v. Enterprise Wheel & Car Corp.*, 363 U.S. 593, 598 (1960).
2. Customarily, labor arbitrators write opinions to accompany their awards providing union and management with guidelines to follow in their future dealings under their collective bargaining agreements.
   The international award may be accompanied by reasons.
3. For example, see New York's No Fault Law (Article 51 of the Insurance Law). The Insurance Department Regulations promulgated thereunder at 11 NYCRR 65.17(b)(5)(xvii) provide: "The award shall be in writing in a format approved by the superintendent. It shall state the issues in dispute and contain the arbitrator's findings and conclusions based on the Insurance Law and Insurance Department regulations."
   See also the United Nations Commission on International Trade Law's (UNCITRAL) Model Law Article 31(2): "The award shall state the reasons upon which it is based, unless the parties have agreed that no reasons are to be given or the award is an award on agreed terms under article 30."
4. In *Meharry v. Midwestern Gas Transmission*, 103 Ill. App. 3d 144, 430 N.E.2d 1138 (1981), the agreement required that findings of fact be stated by the arbitrator, but even then, the court said that the arbitrator is not required to give detailed reasons for the award.
5. *Willow Fabrics, Inc. v. Carolina Freight Carriers Corp.*, 248 N.Y.S.2d 509, 510, *aff'd* 16 N.Y.2d 929, 264 N.Y.S.2d 919 (1965).
6. See, for example, 9 U.S.C. §10 or NYCPLR §7511.
7. *Silverman v. Benmor Coats, Inc.*, 61 N.Y.2d 299, 305, 473 N.Y.S.2d 774, 779 (1984).
8. Robert M. Rodman, *Commercial Arbitration* §21.5 (1984).
9. *Domke on Commercial Arbitration* §29.06 (Rev. Ed.) (1988).
10. *Matter of Tilbury Fabrics v. Stillwater, Inc.*, 57 N.Y.2d 624, 450 N.Y.S.2d 478 (1982).
11. *Willow Fabrics, Inc. v. Carolina Freight Carriers Corp.*, 248 N.Y.S.2d 509, *aff'd* 16 N.Y.2d 929, 264 N.Y.S.2d 919 (1965).
12. *Craig v. Barber*, 524 So. 2d 974 (1988).
13. *Guetta v. Raxon Fabrics Corp.*, 510 N.Y.S.2d 576 (1st Dept. 1987).
14. *Hialeah Park, Inc. v. Ocala Breeders' Sales Co.*, 528 So. 2d 1227 (Fla. Dist. Ct. App. 1988).
15. *Federated Dept. Stores v. J.V.B. Industries*, 894 F.2d 862 (6th Cir. 1990).
16. *Craig v. Barber*, 524 So. 2d 974.
17. *Id.* at 976.
18. *Id.* at 977.
19. *Id.* at 978. See, also, "Immunity and the Arbitration Process," *Lawyers' Arbitration Letter*, vol. 7, no. 1, March 1983.
20. *Guetta v. Raxon Fabrics Corp.*, 510 N.Y.S.2d 576 (1st Dept. 1987).
21. *Willow Fabrics, Inc. v. Carolina Freight Carriers Corp.*, 248 N.Y.S.2d 509, 510, *aff'd* 16 N.Y.2d 929, 264 N.Y.S.2d 919 (1965).
22. *Chasser v. Prudential-Bache Securities*, 703 F. Supp. 78 (S.D. Fla. 1988). The award was rendered by a New York Stock Exchange Arbitration Panel.

23. *Chasser* at 79.
24. *Id.*
25. *Id.*
26. *Hialeah Park, Inc. v. Ocala Breeders' Sales Co.*, 528 So. 2d 1227 (Fla. Dist. Ct. App. 1988).
27. *Silverman v. Benmor Coats, Inc.*, 61 N.Y.2d 299, 308, 473 N.Y.S.2d 774, 779 (1984).

Prejudgment and Postjudgment Interest*

Michael F. Hoellering

From time to time, questions tend to arise relating to the calculation of interest by the court in the confirmation and entry of a judgment on an arbitration award. Three decisions in particular, dealing with the judicial treatment of interest in the context of arbitral proceedings, are of interest. The issue is governed in part by section 1961 of the United States Code, title 28, which permits an award of interest on a judgment entered in federal court. The original section 1961 provided that postjudgment interest would accrue at the rate allowed by state law. In 1982, section 1961 was amended to provide that the calculation of the interest rate be equal to the Treasury bill rate. Two issues that frequently arise in connection with postjudgment interest are when the federal law applies and whether section 1961 is mandatory.

In *Northrop Corp. v. Triad International Marketing, S.A.*,[1] the court was faced with whether an arbitration award requiring Northrop to pay commissions owed to its marketing representative constituted a violation of a "well-defined and dominant" policy of the U.S. Department of Defense. Another issue before the court in a subsequent motion was that of postjudgment interest.[2]

Northrop, a U.S. aircraft manufacturer, entered into a marketing agreement with Triad for the solicitation by Triad of contracts for aircraft, training, and support services for the Saudi Arabia Air Force. Five years after the parties entered into their agreement, Saudi Arabia issued a decree prohibiting the payment of commissions for armament contracts. Northrop, in turn, stopped paying commissions to Triad. A dispute arose over the payment of commissions, and the matter was submitted to arbitration under the rules of the American Arbitration Association pursuant to the arbitra-

* Copyright 1990. The New York Law Publishing Co. Reprinted with permission of the *New York Law Journal* (February 8, 1990). Michael F. Hoellering is General Counsel of the American Arbitration Association.

tion provision in the marketing agreement, which also provided that California law would govern. The arbitrators rendered an award in favor of Triad, concluding, inter alia, that Triad was entitled to its commissions because California law did not prohibit enforcement of the agreement.

The district court vacated the award on public policy grounds, and the appellate court reversed, finding that the policy of the U.S. Department of Defense was not sufficiently "well-defined and dominant" to justify refusal to enforce the award.[3] Following the reinstatement of the award, Triad moved for an amendment of the order to include postjudgment interest.

Federal or State Law

One of the issues before the court was whether prejudgment and postjudgment interest should be calculated at the rate fixed by federal or state law. The court rejected Triad's argument that an exception should be created for diversity actions seeking enforcement of arbitration awards under the Federal Arbitration Act (FAA). It found that Triad's position rested on the premise that suits pursuant to the FAA should lie under federal question jurisdiction, a premise rejected by the Supreme Court in *Southland Corp. v. Keating*.[4] Because the recognized rule is that state law determines the rate of prejudgment interest in diversity actions, the court stated that California law controlled the rate of prejudgment interest. As to postjudgment interest, the court found that even in diversity cases, postjudgment interest is determined by federal law.

Another issue before the court was the date on which postjudgment interest begins to run: that is, whether it should run from the entry of judgment refusing to enforce the arbitration award or from the entry on remand of a judgment enforcing the award.

The court considered section 1961 of 28 U.S.C., which provides that interest "shall be calculated from the date of the entry of the judgment," and noted that the intent of section 1961 was to "ensure that the plaintiff is further compensated for being deprived of the monetary value of the loss from the date of ascertainment of damages until payment by defendent."[5] Because the "failure to allow postjudgment interest from the entry of the original judgment would penalize parties for choosing arbitration rather than jury trial, contrary to the 'national policy favoring arbitration' as an alternative to jury trials," the court concluded that the effective date of judgment for the purpose of calculating postjudgment interest is the date of the district court's order vacating the arbitration award.[6]

Postjudgment interest was also the issue in *Laminoirs-Trefileries-Cableries de Lens, S.A. v. Southwire Co.*[7] Southwire, a manufacturer of cable products, and Laminoirs, a manufacturer of steel wire and rope, entered into a purchase agreement whereby Laminoirs would manufacture and sell galvanized steel wire to Southwire. The agreement contained a world market price adjustment clause, an arbitration clause, and a governing law clause.

A dispute arose as to the interpretation of the world market price adjustment clause. Laminoirs, pursuant to the arbitration clause, demanded arbitration before the International Chamber of Commerce (ICC). Arbitration was conducted, and a partial arbitral award was rendered. A further arbitral award, confirming settlement of one of the issues, was later rendered. Laminoirs moved to confirm the award, and Southwire opposed.

French Interest Rates

One of the grounds on which Southwire attacked the award was that the French legal rate of interest, which the arbitrators had applied on the judgment, should not apply. The court disagreed. It found that the governing law clause stated that Georgia law would apply to the extent that it was in accordance with French law. Because Southwire had agreed to this provision, the court determined that Southwire was on notice that French law had a potential bearing on the outcome of the case. In addition, because arbitrators may draw on their own personal knowledge in making an award, which they did in this case, the court concluded that the manner in which the amount of interest payable was determined by the arbitrators is not grounds for vacation of the arbitration award under 9 U.S.C. §§ 10(c) or (d).

The court also declined to refuse enforcement of the award under Article V. ¶2(b) of the United Nations Convention on the Recognition and Enforcement of Foreign Arbitral Awards. The Article provides that enforcement may be refused if such enforcement would be contrary to the public policy of the country where enforcement is sought. Southwire's argument was that the arbitrators' determination that the applicable annual rate for the time periods in question should be 10.5 percent and 9.5 percent was too high and violated state and federal law. The court disagreed, finding that the Georgia legal rate may be as high as 10.5 percent in some instances.

The court did, however, refuse to enforce a portion of the award providing for an additional 5 percent interest, finding that portion of the award to be penal rather than compensatory in nature. It also rejected Southwire's argument that the arbitrators were allowed to award only preaward interest. The court found, however, that there was no express limitation on the awarding of postaward interest. Consequently, it concluded that there was no error with the decision of the tribunal.

A supplemental opinion was issued by the court in which it discussed, inter alia, the rate of exchange to be applied to convert the French francs due into United States dollars and the rate of postjudgment interest.[8] As to the rate of exchange, the court found that "[w]hen a debt is payable in foreign currency in a foreign country, the proper date of conversion is the judgment date, and the date on which the obligation arose."[9] Consequently, the court determined that the judgment day would be the date of its entry of judgment.

Regarding postjudgment interest, the court found that such interest, when involving a federal judgment, is calculated from the date of entry at the rate allowed by state law. Applying state law under 28 U.S.C. § 1961, the court determined that it could award a rate no higher than the highest lawful rate allowed by the state. In this instance, the rate was 8 percent. Although section 1961 was amended in 1982 to provide that the calculation of the interest rate be equal to the Treasury bill rate, Southwire provides an illustration of how decisions by arbitrators on the issue of postaward interest may be modified based on existing statutory provision.

Credit Card Sales

Another decision involving postjudgment interest is *Carte Blanche (Singapore) PTE, Ltd. v. Carte Blanche International, Ltd.*[10] Carte Blanche (Singapore) PTE (CBS) and Carte Blanche International (CBI) entered into a franchise agreement for the marketing of Carte Blanche credit cards in Malaysia, Singapore, and Brunei by CBS. At some point, the shareholders of CBS transferred their CBS shares to Global Equities PTE, a newly created company controlled by CBS, which then transferred one-half of its stock to the MBF Holdings Berhad Group of Companies.

A dispute subsequently arose and CBS and CBI filed contemporaneous demands for arbitration with the International Chamber of Commerce Court of Arbitration (ICC), with CBI alleging that the transfers were in violation of the franchise agreement.

The panel of arbitrators rendered an interim award in favor of CBS, with one arbitrator dissenting. A final award was also in favor of CBS, which included damages, interest, and injunctive relief. The award was submitted to the ICC for approval pursuant to its procedural rules. After the ICC approved the award, CBS moved to confirm in federal court. CBI opposed. The court confirmed the award, rejecting CBI's contentions that the award should be vacated because the arbitrators manifestly disregarded the law, failed to enforce California law on the availability of damages, and exceeded their authority when they made a valuation determination in connection with the transfer of credit accounts. It also made a determination that the effective date of the award was February 8, 1988, the date on which counsel for the parties received a copy of the award sent to them by the ICC Secretariat.

Following the court's opinion and order, CBS submitted a proposed judgment. CBI objected to the CBS proposal and submitted a proposed judgment of its own. Because the parties disagreed over the form of the judgment to be entered, the court considered the applicability of 28 U.S.C. § 1961 to postjudgment interest since the disagreement centered on the rate of postjudgment interest.[11] More specifically, CBS argued that section 1961 did not apply, while CBI argued that section 1961 is mandatory, even though the arbitrators had purported to establish the rate of postjudgment interest.

Interest Award

The court noted that section 1961 provides for interest on any money judgment in a civil case recovered in a district court and that the interest

> shall be calculated from the date of the entry of judgment, at a rate equal to the coupon issue yield equivalent . . . of the average accepted auction price for the last auction of 52-week United States Treasury bills settled immediately before the date of the judgment.[12]

Relying on the reasons stated in *Parsons & Whittemore Ala. Mach. & Servs. Corp. v. Yeargin Constr. Co.*,[13] the court found that the award of postjudgment interest is governed by section 1961. In doing so, the court rejected the argument that "enforcement of an arbitration award is not a judgment for which interest rates are statutorily regulated,"[14] reasoning that the argument ignores the provisions of 9 U.S.C. § 13, which provides that judgments entered by a federal court confirming, modifying, or correcting an arbitration award be enforced as if it had been rendered in an action in the court in which it was entered.

CBI appealed, and CBS cross-appealed to restore the interest award made by the arbitrators. The appellate court affirmed the district court's order. As to the reduction of interest, the court ruled that the district court judgment affirming the arbitration award was governed by the postjudgment interest rates set forth in 28 U.S.C. § 1961.

Specifically, the court stated that "the universal application of section 1961 to all types of claims makes for logical uniformity [because] once a claim is reduced to judgment, the original claim is extinguished and merged into the judgment; and a new claim, called a judgment debt, arises."[15]

The court also found *Parsons & Whittemore* to be directly on point and disagreed with CBS's contention that *Parsons & Whittemore* was distinguishable because the judgment in the instant case was not a "money judgment" within the meaning of section 1961. The court reasoned that the "essence of post-judgment interest [is] that it assessed upon payments made pursuant to a judgment but subsequent to the entry of the judgment."[16]

In addition, the court rejected CBS's claim that "the arbitrators' interest award was carefully crafted to provide incentives for the parties to comply with the complex injunctive aspects of the award and that failure to enforce arbitral interest awards would lead to forum shopping for the enforcement of arbitral awards among jurisdictions with different rules concerning post-judgment interest."[17] It stated that such an argument "challenges the wisdom of the inflexible, unitary rule provided by § 1961(a) regarding post-judgment interest on money judgments awarded by federal district courts."[18] The court further suggested that Congress is the appropriate forum for CBS to address its claims and noted that 9 U.S.C. § 9 authorizes parties to specify in their arbitration agreement "the court in which any award made pursuant to the agreement shall be enforced."[19] Indeed, further consideration of this issue is probably warranted since an arbitrator's award of interest is customarily within the realm of the arbitrator's powers, and whether the legislature should substitute that power is a debatable question.

Notes

1. 811 F.2d 1265 (9th Cir. 1987).
2. *Northrop Corp. v. Triad International Marketing, S.A.*, No. 84-6480. 88 Daily Journal D.A.R. 3962 (C.D. Cal. Mar. 29, 1988).
3. 811 F.2d at 1271.
4. 465 U.S. 1, 104 S. Ct. 852, 79 LEd.2d 1 (1984).
5. 88 Daily Journal D.A.R. 3963.
6. *Id.* at 3964.
7. 484 F. Supp. 1063 (N.D. Ga. 1980).
8. Supplemental opinion, which was included in the court decision reported at 484 F. Supp. 1063, can be found at 484 F. Supp. at 1070.
9. 484 F. Supp. at 1070.
10. 888 F.2d 260 (2d Cir. 1989).
11. *In the Matter of the Arbitration of Certain Controversies Between Carte Blanche (Singapore) Pte., Ltd. v. Carte Blanche International, Ltd.*, No. 88 Civ. 0662. 1988 U.S. Dist. Lexis 4765 (S.D.N.Y. May 25, 1988).
12. 1988 U.S. Dist. Lexis 4765, p. 3 (citing to 28 U.S.C. § 1961 [1983]).
13. 744 F.2d 1482 (11th Cir. 1984).
14. *Id.* at 4.
15. *Carte Blanche (Singapore) Pte., Ltd. v. Carte Blanche International, Ltd.*, 888 F.2d 260 (2d Cir. 1989).
16. *Id.* at 269.
17. *Id.* at 269, 270.
18. *Id.*
19. *Id.*

Lemon Law Claims for Used Cars*

Carolyn M. Penna

New York was among the first states to enact comprehensive automobile "lemon laws" that protect the consumer who purchases a chronically defective automobile. Such a law covering new automobiles was enacted in 1983,[1] and, in the following year, a similar bill, covering used cars, was enacted.[2] These lemon laws have undergone numerous amendments since then, the most notable of which, in terms of dispute resolution, was the establishment in 1986 of an arbitration mechanism for disputes involving new cars, under the aegis of the State Attorney General.[3]

New Car Arbitration Program

The new car lemon law arbitration program was designed by the Attorney General's office and is administered by the American Arbitration Association (AAA). The program operates under a set of regulations promulgated by the Department of Law.[4] It is a mechanism that provides speedy, final, and binding resolution of a dispute over a "lemon," assuming the consumer has met certain threshold conditions.

The program, if elected by the consumer, is mandatory on the automobile manufacturer, and it is the manufacturer, as opposed to the retail automobile dealer, who must satisfy any award to the consumer.

The arbitration program for new cars has been in operation since February, 1987, with good results:

> [T]he Program has clearly maintained its position as the nation's preeminent lemon law arbitration program. In 1988, over 3,000 applications were processed and recoveries were close to $17 million. Since its inception in February 1987, over 5,600 applications were processed, and recoveries have exceeded $32 million. Cumulatively, consumers have prevailed in 69 percent of the cases when awards and settlements are combined."[5]

Because of the program's success, the Attorney General has been seeking legislation that would extend the program to disputes over used cars. On January 1, 1990, such an amendment to the General Business Law will become effective.

---

* Carolyn M. Penna is Regional Vice President, New York Region, of the American Arbitration Association.

Used Car Lemon Law "Bill of Rights"

Under the "used-car lemon law," a consumer who has spent more than $1,500 on a used car must be given a written warranty by the used car dealer, who is defined under the law as anyone who sells three or more used cars a year.[6] The warranty must extend for at least 60 days or 3,000 miles, whichever comes first, if the car has 36,000 miles or less; or for 30 days or 1,000 miles, whichever comes first, if the car has 36,000–100,000 miles. Cars with more than 100,000 miles are not covered. The seller may limit the warranty by certain conditions, so long as such conditions do not cause the consumer to waive any rights under the law.

Under the warranty, the dealer is responsible to repair, or reimburse the consumer for the cost of repairs, any defects in the basic operating systems of the car, as outlined in the "Bill of Rights." If, after three or more attempts at repair, the problem still exists, the consumer is entitled to return the car for a full refund of the purchase price and related fees, costs, and taxes. A refund is also available if the car is out of service for 15 days or more during the warranty period, due to repair of such a problem. A "reasonable allowance" may be deducted for "damage not attributable to normal usage or wear."[7]

Refund of the purchase price may be refused, however, if the problem does not "substantially impair" the value of the car, or is "caused by abuse, neglect, or unreasonable modification."[8] Also, if the dealer participates in an established arbitration procedure, the consumer's participation in that program may be a precondition to any refund. In any event, the consumer is invited to complain to the State Attorney General where there is a belief that the above rights have been violated.

The newest section of this "Bill of Rights" provides for the alternative arbitration mechanism run by the Attorney General. It provides that

> [A]s an alternative to the arbitration procedure made available through the dealer you may instead choose to submit your claim to an independent arbitrator, approved by the attorney general. You may have to pay a fee for such an arbitration. Contact your local consumer office or attorney general's office to find out how to arrange for independent arbitration.[9]

Administration of the Program

The used car lemon law arbitration program will operate under the same regulations as does the new car program, except that they will be amended to include the various provisions of the used car lemon law. The first sections define the purpose of the regulations, provide certain definitions, and establish a procedure for appointment of a program administrator.

The remaining sections (§§ 300.5–300.19) describe the arbitration procedure itself, from the filing with the Attorney General's office of a Request for Arbitration by the consumer through the ultimate decision of the arbitrator. Under the program, a consumer completes a "Request for Arbitration" form, which is submitted to the Attorney General. The form provides for election by the consumer of, among other things, refund or replacement vehicle, oral hearing or "documents only" proceeding; and desired hearing site. The form also requires attachment of a number of documents which support the consumer's claim.

The form is reviewed by the Attorney General's office for completeness and eligibility. If it passes muster, the case is forwarded to the administrator of the program (the AAA). The consumer must then pay a prescribed filing fee to the administrator, for processing of the claim.[10]

The case moves along a speedy track from the "filing date" (the date the fee is received by the administrator) through the award. The regulations provide that a hearing must be scheduled no later than 35 days from the filing date, and an award is due within 40 days of the filing date.[11] In unusual circumstances, a hearing may even be conducted by telephone.

Procedurally, the hearings generally are conducted as any arbitration hearing. Witnesses are sworn, evidence is taken, and parties may be represented by counsel if desired. Formal rules of evidence do not apply.

The award is final and binding and is subject to review only on the grounds specified in Article 75 of the New York Civil Practice Law. Awards may be converted into judgments by the court through the process of judicial confirmation.

Under the regulations, the arbitrator must be neutral; i.e., without bias or any interest in the outcome of the arbitration. To help ensure neutrality, all communications between the arbitrator and the parties, except at the hearing itself, must be channeled through the administrator. Where grounds can be shown, an arbitrator may be disqualified from serving on a given case.

The arbitrators come from all walks of life, and must be New York State residents or attorneys admitted in the state. They are trained by both the administrator and the Attorney General. Those interested in serving as arbitrators on lemon law cases are encouraged to contact the American Arbitration Association for more information.

As in arbitration generally, the arbitrator has broad powers as to the conduct of the hearing. He may issue subpoenas, examine witnesses or require production of additional documents. He may examine or even ride in the subject automobile, if desired.

Unlike typical commercial arbitration, however, the remedy that the arbitrator can award is limited under the lemon law and the regulations. If the consumer prevails, the arbitrator can award only a refund of the purchase price of the automobile, or a comparable replacement vehicle where desired, plus certain fees, costs, and taxes. If the manufacturer prevails, the case is terminated. No other remedy is available to the consumer, nor may the arbitrator creatively fashion another remedy.

Of course, the parties may settle their dispute outside of arbitration, if desired. Also, if desired, such settlement may be converted into the consent award of the arbitrator, for enforcement purposes.

Projected Caseload

While it is not yet known what the number of cases filed under the used car arbitration program will be, it has been projected that approximately 25 percent of the new car caseload, or 500 cases annually, can be expected. This projection is based on the number of used cars sold statewide on an annual basis, which meet the criteria outlined in the Bill of Rights.

Conclusion

The Attorney General had termed the absence of a state-sponsored arbitration program covering the used car lemon law "a serious deficiency."[12] The need for the same speedy and final mechanism for resolution of used car lemon law disputes is as great as that for new cars. The deficiency has now been remedied with the passage of this new amendment. We are all anxious to see the program prove as successful as the new car lemon law arbitration program has proven and are pleased to see yet another victory for the consumer in the lemon law wars.

Notes

1. Gen. Bus. Law § 198-a; Ch. 444, Laws of 1983.
2. Gen. Bus. Law § 198-b; Ch. 645, Laws of 1984.
3. Gen. Bus. Law § 198-a(k); Ch. 799, Laws of 1986.
4. N.Y. Admin. Code Title 13, Chap. VIII, § 300.1 *et seq*.
5. Attorney General Robert Abrams, from the *Annual Report of the New York Lemon Law Arbitration Program—1988*, Introduction, p. 3 (available from the New York State Attorney General's Office).
6. Gen. Bus. Law § 198-b(f)(1)–(11), otherwise known as the "Used Car Lemon Law Bill of Rights" (hereinafter referred to as Bill of Rights).
7. Bill of Rights, § 5.
8. *Id.*, § 8.
9. *Id.*, § 10.
10. Currently, the fee for new cars is $200. It is expected that the fee for used car arbitrations will be about $100.
11. The actual time frames may vary, however, due to several factors, e.g., either party may request an adjournment of the scheduled hearing; the arbitrator may require additional evidence not provided at the hearing; etc. See the Attorney General's Annual Report for actual statistics as to time frames.
12. Memorandum for the Governor re S. 4744-B, dated July 11, 1989, from Attorney General Robert Abrams.

The Role of the Judiciary in Granting and Supervising Discovery and in Ordering or Enforcing Provisional Measures*

Michael F. Hoellering

I. Arbitration in the United States

1. Strong national policy favors arbitration.
   (a) Arbitration "as a mode of settling disputes should receive every encouragement from the courts." *Burchell v. Marsh*, 58 U.S. 344 (1855).
   (b) "We cannot have trade and commerce in world markets and international waters exclusively on our terms, governed by our laws, and resolved in our courts." *The Bremen v. Zapata Off-Shore Co.*, 407 U.S. 1 (1972).
   (c) "A contractual provision specifying in advance the forum in which disputes shall be litigated and the law to be applied is . . . an already indispensable precondition to achievement of the orderliness and predictability essential to any international business transaction. . . ." *Scherk v. Alberto-Culver Co.*, 417 U.S. 506 (1974).
   (d) "The [Federal] Arbitration Act calls for a summary and speedy disposition of motions or petitions to enforce arbitration clauses." *Moses H. Cone Memorial Hospital v. Mercury Construction Corp.*, 460 U.S. 1 (1983).
   (e) "[W]here entirely foreign interests agree to arbitrate in New York disputes arising out of their commercial relationship, [courts have] jurisdiction under the [U.N.] Convention to compel arbitration and, if need be, appoint an arbitrator." *Bergesen v. Joseph Muller Corp.*, 548 F. Supp. 650 (S.D.N.Y. 1982), *aff'd*, 710 F.2d 928 (2d Cir. 1983).

II. Discovery

A. General Principles

1. Litigation-type discovery is generally unavailable in arbitration.
2. Requests for "[d]iscovery in aid of arbitration under court supervision will not be granted except under extraordinary circumstances

* Paper presented at the ABA Annual Meeting, Honolulu, Hawaii, August 8, 1989. Michael F. Hoellering is General Counsel of the American Arbitration Association. Vicki M. Young, Editor of Court Decisions, American Arbitration Association, assisted in the preparation of this paper.

and then only where it is shown to be absolutely necessary for the protection of the rights of the party." McClendon and Goodman, eds., *International Commercial Arbitration in New York* (Ardsley-on-Hudson, NY: Transnational, 1986), Part II, ch. 7, pp. 74, 88.

B. Federal Statute

1. Federal Arbitration Act (FAA) (9 U.S.C. § 1 *et seq.*) provides that arbitrators may issue subpoenas to cause a person to attend as witness or present any book, record, document, or paper that may be deemed material as evidence in the arbitral proceeding, and that a court order may be obtained to enforce the subpoenas issued. 9 U.S.C. § 7.
2. If parties provide for discovery in their arbitration agreement, enforcement can be had under either the FAA or the United Nations Convention on the Recognition and Enforcement of Foreign Arbitral Awards (also known as the New York Convention, 21 U.S.T. 2517, T.I.A.S. No. 6997, 330 U.N.T.S. 4739. The U.S. acceded to the Convention in 1970, and legislation implementing the Convention is codified at 9 U.S.C. § 201 *et seq.*)

C. Model Arbitration Statute

1. Uniform Arbitration Act (UAA), § 7(b) states that arbitrators may request a court having jurisdiction to direct the taking of a deposition. Currently 48 states, including the District of Columbia, have enacted modern arbitration statutes. Many of these states have modeled their statutes after the UAA.

D. State Arbitration Statutes

1. Domestic commercial arbitration
   (a) Cal. Civ. Proc. Code § 1283.05 provides the manner in which depositions may be taken and discovery may be obtained in arbitration proceedings.
   (b) Conn. Gen. Stat. § 52-412 permits a party to bypass the arbitrator and to proceed directly to the courts to request a deposition.
   (c) N.Y. Civ. Prac. L. & R. § 3102(c) provides that "[b]efore an action is commenced, disclosure to aid in bringing an action, to preserve information or to aid in arbitration, may be obtained, but only by court order. The court may appoint a referee to take testimony."
   (d) Tex. Rev. Civ. Stat. Ann., title 10, art. 235(G) provides that an application may be filed for an order or orders to be entered by the court "seeking from the court in its discretion, order for deposition or depositions needed in advance of the commencement of the arbitration proceedings for discovery, for perpetuation of testimony or for evidence."

2. International arbitration statutes
   (a) Fla. Stat. Ann. § 684.15 allows arbitrators to "issue subpoenas or other demands for the attendance of witnesses or for the production of books, records, documents, and other evidence, may administer oaths, may order depositions to be taken or other discovery obtained, without regard to the place where the witness or other evidence is located, and may appoint one or more experts to report to it," as well as "apply for assistance from any court" in the exercise of these powers.
   (b) Tex. Rev. Civ. Stat. Ann., title 10, art. 249-27(1) allows the arbitral tribunal or a party, with the tribunal's permission, "to request assistance from the district court in taking evidence, and the court may provide the assistance according to its rules on taking evidence. A subpoena may be issued. . . ."
   (c) Cal. Civ. Proc. Code § 1297.271 provides that "[t]he arbitral tribunal, or a party with the approval of the arbitral tribunal, may request from the superior court assistance in taking evidence and the court may execute the request within its competence and according to its rules on taking evidence. In addition, a subpoena may be issued as provided in section 1282.6, in which case the witness compensation provisions of section 1283.2 shall apply."

E. Institutional Rules

1. AAA Supplemental Procedures for International Commercial Arbitration provide for the exchange of information and transmittal of materials in advance to the arbitrator.
2. AAA Commercial Arbitration Rules provide for a prearbitration conference between the AAA and the parties, in which the parties may prearrange such administrative details as the schedule for exchange of information and stipulations as to uncontested facts (AAA Commercial Arbitration Rules, § 10).
3. AAA Commercial Arbitration Rules also provide for a preliminary hearing, at the request of any party or at the discretion of the arbitrator or the AAA, to clarify claims and counterclaims, arrange for and schedule the production and exchange of relevant information and the disposition of other preliminary matters.
4. Arbitration rules of the Hong Kong International Arbitration Centre contain extensive provisions for the discovery of documents, including a list of documents that must be exchanged; whether privilege applies; and inspection by an arbitrator for the purpose of determining the validity of a claim or objection in regard to a document sought to be produced. Rule 17 of the Domestic Arbitration Rules provides, for example:

(a) "a) After the close of the pleadings there shall be discovery by the parties of the documents which are or have been in their possession, custody of power relating to matters in question in the arbitration."

(b) "b) Nothing in this Rule shall be taken as preventing the parties agreeing to dispense with or limit the discovery of documents which they would otherwise be required to make to each other."

(c) "g) A party who has served a list of documents in accordance with this Rule shall allow the other party to inspect the documents referred to in the list and to take copies thereof and accordingly shall when serving the list on the other party also serve a notice stating a time within 14 days (or such longer or shorter period of time as may be agreed or ordered) after the service thereof at which the said documents may be inspected during usual business hours at a place specified in the notice."

(d) "j) If any party who is required to make discovery of documents fails to make such discovery, the Arbitrator may make such order as is just including an order that the claim or counterclaim be dismissed or the defence be struck out and make an award accordingly."

5. Article 25(3) of the UNCITRAL rules provides that "[t]he arbitral tribunal may require a party to deliver to the tribunal and to the opposing party, within a specified period of time, a summary of the documents and other evidence which he will use to support the facts set out in his statement of claim or defense. The arbitral tribunal may require the parties to produce (within a specified period of time) documents, exhibits or other evidence" while article 25(2) provides that "[a]t least 15 days before any oral hearing at which witnesses are to be heard, each party shall communicate to the arbitral tribunal and to the other party the names and addresses of the witnesses to be presented, the subject upon which they will testify, and the language in which they will testify."
6. Article 3(2)(c) of the ICC rules states that "[t]he claimant's request for arbitration should contain such documentation or information necessary to establish clearly the circumstances of the case" and article 4(1) requires that "[w]ithin 30 days from receipt of the request for arbitration, the defendant shall supply relevant documents or seek an extension of time in which to do so."
7. Rule 32 of ICSID requires that "[w]ithin the time limits fixed by the Tribunal, each party shall communicate to the Secretary-General (for

transmission to the Tribunal and to the other party) precise information regarding the evidence which it intends to produce and that which it intends to request the Tribunal to call for, together with an indication of the points to which such evidence is directed.'' According to Rule 35(b), the ''Tribunal may (with the consent of both parties) arrange for the examination of a witness or expert otherwise than before the Tribunal, and the Tribunal shall define the subject of the examination, the time limit, the procedure to be followed and other particulars, and the parties may participate in the examination.'' Rule 23 states that any ''[s]upporting documentation shall be filed with the instrument to which it relates or, in any event, within the time limit for filing the instrument.''

F. Court Decisions

1. A request for discovery was denied for insufficient showing of need in aid of arbitration. *Coastal States Trading, Inc. v. Zenith Navigation S.A.*, 446 F. Supp. 330 (S.D.N.Y. 1977).
2. Lack of discovery was not considered detrimental. *Commercial Solvents Corp. v. Louisiana Liquid Fertilizer Co.*, 20 F.R.D. 359 (S.D.N.Y. 1957) (''By voluntarily becoming a party to a contract in which arbitration was the agreed mode for settling disputes thereunder respondent chose to avail itself of procedures peculiar to the arbitral process rather than those used in judicial determinations'').
3. Federal courts have discretion to permit discovery, and have used their power under ''exceptional circumstances.'' *Recognition Equipment, Inc. v. NCR Corp.*, 532 F. Supp. 271 (N.D. Tex. 1981).
4. The court permitted discovery in aid of arbitration. *Bigge Crane and Rigging Co. v. Docutel Corp.*, 371 F. Supp. 240 (E.D.N.Y. 1973).
5. Discovery was permitted on the issue of arbitrability. *International U. of E.R. & M.W. v. Westinghouse Elec. Corp.*, 48 F.R.D. 298 (S.D.N.Y. 1969).
6. Discovery was permitted because the ship was about to leave port, so that facts might be made available to inspectors. *Ferro Union Corp. v. S.S. Ionic Coast*, 43 F.R.D. 11 (S.D. Tex. 1967).
7. In New York, necessity rather than convenience is the test. *Katz v. Burkin*, 3 A.D.2d 238, 160 N.Y.S.2d 159 (1st Dep't 1957).
8. Where the parties have agreed to make discovery available, the court will enforce the agreement. *Local 99, I.L.G.W.U. v. Corise Sportswear Co.*, 44 Misc. 2d 913, 255 N.Y.S.2d 282 (Sup. Ct. N.Y. Cty. 1964).

III. Provisional Measures

A. General Principles

1. Use
   - (a) To preserve or protect the interests of property that may be in danger of removal or dissipation
   - (b) To settle a preliminary matter in dispute between the parties
2. Purpose
   - (a) protect perishable goods
   - (b) interim custody of goods
   - (c) enjoin the alienation of assets or patent infringement
   - (d) preserve the status quo
   - (e) prohibit the distribution of merchandise
   - (f) mitigate foreseeable damage

B. Federal Arbitration Act

1. The act does not address the many procedural aspects of arbitration practice.
2. The act addresses attachment in maritime-related cases.

C. State Arbitration Statutes

1. Domestic commercial arbitration
   - (a) Georgia provides that the supreme court "may entertain an application for an order of attachment or for a preliminary injunction in connection with an arbitrable controversy, but only upon the ground that the award to which the applicant may be entitled may be rendered ineffectual without such provisional relief." Ga. Code Ann. § 9-9-4(3)(e).
   - (b) New York provides that "[t]he supreme court in the county in which an arbitration is pending, or, if not yet commenced, in a county specified in subdivision (a), may entertain an application for an order of attachment or for a preliminary injunction in connection with an arbitrable controversy, but only upon the ground that the award to which the applicant may be entitled may be rendered ineffectual without such provisional relief. The provisions of articles 62 and 63 of this chapter shall apply to the application, including those relating to undertakings and to the time for commencement of an action (arbitration shall be deemed an action for this purpose) if the application is made before commencement, except that the sole ground for the granting of the remedy shall be as stated above. The form of the application shall be as provided in subdivision (a)." N.Y. Civ. Prac. L. & R. § 7502(c).
   - (c) Texas provides that "[i]n advance of the institution of any arbitration proceedings, but in aid thereof, an application may be filed for order or orders to be entered by the court, includ-

ing but not limited to applications . . . (ii) involving the jurisdiction of the court over the controversy in rem, by attachment, garnishment, sequestration, or any other ancillary proceeding . . . (iii) seeking to restrain or enjoin the destruction of the subject matter of the controversy or any essential part thereof, or the destruction or alteration of books, records, documents, or evidence needed for the arbitration proceeding . . . (v) seeking any other relief, which the court can grant in its discretion, needed to permit the orderly arbitration proceedings to be instituted and conducted and to prevent any improper interference or delay thereof." Tex. Rev. Civ. Stat. Ann., title 10, art. 235(G).

2. State international arbitration statutes
   (a) Tex. Rev. Civ. Stat. Ann., title 10, art. 249-9, which deals with interim measures, provides that (1) a party may request an interim measure of protection from a court before or during arbitral proceedings, (2) a court may order an attachment, grant a preliminary injunction, or take other appropriate action, and (3) a party may request enforcement of an order of an arbitral tribunal granting an interim measure of protection.
   (b) Florida
      (1) Fla. Stat. Ann. § 684.16(1) provides that "the arbitral tribunal may grant such interim relief as it considers appropriate" and that "[t]he power herein conferred upon the tribunal is without prejudice to the right of a party under applicable law to request interim relief directly from any court, tribunal, or other governmental authority, within or without this state, and to do so without prior authorization of the arbitral tribunal. Unless otherwise provided in the written undertaking to arbitrate, such a request shall not be deemed incompatible with, nor a waiver of, that undertaking."
      (2) Fla. Stat. Ann. § 684.23(3) provides that "[u]pon application by an arbitral tribunal or by a party authorized by a tribunal to make the application, a circuit court of this state may grant any interim relief, including, without limitation, temporary restraining orders, preliminary injunctions, attachments, garnishments, or writ of replevin, which it is empowered by law to grant. All actions under this subsection shall be subject to such procedural requirements and other conditions as would apply in a comparable action not pertaining to an arbitration."
   (c) Ga. Code Ann. § 9-9-35 provides that "arbitrators may grant

such interim relief as they consider appropriate . . . [and that the] power conferred in this Code section upon the arbitrators is without prejudice to the right of a party to request interim relief directly from any court, tribunal, or other governmental authority, inside or outside this state, and to do so without prior authorization of the arbitrators.''

(d) Cal. Civ. Proc. Code § 1297.91 provides that ''[i]t is not incompatible with an arbitration agreement for a party to request from a superior court, before or during arbitral proceedings, an interim measure of protection, or for the court to grant such a measure.

D. Model Arbitration Statutes

1. Uniform Arbitration Act has no provision for interim measures.
2. United Nations Commission on International Trade Law (UNCITRAL) Model Law on International Commercial Arbitration, Article 9, provides that ''[i]t is not incompatible with an arbitration agreement for a party to request, before or during arbitral proceedings, from a court an interim measure of protection and for a court to grant such measure.''

E. Institutional Rules

1. AAA Commercial Arbitration Rules § 47(a) provides that when a party applies to a court for a provisional measure, ''[n]o judicial proceeding by a party relating to the subject matter of the arbitration shall be deemed a waiver of the party's right to arbitrate.''
2. Article 8(5) of the ICC rules provides that ''[b]efore the file is transmitted to the arbitrator, and in exceptional circumstances even thereafter, the parties shall be at liberty to apply to any competent judicial authority for interim or conservatory measures, and they shall not by so doing be held to infringe the agreement to arbitrate or to affect the relevant powers reserved to the arbitrator.''
3. UNCITRAL Rules, Article 26
   (a) ''At the request of either party, the arbitral tribunal may take any interim measures it deems necessary in respect of the subject-matter of the dispute, including measures for the conservation of the goods forming the subject-matter in dispute, such as ordering their deposit with a third person or the sale of perishable goods.''
   (b) ''Such interim measures may be established in the form of an interim award. The arbitral tribunal shall be entitled to require security for the costs of such measures.''

F. Court Decisions

1. Prearbitral attachment

(a) Generally, prearbitral attachment cases involve the application of the U.N. Convention.

(b) While no consensus has been reached, recent decisions suggest that a prearbitral attachment is unavailable under the U.N. Convention.

(1) Prearbitral attachment is unavailable under the U.N. Convention. *McCreary Tire & Rubber Co. v. CEAT S.p.A.*, 501 F.2d 1032 (3d Cir. 1974).

(2) Nothing in the text of the U.N. Convention itself suggests that it precludes prejudgment attachment. *Carolina Power & Light Co. v. Uranex*, 451 F. Supp. 1044 (N.D. Cal. 1977).

(3) The reasoning of *McCreary* and *Carolina Power* is not incompatible, as both were adopted in this case, which involved two orders of attachment; the FAA applied, however, instead of the U.N. Convention because the dispute involved a charter party. *Compagnia de Navigacion y Financiera Bosnia, S.A. v. National Unity Marine Salvage Corp.*, 457 F. Supp. 1013 (S.D.N.Y. 1978).

(4) The policy of the U.N. Convention is to minimize the uncertainty of enforcing arbitration agreements and to avoid the vagaries of foreign law for international traders, which would be defeated by allowing prearbitral attachment. *Cooper v. Ateliers de la Motobecane, S.A.*, 57 N.Y.2d 408, 456 N.Y.S.2d 728, 442 N.E.2d 1239 (1982), *rev'g* 446 N.Y.S.2d 297 (App. Div., 1st Dep't 1982).

(5) An order of attachment in aid of arbitration is not available in cases where the U.N. Convention applies because the intent of the Convention is that there be no significant judicial intervention until after an arbitration award is made. *Drexel Burnham Lambert Inc. v. Ruebsamen*, N.Y.L.J., July 28, 1988, at 17, col. 3 (App. Div., 1st Dep't July 21, 1988).

(c) Maritime controversies

(1) The court denied a motion to vacate an order of attachment. *Andros Compania Maritima, S.A. v. Andre & Cir. S.A.*, 430 F. Supp. 88 (S.D.N.Y. 1977).

(2) A party to a maritime cause of action may obtain prearbitration attachment under the U.N. Convention, 9 U.S.C. § 201 *et seq. Atlas Chartering Services, Inc. v. World Trade Group, Inc.*, 453 F. Supp. 861 (S.D.N.Y. 1978).

(3) Attachment of hull insurance proceeds was the type of protective measure traditionally available to a party, even

though the arbitration was governed by the U.N. Convention; the key, however, was that the attachment sought must be for traditional maritime reasons. *Construction Exporting Enterprises, UNECA v. Nikki Maritime, Ltd.*, 558 F. Supp. 1372 (S.D.N.Y. 1983).

(d) Other cases

(1) The fact that the contract between the parties provided for arbitration in London, governed by English law, did not preclude an order or attachment in New York. *Tampimex Oil Ltd. v. Latina Trading Corp.*, 558 F. Supp. 1201 (S.D.N.Y. 1983).

(2) Tanzania was not immune from attachment, since it agreed to arbitration in the United States, and to judicial enforcement of any award rendered. *Birch Shipping Corp. v. Embassy of Tanzania*, 507 F. Supp. 311 (D.D.C. 1980).

2. Partial final awards

(a) Absence of sufficient legal grounds to justify a court order of attachment or injunction need not preclude judicial enforcement of interim measures of protection taken by the arbitral tribunal. *Sperry International Trade v. Government of Israel*, 532 F. Supp. 901 (S.D.N.Y. 1982) (arbitrators were held not to have exceeded their authority in rendering a partial award that required the funds represented by a letter of credit to be placed in escrow by the parties, even though a prior court order enjoining one of the parties from drawing on the letter of credit had been reversed for lack of a showing of irreparable harm).

3. Injunctions

(a) General principles

(1) The traditional test used in litigation is also used in arbitration-related matters to determine necessity.

(2) The party must show irreparable harm and likelihood of success on the merits.

(3) The court will grant a motion for an injunction only if it is reasonably certain that a party's rights will be significantly prejudiced without the aid of an injunction.

(b) Court decisions

(1) A party does not waive its right to arbitrate by seeking injunctive relief to protect its interests. *Sauer-Getriebe KG v. White Hydraulics, Inc.*, 715 F.2d 348 (7th Cir. 1983), cert. denied, 52 U.S.L.W. 3534 (Jan. 16, 1984).

(2) A preliminary injunction and a rule 67 order may also be warranted under appropriate circumstances. *Holborn Oil*

Trading, Ltd. v. InterPetrol Bermuda, Ltd., 658 F. Supp. 1205 (S.D.N.Y. 1987).

(3) The district court had the authority to enjoin payment on a letter of credit pending arbitration before the Iran-U.S. Claims Tribunal. *Rockwell International Systems, Inc. v. Citibank, N.A.*, 719 F.2d 583 (2d Cir. 1983).

(4) The American party was entitled to a preliminary injunction preventing the Korean party from calling a letter of guarantee pending the outcome of arbitration. *Rogers, Burgun, Shahine & Deschler, Inc. v. Dongsan Construction Co., Ltd.*, 598 F. Supp. 754 (S.D.N.Y. 1984).

(5) International comity does not require issuance of a preliminary injunction by U.S. courts where such injunction already has been granted in aid of arbitration by a foreign court. *Pilkington Bros. PLC v. AFG Industries, Inc.*, 581 F. Supp. 1039 (D. Del. 1984).

B. CONSTRUCTION

CASE DIGESTS

ARBITRATION AGREEMENT—ENFORCEABILITY—CONSIDERATION

A motion for a stay pending arbitration was erroneously denied on the basis that the arbitration agreement was an independent and separable contract requiring consideration. Separate consideration is not required for an arbitration provision that is contained within a valid contract.

Wilson Electrical, an electrical contractor, entered into a contract with Minnotte, a commercial contractor, for work as a subcontractor on one of Minnotte's projects. The contract contained a provision allowing Minnotte the option to arbitrate any controversy or claim arising out of the subcontract. Wilson subsequently filed an action against Minnotte for wrongful termination and recovery of money allegedly owed under the contract. Minnotte moved for a stay of the court action pending arbitration. The motion was denied because the court concluded that the arbitration provision was an "independent and separable contract which required mutual consideration. . . ."

The appellate court reversed, directing that a stay pending arbitration be issued. It determined that the lower court erred in its application of *Prima Paint Corporation v. Flood & Conklin Manufacturing Company*, 388 U.S. 395 (1967), "to strike down [an] arbitration clause in [an] otherwise valid contract between Minnotte and Wilson." The court ruled that *Prima Paint* "does not *require* separate consideration for an arbitration provision contained within a valid contract."

In addition, the court noted that Wilson freely signed the contract and "made no claim of fraud or that it was coerced into signing the contract or that the contract was unconscionable." Based on these facts, and because the contract as a whole did not lack consideration, the court concluded that there was no reason why Minnotte's motion for a stay pending arbitration should be denied. ***Wilson Electrical Contractors, Inc. v. Minnotte Contracting Corp.,*** 878 F.2d 167 (6th Cir. 1989).

COLLATERAL ESTOPPEL—ARBITRATION AWARD—FINALITY—SETTLEMENT

Finality of an arbitration award is not vitiated by the fact that it was not confirmed by a court or was later modified by a settlement agreement so as to bar collateral estoppel. In addition, collateral estoppel precludes an action against a third party who did not participate in the arbitration proceeding, even when the arbitrators do not reveal the basis for their decisions.

National Sun Industries and Ibberson Engineering entered into an agreement for the construction of a processing plant. Wellons was hired by National for the construction of two steam boilers. Soon after the boilers were installed, National began encountering problems. Although Wellons modified the boilers to correct the problem, National subsequently filed a lawsuit against Wellons, alleging that Wellons' improper design of the boilers resulted in substantial losses for National. The court action was stayed after Wellons invoked the arbitration clauses in its contract with National. An award was rendered in favor of National, which moved to confirm.

Wellons, in turn, commenced an action against Ibberson, seeking indemnification from the arbitration award and alleging negligent or intentional misrepresentation on the part of Ibberson when Wellons submitted its bid on the project. Before the arbitration award was confirmed, National and Wellons signed a settlement agreement, the terms of which provided for a mutual release of all claims and dismissal of the confirmation suit. Thereafter, Ibberson sought summary judgment against Wellons, claiming that collateral estoppel barred Wellons' suit.

The district court granted Ibberson's motion, finding that the settlement agreement had adopted the arbitration award, which rendered the award "'final' for collateral estoppel purposes." Wellons appealed, arguing that the court erred because there was no final judgment in the action between it and National and because the issues of law and fact in the lawsuit were different from those raised in the arbitration proceeding.

The appellate court affirmed the district court's order in favor of Ibberson. It concluded that "[t]he fact that the award in the present case was not confirmed by a court and was modified by a subsequent settlement agreement [did] not vitiate the finality of the award." Moreover, the court affirmed the district court's finding that the award was not vacated by the subsequent settlement, because the settlement agreement did not contain language providing for vacatur. Accordingly, the court concluded that collateral estoppel applies regardless of a subsequent settlement agreement, provided that the issues have been fully adjudicated.

As to whether the issues of law and fact in the lawsuit are identical to the issues raised at the arbitration proceeding, the court concluded that, even though the arbitrators did not reveal the basis for their decision, they could not have found against Wellons without determining whether Ibberson was liable to Wellons for misrepresentation. Since a determination had to have been made in Ibberson's favor—a determination raised by the same issue in the Wellons/Ibberson action—the court ruled that collateral estoppel applied. In so holding, the court also concluded that estoppel can preclude an action against a third party who did not participate in the arbitration proceeding, even when the panel does not reveal the basis for their decision. ***Wellons, Inc. v. T.E. Ibberson Co.,*** 869 F.2d 1166 (8th Cir. 1989).

PERFORMANCE BOND—INCORPORATION BY REFERENCE—ARBITRATION AGREEMENT

A performance bond that incorporates by reference a subcontract containing an arbitration clause renders the bonding company bound by the provisions of the subcontract, including the arbitration clause.

Collins and Roswell Steel entered into a subcontract obligating Roswell to provide and install steel for a construction project. The subcontract contained an arbitration clause. A performance bond naming Roswell as principal and Collins as obligee was issued by Transamerica Premier Insurance. The bond incorporated by reference the Collins/Roswell subcontract. A dispute arose between Collins and Roswell, and they initiated arbitration proceedings before the American Arbitration Association. Collins filed a Demand for Arbitration requesting that Transamerica be joined in the arbitration. Transamerica moved in state court for a declaratory judgment stating that it was not required to participate in the arbitration and that it should not be bound by the results. It also successfully obtained a temporary restraining order staying arbitration pending the declaratory judgment action. Collins removed the action to federal court.

Because the issue of whether Transamerica, the bonding company, was bound by the arbitration clause in the subcontract that was incorporated by reference in the performance bond was one of first impression in Georgia, the court considered applicable case law from other jurisdictions. It found the Eleventh Circuit decision in *United States Fidelity and Guaranty Co. v. West Point Construction Co.*, 837 F.2d 1507 (11th Cir. 1988), directly on point. The *United States Fidelity* court held that a performance bond that references a subcontract containing an arbitration clause also references the arbitration clause in that subcontract. Since the Federal Arbitration Act will govern the parties' arbitration, and because the " 'strong [Congressional] policy favoring arbitration' that the Eleventh Circuit relied upon in *United States Fidelity* supports a similar outcome in this case," the court held Transamerica bound by the referenced arbitration clause in the subcontract.

Transamerica Premier Insurance Company v. Collins & Company, General Contractors, Inc., 735 F. Supp. 1050 (N.D. Ga. 1990).

SUBCONTRACT—WAIVER OF ARBITRATION—PREJUDICE—COMPROMISE AND SETTLEMENT

A subcontractor that filed a court action and then moved to stay that action and compel arbitration did not waive its right to arbitrate, because the opposing party had not suffered any prejudice. In addition, the court would not dismiss the action, because the parties had not entered into a binding settlement agreement despite serious efforts at negotiation.

AMC Mechanical Contractors was hired by the United States Department of Energy for work on a foam deluge system. Subsequently, Orleans Electric Construction Co. entered into a subcontract with AMC. The agreement between Orleans and AMC contained an arbitration clause. A dispute arose, and Orleans filed suit against AMC. Six months later, Orleans moved for a stay of the proceedings pending arbitration. AMC argued that Orleans had waived its right to arbitrate and claimed prejudice. Orleans argued that AMC could not claim prejudice, noting that settlement negotiations were under way between the parties and citing the applicability of the Miller Act, which places strict time limitations on parties seeking to preserve their rights. In addition, Orleans argued that it had preserved its right to arbitrate in its pleadings.

The court agreed with Orleans, finding that although it was unusual for a party initiating suit also to move for a stay of the action, no steps had been taken toward prosecuting its claim against AMC. Because AMC was not prejudiced in any way, the court ordered arbitration to proceed and stayed the court action brought by Orleans.

The court also denied AMC's motion for a summary dismissal of Orleans' action. AMC had argued that the parties, in their settlement negotiations, had agreed to a valid transaction and compromise of the claim. The court ruled that because a written settlement between the parties had not been executed, the parties had not entered into binding settlement. ***United States v. AMC Mechanical Contractors, Inc.***, 709 F. Supp. 694 (M.D. La. 1989).

AGENCY—PARTNERSHIP—ARBITRATION AGREEMENT—CALIFORNIA

A sole general partner is bound by an arbitration agreement entered into by the limited partnership.

Keller Construction Company entered into an agreement with a California limited partnership to act as general contractor in the construction of a hotel. Kazem Kashani, the sole general partner of the limited partnership, signed the contract on behalf of the partnership. The contract contained a clause providing for the arbitration of disputes in accordance with the American Arbitration Association's rules. A dispute arose, and Keller served a demand against the limited partnership, which subsequently filed for protection under federal bankruptcy law, and Kashani. After the automatic stay was lifted, arbitration proceeded. An award was rendered favoring Keller, who moved to confirm. Kashani opposed, objecting on the ground that he was not subject to the arbitrator's award because he was not a party to the arbitration agreement. The trial court granted Keller's motion, and Kashani appealed.

The court agreed with the trial court and affirmed the decision below. It found that there was a general state policy favoring arbitration and that at least "one California court has enforced an arbitration agreement against unknown parties who were agents of a signatory to an arbitration agreement." The court concluded that Kashani, as sole general partner of the limited partnership, was subject to the arbitration agreement between that partnership and Keller. It reasoned that under California statutory law, a general partner is liable for "all . . . debts and obligations of the partnership," is the agent of the limited partnership, and therefore is logically a beneficiary of any agreement entered into on behalf of the partnership. Consequently, the court concluded that "[a]s the agent and a beneficiary of the partnership, to require [Kashani] to be a party to the arbitration is consistent with . . . [the] 'strong public policy in favor of arbitration.' " ***Keller Construction Company, Inc. v. Kashani,*** 269 Cal. Rptr. 259 (Ct. App. 1990).

INITIATION OF ARBITRATION—CONDITION PRECEDENT—WAIVER—PROCEDURE ON REMAND—STAY OF ARBITRATION—COLORADO

A party's inaction was ruled not a waiver when it failed to notify anyone of its intent to arbitrate, because it was not under any obligation to initiate arbitration. In addition, the proper procedure on remand was to stay the court action pending arbitration.

Mountain Plains contracted with the Torrezes to construct a building. The parties used a standard form agreement containing an arbitration provision. Because of budgetary limitations, the original plans were modified, and a dispute arose over payment of the balance due on the contract. An action for breach of contract and foreclosure on a mechanic's lien was filed by Mountain Plains. The Torrezes moved to dismiss, contending that the dispute was subject to arbitration.

The lower court denied the motion, finding that in neglecting to initiate arbitration the Torrezes had failed to assert their right to arbitration. The Torrezes appealed. The appellate court reversed and the Supreme Court granted certiorari to determine whether the appellate court erred in finding that the Torrezes did not waive their right to arbitration, and whether the proper procedure upon remand was to dismiss the case. It concluded that the appellate court was correct in holding that the Torrezes were entitled to arbitration, but found that the proper procedure was to stay the action pending arbitration.

The court reasoned that because the Torrezes were not obligated to initiate arbitration, they did not have to notify Mountain Plains and the American Arbitration Association as a condition precedent to asserting their right to arbitration. It also disagreed with Mountain Plains' contention that the "Torrezes had waived their right to arbitration by failing to appeal the trial court's denial of their motion to dismiss and proceeding to final judgment." In finding that the appellate court should have stayed the action pending arbitration instead of ordering a dismissal, the high court held that a stay "preserves Mountain Plains' right to foreclose on its mechanic's lien if it prevails in arbitration." ***Mountain Plains Commercial Constructors, Inc. v. Torrez,*** 785 P.2d 928 (Colo. 1990) (en banc).

PREJUDGMENT INTEREST—PUNITIVE DAMAGES—ATTORNEY FEES—UNCONSCIONABILITY—FLORIDA

The trial court erred in confirming an award awarding punitive damages, as well as erred in awarding attorney's fees.

Thomas and Carol Behan and Complete Interiors entered into an agreement for the construction of their home by Complete. Disputes arose over defects in the house as well as Complete's warranty obligations. Complete filed an action against the Behans seeking a judgment declaring what items Complete was obligated to repair under the terms of its warranty. It later moved for an order compelling arbitration pursuant to an arbitration provision in the parties' agreement. The motion was granted. Arbitration was held, and an award was rendered favoring the Behans with compensatory damages and prejudgment interest. The arbitrator also ordered Complete to pay punitive damages. An order confirming the award was entered by the trial court, which also ordered Complete to pay the Behans' attorney's fees. Complete appealed.

Noting that the scope of review of arbitration awards is extremely limited except where, for example, the arbitrator has exceeded his powers, and that the parties' agreement did not provide for an award of punitive damages, the court concluded that the arbitrator had exceeded his powers. Consequently, the lower court had erred in confirming the award of punitive damages. The court found that the state's arbitration code does not authorize attorney's fees. Despite the presence of a clause in the parties' agreement regarding attorney's fees, the court noted the lower court's determination that the clause was unreasonable and unconscionable. Because "there was no evidence from which the trial court could determine unconscionability," the court reversed the award of attorney's fees. ***Complete Interiors, Inc. v. Behan,*** 558 So. 2d 48 (Fla. Dist. Ct. App. 1990).

RIGHT TO ARBITRATION—WAIVER—LACHES— SERVICE OF DEMAND FOR ARBITRATION—GEORGIA

The trial court did not err in enforcing the arbitration agreement between the parties, because the methods of service satisfied the requirements of the applicable statute and contractual provisions.

Ira and Mary Livingston entered into a contract with Knight & Knight of LaGrange for the construction of a new house. The contract contained an arbitration clause requiring that a demand for arbitration be made within five days after a controversy arises. The couple moved into their house and, over the next year and a half, made numerous complaints regarding alleged construction deficiencies. Written communications concerning the dispute were exchanged by the parties during this time. Knight demanded arbitration pursuant to their contract, which the Livingstons rejected. Knight then successfully moved for an order compelling arbitration, and the Livingstons appealed.

The court rejected the Livingstons' claim that Knight's right to arbitration was barred by waiver or laches because it had failed to make the demand at an earlier time. The court found that the evidence supported the trial court's finding that hand delivery of Knight's written demand for arbitration took place within the requisite five days. The court also noted that the demand was later served by certified mail pursuant to the applicable statute. The court found that the statute did not require that service by certified mail be made within any specific time period. Because the methods of service satisfied the requirements of both the contractual provisions and the applicable statute, the court concluded that the trial court did not err in enforcing the arbitration clause. ***Livingston v. Knight & Knight of LaGrange, Inc.,*** 387 S.E.2d 393 (Ga. Ct. App. 1989).

MECHANIC'S LIEN ACT—WAIVER—ILLINOIS

A subcontractor who declined arbitration in a joint action against the property owner and the general contractor under a mechanic's lien was held

not to have waived his right to arbitrate in a separate, subsequent action against the general contractor.

First National Bank and Trust employed Henry Ross Construction as the general contractor to construct a building on its property. Ross, in turn, entered into an agreement with D.E. Wright Electric as subcontractor for the installation of electricity within the building. Subsequently, Electric filed a joint action against First National and Ross claiming that although Electric had fulfilled its part of the agreement, it had not yet been completely paid. Electric also gave them notice of a lien on the property pursuant to the Mechanic's Lien Act of Illinois. Although Electric and Ross's agreement provided for arbitration, the clause had excluded conflicts arising under state and federal mechanic's lien laws. Ross moved to compel arbitration.

Electric and First National subsequently settled. The action against First National was dismissed, leaving the action against Ross. Ross filed a counterclaim against Electric on a breach of contract claim. Because of the settlement with First National, the nature of Electric's suit was no longer based on a mechanic's lien but rather on a breach of contract claim. Ross asked the court to dismiss Electric's complaint, which the court did on the ground that Electric's earlier refusal to arbitrate resulted in prejudice to Ross. Electric appealed.

The appellate court reversed the dismissal and compelled arbitration. The court's opinion highlighted the fact that Electric's initial objection to arbitrate was Electric's right, because their agreement had precluded arbitration of mechanic's lien law disputes. Accordingly, Electric's claim against Ross became arbitrable only when the lien was dropped because of the settlement with First National. Consequently, there was no waiver on the part of Electric for exercising its right to refuse arbitration at the time that the mechanic's lien was in effect. To find otherwise, ruled the court, would be tantamount to punishing Electric for exercising that right. ***D.E. Wright Electric, Inc. v. Henry Ross Construction Co., Inc.,*** 538 N.E.2d 1182 (Ill. App. Ct. 1989).

APPEALABILITY—INTERLOCUTORY ORDER—MECHANIC'S LIEN—MARYLAND

An order staying a mechanic's lien action pending arbitration was not appealable because the court had not entered a final judgment from which an appeal would lie and because the appellant failed to establish that the order was an appealable interlocutory order.

McCormick Construction entered into an agreement with Deerco Partnership for the construction of a single-level park deck. The agreement contained an arbitration clause. A dispute arose over the quality of the construction, and Deerco refused to render payment for the balance due for materials and services. Deerco filed for arbitration, and McCormick sought an order from the circuit court granting it a mechanic's lien. The court heard oral arguments and concluded that it had no discretion to rule on McCormick's action once a petition to arbitrate was filed. McCormick appealed the court order staying his mechanic's lien action.

The appellate court noted that under Maryland law, appeals are generally not permitted until the trial court has rendered a final judgment. While recognizing that certain interlocutory orders are appealable, the court disagreed with McCormick's argument that a mechanic's lien constituted sufficient "possession of property" to render a decision regarding the lien an appealable interlocutory order. The court found that McCormick did not have any present right to possession and that any right that may have existed was purely speculative. In addition, the court stated that "[t]he fact that after foreclosure of a mechanic's lien someone will eventually possess the property does not supply a predicate for allowing an appeal of an interlocutory order 'entered with regard to the possession of property with which the action is concerned.'"

Because McCormick failed to establish a right to appeal and the trial court had not entered a final judgment from which an appeal would lie, McCormick's appeal was dismissed. ***McCormick Construction Co., Inc. v. 9690 Deerco Road Ltd. Partnership,*** 556 A.2d 292 (Md. Ct. Spec. App. 1989).

EVIDENT PARTIALITY—PREAWARD INTEREST—POSTAWARD INTEREST—MICHIGAN

The court found that there was insufficent evidence of arbitrator partiality to warrant vacatur of an award. It also affirmed the lower court's vacatur of preaward interest, as well as the limitation of postaward interest to five percent per annum.

Spence Brothers entered into a construction contract with Gordon Sel-Way. A dispute arose, and the matter was submitted to arbitration. The arbitration panel rendered an award in favor of Gordon, which moved to confirm. Although the trial court confirmed the award, it found that there was no contractual basis for preaward interest. The court modified the award by vacating the preaward interest; however, the court allowed postaward interest limited to five percent per annum from the date of the arbitration award until payment. Spence appealed.

The appellate court rejected Spence's argument that because of the evident partiality of one of the arbitrators, the award should be vacated. The arbitrator's failure to disclose that he had filed a lawsuit against Spence in an earlier unrelated matter on behalf of his consulting firm, the court ruled, was not sufficient grounds for vacating the award. The arbitrator had disclosed in his biographical sketch that he was president of the consulting firm that had brought that lawsuit. The court also concluded that Spence's failure to act on the knowledge of the prior relationship between Spence and the arbitrator constituted a waiver of Spence's objection, and that any possibility of partiality or bias by the arbitrator as a result of the lawsuit was remote and speculative.

The court also upheld the trial court's vacatur of the interest portion of the award, agreeing that there was no provision in the contract for interest while the dispute was pending in arbitration. Further, the court reasoned, "[s]ince the principal damages were not due until the arbitration award was entered, it follows that there was no bias for making an award of interest. . . ." Also affirmed was the lower court's limitation of postaward interest to five percent per annum, on grounds that under applicable state statute, interest begins to accrue on the date of the award, and that the legal rate of interest under the usury statute is five percent per annum. ***Gordon Sel-Way, Inc. v. Spence Brothers, Inc.,*** 440 N.W.2d 907 (Mich. 1989).

PARTIAL SUMMARY JUDGMENT—COLLATERAL ESTOPPEL—MINNESOTA

Because the collateral estoppel doctrine applied, the trial court properly granted a partial summary judgment.

Art Goebel contracted with Arkay Construction for the construction of a new building. Arkay subcontracted with Vidco, Inc., for the masonry work, and Vidco purchased concrete blocks from Anchor Block Company. Two years after completion, Anchor was required to perform cosmetic repair on the building, and two years later it was discovered that the repair was not permanent. Goebel filed an action against Arkay, Vidco, and Anchor. The action was stayed pending arbitration between Goebel and Arkay, which Vidco voluntarily joined. The arbitrator ordered Vidco to pay Goebel and found that Anchor, although not a party to the arbitration proceedings, was the negligent party. Goebel accepted payment from Vidco and moved to lift the stay. Anchor moved for summary judgment. An appealable partial summary judgment was granted by the court, which found Goebel collaterally estopped from litigating damage issues against Anchor.

Goebel contended that summary judgment was precluded because whether the arbitrator considered the possible diminution in value of the building was a genuine issue of material fact. The court disagreed on the ground that because the award was not appealed, the issue of whether certain evidence was presented and considered by the arbitrator was not properly before the court. It also found that the application by the trial court of the collateral estoppel doctrine did not constitute error. The court noted that although the availability of the doctrine in the arbitration context has never been decided by a Minnesota appellate court, the fact that Goebel had accepted payment from Vidco and refrained from appealing the award showed that Goebel had acquiesced to the award. From these facts, the court concluded that the case contained an appropriate factual context in which to apply the collateral estoppel doctrine. Because Goebel was given a "full and fair" opportunity to present evidence of its damage in the arbitration proceeding, and acquiesced to the resulting award, the court affirmed the trial court's order granting a partial summary judgment. ***Art Goebel, Inc. v. Arkay Construction Co.,*** 437 N.W.2d 117 (Minn. Ct. App. 1989).

AIA STANDARD FORM CONTRACT—INCORPORATION BY REFERENCE—AMBIGUOUS TERMS—MISSOURI

Documents that are incorporated by reference into a contract are as much a part of the contract as if they had been included in the main document. The failure to specifically list incorporated documents in a separate part of the contract does not necessarily make the contract ambiguous.

William and Judy Bailey entered into a contract with Jim Carlson Construction for the construction of a house. The agreement utilized a standard form contract prepared by the American Institute of Architects (AIA). The contract stipulated that all contract documents—including the General Conditions of the Contract, which provide for arbitration of disputes—were part of the contract. A provision in the contract called for a listing of the various contract documents, but this was never done. When Carlson filed suit against the Baileys for breach of contract, the Baileys sought to compel arbitration of the dispute, as mandated by the General Conditions document. The court denied the motion, and the Baileys appealed.

The appellate court ruled in favor of the Baileys and remanded the case to the trial court, with directions to order a resubmission of the claim to arbitration. It held that matters that are incorporated by reference into a contract are as much a part of the contract as if they had been included in the main document. Moreover, the court observed, the agreement "definitively state[d] that the general conditions are made fully a part of the contract as if attached to the agreement."

The court also found that failure to list the documents by name did not necessarily render the contract ambiguous, nor did disagreement by the parties on the interpretation of the contract. Consequently, the judgment of the trial court was reversed as erroneous. ***Jim Carlson Construction, Inc. v. Bailey***, 769 S.W.2d 480 (Mo. Ct. App. 1989).

ARBITRATOR MISCONDUCT—VACATUR OF AWARD—REOPENING OF CASE—ADDITIONAL TESTIMONY—NEW YORK

An arbitrator's refusal to reopen the case to take additional testimony did not constitute "misconduct" so as to warrant vacatur of the award.

Menard M. Gertler, a homeowner, entered into a contract with Gabriel Sedlis, an architect, for the renovation and enlargement of his home. Gertler, dissatisfied with the services rendered during construction, withheld payment. Sedlis commenced arbitration pursuant to an arbitration clause in their contract. A six-day hearing was conducted, as well as an on-site inspection. After the hearing was concluded, permission was granted to allow the submission of a real estate appraisal for the limited purpose of establishing the value of the premises. A request was made to reopen the hearing to allow the submission of an engineer's load calculations, but a dispute arose over whether the engineer should be cross-examined. The arbitrator refused to reopen the hearing. An award was rendered, which Sedlis sought to confirm. The trial court confirmed the motion and granted Sedlis prejudgment and postjudgment interest. Gertler appealed.

The appellate court agreed with the trial court's finding that the arbitrator's decision not to reopen the hearing on the ground that the parties had been afforded ample opportunity to fully present all claims was within the arbitrator's authority and did not constitute misconduct. Specifically, the court noted that

> [m]ere refusal to reopen a case to take additional testimony upon an issue which had been addressed at length or to take post-hearing evidence offered to bolster testimony already presented, as in the case at bar, does not constitute misconduct which would allow for vacatur of an award.

Consequently, the lower court's decision confirming the award was affirmed, with a modification of the prejudgment and postjudgment interest award. ***Sedlis v. Gertler,*** 554 N.Y.S.2d 614 (1st Dep't 1990).

INCORPORATION BY REFERENCE—INCONSISTENT TERMS—ARBITRATION AGREEMENT—NEW YORK

Inconsistent terms between an arbitration agreement incorporated by reference in the main contract and the striking out of a similar agreement in an annexed document did not constitute a clear and unequivocal agreement that would warrant the granting of a motion to compel arbitration.

The EIS Group/Cornwall Hill Development Corporation entered into an agreement with Rinaldi Construction for the development of certain residential property. The contract consisted of a standard American Institute of Architects (AIA) form contract and a five-page typewritten rider. The first page of the form contract incorporated by reference an AIA document containing an arbitration clause. However, the actual document was not physically annexed to the form contract. What was annexed was a different AIA document that had been modified, including the striking of a similar arbitration clause. Work began and a dispute arose over an alleged breach of the contract. The EIS Group commenced the action at bar and subsequently moved to stay an arbitration proceeding later commenced by Rinaldi. The trial court refused to compel arbitration, finding that the parties did not have a clear and unequivocal agreement to arbitrate because of the conflicting terms in the parties' contract. Rinaldi appealed.

The appellate court agreed with the trial court's finding, reasoning that inconsistent terms between the incorporation by reference of an arbitration agreement in the main contract and the striking out of a similar agreement in the annexed document did not constitute a clear and unequivocal arbitration agreement. Consequently, the trial court's order was affirmed. ***The EIS Group/Cornwall Hill Development Corporation v. Rinaldi Construction, Inc.***, 546 N.Y.S.2d 105 (2d Dep't 1989).

EVIDENCE IN SUBSEQUENT ACTION—DAMAGES—LEGAL EXPENSES—NEW YORK

A court that ruled that evidence of an arbitration proceeding and award was not to be introduced into evidence in a court action did not commit any error when it allowed the introduction into evidence of a payment ratio, which was relevant to the issues of nonpayment and breach of contract, because the arbitrators ruled only on the issue of nonpayment.

Larry Walter and the City of Elmira entered into a contract for the construction of a parking garage. The contract contained a liquidated damages clause providing that if completion of the project was delayed, Walters would pay the City $1,000 per day, and that if Walters finished the project prior to the stipulated completion date, then the City would pay Walters $1,000 per day. The contract also required the City to make periodic payments to Walters based on estimates Walters made, subject to the approval of Newman & Doll Consulting Engineers. A performance bond for Walters was posted by Travelers Indemnity Company, which became Walters' surety. Construction began, and the City made the first four payment requisitions. On the recommendation of Newman & Doll, a fifth payment requisition was made in part, and the sixth, seventh, and eighth payment requisitions were rejected. Because of nonpayment as well as other issues, Walters discontinued work and sought arbitration. The parties stipulated that the arbitrators would decide only the issue of nonpayment and not whether either party breached the contract. An award was rendered in favor of Walters. Although it was confirmed, the award did not affect Newman & Doll because it was not a party to the arbitration proceeding.

The City commenced an action to recover the excess cost of completion. To eliminate potential prejudice to Newman & Doll, a party in the court action, the trial court ruled that evidence of the arbitration and award was inadmissible. A jury, by special verdict, found that Walters breached its contract with the City and awarded the City actual and liquidated damages. It also found that the City breached its contract with Newman & Doll and awarded the latter damages. The City, Walters, and Travelers appealed.

The court disagreed with the contention of Walters and Travelers that the trial court had erred in permitting the City to introduce evidence regarding the ratio of work completed to the amount the City paid Walters. It reasoned that because the "prior arbitration proceeding determined only whether the City overpaid or underpaid Walters" and "the arbitrators did not decide the precise issue of whether Walters justifiably abandoned the job, [the trial court] cannot be faulted for permitting the City to introduce evidence of the payment ratio." In addition, the court ruled that a reasonable liquidated damages clause is valid, counsel fees are not available absent statutory or contractual authority, and the legal expenses incurred by Newman & Doll to rebid the construction contract after abandonment by Walters are recoverable expenditures. ***City of Elmira v. Larry Walter, Inc.,*** 546 N.Y.S.2d 183 (3d Dep't 1989).

WAIVER—TIMELINESS—NEW YORK

The court held that a party had not waived its right to arbitration because the assertion of that right was made in a timely fashion following resolution of a jurisdictional issue.

Malone Golf Club entered into a construction contract with Moore Golf Incorporated for the construction of a golf course. The agreement contained a broad arbitration agreement. A dispute arose over the amount due Moore under the contract. Malone sued Moore in state court by service of a summons with notice, alleging breach of contract. The matter was removed to federal district court and a demand for a complaint was served on Malone. A complaint was not served and Moore moved for service in federal court. Malone cross-moved for an order of remand based on the contract's forum selection clause, and the motion was granted. Moore again demanded service of a complaint but, before answering the complaint, served a demand for arbitration on Malone. Moore then answered the complaint, asserting that the allegations were subject to arbitration. The trial court held that the contract contained a valid arbitration agreement and that the dispute was arbitrable. Malone appealed.

Malone argued on appeal that Moore had waived its right to arbitrate by removing the matter to federal court and by delaying its filing of the demand for arbitration. The court found that in the case at bar, "the assertion of the right to arbitration followed closely on the heels of [Moore's] legitimate testing of the subject matter jurisdiction of both the State and Federal courts" and that Moore, "in its petition for removal, asserted the broad arbitration agreement and that it was unable to determine if some of [Malone's] allegations were arbitrable." Because the petition sought service of the complaint and the merits were not placed in issue, the court concluded that no waiver had occurred. It found that "[o]nce the jurisdiction issue was resolved and the complaint was served, [Moore] raised the defense of arbitration in a timely fashion." ***Malone Golf Club, Inc. v. Moore Golf Incorporated,*** 538 N.Y.S.2d 100 (3d Dep't 1989).

WAIVER—TIMELINESS—TEXAS

The trial court did not commit any error in determining that a party had waived its right to arbitration on the ground that the party had failed to request arbitration at the appropriate times during the course of the court proceedings.

Wigley Construction Company was a subcontractor under a written contract with Bramcon General Contractors. After partial payment was made by Bramcon, a dispute arose over the remaining balance. Bramcon defended on the ground that the contract was a contingent payment contract and that because it had not been paid, Bramcon was under no obligation to pay Wigley. Wigley sought to recover the balance and successfully moved for summary judgment. Bramcon appealed.

Because the contract that the parties signed contained a clause subjecting the contract to the Texas Arbitration Act, the appellate court considered whether Bramcon had waived its right to arbitrate the dispute. It found that the trial court had committed no error in determining that Bramcon had waived its right to arbitrate on the basis that it had failed to request arbitration at the appropriate times during the course of the court proceedings. The appellate court also agreed with the trial court's finding that to allow arbitration would cause prejudice to Wigley and that such would not be in the interest of justice. Since the trial court's decision as to arbitration was supported by the evidence, it was affirmed by the appellate court. ***Bramcon General Contractors, Inc. v. Wigley Construction Company,*** 774 S.W.2d 826 (Tex. Ct. App. 1989).

RES JUDICATA—EVIDENCE—MATERIALITY AND SUBSTANTIAL PREJUDICE—VERMONT

Res judicata does not apply to a matter that was never tried on its merits. In addition, an award will not be vacated on the ground that the arbitrators

failed to consider material evidence when there is no proof of either materiality or substantial prejudice.

Matzen Construction entered into a contract with United McGill Corporation to construct a pre-engineered building. Matzen subcontracted the construction to Leander Anderson Corporation. The subcontract contained an arbitration clause. McGill encountered difficulties with Leander's crews at the job site, which resulted in damage to a partially completed roof during a windstorm. McGill subsequently demanded that Matzen terminate the subcontract, which it did. An action was brought by McGill against Leander, which was later settled. Matzen completed the job with its own personnel, and Leander demanded arbitration for wrongful termination and monies due on the contract. During the arbitration, Matzen sought to introduce documents regarding the responsibilities of the parties, which the arbitrators declined to accept as evidence. An award was rendered in favor of Leander, and Matzen moved to vacate the award. The court affirmed the award, and Matzen appealed.

Matzen alleged that the award should be vacated on grounds that it was precluded by res judicata and that the arbitrators prejudiced Matzen's case by their refusal to hear material evidence. As to the issue of res judicata, the court determined that the McGill action was never tried on its merits and that "[b]ecause the matter was resolved through a settlement agreement, no defenses were waived nor admissions made that would have a res judicata effect." Noting that Matzen was not a party to that action, the court ruled that the lower court "properly found that the McGill action did not control the outcome of the arbitration by res judicata."

As to the claim that the arbitrators failed to consider material evidence, the court noted that in order to successfully argue its case, Matzen must prove both materiality and substantial prejudice. The court determined that Matzen failed to demonstrate either. Accordingly, the lower court's order confirming the award was affirmed. ***Matzen Construction, Inc. v. Leander Anderson Corp.***, 565 A.2d 1320 (Vt. 1989).

SUMMARY JUDGMENT—SETOFF—LIQUIDATED DAMAGES—VIRGINIA

Summary judgment was erroneously granted because a material fact was genuinely in dispute. In addition, the general contractor was allowed to offset an unliquidated debt from a separate contract against the subcontractor's claim for liquidated damages.

League Construction was the subcontractor on two projects with Piland, the general contractor. League subsequently sued Piland for money allegedly due under one of the project contracts. Piland sought a stay pending arbitration pursuant to an arbitration clause in the contracts. In an attempt to offset the amount of damages that League claimed in the action, Piland filed a counterclaim alleging that League owed Piland damages arising from the other project contract. The trial court awarded League summary judgment in the amount that League claimed in its action. It did not address Piland's demand for arbitration and ruled that Piland could not offset its debt to League because League's claim was a liquidated debt whereas Piland's claim was an unliquidated debt. Piland appealed.

The appellate court determined that summary judgment had been inappropriate because there was a material fact that was genuinely in dispute—namely, the parties' dispute over alleged delays and back charges. The trial court also erred in failing to order arbitration, because Piland was entitled to arbitration of its claim for damages against League. Finally, the court considered whether Virginia law permitted Piland to offset, by counterclaim, an unliquidated debt against a liquidated debt. Finding that the language in the applicable Virginia Rules of Court "explicitly allows a defendant to plead, as a counterclaim, any cause of action at law whether or not it is for liquidated damages," the court held that Piland could seek to offset the unliquidated debt that arose from another contract. ***Piland Corp. v. League Construction Co., Inc.,*** 380 S.E.2d 652 (Va. 1989).

COMMENTARY

Alternative Dispute Resolution: Construction Disputes*

Michael F. Hoellering

Extrajudicial means of dispute resolution are used as supplementary avenues of justice in the United States. The American Arbitration Association (AAA), which was founded in 1926 and is headquartered in New York, is a not-for-profit organization providing a wide range of dispute resolution services. Administering over 50,000 disputes annually, and over 5,000 in the construction area, the AAA and the construction industry have worked together for many years to ensure the best possible system for the resolution of construction contract disputes.

* Paper presented at the American Water Works Association 1990 Annual Conference, Cincinnati, Ohio, June 20, 1990. Michael F. Hoellering is General Counsel of the American Arbitration Association. Vicki M. Young, Editor of Court Decisions, American Arbitration Association, assisted in the preparation of this paper.

ADR Options

While litigation remains as the primary method of dispute resolution, alternatives to litigation are being employed with regularity to meet the burgeoning complexities of modern day society and provide a meaningful redress of grievances. This is especially so since the public court system, overwhelmed by crushing caseloads, insufficient resources, and inefficient traditional litigation methods, simply can no longer cope with the wealth of human problems that clamor for judicial attention.

It should be stated at the outset that I regard the term *alternative dispute resolution* (ADR) as encompassing all litigation alternatives, whether quasi-judicial in nature or aimed primarily at furthering the negotiation process, with the outcome controlled by the parties themselves rather than a neutral decision maker.

There are a number of ADR options which the AAA administers for parties desiring an alternative to litigation. Of these alternatives, which include mediation, dispute review boards, med-arb, and the mini-trial, arbitration is by far the most widely used. Arbitration is broadly utilized by the construction industry for a number of reasons. It is an extremely flexible procedure that allows parties the freedom to tailor the procedure to their needs. Arbitration is also final in that the parties agree to be bound by the result. Other advantages of a properly conducted arbitration process are economy, speed, and privacy. In addition, because industry disputes frequently involve technical questions best understood by construction experts, the procedure is favored as it allows the parties to select industry experts to act as the decision makers.

When the American Institute of Architects (AIA) was founded in 1911 and began printing its standard forms, arbitration provisions were included in those forms. The forms were later amended, after the AAA was established, to provide parties with a choice of arbitrating either under the AIA procedures or the AAA's *Commercial Arbitration Rules*. Because of shortcomings under both systems, the AAA's *Construction Industry Arbitration Rules* were designed. Administered by the AAA, the new system is supervised by a National Construction Industry Arbitration Committee (NCIAC).

The NCIAC, a highly active body which provides the AAA with policy guidance in relation to the construction industry dispute resolution system, consists of various industry and professional association representatives and regional advisory committees from 43 metropolitan areas throughout the United States. The American Consulting Engineers Council, American Institute of Architects, American Society of Civil Engineers, American Society of Interior Designers, American Society of Landscape Architects, American Subcontractors Association, Associated Builders and Contractors, Associated General Contractors, Associated Specialty Contractors,

Business Roundtable, Construction Specifications Institute, National Association of Home Builders, National Society of Professional Engineers, and National Utility Contractors Association are the NCIAC member organizations.

Mediation, sometimes referred to as conciliation and second in popularity to arbitration, involves the use of an impartial third party. This individual, known as a mediator, assists the parties in reaching a settlement through direct negotiation, preferably in the early stages of the dispute, so as to avoid the need of adversary proceedings, whether litigation or arbitration. The mediator actively participates in the negotiations, often advising and consulting with the parties. The construction industry, which is showing keen receptivity to this mechanism, has worked with the AAA in developing the AAA's *Construction Industry Mediation Rules* and in training qualified industry mediators. AIA documents now provide for the use of mediation under AAA auspices "in addition to and prior to arbitration." AAA statistics reflect that of the cases mediated under AAA auspices, over 80 percent have resulted in settlement between the parties. Note that although mediation is strictly voluntary and nonbinding because the mediator does not have the authority to impose a settlement on the parties, one important attribute of the procedure is confidentiality. As a result of information imparted to a mediator in a caucus that might be left unsaid during an arbitration, the mediator is often able to suggest creative solutions that might not otherwise be considered and that might lead to a settlement.

The disputes review board is an ADR technique that was initially developed to aid in the resolution of disputes involving underground construction. This technique involves a three-member board, consisting of industry experts, that is organized soon after the award of the contract and before any disputes arise. The purpose of the on-site board is to provide an assessment of the merits of the disputes. While the recommendations are purely advisory and nonbinding on the contracting parties, there appears to be a trend toward acceptance of the board's findings and recommendations. When this technique is used, however, it seems desirable for the parties to provide for arbitration in their contract in the event that the board's recommendations are not voluntarily accepted or implemented by the parties.

The mini-trial is a structured settlement procedure that facilitates an abbreviated, confidential, nonbinding information exchange aimed at assisting the parties in settling their dispute(s). A noted feature of this ADR technique is the participation of high-level executives with settlement authority. The parties can structure the mini-trial in whatever way they wish. Should they desire, the AAA's *Mini-trial Procedures* may be used. Usually, the parties enter into a voluntary agreement that sets forth the guidelines under which the mini-trial is to be conducted.

AAA Panel of Arbitrators

One notable feature of AAA-administered industry arbitration is the existence of the National Panel of Construction Industry Arbitrators. This panel currently consists of over 30,000 construction arbitrators, representing the construction and construction-related fields. For example, the panelists include accountants, architects, attorneys, construction managers, engineers, general contractors, geologists, insurers, manufacturers and suppliers, real estate appraisers, and subcontractors. The AAA continuously recruits qualified individuals to the panel. This is done both at the AAA headquarters in New York and locally at the AAA regional offices. Assisting in the recruitment are the staff representatives of NCAIC member organizations and the regional NCIAC advisory committees.

Arbitrator Selection

Parties to an AAA-administered arbitration are given the up-to-date information about the arbitrators to enable them to select the most qualified individuals for their case. Those individuals who are members of the AAA panel agree to be bound by the AAA's procedures and the provisions of the Code of Ethics for Arbitrators in Commercial Disputes. Note that AAA procedures also impose upon arbitrators the duty to disclose potentially disqualifying relationships. This requirement is to ensure impartiality on the part of the arbitrators. Upon such disclosure, which is communicated to the parties, the parties then are given the option to agree to proceed or to challenge the arbitrator's continued service on the panel for that particular case.

The AAA employs a flexible approach when ruling on arbitrator challenges. This approach balances the concept of impartiality against the inevitable business relationships of experts who are prominent and experienced members of the construction and construction-related fields. Considerations include a weighing of whether a relationship is "direct" rather than "remote," or "substantial" or "significant" and "ongoing" rather than "speculative" or "uncertain." Certainly, a personal or financial interest in the result of an arbitration would always prevent service of an arbitrator, as would other close business, social, and family relationships. Of course, parties with full and complete knowledge can always elect to waive such disqualifications in writing, prior to the first hearing.

Note that the above standard for neutral arbitrators is slightly different when dealing with party-appointed arbitrators. Partisan predisposition of the latter, while limiting partiality as a ground for *vacatur* of a resulting award, in no way excuses the arbitrator(s) from upholding the fairness and integrity of the arbitration process.

Arbitrator Training

AAA arbitrators, besides being experts in their respective fields, also need a thorough understanding of the arbitral process. To achieve that end, the AAA conducts a variety of arbitrator training programs. The NCIAC assists the AAA in the implementation of the programs. These annual training programs are conducted nationally by the AAA's 35 regional offices. In 1989, 72 such programs were held. Through lectures, workshops, mock arbitration films, and role playing, arbitrators are provided with an understanding of arbitration law and procedure. A series of three training tapes involving construction arbitration issues is used in the training of construction arbitrators.

Expediting Large and Complex Cases

Large and complex cases consist of disputes involving large sums of money, a variety of claims and counterclaims, and complex issues. The AAA administers about 15 percent of such cases annually. To facilitate prompt resolution of this type of case, the AAA, with the assistance of the NCIAC, has developed *Guidelines for Expediting Larger, Complex Construction Arbitrations*. The *Guidelines* provide for two mechanisms for the advance exchange of information aimed at expediting the actual hearings, an administrative conference and a preliminary hearing. In addition, the *Guidelines* contain information regarding construction arbitrators especially suited to hearing large and complex cases, the availability of mediation and consecutive hearings, and form of award.

Consolidation

A question that arises is whether the AAA's rules should be amended to provide for consolidation of multiple-party construction claims involving the same construction project but containing separate agreements between the parties. After extensive consideration, the NCIAC found that consolidation was appropriate in some instances but not in others. It therefore concluded that the parties themselves should regulate the issue of consolidation. This is accomplished either in the parties' arbitration agreement or at the time of arbitration.

International Disputes

The AAA administers a number of international construction disputes each year. Arbitration is particularly favored in international disputes because the current law allows participants to avoid the national courts of the other party as well as to tailor the arbitration proceeding according to the parties' special needs. Because many nations are contracting states to multilateral treaties and conventions that support arbitration, parties know that the arbitration agreement and the resulting award will be enforced by any contracting state, regardless of the relationship of the parties to that state. In addition, to meet the special concerns and needs of parties involved in international disputes, the AAA has developed *Supplementary Procedures for International Commercial Arbitration*. The *Supplementary Procedures* contain provisions regarding language, nonnational arbitrators, exchange and transmittal of documents, and opinions explaining the reasons of the award.

AAA Staff Training

The AAA regularly conducts staff training programs of case administrators both to increase user satisfaction and to provide users with a level of administrative services that is desired and expected. The training programs are intensive two-day sessions consisting of videotapes, question-and-answer periods, role playing, and discussions by experts on the substantive aspects of construction dispute resolution.

User Surveys

Regular AAA surveys of users of its construction arbitration and mediation services indicate general satisfaction with the operation of the system, citing quality of performance as the major advantages.

Conclusion

As this brief survey has sought to indicate, arbitration continues to be the most frequently used ADR technique in the resolution of inevitable construction disputes. At the same time, the term ADR has become a household word, with much valuable experimentation under way, particularly in the area of dispute avoidance through the early identification of problem areas. Clearly, the newer techniques, except perhaps for mediation, are still in their infancy. They deserve our full support, for it makes eminent good sense to promote earlier resolutions, before positions harden and claims escalate. Ultimately, however, to fully realize the advantages of the various techniques will require an informed appreciation of their particular characteristics and suitability under given circumstances.

Appendix

Number and Size of Construction Cases

The following numbers reflect the steady growth in number of cases arbitrated under AAA auspices for the last ten years:

1980	2,831
1981	2,817
1982	2,683
1983	2,675
1984	3,150
1985	3,735
1986	4,317
1987	4,582
1988	4,940
1989	5,132

In 1989 alone, the 5,132 arbitrated cases involved a total of $873,053,302 in claims and counterclaims.

Breakdown by Amounts and Percentages

Amount of Claim	Number of Cases	Percentage of Cases
$1-10,000	1,456	28%
$10,001-50,000	1,858	36%
$50,001-100,000	714	14%
$100,001-500,000	723	14%
$500,001-1,000,000	108	2%
$1,000,001 and over	111	2%
No Amount Disclosed	161	3%

Geographic Distribution of Cases

Atlanta	150	Cleveland	83
Boston	421	Dallas	138
Charlotte	154	Denver	69
Chicago	178	Detroit	120
Cincinnati	100	Garden City, NY	80

Hartford	161	Orlando	0
Hawaii	38	Philadelphia	244
Houston	0	Phoenix	127
Kansas City	46	Pittsburgh	88
Los Angeles	553	Puerto Rico	12
Miami	259	Salt Lake City	10
Minneapolis	93	San Diego	137
Nashville	45	San Francisco	31
New Jersey	341	Seattle	118
New Orleans	3	St. Louis	31
New York	259	Syracuse	91
Orange County, CA	116	Washington, DC	405
		White Plains, NY	96

Parties to and Number of Cases

Parties to Cases	Number of Cases
ARCHITECT (230) or ENGINEER (20) v. OWNER	250
OWNER v. ARCHITECT (161) or ENGINEER (12)	173
CONTRACTOR(1,523) or SUBCONTRACTOR (80) v. OWNER	1,603
OWNER v. CONTRACTOR (711) or SUBCONTRACTOR (26)	737
CONTRACTOR v. SUBCONTRACTOR	247
SUBCONTRACTOR v. CONTRACTOR	779
OTHER—Consisting of Multiparty Cases, and Including Other Than the Above Categories	1,346

Duration of Arbitrated Cases

The following information is compiled from the results of a 1988 survey.

Claim Range	Number of Cases	Percentage of Total	Median Number of Days from Filing to Award
$1-15,000	873	37%	116
$15,000-50,000	660	28%	189
$50,001-100,000	274	12%	240
$100,001-500,000	319	13%	327
$500,001-1,000,000	45	2%	413
$1,000,001 and over	40	2%	575
Undetermined	151	6%	216
TOTAL or AVERAGE	2,362	100%	182

C. INSURANCE AND MEDICAL MALPRACTICE

CASE DIGESTS

CONSOLIDATION—ARBITRATION AGREEMENT

Federal courts may not read a consolidation provision into the arbitration agreement when such a provision is absent.

A district court ordered the consolidation of arbitration of Lincoln's dispute with Protective, as well as the arbitration of claims between Protective and a third party. Lincoln appealed.

Vacating the lower court's ruling, the appellate court held that a district court may not consolidate arbitration proceedings if the parties had not provided for consolidation in their arbitration agreement. It noted that the federal courts are limited to ordering parties to proceed to arbitration if an arbitration agreement is found to exist. The court also specifically stated that because parties may negotiate for and include provisions for consolidation in their arbitration agreements, federal courts may not read in consolidation provisions when such provisions are absent from the arbitration agreements. Consequently, the ruling below was found to be improper, and the court remanded the matter. ***Protective Life Insurance Corp. v. Lincoln National Life Insurance Corp.,*** 873 F.2d 281 (11th Cir. 1989).

UNINSURED MOTORIST—REMEDIES—MOTION TO COMPEL ARBITRATION—ATTORNEY FEES—FLORIDA

Overriding the lower court, the appellate court held that because the state arbitration statute superseded the statutory uninsured motorist coverage provision, a party was entitled to remedies.

A motion to compel arbitration of an uninsured motorist claim against State Farm was filed by Kathleen Leaf, an insured. State Farm argued that it had not agreed to arbitration pursuant to the terms of the insurance policy. The issue was submitted to a jury, which returned a verdict finding that State Farm had in fact consented to arbitration. State Farm then moved to strike Leaf's claim for attorney fees. The motion was granted on the ground that there was no statutory basis for such a claim. Leaf appealed.

The appellate court disagreed with the lower court's ruling to strike the claim for attorney fees, and reversed. It determined that the Florida arbitration statute governed, not the statutory uninsured motorist coverage provision. Leaf's action, the court held, was not a request for payment of uninsured motorist coverage benefits, but rather a demand that the determination of the amount of such benefits be arbitrated rather than litigated. Consequently, Leaf was entitled to a remedy under the arbitration statute. ***Leaf v. State Farm Mutual Automobile Insurance Co***., 544 So. 2d 1049 (Fla. Dist. Ct. App. 1989).

APPRAISAL—ARBITRATION AGREEMENT—FLORIDA

An appraisal clause qualifies as an arbitration agreement under the Florida Arbitration Code when it sufficiently identifies the matters to be submitted to arbitration and provides procedures by which arbitration is to be effected.

Intracoastal Ventures was insured by Safeco Insurance. The insurance policy contained a provision allowing appraisers to determine the amount of loss in the event Intracoastal and Safeco could not agree. The provision also contained information as to how the appraisers would be selected, the issues to be submitted for appraisal, and apportionment of related expenses. A dispute arose over the amount of loss, and Intracoastal filed a complaint in court. The complaint was subsequently dismissed by the trial court on the ground that the language of the policy compelled arbitration. Intracoastal appealed.

The appellate court affirmed. It rejected Intracoastal's argument that the provision at issue "contemplate[d] nothing more than an informal process" that did not qualify as an arbitration agreement under Florida's Arbitration Code. Finding that several Florida courts have equated appraisal clauses with arbitration clauses in cases where substantially the same policy language was used as in the case before it, the court ruled that the appraisal provision constituted an arbitration agreement because it sufficiently identified the matters to be submitted to the arbitration as well as the procedures by which arbitration was to be effected. ***Intracoastal Ventures Corp. v. Safeco Insurance Co. of America,*** 540 So. 2d 162 (Fla. Dist. Ct. App. 1989).

UNDERINSURED MOTORIST—ARBITRATION AGREEMENT—INCONSISTENT RESULTS—SUBROGATION—MASSACHUSETTS

Absent a provision to the contrary in the underinsurance statute or in the insurance policy, a party may seek arbitration of a claim for underinsured

motorist benefits prior to the exhaustion of claims against the alleged tortfeasors.

Kevin Faris, a minor, was injured when a rented car driven by his father, James Faris, collided with an auto driven by Linda Moniz. A tort action was filed on Kevin's behalf against both his father and Moniz, resulting in a settlement of $10,000 from Moniz's insurer. An additional liability claim against James Faris, which invoked an insurance policy issued by Aetna Casualty and Surety Company on a car owned by Faris, remained unresolved. A demand was made on Kevin's behalf for arbitration, which Aetna refused. Instead, Aetna filed an action seeking a preliminary injunction and a declaration that the demand was premature because of the failure to exhaust all claims for liability first.

The trial court rejected both requests by the insurer, ruling that a party injured in an automobile accident has a right to arbitration of claims for underinsurance benefits because there is nothing in the underinsurance statute or the insurance policy requiring that all other claims against the tortfeasors be settled prior to arbitration. Aetna appealed.

The appellate court affirmed the trial court's ruling, reasoning that the advantages of speed, efficiency, and cost offered by arbitration would be thwarted by a contrary ruling. In addition, the parties had agreed in their policy that an arbitrator could determine the issues of liability and damages. To the extent that arbitration might precede an inconsistent judicial resolution of the tort claim, the court noted that the insurer was protected by its subrogation rights in the policy and the statute. ***Aetna Casualty and Surety Co. v. Faris,*** 536 N.E.2d 1097 (Mass. Ct. App. 1989).

NO-FAULT—UNDERINSURED MOTORIST—RES JUDICATA—MINNESOTA

The trial court did not err in giving res judicata effect to an arbitration award, because to do otherwise would have resulted in a double recovery.

Jay Quam was involved as a passenger in a single-vehicle accident. He reached a settlement with the driver and then filed a claim against his own insurer, United Fire & Casualty, for underinsured motorist benefits. United paid a portion of Quam's no-fault medical benefits. The issue of damages was submitted to arbitration.

The arbitration panel, although asked to specify the components of its award, instead issued a general award covering all past and future damages. This award was subsequently reduced by the amount of medical benefits paid by United and by the settlement paid by the driver's insurer. Both parties moved to confirm, making no request that the arbitrators specify the dollar amounts for future wage loss and medical expenses.

Following arbitration, Quam sought further medical treatment, and submitted the bills to United for payment. United refused to pay and moved to quash Quam's petition for a second arbitration hearing on the issue of subsequent treatment. The trial court granted United's motion, ruling that the arbitration award had already compensated Quam for future medical expenses. Quam appealed.

The appellate court affirmed, finding that the "trial court did not err when it gave res judicata effect to the arbitrators' determination of all past and future damages." The court noted that *Richardson v. Employers Mutual Casualty Co.*, 424 N.W.2d 317 (Minn. Ct. App. 1988)—wherein the court refused to allow additional claims after a prior arbitration award because to do so would allow a double recovery—was determinative of Quam's dispute. The appellate court found that there was no error, reasoning that when the dollar amount of damages is not specified and an award specifically states that it is for "all future damages," it would be impossible to avoid a double recovery without giving preclusive effect to the arbitration award. ***Quam v. United Fire & Casualty Co.***, 440 N.W.2d 131 (Minn. Ct. App. 1989).

UNINSURED MOTORIST—UNINSURED VEHICLE—COVERAGE—STAY OF ARBITRATION—NEW YORK

The court held that the question of whether a vehicle was uninsured was one for the courts to decide. It also ruled that a stay of arbitration was not warranted because the insurer failed to show that the vehicle was insured under a homeowner's policy.

Marie Taibbi was struck by a motorized bicycle driven by Edward Serrao. Aetna Casualty and Surety, the insurer of Serrao's parents under a homeowner's policy, disclaimed coverage. Taibbi then commenced an arbitration proceeding, seeking to recover uninsured motorist benefits from her automobile insurance carrier, Allstate. Allstate moved for a stay of arbitration, which was denied on the ground that the issue of whether the bicycle was uninsured was one for the arbitrator to decide.

On appeal, the lower court's determination was reversed. The appellate court ruled that the question of whether a vehicle is insured is one for the courts. The lower court's order denying the stay was affirmed, nevertheless, because Allstate failed to show that the bicycle was insured under the homeowner's policy of Serrao's parents. Consequently, the court ruled that a stay was not warranted. ***Allstate Insurance Co. v. Taibbi***, 550 N.Y.S.2d 56 (2d Dep't 1990).

NO-FAULT—ARTICLE 75 PROCEEDING—ARBITRATION AWARD—VACATUR—MASTER ARBITRATION AWARD—INTERESTS OF JUSTICE—NEW YORK

The master arbitrator exceeded his authority in vacating a hearing arbitrator's award in the interests of justice absent a finding either of misconduct or that the hearing arbitrator acted in an "arbitrary, capricious or irrational" manner.

A dispute between Hempstead General Hospital and National Grange Mutual Insurance Company over an unpaid hospital bill was submitted to arbitration. The arbitrator's award of no-fault benefits was later vacated by the master arbitrator. A subsequent proceeding to vacate the master arbitrator's award in accordance with article 75 of the New York Civil Practice Law & Rules was in turn dismissed, and the decision was appealed.

The appellate court noted that judicial review of a master arbitrator's vacatur of an award was limited to whether the master arbitrator exceeded his power. It found that in the instant case, the master arbitrator did not have the authority to vacate the original award "in the interests of justice." The court determined that the master arbitrator exceeded his authority by substituting his discretion for that of the hearing arbitrator without either finding misconduct by the arbitrator or ascertaining that he had acted in a manner that was "arbitrary, capricious or without rational basis." Accordingly, the court vacated the master arbitration award. ***Hempstead General Hospital v. National Grange Mutual Insurance Co.,*** 542 N.Y.S.2d 780 (2d Dep't 1989).

NO-FAULT—JUDICIAL REVIEW—MASTER ARBITRATOR—PUBLIC POLICY—AWARD—NEW YORK

Failure to appeal an award to the master arbitrator renders a court ineligible to decide or review the issues that the master arbitrator would have reviewed. Judicial review of a no-fault award is limited to ascertaining whether there was a final and definite resolution of the dispute; if there was no final and definite award, the proper course of action is to remand the case back to the arbitrator. The court also determined that public policy considerations warranted a reduction of the award to the maximum allowed by statute.

Carty appealed an order denying his petition to confirm his insurance award. In its denial of the petition to confirm, the court noted that the award was "arbitrary," "contrary to the evidence," and clearly "unintelligible" with respect to the insurance company's duty to repay Carty for lost work.

The appellate court agreed with Carty's argument that the lower court did not have the requisite authority to review the award on the basis of its rationality. It noted that the insurance company should have appealed the award to a master arbitrator, whose scope of review includes the rationality of the award as well as errors of law. Because the insurance company failed to do so, the lower court was precluded from inquiring on any matter other than the award's finality. The court, nevertheless, lowered the award to the maximum statutory amount, reasoning that an award which required the insurance company to "compute and pay" the interest was not a final and definite award. In addition, because the award was in excess of the statutory limit, public policy considerations warranted a reduction in the award to the maximum amount allowed by law.

The court also found that in order for the insurance company to "compute and pay" Carty, Carty had to present "proof of the fact and amount of loss sustained." Since Carty had not submitted such proof to the insurance company or the court, a remand to the arbitrator for a determination of the issue was necessary before the court could deem the award final. ***In re Carty,*** 539 N.Y.S.2d 374 (1st Dep't 1989).

NO-FAULT—TIMELINESS—ARBITRATION AGREEMENT—MOTION TO STAY ARBITRATION—NEW YORK

When there is a question regarding whether an agreement to arbitrate actually exists, a petition to stay arbitration is appropriate regardless of whether the proceeding was timely brought.

A driver wanted to arbitrate a claim under the uninsured motorist benefits provision of a Countrywide Insurance Company policy. The driver sought to recover damages that his car sustained when "struck by a concededly uninsured and unregistered car." Countrywide disputed the fact that the vehicle was insured under a policy, claiming that the insured driver had transferred his policy from the vehicle in question to another vehicle in his possession sometime prior to the date of the accident. The court decided to permanently stay the arbitration proceedings. Upon rehearing, the court upheld its previous decision, even though the driver contended that Countrywide's stay of arbitration was untimely.

When the driver appealed the court's decision, the appellate court stated that the driver's claim about the untimeliness of the stay was irrelevant because the statutory time limitation that the driver relied upon "presumes the existence of a viable agreement to arbitrate." Because the agreement to arbitrate was questionable, the court could not enforce such a time bar to prohibit the proceedings for the stay. Consequently, the court affirmed the lower court's ruling to stay arbitration and modified it to include a hearing on the issue of insurance coverage. ***In re Countrywide Insurance Co.,*** 539 N.Y.S.2d 366 (1st Dep't 1989).

UNINSURED MOTORIST—CONDITION PRECEDENT—MOTION TO COMPEL ARBITRATION—OREGON

The Supreme Court of Oregon held that an insurer's failure to agree with the insured on the amounts due under an uninsured motorist provision did not constitute a failure, neglect, or refusal to perform so as to provide grounds for a filing of a petition to compel arbitration under Oregon Law.

Moresi and Nationwide Mutual entered into an automobile insurance agreement that contained an arbitration clause. Moresi was involved in an automobile accident. Nationwide rejected Moresi's demand pursuant to the policy's uninsured motorist coverage for $50,000 and offered $4,000. Five days before the applicable two-year statute of limitations period was due to expire, Moresi petitioned to arbitrate in state court. The court denied Moresi's petition, finding that Nationwide did not breach the arbitration clause and that Moresi's petition did not constitute a written demand for arbitration as required by the clause. Moresi appealed the decision.

The appellate court ruled that the lower court had erred in dismissing the petition when it wrongly concluded that a particular requirement was a condition precedent to arbitration rather than a procedural condition of arbitration. However, on appeal to the state's highest court, the decision of the appellate court was reversed and the judgment of the lower court was reinstated.

The high court ruled that under the applicable statute, courts are authorized "to compel arbitration only where a party has failed, neglected or refused to arbitrate in accordance with a contract arbitration provision." In this case, the court concluded that Nationwide's failure to agree on the amount due under the uninsured motorist clause did not constitute failure, neglect, or refusal to perform.

Thus, the court concluded that while disagreement over the damages provided grounds for either party to demand arbitration under the contract, it did not provide grounds for the filing of the petition to compel arbitration. Because Moresi had not made a written demand for arbitration, and because Nationwide had not failed, neglected, or refused to perform under the terms of the arbitration provision, Nationwide's duty to perform contract had not arisen. ***Moresi v. Nationwide Mutual,*** 309 Or. 619, 789 P.2d 667 (1990).

UNINSURED MOTORIST—CONDITION PRECEDENT—PROCEDURAL CONDITION—MOTION TO COMPEL ARBITRATION—OREGON

The trial court erred in dismissing a petition to arbitrate when it wrongly concluded that a particular requirement was a condition precedent to arbitration rather than a procedural condition of arbitration.

Moresi and Nationwide Mutual entered into an automobile insurance agreement that contained an arbitration clause. The clause provided for arbitration when the two parties "do not agree about the insured's right to recover damages or the amount of damages." Moresi was involved in an automobile accident and was offered $4,000 in damages by Nationwide. Nationwide stipulated that failure to agree on the settlement amount by a certain date would leave Moresi with no legal recourse pursuant to Oregon law. Moresi subsequently filed a petition to arbitrate in state court. The trial court denied Moresi's motion to compel arbitration, finding that Nationwide did not breach the arbitration clause because Moresi's petition did not constitute a written demand for arbitration as required by the clause. Moresi appealed the decision.

The appellate court ruled that in a proceeding to compel arbitration, the trial court may consider only whether an agreement to arbitrate existed and whether a party breached this agreement. The court noted that in this case, a clause to arbitrate definitely existed. It also noted the difference between conditions precedent and procedural conditions, the former to be determined by a court and the latter to be determined by an arbitrator. Nationwide argued that it was not in default because Moresi did not meet the condition precedent of a written demand. The court, however, determined that the requirement of a written demand was a procedural condition for the arbitrator to decide.

The court also clarified that the actual and only condition precedent that was required before the parties could gain access to the arbitral forum was their failure to agree on damages. Because it was this failure that invoked the arbitration clause, the court held that the other conditions were procedural conditions related to the conduct of the arbitration proceedings. Consequently, because the trial court erred in concluding that the requirement of a written demand was a condition precedent to arbitration rather than a procedural condition of arbitration, the appellate court remanded the case to the lower court with a directive compelling arbitration. ***Moresi v. Nationwide Mutual,*** 771 P.2d 301 (Or. Ct. App. 1989).

UNINSURED MOTORIST COVERAGE—DECLARATORY RELIEF—PENNSYLVANIA

The court determined that declaratory relief was appropriate and that the complaint was properly authorized.

Barbara Johnson suffered severe injuries as a result of a motor vehicle accident. Because Johnson's first-party benefits, provided by Prudential Property and Casualty Insurance Company, were insufficient to meet all the bills, the Department of Public Welfare (DPW) paid a portion of her medical bills through its medical assistance program. Prudential was willing to tender $25,000, the policy limit under Johnson's uninsured motorist coverage. A dispute arose between the DPW and Johnson over their respective rights to the monies paid by Prudential. DPW filed an action for a declaratory judgment.

Johnson initially argued that the DPW could not pursue its statutory cause of action for reimbursement of medical benefits because it failed to request the attorney general to bring suit against her and that the attorney general was the only party that could bring such a suit. The court rejected this argument, noting that the complaint was verified by an attorney for the Commonwealth of Pennsylvania and that the complaint was brought in the name of the Commonwealth as required by the Pennsylvania civil procedural rules. The court determined that verification was sufficient and that the attorney general's authorization need not be specifically pleaded.

Johnson also argued that "her initiation of an arbitration proceeding pursuant to her liability insurance policy is a prior action prohibiting DPW from pursuing declaratory action." The court disagreed, finding that the duty to arbitrate arose out of the contract of insurance between Johnson and Prudential. Because the DPW was not a party to that contract, the court reasoned it was not obligated to arbitrate its claim for reimbursement. In addition, because the DPW and Johnson were the only parties making a claim on the policy limits, the court found that there was no pending action which barred the DPW's request for declaratory relief. Since the dispute between the DPW and Johnson was current and ongoing, the court ruled that declaratory relief would end that dispute. ***DPW v. Prudential Property & Casualty Insurance Co.,*** 564 A.2d 523 (Pa. Commw. Ct. 1989).

ASSIGNMENT—APPRAISAL—PREJUDGMENT INTEREST—CONFIRMATION OF AWARD—ARBITRAL AUTHORITY—RHODE ISLAND

A dispute resolution procedure in an insurance policy providing for an appraisal constitutes arbitration under Rhode Island law. In addition, awarding prejudgment interest is within the arbitrator's authority.

Wear/Friction is the insured under an insurance policy issued by Aetna for fire, theft, and business interruption loss. A fire destroyed Wear/Friction's premises and Wear/Friction sustained losses. A dispute arose over Wear/Friction's loss claims. Because of reorganization, George Waradzin was assigned Wear/Friction's claims against Aetna. Pursuant to a dispute resolution procedure in the policy providing for an appraisal, an umpire and two appraisers were selected. The appraisal proceeding resulted in an award in favor of Waradzin, who commenced an action to confirm the award. Aetna moved to modify or correct the award, contending that the prejudgment interest added to the award by the appraisers was in error and not within their authority. The court denied the motion and placed the matter on a special cause calendar for confirmation of the award. Aetna again challenged the award of prejudgment interest and also argued that subjecting the award to the arbitration confirmation proceeding was incorrect because the appraisal-evaluation proceeding was not arbitration. The court rejected Aetna's arguments and upheld the award.

Aetna appealed the decision and raised the same arguments on appeal. The appellate court, stating that an appraisal procedure can be equated with arbitration, found that the appraisal procedure called for in the policy at issue was arbitration. It further clarified that the label used to describe a procedure is not controlling because what is more important is the substance of the transaction that determines its character.

The court also found that Aetna had recognized the valuation proceedings as arbitration in several of its pleadings. Because of this, the court stated that "a party wishing to object to the arbitrability of a dispute must state his objection on those grounds at the arbitration hearing or refuse to submit to the process and pursue his remedy in court." In addition, the court determined that under Rhode Island law, arbitrators have the authority to award prejudgment interest. Because the terms of the policy did not prohibit the awarding of prejudgment interest, the court rejected Aetna's claim that the arbitrators exceeded their authority. The judgment confirming the award was affirmed. ***Waradzin v. Aetna Casualty and Surety Company,*** 570 A.2d 649 (R.I. 1990).

UNINSURED MOTORIST ACT—MCCARRAN-FERGUSON ACT—FEDERAL ARBITRATION ACT—STATE ARBITRATION ACT—VERMONT

The McCarran-Ferguson Act does not preclude application of the Federal Arbitration Act (FAA) to a claim made under the uninsured motorist provision of an automobile insurance policy.

Michael and Linda Preziose were involved in an accident in New York and initiated an action in a Vermont court against Lumbermen's Mutual

Casualty Company for recovery under the uninsured motorist provision of their insurance policy. The policy contained a clause providing for arbitration of disputes over the Prezioses' entitlement to damages. Lumbermen's moved to compel arbitration, which the court granted on the ground that the FAA applied to the policy.

The Prezioses disagreed, claiming that the FAA does not specifically relate to the business of insurance. In their appeal, they argued that the McCarran-Ferguson Act barred application of the FAA and that the lower court's ruling "invalidated, impaired or superseded Vermont laws, in violation of the McCarran-Ferguson Act." The two Vermont laws at issue were the Vermont Arbitration Act (VAA) and the state Uninsured Motorist Act (UMA). The Prezioses also argued that the VAA and the UMA were created to regulate the business of insurance and could be used to revoke the arbitration provision in their insurance policy.

The court determined that as to the invalidation, impairment, or supersession of Vermont law, the Prezioses' insurance contract was not subject to the VAA. The court found that the VAA applies only to agreements entered into and executed on or after July 1, 1985, while the Prezioses' insurance contract was entered into prior to that date. As for the UMA, the court found that there was no express requirement that disputes regarding uninsured motorist coverage be resolved in court. Because enforcement of the arbitration clause did not invalidate, impair, or supersede either the VAA or the UMA, the court ruled that the McCarran-Ferguson Act did not bar application of the FAA. ***Preziose v. Lumbermen's Mutual Casualty Co.,*** 568 A.2d 397 (Vt. 1989).

PREJUDGMENT INTEREST—APPEALABILITY—STATUTORY OFFER OF SETTLEMENT—JUDICIAL ARBITRATION—COURT-ANNEXED ARBITRATION—CALIFORNIA

Under California law, prejudgment interest is recoverable in judicial arbitration proceedings.

Stacey and Michael Joyce filed an action against Sherwin Black for dental malpractice. They made a statutory offer of settlement, which Black declined. The case went to judicial arbitration, and an award was rendered in favor of the Joyces. The award was subsequently entered as a judgment, after which the Joyces filed a cost memorandum that included prejudgment interest. Under California law, if a defendant in a personal injury action fails to accept a settlement offer pursuant to applicable statutory law and the plaintiff obtains a more favorable judgment, the judgment is to bear interest from the date of the offer. Black, in turn, successfully moved to strike the costs. The Joyces appealed.

The court rejected Black's argument that the lower court's order was nonappealable. Finding that the order was the "only judicial ruling in the case" and concluding that "the substance and effect of the order, not its label or form, determines whether it is appealable as a final judgment," the court determined that the order "ha[d] all the earmarks of a final judgment."

As to the issue of prejudgment interest, the court considered an analysis of the issue in *Woodard v. Southern California Permanente Medical Group*, 171 Cal. App. 3d 656, 217 Cal. Rptr. 514 (1985). The court, although finding that that reasoning in *Woodard* is sound within the context of contractual arbitration, "reject[ed] any interpretation of *Woodard*'s broad-sweeping language as applying to judicial arbitration." It held that under applicable statute, prejudgment interest is recoverable in judicial arbitration proceedings. Consequently, the lower court's order striking costs was reversed, and the lower court was directed to award prejudgment interest. ***Joyce v. Black,*** 266 Cal. Rptr. 8 (Ct. App. 1990).

WRIT OF MANDAMUS—SCOPE OF MARYLAND HEALTH CARE MALPRACTICE CLAIMS ACT—MANDATORY ARBITRATION—PLAIN MEANING RULE—MARYLAND

The trial court did not abuse its discretion when it declined to issue a writ of mandamus. In addition, a non-health care provider is subject to mandatory arbitration where the claim is joined with and incorporated in an arbitrable claim against health care providers.

Bradley Crites received a consultation from Joseph Kies, an employee of Dr. Jeffrey Weidig, regarding hair transplant surgery. Crites subsequently underwent surgery, which proved to be unsuccessful. Pursuant to the Health Care Malpractice Claims Act (Act), Crites filed a complaint for medical malpractice with the Health Claims Arbitration Office against Kies, Weidig, and Weidig's corporation. Kies moved for summary judgment on the ground that the claim against him was beyond the scope of the Act, because he was not a health care provider. The panel chairman denied the motion. Kies sought a writ of mandamus to prohibit the Health Claims Arbitration Office from exercising jurisdiction over him. The motion was denied and Kies appealed.

Because mandamus is an extraordinary remedy reserved for those claims where there is no other available procedure for obtaining review, and because Kies had the option of seeking review upon the disposition of arbitration proceedings, the court ruled that the trial court did not abuse its discretion when it declined to issue the writ.

As to the issue of whether a non-health care provider, when joined as a party defendant with a health care provider in an action to recover for medical injuries, is included within the Act, the court concluded in the affirmative. In doing so, it rejected Kies's argument that non-health care providers are excluded when the "plain meaning" rule is applied.

The court stated that "statutory language [that] is clear and unambiguous does not preclude [it] from consulting external evidence to determine the goal or purpose of the Act." After reviewing the legislative history of the Act, the court concluded that the "plain meaning of the words used [in the Act] should not be afforded their literal effect." In support of its decision, the court stated that it reviewed applicable case law interpreting the scope of the Act and found "nothing . . . to suggest that a claim against a non-health care provider should not be arbitrable along with a claim against a health care provider where the claim stems from an aggregate of facts alleging the negligent performance of a health care procedure."

In conclusion, the court wrote that "we think that it would be unreasonable, illogical, and inconsistent with common sense, on the facts before us, to construe the Act so as to exclude appellant from its coverage." Accordingly, the judgment of the trial court was affirmed. ***Weidig v. Tabler,*** 568 A.2d 868 (Md. Ct. Spec. App. 1990).

VENUE—WRIT OF MANDAMUS—WRIT OF CERTIORARI—APPEALABILITY—INTERLOCUTORY ORDER—MARYLAND

Under Maryland law, neither a writ of mandamus nor a writ of certiorari is available to a party seeking to reverse an arbitrator's denial of a request for a change of venue. Moreover, the interlocutory nature of the arbitrator's decision was not appealable until after the arbitrator had rendered his award.

Janice Wright was admitted to Dorchester General Hospital. She was diagnosed as having kidney disorder and suffering from shock. Wright alleged that because of negligent monitoring and treatment, she suffered additional ailments that necessitated her transfer to a shock trauma unit in another part of town and ultimately caused her permanent paralysis. A claim was filed by Wright with the Health Claims Arbitration Office against the hospital and medical staff that treated her.

Dennis Sober, chairperson of the Health Claims Arbitration Panel, made a determination that Baltimore City was the proper venue, since this was where the shock trauma unit and most of the defendants were located. Dorchester General moved for a change of venue to Dorchester County but Sober denied the motion. A complaint was filed in state court by Dorchester General for either a writ of mandamus or a writ of certiorari, requesting that the venue be changed. The court denied the requested relief, maintaining that it was unaware of any case law that allowed the appealability of "an interlocutory order of this nature. . . ." The court further noted that even if the arbitrator's decision was appealable, there was no "clear abuse of discretion [as] would justify the granting of the complaint. . . ."

Dorchester filed an appeal which the appellate court dismissed. The court determined that an order denying a motion for change of venue in a medical malpractice arbitration proceeding is not reviewable by a circuit court through an action for a writ of either mandamus or certiorari. It further stated that to "allow such a use of these writs with respect to a matter within the panel chairman's discretion [would] circumvent the rule prohibiting appeals from certain types of interlocutory orders, and . . . would open the door to unnecessary judicial interruption." Finally, the court noted that Dorchester General could seek review of the venue decision upon final disposition of the case. ***Dorchester General Hospital v. Sober,*** 555 A.2d 1074 (Md. Ct. Spec. App. 1989).

D. SECURITIES

CASE DIGESTS

PREEMPTION—ARBITRATION AGREEMENT—FEDERAL ARBITRATION ACT

The court affirmed the lower court's determination that a state's regulations concerning pre-dispute arbitration agreements were preempted by federal law.

The state of Massachusetts promulgated regulations governing securities brokers' use of pre-dispute arbitration agreements. The Securities Industry Association filed an action contending that the regulations were preempted by the Federal Arbitration Act (FAA). The issue before the court was "whether Congress did or meant to displace state law concepts in enacting the federal scheme set up by Congress." The court determined that the FAA preempted the Massachusetts regulation singling out pre-dispute arbitration agreements for more demanding standards than are imposed under the state's general law of contracts. The Commonwealth appealed.

The appellate court affirmed the district court's finding of preemption, rejecting claims that the regulations were not preempted by the FAA and that Congress had carved out an exception to the FAA by permitting states concurrently to regulate securities transactions. The court found no evidence of a clear congressional command to override the unambiguous proarbitration mandate of the FAA in the securities field. The court also found that there was "nothing in the Securities Act [of 1933], the [Securities] Exchange Act [of 1934], or the grant of concurrent power to the states to regulate securities [that] manifests a congressional intent to limit or prohibit waiver of a judicial forum for a particular claim, or to abridge the sweep of the FAA."

In addition, the court expressly stated that it was not "willing to infer implicit congressional approval of the Commonwealth's policy simply because the Commodities Futures Trading Commission (CFTC) has adopted rules . . . not dissimilar in spirit from the Massachusetts regulations." Even though the Securities and Exchange Commission (SEC) also approved similar rules submitted by three self-regulatory organizations, the court determined that the CFTC's rulemaking and the SEC's acquiescence are distinguishable from the present action, because the CFTC and the SEC are products of federal, not state, authority.

As for the regulations themselves, the court determined that they contained a value judgment that the state was foreclosed from making "precisely because the FAA ordains that the state's appulse toward arbitration agreements must be the same as its approach to contracts generally." In addition, the value judgment that was made was "within the congressional domain and only Congress, not the states, may create exceptions to it." In conclusion, the court ruled that the regulations were preempted because they treat standard-form pre-dispute arbitration agreements in the securities industry more severely than standard-form contracts are generally treated under state law. In addition, because the policies underlying the regulations and the methods of enforcement conflict with the national policy favoring arbitration, the state scheme is too discommoding to the federal plan. ***Securities Industry Association v. Connolly,*** 883 F.2d 1114 (1st Cir. 1989).

APPEAL—JURISDICTION—COLLATERAL ORDER DOCTRINE

The appellate court ruled that it lacked jurisdiction to hear the appeal. It also concluded that the requirements for appealability under the collateral-order doctrine were not met in the case at bar.

Juanita Queipo was a client of Prudential Bache Securities. A dispute arose and Prudential moved to stay the proceedings and to compel arbitration. Both motions were denied and Prudential appealed. Queipo, in turn, moved to dismiss the appeal for lack of jurisdiction.

The appellate court granted the motion to dismiss. It concluded that the order denying the motion to stay the proceedings and the order denying the motion to compel arbitration were not appealable either as final judgments under 28 U.S.C. § 1291 or as injunctions under 28 U.S.C. § 1292(a)(1). The court also concluded that the requirements for appealability under the collateral-order doctrine were not met in the case at bar because the orders at issue were "not effectively unreviewable on appeal from a final judgment entered after the conclusion of arbitration." It further reasoned that

> [i]f on appeal from a final judgment [those orders are] overturned, denial of immediate review will have required [Prudential] to have incurred the expense of court proceedings, but this potential inconvenience does not constitute irreparable harm and therefore does not render the order appealable as a collateral order.

Queipo v. Prudential Bache Securities, Inc., 867 F.2d 721 (1st Cir. 1989).

INTERLOCUTORY APPEAL—FEDERAL ARBITRATION ACT

As a result of the new congressional amendment to the Federal Arbitration Act, an appeal from an order refusing to stay an action pending arbitration is an appeal as of right. Consequently, the exercise of judicial

discretion under section 1292(b) of title 28 of the United States Code was not necessary.

Aaron Fleck filed an action against E.F. Hutton. Hutton moved for a stay of the action pending arbitration. The motion was denied and Hutton appealed. The district court judge certified his order for an appeal, and Hutton petitioned the appellate court for permission to appeal the subsequent petition as unnecessary because of the congressional amendment to the Federal Arbitration Act that added a new section 15. Under this new section, an appeal from an order refusing to stay an action pending arbitration is an appeal as of right. Consequently, the court ruled that it was no longer necessary for it to exercise its discretion under section 1292(b) of title 28 of the United States Code. ***Fleck v. E.F. Hutton Group, Inc.,*** 873 F.2d 649 (2d Cir. 1989).

AMERICAN ARBITRATION ASSOCIATION RULE 42—RATIONALE FOR AWARD—JUDICIAL REVIEW

American Arbitration Association (AAA) Securities Arbitration Rule 42, which provides that an award include a statement regarding the disposition of any statutory claims, does not mandate that arbitrators must articulate reasons for their award.

Harold and Joeanne Antwine engaged in options trading through the firm of Prudential Bache Securities. The account agreement they signed contained an arbitration provision. After they sustained losses in their account, the Antwines filed an action against Prudential, alleging violations of federal and state securities law. The district court stayed the litigation pending arbitration, pursuant to the parties' arbitration agreement. The matter was submitted to the AAA, and an award was rendered denying the Antwines' claims. The arbitrators refused the Antwines' request for a clarification of the award. The Antwines then moved to vacate the award on the grounds that the arbitrators imperfectly executed their powers because a mutual, final, and definite award was not made. They also argued that the AAA's Securities Arbitration Rule 42, requiring that a statement regarding the disposition of any statutory claims be included in the award, mandated the arbitrators to provide reasons for their award.

The court disagreed with the Antwines, finding that it "has been long settled that arbitrators are not required to disclose or explain the reasons underlying an award" and that if the arbitrators were required to do so, "the very purpose of arbitration—the provision of a relatively quick, efficient and informal means of private dispute settlement—would be markedly undermined." As for the language of Rule 42, the court interpreted that the statement requirement "does not imply that an arbitration panel must articulate reasons for an award."

In addition, the court noted that even if it were to find otherwise, "any perceived error in this case does not rise to the level which would warrant judicial intervention." It concluded that a mutual, final, and definite award was made because the award and statement provided by the arbitrators in this case were clear, concise, and unambiguous. ***Antwine v. Prudential Bache Securities, Inc.,*** 899 F.2d 410 (5th Cir. 1990).

WAIVER—MOTION TO COMPEL ARBITRATION—INTERTWINING DOCTRINE

The intertwining doctrine did not justify a brokerage firm's delay in seeking arbitration. In addition, participation by that firm in discovery and pretrial proceedings was sufficient to constitute prejudice to the opposing party and the firm was deemed to have waived its right to arbitration.

Nancy Frye opened a securities account with Paine, Webber, Jackson & Curtis, signing an agreement which contained an arbitration agreement. A dispute arose and Frye filed an action against Paine Webber, alleging federal securities law violations. During the year-and-a-half discovery period and other pretrial activity in connection with the court action, Paine Webber failed to assert any right to arbitration. It finally demanded arbitration following the U.S. Supreme Court's decision in *Dean Witter Reynolds, Inc. v. Byrd,* 470 U.S. 213, 105 S. Ct. 1238, 84 L. Ed. 2d 158 (1985), wherein the Court rejected the doctrine of intertwining, held that arbitrable pendent claims must be arbitrated, and moved to compel arbitration pursuant to the parties' agreement. Frye opposed, arguing that Paine Webber had waived any right to arbitration based on its full participation in discovery. The trial court granted Paine Webber's motion, and subsequently denied Frye's motion for reconsideration. An arbitration panel was convened, which denied Frye relief. The award was confirmed and Frye appealed.

The appellate court found that the lower court had "erred by finding that the intertwining doctrine rejected in *Byrd* justified [Paine Webber's] delay in seeking arbitration of Frye's claims." It also noted that both delay and extent of the moving party's participation in judicial proceedings are material factors in assessing whether a party suffered sufficient prejudice so as to warrant a finding that the moving party waived its right to arbitration. In the case at bar, the court determined that Frye was sufficiently prejudiced by Paine Webber's actions and participation in the judicial proceedings. Therefore, it ruled that Paine Webber had waived its right to arbitration and reversed the lower court's order compelling arbitration. The matter was remanded to the lower court for trial. ***Frye v. Paine, Webber, Jackson & Curtis, Inc.,*** 877 F.2d 396 (5th Cir. 1989).

INTERLOCUTORY ORDER—JURISDICTION—APPEAL—CERTIFICATION—FEDERAL ARBITRATION ACT

The appellate court was without jurisdiction to hear an appeal over an interlocutory order concerning arbitration because the appellant had failed to obtain district court certification.

Jerald Turboff is a debtor-in-possession whose estate owned a margin account with Merrill Lynch, Pierce, Fenner & Smith. He filed suit against Merrill Lynch, alleging various state law causes of action. The action was moved to federal court on motion by Merrill Lynch, which also sought an order compelling Turboff to arbitrate his claims pursuant to the arbitration agreement he had signed. The district court denied Turboff's motion to remand the matter to state court and ordered Turboff to proceed to arbitration. Turboff appealed.

The court considered the newly amended Federal Arbitration Act (FAA), which now contains a provision regarding appeals. It concluded that it had no jurisdiction to hear the appeal over an interlocutory order concerning arbitration because a section 1292(b) certificate from the district court was never obtained by Turboff. The court also noted that it

> must apply the law in effect at the time it decides the case. . . . When Congress adopts statutory changes while a suit is pending, the effect of which is not to eliminate a substantive right but rather to "change the tribunal which will hear the case," those changes—barring specifically expressed intent to the contrary—will have immediate effect.

Because the amendment to the FAA "introduces procedural changes to the enforcement of arbitration clauses [and] does not affect substantive rights," the court concluded that the amendment applied to the case at bar even though it was passed after the district court ruled in the case. Consequently, the appeal was dismissed. ***Turboff v. Merrill Lynch, Pierce, Fenner & Smith, Inc.,*** 867 F.2d 1518 (5th Cir. 1989).

JURISDICTION—APPEAL—INTERLOCUTORY ORDER—CERTIFICATION

The appellate court declined to hear an appeal on the ground that it lacked jurisdiction because the appellant failed to obtain district court certification. In addition, the court stated that it was without jurisdiction even though appellant had filed notice of appeal before the effective date of the law depriving it of jurisdiction because a statute that addresses remedies or procedures is applied to pending cases.

Charles P. Nichols filed an action against Thomas E. Stapleton and others, claiming damages and alleging securities and commodities fraud, breach of fiduciary duties, and breach of contract. Stapleton moved to compel arbitration pursuant to an arbitration agreement signed by Nichols in his customer agreement. The court issued an order compelling Nichols to arbitration and Nichols appealed.

The court determined that it had to dismiss the appeal because of the recent amendment to the Federal Arbitration Act (FAA) regarding appeals over interlocutory orders concerning arbitration. It found that Nichols had failed to obtain district court certification for the appeal as required under the amendment. The court also ruled that even though Nichols had filed his notice of appeal before the amendment's effective date, the court was still deprived of jurisdiction. It reasoned that "when a statute is addressed to remedies or procedures and does not otherwise alter substantive rights, it will be applied to pending cases." Consequently, the court remanded the case to the district court with instructions to allow Nichols to apply for certification. ***Nichols v. Stapleton,*** 877 F.2d 1401 (9th Cir. 1989).

JURISDICTION—APPEAL—FEDERAL ARBITRATION ACT—RETROACTIVE APPLICATION

Because retroactive application of a statute is presumed, a court lacks jurisdiction to hear an appeal over an interlocutory order concerning arbitration even though the appeal was filed before the new statute was enacted, since the statute became effective upon enactment and is applicable to cases pending upon its enactment.

Thomas and Theresa Campbell filed an action against Dominick Investor Services Corporation, seeking money damages for federal securities law violations. Dominick moved to stay the court action and to compel arbitration. The motion was granted and the Campbells appealed.

While the appeal was pending, the Federal Arbitration Act (FAA) was amended to included a provision governing appeals. Because the provision became effective upon enactment and applied to cases pending upon enactment, the court dismissed the appeal. ***Campbell v. Dominick & Dominick, Inc.,*** 872 F.2d 358 (11th Cir. 1989).

CHOICE-OF-FORUM—LOCALE—AMERICAN ARBITRATION ASSOCIATION—ARBITRAL AUTHORITY

Once it is determined that the parties are bound to submit their dispute to arbitration, the court held, all procedural questions which grow out of the dispute and bear on its final disposition are to be resolved by the arbitrator.

Robert Boudreau and L.F. Rothschild were parties to a contract. The contract did not contain an arbitration agreement. Nevertheless, Boudreau's right to arbitration arose from and was governed by the constitution of the American Stock Exchange, of which L.F. Rothschild was a member. Under the constitution, Boudreau, as a customer, had the choice of demanding arbitration and the option of electing to arbitrate before the American Arbitration Association (AAA) "in the City of New York."

The parties disputed over the interpretation of the language "in the City of New York," with L.F. Rothschild asserting that the language fixed venue in New York and Boudreau claiming that the language is only descriptive of the location of the AAA. The court stated that once there is a determination that the parties must submit their dispute to arbitration, it is the arbitrator who then determines the procedural questions that grow out of the dispute. Because there was no doubt that the parties were obligated to proceed to arbitration, the court ruled that the question of where the arbitration hearing was to be held was a matter for determination by the arbitrator. ***Boudreau v. L.F. Rothschild & Co., Inc.,*** No. 89-250-CIV-ORL-18 (M.D. Fla. Feb. 23, 1990).

FAILURE TO DISCLOSE—EVIDENT PARTIALITY—VACATUR OF AWARD—DAMAGES—AMOUNT OF AWARD—IRRATIONAL DETERMINATION OF AWARD—BURDEN OF PROOF

Failure to disclose a past association that has long since been severed is insufficient to vacate an arbitration award on grounds of evident partiality. In addition, the size of an award is neither a sufficient basis for a finding of partiality nor a statutory ground for vacating an arbitration award.

Marjory Kaye opened an investment account with Dean Witter Reynolds. She subsequently filed an action against Dean Witter for mismanagement of her account. This action was stayed pending arbitration. An arbitration award was rendered in Kaye's favor, and she moved to confirm. Dean Witter countered with a motion to vacate, alleging evident partiality by the arbitrator and that the amount of the award was determined irrationally.

The court denied Dean Witter's request for an evidentiary hearing, finding that Dean Witter had failed to sustain its burden of proof on the issue of evident partiality. It also rejected Dean Witter's complaint of arbitrator corruption, which Dean Witter had based on the arbitrator's failure to disclose a past association with another securities company. The court found that the arbitrator had long since severed his ties with that company and that there was no demonstration of bias, either direct or definite. It also stated that Dean Witter's 15-page motion papers "exclaiming their shock and outrage at the injustice they contended has occurred . . . is unduly extreme and completely unwarranted [and that w]hen all bombastic exhortation is pared away, little of substance remains.''

The court also rejected Dean Witter's claim that the arbitration award should be vacated because the size of the award was determined irrationally. It found that ''[a]s an initial matter, the size of the award is not a statutory ground for vacating an arbitration award.'' Moreover, the court stated that ''the size of the award, even if unduly large, is an insufficient basis for a finding of partiality.'' In accordance with its findings, the court denied Dean Witter's motion to vacate and confirmed the arbitration award. ***Kaye v. Dean Witter Reynolds, Inc.,*** No. 85-378-Civ.-T-15 (M.D. Fla. Feb. 20, 1990).

ARBITRAL IMMUNITY—FEDERAL ARBITRATION ACT

The court held that an action could not be maintained against the Chicago Board Options Exchange for mental anguish and expenses arising from defending a motion to confirm an arbitration award, because the denial of the motion to confirm was the corrective review provided for by the Federal Arbitration Act.

Esther Austern, wife of S. Ezra Austern, was a party to a limited partnership agreement with Fried Trading Company. When a dispute arose, Fried filed a petition with the Chicago Board Options Exchange (CBOE) for arbitration pursuant to the limited partnership agreement; the CBOE accepted the matter. The Austerns subsequently withdrew their appearance, answer, and counterclaim in the arbitration when they learned that Fried was a differently configured entity from the company with which they expected to arbitrate.

A panel of arbitrators designated by the CBOE nevertheless held a hearing and ruled in favor of Fried. Fried moved to confirm the award, and the Austerns opposed. A federal district court in Illinois denied the confirmation petition on the ground that the Austerns had not had adequate notice of the hearings. The Austerns subsequently filed an action for damages for mental anguish and for expenses incurred in defending against Fried's confirmation petition.

The CBOE asserted that it was protected from suit under the quasi-judicial immunity doctrine. The court noted that the doctrine of arbitral immunity arose from policy considerations underlying judicial immunity—namely, to protect the ''integrity of the decision-making process from the fear of reprisals by dissatisfied litigants.'' Immunity, the court continued, was ''extended to arbitrators [because of] the functional comparability of the arbitrators' decision-making process and judgments to those of judges. . . .'' In addition, the court stated that a second policy reason for the extension of immunity was to develop and maintain a pool of qualified individuals willing to act as arbitrators. Because notice of the proceeding is "integrally related to the process of arbitration," the court rejected the Austerns' argument that mailing notice of the hearing was a ministerial and not quasi-judicial act.

The court also ruled that because corrective review was provided by the Federal Arbitration Act, the Austerns could not maintain their action. Specifically, "[b]y defeating confirmation of the arbitration award, the Austerns have already obtained a remedy from another federal court for the wrongs of which they complain." Consequently, the court dismissed the Austerns' complaint for failure to state a claim upon which relief can be granted. ***Austern v. The Chicago Board Options Exchange, Inc.***, 716 F. Supp. 121 (S.D.N.Y. 1989).

AMEX WINDOW—ARBITRAL FORUM—AMERICAN ARBITRATION ASSOCIATION

In this omnibus opinion covering a common issue in three cases, the court held that the constitution of the American Stock Exchange (AMEX), which provides for the arbitration of disputes before the American Arbitration Association (AAA) as an option for customers, is not a rule for purposes of determining the choice of arbitral forums available to customers who sign brokerage account agreements containing a statement that they submit their disputes to arbitration "in accordance with the rules, then obtaining."

James Pitchford, Joseph Beuchot, and Bert and Elizabeth Bishop were customers of Paine Webber. Each signed customer agreements containing a clause requiring the arbitration of disputes "in accordance with the rules, then obtaining, of either the Arbitration Committee of the New York Stock Exchange, American Stock Exchange, National Association of Securities Dealers. . . ." Disputes arose and each subsequently filed a demand for arbitration against Paine Webber with the AAA.

The issue before the court was whether the AAA is an appropriate forum. Because each of the customer agreements limited arbitration "in accordance with the rules, then obtaining," resolution of the issue centered on whether section 2 of the AMEX constitution is a rule of the AMEX that would enable parties to elect arbitration before the AAA. The court concluded that the constitution is not a rule, finding that the "rules" referred to in their agreements "refer to the arbitration procedures of the [named organizations], not to their constitutions or other general provisions for resolving member disputes." In addition, the court noted that neither Pitchford, Beuchot, nor the Bishops showed any prejudice in proceeding before an organization other than the AAA. Consequently, the parties were not allowed to proceed on their claims before the AAA. ***Paine Webber, Inc. v. Pitchford***, 721 F. Supp. 542 (S.D.N.Y. 1989).

ARBITRATION AGREEMENT—RETROACTIVITY

The court held that the Supreme Court's *McMahon* decision applied retroactively to an arbitration agreement that was executed prior to the *McMahon* decision.

Vincent R. Iacono opened four securities accounts at Drexel for himself and the three business entities that he controlled. For each account, Iacono executed a customer agreement that included an arbitration provision. Iacono subsequently filed suit against Drexel, alleging that Drexel violated the Securities Exchange Act of 1934, the Employee Retirement Income Security Act of 1974, the Racketeer Influenced and Corrupt Organizations Act, and several state law claims. Drexel moved to stay the court action pending arbitration in accordance with the arbitration provisions in the customer agreements. Iacono objected on the ground that the arbitration provisions in the agreements were void and unenforceable. He argued that at the time he signed the agreements, the Securities and Exchange Commission had a rule that rendered the arbitration provisions illegal. The rule was rescinded following the U.S. Supreme Court's decision in *Shearson/American Express, Inc. v. McMahon*, 482 U.S. 220 (1987).

The court concluded that Iacono should not be released from his promise to arbitrate disputes arising under the brokerage agreements, even though the agreements were based on a rescinded and repudiated SEC rule. It reasoned that *Rodriguez de Quijas v. Shearson/American Express, Inc.*, __ U.S. __, 109 S. Ct. 1917 (1989), supported such a determination because the *Rodriguez* court, which held that controversies arising under the Securities Act of 1933 are arbitrable, determined that its decision should be applied retroactively so as to validate existing arbitration agreements. The court further noted that "in *Rodriguez,* the Supreme Court emphasized that arbitration clauses affecting causes of action under the 1933 and 1934 Acts should be treated similarly." In line with the Supreme Court's emphasis, the court applied the *McMahon* decision retroactively in this case and granted Drexel's motion to stay the court action pending arbitration. ***Iacono, M.D., Inc. v. Drexel Burnham Lambert, Inc.,*** 715 F. Supp. 18 (D.R.I. 1989).

RIGHT TO ARBITRATE—WAIVER

A brokerage firm waived its right to arbitrate when it substantially invoked the judicial process and failed to give the opposing party notice of its intent to arbitrate, causing prejudice to the opposing party.

The Stevensons opened brokerage accounts with Prudential-Bache Securities. Their brokerage customer agreement contained an arbitration clause. Prudential subsequently alleged that the Stevensons owed money to meet a margin call and sought to recover the sums owed by filing a complaint against them. The Stevensons, in turn, responded by filing a counterclaim against Prudential on the grounds that the brokerage firm violated the Securities Exchange Act of 1934 and committed common law fraud, negligence, and breach of contract. About six months later, Prudential moved to compel arbitration and stay the court action that it had begun.

The court denied the motion, allowing the court proceedings in the initial action to proceed. It admitted that although courts disfavor waiving arbitration, the circumstances in this case did not support enforcement of Prudential's right to arbitrate. The court stated that although no settled rule exists as to what constitutes a waiver, a waiver probably would be found when there is a determination that the party seeking arbitration has substantially invoked the judicial process to the detriment or prejudice of the other party. Noting that a finding of prejudice could be derived from the lack of notice to the nonmovant of the movant's intent to arbitrate, the court found that the facts indicated that the Stevensons had no notice of Prudential's intent to arbitrate. As a result, they suffered prejudice when they employed an attorney at considerable expense in the preparation of their answer and counterclaim. Because Prudential should have explicitly reserved its right to arbitrate in its complaint to the Stevensons, and because Prudential failed to dismiss the pending court action for which a scheduling conference date had been set in compliance with the Federal Rules of Civil Procedure, the court held that Prudential had substantially invoked the judicial process, causing prejudice to the Stevensons. Accordingly, Prudential's actions constituted a waiver of its right to arbitrate. ***Prudential-Bache Securities, Inc. v. Stevenson,*** 706 F. Supp. 533 (S.D. Tex. 1989).

WAIVER—ENFORCEMENT OF ARBITRATION AGREEMENT—COLORADO

Failure to timely and affirmatively plead the right to arbitration, and participation in pretrial discovery, constitute a waiver of that right.

Thomas C. Bashor executed a standard form customer agreement in connection with an account he established with Bache Halsey Stuart Shields. He later filed a complaint against Bache, alleging breach of fiduciary duty and violation of various state and federal securities laws. He filed an amended complaint as well as a second amended complaint. Some of his causes of action were summarily dismissed by the court. The matter was submitted to arbitration and the panel found in favor of Bache on all issues. Bashor unsuccessfully moved to vacate the award and appealed.

The issue before the court was whether Bache had waived its right to arbitration. The court determined that Bache's actions and participation in the preparatory trial proceedings were sufficiently inconsistent with arbitration and constituted a waiver of that right. In addition, the court ruled that the "advantage [Bache] gained by judicial discovery not available to them in arbitration proceedings constitutes sufficient prejudice to [Bashor] to infer waiver of [Bache's] right to require arbitration." Also, the court ruled that the time when Bache should have asserted its right to arbitration was when it moved to dismiss the nonarbitrable claims in Bashor's complaint and amended complaints. Accordingly, the order compelling arbitration and order confirming the subsequent award were reversed. ***Bashor v. Bache Halsey Stuart Shields, Inc.***, 773 P.2d 578 (Colo. Ct. App. 1989).

AMEX WINDOW—AMERICAN ARBITRATION ASSOCIATION

The court held open the "AmEx Window," allowing investors the option to choose arbitration before the American Arbitration Association (AAA), unless they have agreed in writing to submit only to the American Stock Exchange's arbitration procedure.

Jeffrey Anderson opened securities accounts with Cowen & Company. He signed an option agreement and a margin agreement, both of which contained clauses providing for the arbitration of disputes in "accordance with the rules then in effect" of the New York Stock Exchange, American Stock Exchange, or the National Association of Securities Dealers. The two agreements gave Anderson the option of choosing the forum. A dispute arose and Anderson served notice of his intent to arbitrate his claims before the AAA. Cowen moved for a stay of arbitration on the ground that the AAA was an improper forum. The trial court denied the stay, ruling that Anderson was allowed the option of arbitrating before the AAA per the American Stock Exchange constitution ("AmEx Window") because he had not in any way limited himself to arbitration only before the American Stock Exchange. The appellate division affirmed and Cowen appealed.

The appellate court affirmed, finding that because Anderson "did not agree to limit the arbitration to the self-regulating organizations, the plain language of the stock and margin agreements grants him under the AMEX Constitution to elect to arbitrate the dispute before the AAA." It disagreed with Cowen's reliance on existing case law regarding the "AmEx Window," concluding that those cases were distinguishable because "[a]lthough the 'Amex Window' allowed the customer to arbitrate before the AAA, the parties had agreed otherwise and their agreement was held controlling." In addition, the court determined that because the term "rules," as used in their agreements, was neither defined nor limited by the agreements, Anderson was entitled to rely on the provision in the constitution allowing him the option to arbitrate before the AAA. Finally, the court stated that even if "the language of [Cowen's] agreements could be considered ambiguous, we would construe it most strongly against [Cowen] and favorably to [Anderson] because [Cowen] drafted the agreement." ***In the Matter of Cowen & Company v. Anderson,*** 76 N.Y.2d 318, 558, N.E.2d 27 (1990).

ENFORCEMENT OF SUBPOENAS—WAIVER—NEW YORK

The court declined to enforce subpoenas issued in connection with an arbitration proceeding because the party requesting enforcement had waived any court involvement by first requesting enforcement by the arbitration panel. It reasoned that such an action constituted an election of remedy resulting in the waiver of the right to pursue any remaining relief procedures.

William and Grace Cotter opened an index option brokerage account with Shearson. They suffered losses in the account and commenced an arbitration proceeding against Shearson. In connection with that proceeding, they had subpoenas issued to several individuals, who failed to respond. The Cotters sought enforcement of the subpoenas from the arbitration panel, which ruled that the Cotters could request witnesses and documents. The Cotters interpreted the ruling as a refusal to enforce the subpoenas and commenced a proceeding in court for enforcement.

The court determined at the outset that the rules of the National Association of Securities Dealers, under which the arbitration was being conducted, precluded enforcement of the subpoenas by the court. The court later declined enforcement, ruling that the Cotters had waived court involvement by first submitting the issue to the arbitration tribunal. In doing so, the court ruled, the Cotters had elected their remedy and waived their right to pursue the relief procedures that remained. The court noted that recognizing such a waiver was "in keeping with the policy that the court should order enforcement only to effectuate a decision of the arbitrators . . . and should avoid intermeddling in the arbitrators' procedural regulation of their own arbitration, particularly in matters of disclosure and the production of evidence." ***Cotter v. Shearson Lehman Hutton, Inc.,*** 546 N.Y.S.2d 319 (S. Ct., N.Y. Cty. 1989).

CONSOLIDATION—JUDICIAL AUTHORITY—FEDERAL ARBITRATION ACT—NEW YORK

Consolidation of seven arbitration proceedings was appropriate not only to maintain efficiency in time and cost but also to reduce the possibility of conflicting awards based on the same alleged pattern of activity.

As a requirement to opening a brokerage customer account, Drexel had its customers sign a brokerage agreement containing an arbitration clause. Several disputes arose, and Drexel's customers sought to compel consolidation of seven arbitrations in state court. The basis for each dispute involved charges of fraudulent transactions by one of Drexel's agents in violation of federal securities laws and of the Racketeer Influenced and Corrupt Organizations Act (RICO).

Drexel opposed the investors' petition for consolidation and sought to hold seven separate arbitration proceedings. After considering whether it had the authority to order the American Arbitration Association (AAA) to consolidate the claims, and, if so, whether consolidation was indicated in this case, the court granted the customers' application for consolidation.

Drexel's customers originally filed suit in federal court. The suit was stayed pending the Supreme Court's decision in *Shearson/American Express, Inc. v. McMahon*, 482 U.S. 220 (1987), which held securities claims arbitrable. As a result of the *McMahon* decision, the customers discontinued the federal action and filed a consolidated petition with the AAA, alleging the same causes of action. The AAA asked the petitioners to proceed individually, which prompted the state court petition.

Drexel contended that the decision of the AAA not to consolidate was unreviewable, because it was against the AAA's policy to permit consolidated claims. The court, however, found no evidence of such a policy. Drexel also disputed the customers' claim that courts have the authority to order consolidation of arbitration proceedings under state and federal law.

The court stated that procedural issues such as consolidation are within power of the court, as long as the manner in which a state court enforces an arbitration agreement subject to the Federal Arbitration Act does not determine the outcome of the case. The court also noted that there is no uniform federal policy or rule prohibiting consolidation of separate arbitration proceedings, even where the agreements to arbitrate do not mention consolidation. Because common issues of law and fact existed among the various disputants, and because separate hearings would require multiple testimony by the customers and expert witnesses, possibly resulting in conflicting awards based on the same alleged pattern of activity, the court ruled that a consolidated hearing was appropriate. ***Bock v. Drexel Burnham Lambert, Inc.,*** 541 N.Y.S.2d 172 (S. Ct., N.Y. Cty. 1989).

COMMENTARY

Securities Case Law, Recent Developments*

George H. Friedman

In the past two years, securities disputes have had a major role in shaping the development of arbitration case law. This article examines some of the more interesting recently decided cases.

Two United States Supreme Court decisions, handed down about two years apart, set the stage for some of the more recent cases relating to securities arbitration. The first was *Shearson/American Express, Inc. v. McMahon*,[1] decided on June 8, 1987. There, the Court held that pre-dispute arbitration clauses contained in customer-broker agreements were valid and enforceable as to disputes involving the 1934 Securities Exchange Act.[2] About two years later, the Court dealt with this issue concerning claims arising out of the 1933 Securities Act,[3] in *Rodriguez de Quijas v. Shearson/American Express, Inc.*[4] holding that such arbitration agreements were valid. In so doing, the Court expressly overruled its 1953 decision in *Wilko v. Swan*.[5]

Forum Choice: The ''Amex Window''

A major issue not directly addressed in either of the two Supreme Court decisions discussed above was the degree to which the consumer is permitted to elect the arbitral agency under whose rules the dispute is to be determined. The typical arbitration clause contained in a customer-broker agreement usually permits the customer to choose the arbitration forum from among several listed in the clause (e.g., National Association of Securities Dealers [NASD], New York Stock Exchange [NYSE], American Stock Exchange [ASE], or the American Arbitration Association [AAA]). A majority of the existing arbitration agreements, however, do not provide for AAA-administered arbitration, in effect forcing the customer to elect from among several industry-sponsored arbitration forums.

Some customers' attorneys took note of a little-known provision of the constitution of ASE, which reads as follows:

---

* George H. Friedman is Vice President, Case Administration, of the American Arbitration Association and formerly was director of the association's New York office. Vicki Young, Editor of Court Decisions at the American Arbitration Association, assisted in the preparation of this article.

> If any of the parties to a controversy is a customer, the customer may elect to arbitrate before the American Arbitration Association in the City of New York, unless the customer has agreed, in writing, to submit only to the arbitration procedure of the Exchange.[6]

Customers whose arbitration clauses did not provide for AAA arbitration, but whose disputes involved members of the ASE, began to file arbitrations with the AAA based on the provision quoted above. This led to litigation over two basic issues: (1) whether the clause could be invoked in the face of an arbitration clause that did not provide for AAA-administered arbitration; and (2) whether arbitrations had to take place in New York City.

There have been several decisions dealing with the Amex Window, or related issues, this year. The first decision was apparently rendered by the Supreme Court, New York County, in the matter of *Cowen & Co. v. Anderson*,[7] in April. The arbitration clause between the customer and the broker provided for arbitration in accordance with the rules of the NYSE, the ASE, or the NASD. The AAA was not listed as an option. After the customer commenced arbitration, the brokerage firm moved to stay arbitration. The court, in denying the stay for arbitration, stated:

> The rules of the American Stock Exchange include a right on the part of the customer "to elect to arbitrate before the American Arbitration Association in the City of New York unless the customer has expressly agreed . . . to submit only to the arbitration procedure of the Exchange." I do not read the arbitration clauses of the agreements to establish that the claimant was agreeing to arbitrate only before the Amex, and therefore the exception precluding arbitration before the AAA does not apply here.[8]

The outcome in the federal district court cases dealing with this issue has been different, however. The first reported case was *Hybert v. Shearson/Lehman/American Express, Inc.*[9] decided on June 7, 1989, in the Northern District of Illinois. The relevant arbitration provision stated that arbitrations would be conducted under the rules of the NASD, the NYSE, or the ASE. Notwithstanding this language, one of the customers notified the broker that it was electing to arbitrate disputes under the rules of the AAA, by virtue of the Amex Window. The customer noted the rules of the ASE were among one of the three referred to in the arbitration agreement. It contended that the constitution of the ASE that permitted customers to elect AAA arbitration was a "rule" of the Amex and that their selection of the AAA was in accordance with the terms of the parties' contract. In addition, the customer contended that the limitation contained in the Amex Window that did not permit AAA arbitration where the parties "expressly agreed" to submit only to the procedures of the Exchange would not apply in this case, since the parties had expressly agreed to three different arbitration forums.

The court rejected both of the plaintiff's contentions. As to the former, the court stated,

> the "rules" referred to in the contract, we believe, referred to the arbitration procedures of the three organizations, not their constitutions or other general provisions for resolving member disputes. The intent expressed in the language of the contract, we find, is to create a choice of three arbitration forums, and it is that intent we must effectuate.

In rejecting the customer's second argument, the court broadly construed the language "to submit to the arbitration procedure of the Exchange" contained in the ASE's constitution. "We believe that [this] language . . . means 'unless the customer has expressly agreed in writing to submit only to specified arbitration forums.'"[10] To interpret otherwise, the court stated, would too easily subvert the parties' expressed intention to limit the choice of potential arbitration forums.

Signed, Unsigned Contracts

The most recent federal district court decision on this issue was rendered in the Southern District of New York in the matter of *Paine Webber, Inc. v. Pitchford*,[11] decided September 14, 1989. In this case, which involved several unrelated, but factually similar disputes, the court essentially followed the holding in *Hybert*, above. The court differentiated its analysis, however, between those cases involving a signed contract between the parties and those that did not. The arbitration agreements in question provided for arbitration under the rules of the NYSE, AMEX, or NASD. The AAA, specifically, was not listed as an option. Noting that the matter of selection of arbitral forum was of "increased importance" in view of the *McMahon* and *Rodriguez* decisions, the court, following *Hybert*, held that "the Constitution [of Amex] is not a rule, and, therefore, all of the claimants with arbitration clauses in their [signed] customer agreements may not arbitrate their claims before the AAA." Where the parties have signed a customer-broker agreement delineating specific arbitration forums, the court ruled that it was appropriate to assume that these forums were the only ones the parties intended to utilize. "If we held that the constitution of the Amex is a 'rule,' we would be creating a fourth electable forum, a result we believe was not envisioned by either the drafters of the clause or the parties." Accordingly, the description of arbitration forums contained in the parties' signed arbitration agreement was held to override the Amex Window's apparent option of selecting the AAA.

The court, however, ruled differently with respect to unsigned arbitration agreements. In such instances, the court found that claimants "can avail themselves of the Amex Window provision in the Amex constitution if they so choose." Such election of AAA arbitration, however, required that arbitrations take place in New York City, as stated in the aforementioned language contained in the ASE constitution. While the customers contended that the term "before the American Arbitration Association in the City of New York" was merely a forum selection clause, the court found that the term clearly and unequivocally required arbitrations to take place in New York City. "There is no other reasonable way that this term could be construed without being superfluous."

While no federal circuit court has yet to rule directly on the Amex Window, the Sixth Circuit's May, 1989 decision in *Roney and Co. v. Goren*,[12] deserves careful attention. The arbitration agreement between the parties specified that arbitrations would take place under the rules of the NYSE. When a dispute arose between the parties, however, the customer filed for arbitration pursuant to the rules of the NASD, basing such filing on section 12(a) of the NASD's Code of Arbitration Procedure, which reads:

> Any dispute, claim, or controversy eligible for submission under Part I of this Code between a customer and a member and/or associated person arising in connection with the business of such member or in connection with the activities of such associated persons shall be arbitrated under this Code, as provided by any duly executed and enforceable written agreement, or upon the demand of the customer.

The customer asserted that this provision of the NASD Code of Arbitration permitted her to demand arbitration with Roney, a member of the NASD, irrespective of the parties' arbitration agreement, which required NYSE arbitration. The NASD accepted a motion by Roney in the district court to compel arbitration pursuant to the rules of the NYSE. The customer filed a cross-petition to compel NASD arbitration. The district court held that the customer had waived any right to NASD arbitration by entering into an agreement that expressly provided for NYSE arbitration. On appeal, the Sixth Circuit affirmed the lower court's decision, finding "nothing objectionable in a voluntary agreement limiting the customer's forum to the NYSE."

While recognizing the language of the NASD Code of Arbitration, which seemed to permit the customer to insist upon NASD arbitration with an NASD member, the court stated

> the customer's ability to demand arbitration before the arbitral forum of his choice dictates that he is equally free to limit his recourse to a particular arbitration forum. . . . A forum selection clause in an arbitration agreement, just like any other contract provision, is entitled to complete enforcement absent evidence that the contract was procured through fraud or excessive economic power.

Thus, the customer was bound to arbitrate this dispute pursuant to the rules of the NYSE.[13]

To date, the Amex Window question has not been decided beyond the trial level. Appeals are possible in some of the cases discussed above. Certainly, this issue warrants close attention by securities practitioners.

In the wake of the *McMahon* and *Rodriguez* decisions, some states turned their attention to regulating the arbitration of customer-broker disputes. One such state was Massachusetts, which in 1988 promulgated regulations covering these arbitration agreements.[14] The regulations promulgated by the Massachusetts division of securities had three major aspects: (1) they prohibited firms from forcing customers to sign pre-dispute arbitration agreements as a condition to doing business; (2) they required disclosure to customers of this prohibition; and (3) they required full disclosure in writing on the "legal effect" of the signing of a pre-dispute arbitration agreement. These regulations, among others, applied to those who sold securities in the Commonwealth of Massachusetts.

In December, 1988, the United States District Court for the District of Massachusetts declared these regulations unconstitutional, on the ground of preemption, in the case of *Security Industry Association v. Connolly*.[15] On appeal, the First Circuit affirmed on August 31, 1989.[16] Noting that the contracts to which the regulations were meant to apply involved interstate and international commerce, the court held that they were subjected to the terms of the Federal Arbitration Act. The "critical inquiry" to be made by the court was "whether the FAA is an enactment which Congress meant to remain relatively unfettered; and if so, whether the Regulations intrude impermissively." Finding that the plain meaning of the Federal Arbitration Act[17] was to broadly enforce the parties' agreement to arbitrate, the court ruled that

> nothing in the securities act, the exchange act, or the grant of concurrent power to the states to regulate securities manifests a congressional intent to limit or prohibit waiver of a judicial forum for a particular claim, or to abridge the sweep of the federal arbitration act (cit. *Rodriguez* and *McMahon*).

In view of the regulations' impingement on the parties' right to arbitrate, and the inherent conflict with the broad federal policy favoring arbitration, the court held that the regulations were specifically preempted.

> Because the Regulations treat standard form [pre-dispute arbitration agreements] in the securities industry more severely than standard-form contracts are generally treated under Massachusetts law, and because the policies underlying the Regulations, and their method of enforcement, conflict with the national policy favoring arbitration, the state's scheme is too discommoding to the federal plan. The Regulations are, therefore, pre-empted.[18]

Notes

1. 482 U.S. 220 (1987).
2. 15 U.S.C. § 78j(b).
3. 15 U.S.C. §§ 77a *et seq*.
4. __U.S.__, 109 S. Ct. 1917 (1989).
5. 346 U.S. 427 (1953).
6. Amer. Stock Exch. Const., art. VII, ¶9063(2)(c).
7. *New York Law Journal*, Apr. 4, 1989, p. 22, col. 4 (Sup. Ct., N.Y. Cty.) (currently under appeal).
8. *Id.*
9. No. 84 C 10327 (N.D. Ill. June 7, 1989).
10. *Id.*
11. 88 Civ. 4400 (S.D.N.Y. Sept. 14, 1989). See also *Lapayre v. Shearson/Lehman Bros., Inc.*, No. 87-0330 (E.D. La. Aug. 24, 1989) (forums listed in arbitration clause incorporate not only the rules of the various forums, but administration as well). But see *Shearson Lehman Hutton, Inc. v. Lee*, 89 Civ. 4523 (S.D.N.Y. Sept. 29, 1989) (broker's request for preliminary injunction in response to customer's "Amex Window" filing with AAA denied; no irreparable injury will result from AAA assertion of jurisdiction; relief may be obtained via petition to vacate the ultimate award).
12. 875 F.2d 1218 (6th Cir. May 26, 1989).
13. *Id.* In an apparent attempt to legislatively override the decision in *Roney*, the FCC in August issued a "litigation release" prohibiting arbitration agreements that limit customers to a single arbitration forum. See FCC litigation release number 12198, Aug. 7, 1989, Fed. L. Rep. (CCH), ¶84,437 at 80,377. This release, however, would appear to have no impact on an agreement listing a choice of several arbitration forums.
14. Mass. Regs. Code tit. 950, §§ 12.204(g) (1) (a)–(c) (Regs. 1988).
15. 703 F. Supp. 146 (D. Mass. Dec 19, 1988).
16. 883 F.2d 1114 (1st Cir. 1989).
17. 9 U.S.C. § 1 *et seq*.
18. *Id.*

2

Labor Arbitration

CASE DIGESTS

UNFAIR LABOR PRACTICE—NATIONAL LABOR RELATIONS BOARD—NATIONAL LABOR RELATIONS ACT—DEFERRAL TO ARBITRATION

An employee who files an unfair labor practice (ULP) complaint that does not require contractual interpretation of the collective bargaining agreement (CBA) against his employer is not required to present the grievance to an arbitration committee, because Congress did not contemplate the deferral of individual ULP claims to arbitration. Such deferral is warranted only when resolution of the ULP claims under the National Labor Relations Act (NLRA) require an interpretation or application of the language of the CBA.

Paul Hammontree was employed as a truck driver for Consolidated Freightways Corporation. Consolidated entered into a CBA with the teamsters union. Hammontree was involved in several disputes over the posting of driving duties. After being assigned a number of undesirable runs, he filed a ULP charge. The National Labor Relations Board (NLRB), which did not reach the merits of the case, held that the grievance should have been presented first to a joint labor-management arbitration committee, reasoning that the ULP charge could be brought before the committee under the antidiscrimination provisions of the CBA. Hammontree petitioned the court for review by the NLRB.

The court noted at the outset that the case involved the interaction of two congressional policies: the prevention of unfair labor practices and the fostering of the collective bargaining process. It found that the dispute could not proceed to arbitration because Hammontree did not agree to arbitrate his ULP claims. The court stated that the NLRB may defer only where the employee acts to subsume his ULP claims or his ULP claims rest upon otherwise arbitrable matters. The court reasoned that arbitration would have been approved had Hammontree either waived his ULP rights or provided an express statement that those rights were subsumed in the parallel contractual protection in the CBA. Accordingly, the court rejected the NLRB's argument that the ULP claims are parallel to the inclusion of nondiscrimination language in the CBA.

The court determined from the legislative history of the NLRA that there was strong congressional concern for the protection of the individual employee. Because of this concern, it concluded that the NLRB's "current policy of deferring individual ULP claims to arbitration committees interdicts its responsibility to protect the rights of individual employees." In clarifying its decision, the court stated that

> we only require that individuals whose ULP claims do not require contractual interpretation be given an opportunity to present such claims to the Board . . . moreover, our ruling does not prevent an individual from voluntarily choosing to arbitrate his grievance. . . . Deferral to arbitration is perfectly legitimate when the issues submitted to the arbitrator require contractual interpretation.

Hammontree v. National Labor Relations Board, 894 F.2d 438 (D.C. Cir. 1990). **[Editor's note**: Rehearing was granted.]

PREEMPTION—LABOR MANAGEMENT RELATIONS ACT—STATE-LAW TORT ACTION

State-law tort claims not independent of the collective bargaining agreement (CBA), and whereby the employer's obligations are inextricably intertwined with the CBA, are arbitrable and are preempted by the Labor Management Relations Act (LMRA).

Kathleen Dougherty and others were employed by the New York Telephone Company (NYT), which was at the time owned by the American Telephone and Telegraph Company (AT & T). The CBA in existence contained terms and conditions of employment, including layoffs, reassignments, and transfers. The CBA also contained broad grievance and arbitration clauses. A settlement of an antitrust litigation in the early 1980s resulted in divesting AT & T of its telephone operating companies, including NYT. AT & T negotiated modification of its various CBAs in anticipation of the reorganization. Dougherty was transferred to an AT & T subsidiary at its Buffalo location. Two years later, experiencing a business reversal, the subsidiary consolidated all residential operations at its Pearl River location. Dougherty was offered, but declined, continued employment at the Pearl River location. An action was filed by Dougherty, alleging common-law fraud and negligent misrepresentation. AT & T moved for summary judgment on the ground that Dougherty had failed to exhaust the grievance and arbitration procedures provided in their CBAs, which the district granted. Dougherty appealed.

The appellate court noted at the outset that section 301 of the LMRA governs actions by an employee against an employer for breach of a CBA and that the employee must exhaust all grievance procedures provided for in the CBA before bringing the action. Dougherty argued that although she failed to exhaust all pertinent grievance procedures, her claim was instead an assertion of a state-law tort claim independent of her rights under the CBA. The court stated that "federal interest in uniform interpretation of collective bargaining agreements may preempt certain state-law tort actions." It found that the state-law claims were not independent of the CBA and that AT & T's obligations were inextricably intertwined with the CBA, thereby rendering Dougherty's claims arbitrable and preempted under the LMRA. Because Dougherty had failed to exhaust the applicable grievance procedures, the court affirmed the district court's order granting AT & T its motion for summary judgment. ***Dougherty v. American Telephone and Telegraph Co.,*** 902 F.2d 201 (2d Cir. 1990).

FINALITY OF AWARD—JURISDICTION—LABOR MANAGEMENT RELATIONS ACT—COMPLETE ARBITRATION RULE

The court held that the existence of a "final" arbitration award is not a prerequisite to federal court jurisdiction in an action under section 301 of the Labor Management Relations Act to enforce or vacate an arbitration award.

Union Switch and Local 610 entered into a collective bargaining agreement. When a dispute arose, an arbitrator sustained the grievance, ordered make-whole relief, directed the parties to negotiate that relief, and retained jurisdiction over unresolved issues regarding the remedy. Judgment was entered enforcing the award, but remedial issues remained; the union filed an unsuccessful postjudgment motion that sought an order returning a dispute over the remedial issues back to the same arbitrator who had established the liability. The union appealed.

The court clarified the issue before it as whether the existence of a final award of an arbitrator is a prerequisite to federal district court jurisdiction under section 301 of the Labor Management Relations Act. The court found the complete arbitration rule to be one of prudence and not jurisdiction. It stated that there was nothing in section 301 similar to the appellate jurisdiction limits of 28 U.S.C. § 1291 that would limit judicial review to "final" arbitration awards. Because it is a prudential rule, the court stated that it was obligated to accept the judgment as valid and determine whether the district court erred in refusing to remand the remedial issues to the arbitrator.

The court found that the district court had jurisdiction to entertain the union's motion and had abused its discretion in refusing to remand the dispute over remedial matters to the same arbitrator who established liability. It found that the dispute was not a new, arbitrable dispute, and reasoned that the company should be held to its bargain to arbitrate. ***Union Switch & Signal Division, American Standard, Inc. v. United Electrical Radio and Machine Workers of America, Local 610***, 900 F.2d 608 (3d Cir. 1990).

COLLECTIVE BARGAINING AGREEMENT—DUTY TO ARBITRATE—SINGLE-EMPLOYER DOCTRINE

The court held a nonsignatory to a collective bargaining agreement duty bound to arbitrate a dispute under the single employer doctrine.

National Distillers, an organization divided into the liquor and chemical divisions, entered into a collective bargaining agreement (CBA) with a union. The CBA provided that the liquor division would employ only union members and that any unresolved dispute would be subject to arbitration. About 25 liquor division employees were sent to do maintenance work in the chemical division. These employees retained their classification as employees of the liquor division.

James J. Beam Distilling Company subsequently bought the liquor division from National and replaced National as the employer party to the CBA. The employees sent to the chemical division were recalled, and the chemical division hired nonunion employees as replacements. The union filed a grievance with the chemical division, which returned the grievance, and the union then filed a charge with the National Labor Relations Board (NLRB) against the liquor and chemical divisions and James J. Beam. Because the NLRB refused to issue a complaint, the union moved to compel arbitration. National moved for a summary judgment directing the union's grievance to James J. Beam. The court denied the motion and ordered National to submit to arbitration. National appealed.

The issue before the appellate court was whether National, including its remaining chemical division, was bound by the arbitration provision of the CBA. Even though the chemical division was not explicitly named in the CBA, the court found that it was bound by the arbitration provision because it is a division of National, a signatory to the CBA. The court also concluded that the issue of hiring nonunion maintenance employees is subject to arbitration. It stated that

> because the collective bargaining agreement at issue in this case might reasonably be interpreted to include former maintenance employees working jointly at the Liquor and Chemical Division, we find that this grievance should be arbitrated.

In addition, the court considered four factors to determine whether two or more related entities can be considered a single employer: "(1) interrelation of operations, (2) common management, (3) centralized control of labor relations, and (4) common ownership." Taking the circumstances as a whole and the past matters that were arbitrated, the court found that there was a sufficient basis for a finding of a single-employer status. As a result, the court held that "even though the Chemical Division was not a signatory to the collective bargaining agreement, it will still be bound by virtue of its single employer status with the Liquor Division under the umbrella of National Distillers." Accordingly, the judgment of the lower court compelling National to arbitrate was affirmed. ***Distillery, Wine & Allied Workers Int'l Union, Local Union No. 32, AFL-CIO v. National Distillers & Chemical Corp.,*** 894 F.2d 850 (6th Cir. 1990).

VESTING OR ACCRUING OF RIGHTS—EXPIRATION OF COLLECTIVE BARGAINING AGREEMENT—RELATION BACK

A union was held not entitled to arbitration of certain grievances because the disputes, which arose after the expiration of the collective bargaining agreement (CBA), did not involve any rights that vested or accrued during the CBA's term.

The union entered into a CBA with Gold Star Sausage Co. After the CBA expired, a series of seven disputes arose. Following unsuccessful attempts at resolving the disputes, the union demanded arbitration under the broad arbitration clause of the expired CBA. It also sought to compel arbitration of the grievances in two different lawsuits. In the first lawsuit, the court was influenced by the U.S. Supreme Court's decision in *Nolde Brothers Inc. v. Local No. 358, Bakery & Confectionery Workers Union*, 430 U.S. 243 (1977), recognizing "a strong presumption favoring arbitrability in union contracts, even after the contract ha[s] terminated" and ordered the grievances submitted to arbitration. In the second lawsuit, the court took a different approach and did not order arbitration, concluding that courts must first determine whether the disputed right arose under the CBA before applying the *Nolde Bros.* presumption.

The appellate court rejected the union's interpretation of *Nolde Bros.* that a "dispute 'arises under' the expired agreement if it would have been arbitrable had it arisen during the term of the [collective bargaining] agreement." It noted that decisions generally hold that to "arise under" the expired CBA, the dispute must involve rights that have vested or accrued during the life of the CBA or relate to events which have occurred in part while the CBA was still in effect. The court concluded that this interpretation, requiring the dispute to relate back in time during the CBA's existence before concluding that it arises under that CBA, was the better approach. It consequently ruled that the union was not entitled to arbitration of the grievances because none of the disputes involved rights that extended beyond the CBA's expiration. ***Food & Commercial Workers Local 7 v. Gold Star Sausage Co.,*** No. 88-1951 (10th Cir. Mar. 1, 1990).

MOTION TO COMPEL ARBITRATION—ARBITRABILITY—UNION DUES—NATIONAL LABOR RELATIONS BOARD

The court held arbitrable a dispute over whether union dues were still owed for a certain group of employees that were originally part of the bargaining unit, even after the National Labor Relations Board issued a decision excluding those employees from the bargaining unit.

Local 74 of the Denver Newspaper Guild and the Denver Publishing Company were parties to a collective bargaining agreement (CBA). The CBA, which contained an arbitration agreement, covered the publishing company's district managers and other employees. While the CBA was still in effect, the regional director of the National Labor Relations Board (NLRB) issued a clarification decision ruling that the company's "district managers were managerial employees and should be excluded from the [guild's] collective bargaining unit." Immediately thereafter, the company ceased to pay union dues on behalf of its district managers as required by the CBA. The guild moved to compel arbitration.

The issues before the court were whether a valid enforceable arbitration agreement existed and whether the dispute was covered by the CBA. Because neither party contested the validity of the arbitration agreement, the court determined that the agreement was valid and enforceable. As to the arbitrability of the dispute over the payment of union dues, the company urged that there was no duty to arbitrate because the NLRB decision to exclude district managers from the bargaining unit effectively removed them from the CBA and its provisions. The court, however, determined that the arbitration agreement was broad enough to require the parties to submit their dispute to arbitration. Accordingly, the court ruled that it was the "arbitrator's role to determine whether the agreement continued to cover [the company's] district managers after the [NLRB] decision was issued." ***Denver Newspaper Guild, Local 74 v. Denver Publishing Co.,*** 714 F. Supp. 448 (D. Colo. 1989).

ARBITRABILITY—INTERPRETATION OF COLLECTIVE BARGAINING AGREEMENT

The arbitration clause in the collective bargaining agreement was broad enough to cover the grievances filed by the union. In addition, matters relating to the interpretation of the collective bargaining agreement are for the arbitrator to decide.

Evergreen Cemetery entered into a collective bargaining agreement (CBA) with a union representing Evergreen's employees. The CBA contained a provision requiring mandatory arbitration of certain grievances. Two disputes arose: one over whether an employee designated as a superintendent and not covered by the CBA can be assigned to do production work, and the other one over whether the employer, having designated a person as a working foreman, is obligated to fill that position. When grievances were filed, Evergreen argued that the arbitration provision in the CBA did not cover the two disputes.

The court compelled the arbitration of both disputes, finding that the parties did agree to arbitrate. It noted that the arbitration provision was a broad clause and that absent any provision excluding a specific grievance from arbitration, "only the most forceful evidence of a purpose to exclude the claim from arbitration can prevail" (citing *AT&T Technologies, Inc. v. Communications Workers of America*, 475 U.S. 643, 650 (1986)).

Upon further review, the court found that an article in the CBA appeared to preserve the union's jurisdiction over production workers, even when they are promoted to supervisory positions. Noting this, the court ruled that the first dispute over the assignment of production work was arbitrable. As to the second dispute, the court found that the issue, based on the parties' opposing viewpoints, was really about the proper interpretation of a provision in the CBA. The issue, the court ruled, was best left to the arbitrator. Accordingly, the court granted the union's motion to compel arbitration of both grievances. ***Local 106, Service Employees International Union, AFL-CIO v. Evergreen Cemetery,*** 708 F. Supp. 917 (N.D. Ill. 1989).

GRIEVANCE PROCEDURES—DUTY OF FAIR REPRESENTATION

A labor union did not breach its duty of fair representation merely because it decided not to process a grievance over discharge to arbitration. In fact, even a mistake in judgment on the union's part is insufficient to show a breach of such a duty.

Carolyn Baker was employed by the Postal Service as a letter sorting machine trainee. After failing to pass some required tests, she was discharged. Baker pursued the grievance and went so far as step three of the grievance procedure available to her. At some point, the union decided not to certify her case for arbitration. Baker filed an action against the Postal Service and the two unions involved (the two unions were involved in different steps of the grievance procedure), alleging that she was discharged without just cause and that the unions had breached their duty of fair representation. The Postal Service and the unions moved to dismiss or, in the alternative, for summary judgment.

The court found Baker's contentions that she had failed to pass her tests because of training irregularities to be meritless. In addition, the court rejected her claim that she should have been transferred, rather than discharged. Also problematical to her action, the court found, was the fact that Baker had failed to exhaust the grievance procedures available to her. Finally, the court stated that the only way Baker could get around her failure to exhaust her grievance remedies was by showing that the unions had breached their duty of fair representation. It concluded that based on the evidence before it, the unions had investigated her grievance thoroughly and had not breached any duty. The court noted that unions need not arbitrate every case and that even a mistake in judgment is not sufficient to make out a breach of its duty of fair representation. ***Baker v. Frank,*** 723 F. Supp. 1183 (W.D. La. 1989).

INTEREST ON AWARD—BACK PAY ACT

An arbitration award that becomes final two days before the effective date of a federal law does not entitle a party to the benefits afforded under that law.

Nancy Soiett, a public employee, received an arbitration award of back pay. She filed suit for interest on the award under the Back Pay Act (BPA), which requires the payment of interest on back-pay awards. The Veterans Administration successfully moved for summary judgment. The issue before the court was the proper time period in which an arbitration award can be appealed before it becomes a final award. Soiett reasoned that the proper time period was the 35-day appeal period prescribed by 5 C.F.R. § 1201.113.

The court decided that because an arbitration award stands on an equal footing with a decision of the Merit System Protection Board, the 30-day time period under 5 U.S.C. § 7703 is the appropriate appeals period to calculate when the award becomes final. The court concluded that because the award became final two days before the effective date of the amendment to the BPA that Soiett relied upon, she was not entitled to interest on her award. ***Soiett v. Turnage,*** 708 F. Supp. 429 (D. Me. 1989).

VENUE—VACATUR—MODIFICATION OF AWARD—LIQUIDATED DAMAGES—FEDERAL ARBITRATION ACT

When two special venue provisions seem to conflict, the more restrictive venue provisions of the Federal Arbitration Act (FAA) should govern.

Deleeuw Murcko Ferguson and the Screen Actors Guild (SAG) entered into a collective bargaining agreement. SAG subsequently claimed that Deleeuw failed to pay performers for services rendered, failed to contribute to SAG's health and pension plans, and violated union security provisions of the agreement. SAG sought arbitration, which Deleeuw failed to enjoin. Arbitration was held in New York, where an award in favor of SAG was rendered.

A portion of the arbitrator's award included an award of liquidated damages to SAG, which Deleeuw sought to vacate in the federal district court for the Eastern District of Michigan. Deleeuw claimed that federal court jurisdiction was based on section 301(a) of the Labor Management Relations Act and section 10 of the FAA. SAG, in turn, claimed that the court did not have jurisdiction because under section 10, the district court where the arbitration award is granted has exclusive jurisdiction to hear proceedings to vacate. In this instance, SAG argued, the appropriate venue is the Southern District of New York, where the award was rendered.

The court rejected Deleeuw's argument that the venue provisions of the FAA are permissive rather than exclusive. It found that under federal labor law (29 U.S.C. § 185 (a)), venue is proper in both the Eastern District of Michigan and the Southern District of New York. The court found, however, that under the FAA, venue is proper only in the Southern District of New York. It ruled that when there are two special venue provisions which seemingly conflict, the more restrictive venue provisions of the FAA should govern. Accordingly, the action was transferred to the Southern District of New York. ***Deleeuw Murcko Ferguson v. Screen Actors Guild, Inc.,*** No. 89-73298 (E.D. Mich. Feb. 2, 1990).

VACATUR OF AWARD—PUBLIC POLICY

A court may vacate an arbitration award on grounds of public policy violation only if the policy relied upon is well defined and dominant, and a clear link exists between enforcement of the award and violation of the public policy.

Russell Memorial Hospital and the United Steelworkers of America were parties to a collective bargaining agreement (CBA). Sharon Repke, a licensed practical nurse at Russell, was discharged for negligence in administering medication. United grieved her discharge. The arbitrator, ruling in favor of United, ordered Repke's reinstatement. Russell moved to vacate the award, contending that its enforcement would violate public policy. United opposed, claiming that the integrity of the collective bargaining process required the court to defer to the arbitrator's interpretation of the CBA.

Although judicial review of arbitration awards is generally extremely limited, the court noted that the U.S. Supreme Court has recognized an exception to such limited review. Specifically, under *W.R. Grace & Co. v. Local Union 759*, 461 U.S. 757, 103 S. Ct. 2177, 76 L. Ed. 2d 298 (1983) and *United Paperworkers Int'l Union v. Misco, Inc.*, 484 U.S. 29, 108 S. Ct. 364, 98 L. Ed. 2d 286 (1987), a court may not enforce a CBA that is contrary to public policy that is "well defined and dominant" and ascertained "by reference to the laws and legal precedents and not from general considerations of supposed public interests." The court noted that so long as the policy relied upon was well defined and dominant and a clear link existed between the award's enforcement and public policy violation, it could vacate the award.

As for Michigan public policy, the court identified several factors suggesting that there was a policy ensuring safe and competent nursing. It also found that the arbitrator had reinstated Repke in spite of his express finding that Repke's conduct was negligent and that she "has a propensity for misconduct and that she is reluctant to change her ways." Because the order of reinstatement conflicted with the arbitrator's findings and violated Michigan's public policy regarding safe and competent nursing care, the court vacated the arbitration award. ***Russell Memorial Hospital v. United Steelworkers of America,*** 720 F. Supp. 583 (E.D. Mich. 1989).

EMPLOYEE RETIREMENT INCOME SECURITY ACT OF 1974—MULTIEMPLOYER PLAN CONTRIBUTIONS—PRECLUSIVE EFFECT OF ARBITRATION AWARD

An arbitration award has a preclusive effect on a subsequent Employee Retirement Income Security Act (ERISA) action for contributions allegedly owed under a collective bargaining agreement (CBA).

WCCO Television is a party to a CBA with the American Federation of Television and Radio Artists (AFTRA). The parties negotiated successive CBAs since 1969. When the new CBA was negotiated in 1986, the issue of pension and welfare payment went to arbitration. Prior to 1986, WCCO had not made any such payments. The arbitrator found that the CBA required WCCO to make contributions to the AFTRA funds—multiemployer fringe benefit funds—on behalf of its freelance employees. However, the arbitrator ordered WCCO only to pay contributions prospectively from August 1, 1988. AFTRA neither moved to vacate nor to modify the arbitrator's awards. The trustees of the AFTRA funds, however, subsequently filed an action instead to enforce payment of contributions for freelancers employed by WCCO prior to August 1, 1988, as well as obtain full ERISA statutory remedies on behalf of the AFTRA funds. The trustees moved for a partial summary judgment, stating that it was entitled to judgment, with the amount to be determined at trial. WCCO also moved for summary judgment.

The issue before the court was the preclusive effect of an arbitration award on a subsequent ERISA action for contributions allegedly owing under a CBA. The court found that the arbitration award resolved a right arising out of the CBA. Therefore, the court stated, it was not free to substitute its own judgment for that of the arbitrator's absent a finding that the arbitrator acted arbitrarily or capriciously. Consequently, the trustees' motion was denied and WCCO's motion was granted because the arbitration award was given a preclusive effect. ***American Federation of Television and Radio Artists Health and Retirement Funds v. WCCO Television, Inc.***, 734 F. Supp. 893 (D. Minn. 1990).

ARBITRATION AWARD—VACATUR—CONSTRUCTION OF COLLECTIVE BARGAINING AGREEMENT

The arbitration award was vacated because the arbitrator relied on previous interpretations of the collective bargaining agreements (CBAs), rather than on his own reading and interpreting of the CBAs.

Six trustees—three union-appointed trustees and three employer-appointed trustees—manage a trust fund on behalf of an employees' union. The union-appointed trustees repeatedly attempted to obtain employer contributions to the trust fund per the applicable CBAs. The parties were ordered to arbitrate their dispute pursuant to the procedures described in the trust agreements. The issue presented before the arbitrator was

> [s]hould Employer-Appointed trustees be ordered to join Union-Appointed trustees in a lawsuit to compel certain employers to contribute to the insurance and annuity funds pursuant to a contractually defined obligation set forth in [the CBAs]?

An award was rendered, of which the employer-appointed trustees sought confirmation.

The court noted that the arbitrator had divided the employers from whom contributions were sought into three groups: defendants in cases before two different judges and those who had not been defendants in any lawsuit. It found that in this case, the arbitrator did not arguably construe or apply the CBA but made his decision based on what the judges in question had said about the CBA. Because the parties bargained for the arbitrator's interpretation of the CBA, which the arbitrator in this case did not provide, the court vacated the arbitration award and remanded the dispute to the arbitrator for proceedings consistent with the court's order. ***Union Appointed Trustees of the Tapers Industry Insurance and Annuity Funds v. Employer-Appointed Trustees of the Tapers Industry Insurance and Annuity Funds,*** 714 F. Supp. 104 (S.D.N.Y. 1989).

ARBITRATOR AUTHORITY—GRIEVANCE PROCEDURE—SEXUAL HARASSMENT—COLLECTIVE BARGAINING AGREEMENT

An arbitrator's finding that a filing of a formal grievance was not required and award of severance pay were upheld because the arbitrator did not exceed his authority.

Elizabeth Randolph was a news director at a radio station owned and operated by EZ Communications, which was a party to a collective bargaining agreement with the American Federation of Television and Radio Artists (AFTRA). During one workday, Randolph walked off her job because she was too distraught to do her news report as a result of sexual harassment by her coworkers. Randolph had complained to her superiors of prior incidences of harassment. She returned to work later that day, but was terminated a week later for flagrant neglect of her duty. AFTRA represented Randolph at an arbitration hearing; the arbitrator ruled in favor of Randolph and awarded her severance pay.

EZ sought to vacate the award on the ground that the arbitrator exceeded his authority. The court, however, declined to do so, finding that the collective bargaining agreement gave the arbitrator the authority to determine whether the act of walking off the job was a flagrant neglect of employment duties. The court also rejected EZ's arguments that Randolph was not entitled to severance pay and that she was required to file a formal grievance rather than resort to self-help by walking off the job. It noted that the arbitrator found that EZ was aware of—or at least strongly suspected—that Randolph was offended by the harassment. Because the court found that the arbitrator did not substitute his own notions of industrial justice for the terms of the parties' agreement, it declined to vacate the arbitration award. ***EZ Communications, Inc. v. American Federation of Television and Radio Artists,*** 722 F. Supp. 232 (W.D. Pa. 1989).

SCOPE OF ARBITRATION AGREEMENT—DISTRICT OF COLUMBIA

The trial court properly stayed arbitration because the parties did not intend to arbitrate disputes over the termination of probationary employees.

The American Federation of Government Employees, Local 3721, and the District of Columbia, through its Fire Department, were parties to a collective bargaining agreement (CBA). The Fire Department notified Russell Jones, a probationary employee, that his employment would be terminated. Jones filed a grievance, through American, and arbitration was demanded. The District of Columbia successfully sought a stay of arbitration. American appealed.

The appellate court affirmed the trial court's ruling, finding that the parties did not agree to arbitrate the dispute at issue. It considered whether the arbitration clause in the CBA was "susceptible of an interpretation" that covered the dispute at issue. What the court found was that "management rights" were specifically excluded from the grievance procedure in the CBA. These rights included the right to hire, promote, and retain employees, as well as the right to demote and discharge employees for cause. The court also found that the arbitration clause was not susceptible of an interpretation that would cover disputes concerning the termination of probationary employees. ***American Federation of Government Employees, Local 3721 v. District of Columbia,*** 563 A.2d 361 (D.C. Ct. App. 1989).

PUBLIC EMPLOYMENT—SUPPLEMENTAL AWARD—ENFORCEMENT OF AWARD—IOWA

An arbitrator's supplemental award cannot be disturbed simply because the party attempting to vacate the award disagrees with the arbitrator's interpretation of the collective bargaining agreement.

Central Iowa Public Employees Council and the City of Des Moines were parties to a collective bargaining agreement (CBA). The agreement contained an arbitration provision and provided coverage for the employees working at the city's central maintenance garage. After the city contracted out its garage to a private business, a dispute arose over whether "the laid off employees could bump into any lesser classification bargaining unit jobs for which they had a greater seniority than the incumbent if they were qualified and able to perform those duties. . . ."

The question of whether the dispute was arbitrable was submitted to an arbitrator, who determined that it was. A different arbitrator directed the city to allow the laid-off employees to bump into lesser-class positions. Iowa later amended its code to extend civil service coverage to practically all permanent full-time city employees.

A separate dispute arose when an attempt was made to implement the arbitrator's decision. The dispute was submitted to arbitration, and the arbitrator issued a supplemental decision ordering the city to "grandfather a former employee into civil service employment or to create employment outside of civil service for him." The employee notified the city of his desire to exercise his rights for re-employment, and the city denied relief. Central brought an action to enforce the supplemental award, and the district court ordered the city to comply.

On appeal by the city, the court decided that the dispute was arbitrable because the dispute issue was within the scope of the arbitration agreement. It also disagreed with the city's argument that "the arbitrator exceeded his authority and altered terms of the collective bargaining agreement in ordering the City to grandfather [the ex-employee] into civil service employment." The court found that the decision to order grandfathering resulted from the arbitrator's application of the entitlement section of the Iowa Code when he found that the former employee was covered by the provision. Because the city's position on appeal was based only on a disagreement with the arbitrator's interpretation of the CBA, the court deemed that the city's assertion was insufficient to disturb the arbitrator's supplemental award. Consequently, the lower court's order was affirmed. ***Central Iowa Public Employees Council v. City of Des Moines,*** 439 N.W.2d 170 (Iowa 1989).

CUTLER-HAMMER DOCTRINE—TIME LIMITATIONS—NEW YORK CIVIL PRACTICE LAW AND RULES—NEW YORK

The trial court erred in denying a stay of arbitration.

The Metropolitan Opera Association (MOA) was a party to a collective bargaining agreement (CBA). One of the union's members claimed that it was unjustly discharged and the union demanded arbitration. The MOA sought a stay of the arbitration, claiming that the union did not comply with certain time limitations contained in the CBA and that these limitations were conditions precedent to arbitration. The union opposed, claiming that the limitations were merely procedural stipulations incidental to the arbitration proceeding and that failure to comply is a question for the arbitrator to decide, not the court. The MOA's application for a stay was denied, and it appealed.

The appellate court reversed, finding that the stay was appropriate. It noted the unusual arbitration clause in the CBA and the parties' intent to resurrect the *Cutler-Hammer* doctrine (which allows courts to screen out any meritless and frivolous claims a party would have submitted to arbitration), despite its abrogation by N.Y. Civ. Prac. L. & R. § 7501. As for the question of who should decide the issue of compliance with the time limitations, the court stated that it would still stay the arbitration even if the issue were one for the arbitrator to decide because "we do not see how this question can be decided in [the union's] favor by a rational arbitrator." ***Metropolitan Opera Association, Inc. v. Chaiken,*** 554 N.Y.S.2d 557 (1st Dep't 1990).

RATIONALITY OF AWARD—STANDARD FOR VACATUR OF AWARD—NEW YORK

The trial court properly affirmed an arbitration award that was in keeping with the spirit of the contract.

M. Slavin & Sons employed George Medina as a delivery person. Slavin terminated Medina, alleging that Medina "goofed off" and made only six deliveries in a full day's work. When the matter proceeded to arbitration, Medina presented evidence that he completed more than six deliveries. The arbitrator decided in Medina's favor, stating that Slavin did not have just cause to dismiss Medina. Slavin filed to vacate the arbitration award pursuant to article 75 of the New York Civil Practice Law & Rules. The court, however, confirmed the award. Slavin appealed.

The appellate court noted that the test for vacating an award depended on whether the arbitrator acted so irrationally as to create "a new contract for the parties." Relying on Medina's evidence of deliveries to conclude that the arbitrator rationally decided that Medina's breach of his duties was insufficient to warrant dismissal, the court found that the arbitrator's decision was in harmony with the spirit of the contract and did not create a new one. Consequently, the appellate court affirmed the trial court's order confirming the arbitration award. ***M. Slavin & Sons, Ltd. v. Cirillo,*** 539 N.Y.S.2d 78 (2d Dep't 1989).

INJUNCTIVE RELIEF—CIRCUMVENTION OF ARBITRATION—OKLAHOMA

A city may not circumvent arbitration with the police union by claiming a budget deficit.

The City of Del City (City) and the police union, the Fraternal Order of Police Lodge #114 (FOP) were involved in collective bargaining. As the negotiations progressed, two issues remained, wages and longevity pay, that were to be submitted to arbitration. The day before the scheduled arbitration hearing, the City petitioned for a temporary injunction to enjoin arbitration. The petition was granted and FOP appealed.

The court vacated the trial court's order granting the temporary injunction enjoining FOP from submitting certain issues to arbitration. Under Oklahoma law, firefighters and police officers are accorded the right to collectively bargain because public policy does not allow these groups the right to strike. The court found that this included arbitration hearings. Because the duty to bargain in good faith is mandatory, refusal to bargain is deemed an unfair labor practice. Consequently, the City may not circumvent arbitration on the ground that it is suffering a budget deficit. It reasoned that applicable law allows the "arbitrator to find for the City if financial distress is found. Otherwise, the City has an adequate remedy at law in its ability to reject the arbitrator's findings." ***FOP Lodge No. 114 v. City of Del City,*** 785 P.2d 753 (Okla. Ct. App. 1989).

VACATUR OF AWARD—ARBITRATOR AUTHORITY—JURISDICTION

The trial court properly set aside the arbitration award because the arbitrator lacked the jurisdiction and authority to determine the issue submitted.

Robert Redden was employed as a bus driver by the Garnet Valley School District, which was a party to a collective bargaining agreement (CBA) with Garnet Valley Service Personnel Association. Redden was involved in an automobile accident and after an investigation by District, was recommended for discharge. Redden was subsequently terminated, and he filed a grievance. The grievance was denied at levels one and two. No action was taken at level three by the parties' agreement and the matter was moved directly to arbitration. The arbitrator determined that the matter was arbitrable and reversed Redden's discharge. The District moved to vacate the award. The motion was granted and Redden appealed.

The appellate court affirmed the lower court's determination, finding that the parties did not intend, in their CBA, to submit the issue of Redden's disciplinary dismissal to an arbitrator's jurisdiction. It also found that the arbitrator had confused two sections of the CBA. Because the arbitration of the disciplinary dismissal of a nonprofessional employee was specifically excluded from the CBA, the arbitrator lacked jurisdiction and authority to determine the issue, and the lower court properly set aside the arbitration award. ***Garnet Valley Service Personnel Association v. Garnet Valley School District,*** 563 A.2d 207 (Pa. Commw. Ct. 1989).

COMMENTARY

Employment Contracts: The Misunderstood Labor Cases*

Robert Coulson

An interesting issue has been created by the collision between the libertarian policies of the Federal Arbitration Act (FAA) (that parties who agree to resolve their disputes privately will have that agreement enforced) and the social commandments of the various antidiscrimination laws. A case in point involves a corporate lawyer who entered into an employment contract specifying that disputes with his employer would be arbitrated. Should he be obliged to arbitrate a claim based on the Age Discrimination in Employment Act?

That question was decided in the negative by a three-judge panel of the United States Court of Appeals, Third Circuit, in *James J. Nicholson v. CPC International* No. 88-5588 (June 2, 1989), opinion by Circuit Judge Sloviter. Circuit Judge Becker filed a strong dissent.

In this article, I will explain why I expect Judge Becker's dissenting views to be upheld by the Supreme Court; they reflect the current, pragmatic, and conservative views of the Court and express the intent of the FAA, 9 U.S.C. § 1 *et seq*.

Public or Private Arena

By enforcing arbitration clauses in contracts in interstate commerce, the FAA is consistent with the concept that parties should be able to terminate business relationships and resolve level disagreements without government interference. This is a libertarian idea. Arbitration allows parties to settle their disagreements privately rather than forcing them into official tribunals.

In contrast, antidiscrimination statutes provide government protection to various, defined categories of beneficiaries, providing additional legal rights and authorizing specific delegated administrative intervention. The extent of such intervention is determined by the particular statute.

In the *Nicholson* case, the employee's protection under the Age Discrimination in Employment Act of 1964 (ADEA) 29 U.S.C. § 621 *et seq*. (1982

---

* Robert Coulson is President of the American Arbitration Association.

and Supp. 1986) clashed with the employer's right to enforce the employee's agreement that all disputes would be resolved through arbitration.

In recent years, the Supreme Court has rolled back judicial intervention against arbitration agreements in a series of decisions, enforcing arbitration clauses in a broad range of contractual relationships. *Mitsubishi Motors Corp. v. Soler Chrysler-Plymouth, Inc.*, 473 U.S. 614 (1985), enforced an arbitration clause in an international contract in a dispute involving the Sherman Act. *Shearson/American Express v. McMahon*, 107 S. Ct. 2332 (1987), did the same in another dispute involving the Racketeer Influenced and Corrupt Organizations Act (RICO) and the Securities Exchange Act of 1934. More recently, *Rodriguez de Quijas v. Shearson/American Express, Inc.* 57 U.S.L.W. 4539 (U.S. May, 1989), applied the same principle to section 12(2) of the Securities Act of 1933.

Earlier, the Court had determined that state statutes would not be permitted to stand in the way of enforcement of an arbitration clause in a contract in interstate commerce, even when that statute made litigation the exclusive remedy. *Southland Corp. v. Keating*, 465 U.S. 1 (1984). In *Nicholson*, for example, the court ordered claims under the New Jersey age discrimination statute to be arbitrated.

One line of cases continues to resist the trend, those involving an interplay between collective bargaining and the individual rights of workers, as expressed in various federal statutes. The leading cases are *Alexander v. Gardner-Denver Co.*, 415 U.S. 36 (1974), under title VII of the Civil Rights Act of 1964; *Barrentine v. Arkansas-Best Freight System, Inc.*, 450 U.S. 728 (1981), under the Fair Labor Standards Act (FLSA); *McDonald v. City of West Branch*, 466 U.S. 284 (1984), under 42 U.S.C. § 1983.

All of these cases are being cited for the proposition that Congress did not intend such issues to be arbitrated, that the Supreme Court will not enforce arbitration clauses involving those kinds of statutes.

Judge Becker discusses that point in his dissent in the *Nicholson* case. The three cases listed above all involve collective bargaining. The issue in those decisions is not whether an arbitration clause in an individual employment contract will be enforced. Rather, it was whether an arbitration award against the employee's union will prohibit the individual employee/grievant from asserting his statutory rights in court. They are not relevant to the situation in *Nicholson*.

Enforceable Obligation

Setting those cases aside, the issue of whether an employee has an enforceable obligation to arbitrate a particular statutory claim must be determined by an examination of the applicable federal statute.

The Supreme Court has stated that the FAA mandates enforcement of agreements to arbitrate claims covered by an arbitration clause. Absent a contrary congressional command, that is the law of the land.

The majority acknowledged that "No language in ADEA speaks directly to the effect of an arbitration agreement."

The majority in the *Nicholson* decision relied upon the *Barrentine* case since FLSA was adopted as the remedial model for ADEA, but it failed to note that *Barrentine* was a collective bargaining case when it observed that "nothing . . . suggests that the Court was overruling its prior holdings that arbitration agreements do not preclude access to a judicial forum for resolution of claims arising under the Fair Labor Standards Act (FLSA)." This was misleading.

The holding in *Barrentine* was that "not all disputes between an employee and his employer are suited for binding resolution in accordance with the procedures established by collective bargaining," specifically referred to collective bargaining situations. The arbitration clause in *Nicholson* has no relationship to collective bargaining. It is a negotiated term of an employment contract between a senior executive and his corporate employer. Thus, *Barrentine* was not relevant.

A more recent decision by the Supreme Court in another case promises that this last redoubt of hostility to arbitration may soon be over-run. In *Frank L. Bird v. Shearson/Lehman/American Express, Inc.*, 871 F.2d 292 (1989), the Second Circuit Court of Appeals was asked to decide whether a claim under the Employee Retirement Income Security Act (ERISA) should be processed under an agreement to arbitrate disputes between the retirement fund and its broker. The trial judge determined that the arbitration clause was valid and enforced it as to 1934 Act claims, but said that the pension trustees were not required to arbitrate ERISA claims. The Second Circuit agreed, with Circuit Judge Kaufman explaining that "ERISA violations can be brought in a federal forum notwithstanding an agreement to arbitrate." p. 294.

Acknowledging that the FAA is "a congressional declaration of a liberal federal policy favoring arbitration agreements," Judge Kaufman nevertheless said that ERISA fell outside that intent because there was "an inherent conflict between arbitration and the statute's underlying purposes." p. 295.

Again, *Barrentine* was cited to show that Congress intended to prohibit waiver of a judicial forum when enacting remedial legislation. The *Alexander* case was also used to illustrate that proposition. According to Judge Kaufman, "The remedial intent of Congress tempers the right to privately order one's affairs."

In fact, Justice Brennan's opinion in *McDonald* explains exactly why the collective bargaining cases should not apply: "when the union has control over the grievance procedure, the interests of the union and those of the individual employee may conflict." p. 1804.

No Whittling at Rights

ERISA provides access to the federal courts for pension claimants and other beneficiaries. The majority opinion written by Circuit Judge Kaufman in *Bird* concluded that Congress intended the federal courts to be the sole tribunal, citing a district court decision to that effect. *Lewis v. Merrill Lynch, Pierce, Fenner & Smith, Inc.*, 431 F. Supp. 271 (E.D. Pa 1977). "In passing ERISA, Congress intended to protect plan participants from arbitration and similar agreements often unilaterally imposed, which 'snip and whittle' at federally granted rights." The court also argued that Congress had expressed a need to develop a federal common law on pensions, best created in the federal courts.

In a strong dissent, Circuit Judge Cardamone explained that the Supreme Court had abandoned such restrictive theories. He cited the "liberal federal policy favoring arbitration agreements." *Moses H. Cone Memorial Hospital v. Mercury Constr. Corp.*, 460 U.S. 1, 24 (1983), as well as the two *Shearson/American Express* decisions cited earlier.

He said that in the absence of a specific congressional prohibition, the policy expressed in the FAA should be honored. The fact that ERISA specifies federal rather than state jurisdiction should not inhibit private parties from agreeing to arbitrate their disputes. Judge Cardamone pointed out that neither the text nor the legislative history of ERISA even mentions arbitration, so there is no indication "that when Congress gave ERISA plaintiffs 'ready access' to the federal courts, it was issuing an invitation to plaintiffs that they could not refuse." p. 299. A party who agrees to arbitrate does not forgo substantive rights under a statute, but merely changes the method of resolving the dispute. The majority's portrayal of ERISA as remedial did not rebut the heavy presumption in favor of the freedom to arbitrate. Judge Cardamone read an Eighth Circuit case, *Sulit v. Dean Witter Reynolds, Inc.*, 847 F.2d 475 (1988) as supporting his view.

When the *Bird* case was taken to the Supreme Court on certiorari, Judge Cardamone's views prevailed. 58 Law Week 3239 (October 10, 1989) reports that, by summary disposition, the Supreme Court vacated the judgment below and remanded the case to the Second Circuit for further consideration in light of *Rodriguez de Quijas v. Shearson/American Express, Inc.* Justices Brennan, Marshall, and Stevens dissented.

Limited Application

The collective bargaining cases (*Alexander, Barrentine,* and *McDonald*) should now be limited in their application to collective bargaining situations. They should no longer be cited in cases where arbitration clauses are used in contracts between individuals and employers. This ought to encourage the use of private arbitration to determine the disputes involving title VII, ADEA, and ERISA under broad arbitration clauses in individual employment contracts.

The citation of the collective bargaining cases reflects a judicial hostility to arbitration that has been abolished by the Supreme Court in recent years. The choice of tribunal does not reduce the substantive rights of the plaintiff. The *Mitsubishi* decision makes that exact point: "By agreeing to arbitrate a statutory claim, a party does not forgo the substantive rights afforded by the statute; it only submits to their resolution in an arbitral, rather than a judicial forum." 473 U.S. at 628.

The full panoply of statutory remedies should be available to an arbitrator authorized to award a remedy to a claimant in such a case, whether it be double (ADEA) or triple (Sherman Act) or punitive damages.

The FAA says that arbitration agreements "shall be valid, irrevocable, and enforceable, save upon such grounds as exist at law or in equity for the revocation of any contract." 9 U.S.C. § 2. Unless a party can show that a statute precludes a waiver of judicial remedies, or that such a waiver "conflicts with the underlying purposes" of the statute, a valid arbitration clause must be enforced. The collective bargaining cases relied upon by Judge Sloviter in the *Nicholson* case are no more relevant there than when they were relied upon by Circuit Judge Kaufman in his recently vacated decision in the *Bird* case.

Federal Preemption of State-Law Wrongful Discharge Actions by Agreements to Arbitrate*

Charles G. Bakaly, Jr., and Jeffrey I. Kohn

Synopsis

* Reprinted from *Proceedings of New York University Forty-first Annual National Conference on Labor* (B. Stein, ed.), 1988 at 9-1. Charles G. Bakaly, Jr., is a partner and Jeffrey I. Kohn is an associate with O'Melveny & Myers. Dana H. Biberman, a summer associate with O'Melveny & Myers, assisted in the preparation of this article.

§9.01 Introduction

During the past decade there has been an explosion of state-law actions by employees asserting that they have been wrongfully terminated from their jobs. The abundance of wrongful or retaliatory discharge lawsuits[1]—under the rubric of various contract and tort law theories—has led to a gradual erosion of the traditional employment-at-will doctrine, which allows either the employer or the employee to terminate the employment relationship at any time, with or without cause.[2]

State-law wrongful discharge actions have their genesis in the protection of employees who are not covered by a collective bargaining agreement. Traditionally, the nonunion employee has been afforded neither the right to be terminated only for just cause nor the right to challenge the termination decision by an agreement to arbitrate. Thus, employees not protected by a labor agreement had no other choice but to resort to judicial procedures to contest a decision to terminate their employment. In contrast, agreements between unions and companies historically have provided for an employer's right to discharge only for just cause and an employee's right to challenge his or her termination under a grievance and arbitration procedure, thereby protecting unionized employees from the possibility of termination at will.

Wrongful or retaliatory discharge actions have been viewed therefore as a substitute for the protections generally accorded to union employees.[3] However, as courts continue to eviscerate the employment-at-will rule, employees protected by comprehensive collective bargaining agreements have begun to recognize that there are advantages to state-law tort actions against their employers for wrongful or retaliatory discharge. Even though the exceptions to the at-will rule were intended to take the place of the protections afforded by grievance and arbitration provisions under collective bargaining agreements, union sector employees have sought to bypass their labor agreements in favor of state-law claims which give them access to juries and punitive damages not available under their labor contracts.

The Supreme Court's June 6, 1988 decision in *Lingle v. Norge Division of Magic Chef, Inc.*[4] gave limited judicial approval to this recent development. The Court's holding signaled a weakening of the strong federal labor policy favoring arbitration as the preferred means of resolving discharge disputes between parties to a labor agreement. In *Lingle*, the Court allowed a union employee to avoid the grievance and arbitration procedures of the labor agreement and to commence a state-law tort claim for retaliatory discharge under a state workers' compensation statute, even though she had grieved her discharge and was ultimately ordered reinstated with full back pay by an arbitrator.[5] The Court rejected the argument that plaintiff's claim was preempted by federal law in favor of agreements to arbitrate.

This Article will discuss the extent to which state-law wrongful discharge actions by union and nonunion employees are preempted under federal law by agreements to arbitrate. Section 9.02 provides an overview of the employment-at-will doctrine and its recognized exceptions. The federal labor preemption doctrine as it relates to agreements to arbitrate is discussed in Section 9.03. The impact of the Court's *Lingle* decision will be addressed in this part of the Article. Section 9.04 of this Article briefly explores the expanding use of grievance and arbitration procedures for nonunion employees and the preemptive effect of such procedures on state-law wrongful discharge actions. This Article concludes that, under the existing state of the law, including the Court's recent *Lingle* decision, there has been and there will continue to be a division among the courts over the kinds of wrongful discharge claims preempted by federal law, thereby damaging the federal scheme of labor-management relations, including the exclusivity and finality of agreements to arbitrate. This Article explores the implications of this approach and suggests that the courts would serve federal labor policy better by promoting a more sweeping preemption doctrine of state-law wrongful discharge actions.

§ 9.02 Wrongful Discharge: The Employment-at-Will Doctrine and Its Exceptions

In contrast to the protection afforded to employees who are represented by a union, most United States employees are subject to the employment-at-will rule.[6] This rule of employment law evolved during the social and economic changes brought on by industrialization during the 19th century. The laissez-faire ideology prevalent in those days was extended to employment relationships which were subject to little, if any, external controls.[7]

Legislation in the 20th century, beginning with the New Deal legislation of the 1930s, was the first response to the employment-at-will rule. The National Labor Relations Act (''NLRA''),[8] passed in 1935, protects the rights of employees to be represented by a union, to bargain collectively with their employer and not to be terminated for engaging in protected union activity. In *NLRB v. Jones & Laughlin Steel Corporation*,[9] the U.S. Supreme Court upheld the constitutionality of the NLRA and declared it unlawful for an employer to discharge an employee solely because of his union activities.[10]

Through legislation, the federal and state governments have expanded the statutory limitations on the employment-at-will rule. Employees are protected not only from discharge based on their union activities, but also may not be terminated under federal law, and many analogous state laws, on the basis of their race, color, religion, sex or national origin.[11] Discharge because of an employee's age is legislatively proscribed by the Age Discrimination in Employment Act of 1978 and analogous state laws.[12] Many states also prohibit dismissal of employees for filing a workers' compensation claim,[13] having a disability or handicap,[14] disclosing an activity of the employer which violates public health or safety[15] or serving on a jury.[16] In short, state legislatures and the federal government have responded to the employment-at-will rule by imposing limitations on the employer's previously unrestricted right to terminate employees for any reason.[17]

The judiciary has also played a significant role in limiting the scope of the employment-at-will rule. In one of the early judicial rejections of the employment-at-will rule, the California Court of Appeal held in *Petermann v. International Brotherhood of Teamsters*[18] that it ''would be obnoxious to the interests of the state and contrary to public policy''[19] to allow an employer to discharge an employee because of his refusal to commit perjury at the behest of his employer. Several years later, the New Hampshire Supreme Court, in *Monge v. Beebe Rubber Co.*,[20] ruled that employment arrangements implicitly protect workers against terminations ''motivated by bad faith or malice or based on retaliation.''[21]

Since *Petermann* and *Monge*, many courts have identified exceptions or limitations on the traditional employment-at-will rule. Using a variety of state-law contract and tort theories, courts have recognized causes of action by discharged employees for tortious discharge in violation of public policy,[22] breach of an implied or express promise of job security,[23] breach of an implied covenant of good faith and fair dealing,[24] prima facie tort[25] and intentional infliction of emotional distress.[26]

[1]—Tortious Discharge in Violation of Public Policy

Looking to afford nonunion employees with protection similar to that offered by a labor agreement, several state courts have recognized that a discharge in violation of public policy may be an exception to the employment-at-will rule.[27] The reported cases under this exception fall generally into three areas: discharge for a refusal to commit an illegal act in violation of a statute, discharge for the exercise of a legal right and discharge arising from "whistleblowing" activities.

California courts, for example, have recognized tort actions for wrongful discharge when an employee was discharged for refusing to engage in illegal conduct at his employer's request.[28] A Michigan court has held that an employer may not discharge an employee in retaliation for his exercising the legal right of filing a workers' compensation claim.[29] And a Connecticut court has recognized a cause of action for tortious discharge for an employee's objecting to the employer's mislabeling of frozen meat and vegetables.[30]

The public-policy exception to the employment-at-will rule has given courts by far the most difficulty. On a case-by-case basis, courts have struggled primarily with the source and meaning of public policy under state law and in some cases have either declined to recognize the public policy exception to the at-will rule or have limited the exception to a clear public policy mandate from the state legislature.[31] Other courts, in contrast, have recognized causes of action based upon a broad reading of public policy.[32] As will be discussed in Section 9.03 of this Article, the public-policy exception has also given the courts the most difficulty under federal preemption analysis.

[2]—Implied or Express Promise of Job Security

Many state courts now recognize a cause of action when the discharge of an employee is contrary to an employer's express or implied promise or assurance of job security.[33] For example, promises of job security may be inferred from the employee's longevity of service or from commendations and promotions received by the employee.[34] Promises of job security also may be made to employees by supervisors or contained, by express statement or by implication, in employer policies or handbooks.[35]

Courts in several jurisdictions have held that such promises or assurances create contractual rights.[36] This result can be explained as an application of the contract-law principles of offer and acceptance. When an at-will employee is made aware of personnel policies or procedures, those policies or procedures are deemed to be offers which the employee then accepts by continuing his or her employment. Thus, a unilateral contract may be formed. The employer's consideration is the new policy (e.g., grievance procedure) and the employee's consideration is his agreement to keep working as an at-will employee, though he may quit at any time. This analysis becomes important in the discussion of nonunion grievance and arbitration procedures in Section 9.04 of this Article.

[3]—Breach of the Implied Covenant of Good Faith and Fair Dealing

A cause of action based upon the breach of an implied covenant of good faith and fair dealing has been recognized by some states as an exception to the employment-at-will rule.[37] As a principle of contract law, courts generally recognize that parties to a contract implicitly promise the other party to act in good faith.[38] Some courts, including the courts of California and Michigan, have extended that principle to protect at-will employees not covered by a "just cause" provision in a labor agreement. These courts now recognize, under certain circumstances, a good-faith obligation on the part of employers when discharge decisions for at-will employees are made.

In the first significant decision recognizing this exception, the Supreme Judicial Court of Massachusetts in *Fortune v. National Cash Register Company*[39] held that an at-will-employment relationship "contains an implied covenant of good faith and fair dealing, and a termination not made in good faith constitutes a breach of the contract."[40] In *Fortune*, the plaintiff employee charged his employer with a bad-faith termination when the timing of his discharge from a sales position served to deprive him of earned bonus commissions.[41]

Since *Fortune*, this exception to the at-will rule has been recognized by courts in a handful of states. Recently, however, at least the California courts have been taking a more limited view of this exception. The California Court of Appeal in *Koehrer v. Superior Court*,[42] while recognizing this exception, found that in order for an action for breach of the implied covenant of good faith and fair dealing to lie, the employer must be "without probable cause and in bad faith, that is, without a good faith belief that good cause for discharge in fact exists."[43] And in a case currently pending before the Supreme Court of California,[44] the Court of Appeal declined to recognize a cause of action for breach of the implied covenant of good faith and fair dealing, stating that "[t]o prove a violation of the covenant, plaintiff must show longevity of service, and breach of an express employer policy regarding the adjudication of employee disputes."[45] According to the court, the plaintiff in that case had failed on both counts.

Other courts have refused to recognize an implied covenant of good faith and fair dealing as an exception to the employment-at-will rule.[46] One court, although acknowledging that a covenant of good faith and fair dealing may be implied in an employment contract, held that breach of such a covenant "cannot be predicated simply upon the absence of good cause for a discharge."[47] To hold otherwise, the court explained, "would render the court bargaining agent for every employee not protected by statute or collective bargaining agreement."[48]

§ 9.03 Effect of a Collective Bargaining Agreement's Grievance and Arbitration Procedure on Wrongful Discharge Actions

The just-cause provision in a labor agreement represents the parties' mutual understanding as to the grounds on which employment may be terminated. When a dispute arises over whether cause for termination is present, labor agreements bind employers and employees to resolve through a grievance and arbitration mechanism any questions about whether valid grounds for discharge exist and what remedies for a violation would be appropriate. The parties expect that all discharge disputes will be governed by the just-cause provision and resolved through the grievance and arbitration procedures. Therefore, any state-law cause of action for wrongful discharge which allows union employees to avoid the contractual dispute resolution mechanism contained in their labor agreements will have a direct bearing on the parties' binding commitment to resolve their differences through arbitration.

The federal labor preemption doctrine as it relates to state-law wrongful or retaliatory discharge actions has been evolving in recent years. For several years, the courts seemed to be moving toward a more-sweeping rule of federal preemption of state-law wrongful or retaliatory discharge actions, thereby reinforcing the strong federal labor policy in favor of agreements to arbitrate. The Supreme Court's recent *Lingle* decision made it clear, however, that the Court would permit certain types of retaliatory discharge actions to go forward in state court notwithstanding the parties' agreement to resolve all discharge disputes through arbitration.

In this Section, we briefly explore the evolving federal preemption doctrine with respect to state-law wrongful or retaliatory discharge actions.

[1]—Federal Preemption Doctrine in General

The supremacy clause of the United States Constitution,[49] which is at the core of federal preemption analysis, grants Congress the power to preempt state law which conflicts with federal legislation.[50] Congress may preempt state law expressly.[51] Congressional intent to preempt state law may also be inferred. Federal law may be sufficiently comprehensive to permit the inference that Congress left no room for state regulation.[52] Federal law may also displace state law where it actually conflicts with federal law or because the state law hinders the accomplishment and execution of the full purpose and objectives of Congress.[53]

The Supreme Court has recognized, however, that the NLRA provides little or no guidance as to the degree of preemption of state law affecting labor relations. In *Garner v. Teamsters, Chauffeurs & Helpers*,[54] the Supreme Court observed that the NLRA "leaves much to the states though Congress has refrained from telling us how much."[55] Consequently, the Court has attempted to establish the scope of federal labor law preemption with little specific congressional direction.

Under Sections 7 and 8 of the NLRA, the Court at one point created a sweeping labor preemption doctrine that vested the National Labor Relations Board with exclusive jurisdiction to decide the full panoply of labor activities either clearly or arguably prohibited or protected by the NLRA. In *San Diego Building Trades Council v. Garmon*,[56] the Court focused on general areas of federal-state conflict in a broad sense holding that "[w]hen an activity is arguably subject to § 7 or § 8 of the [NLRA], the States as well as the federal courts must defer to the competency of the . . . Board."[57] The rule enunciated in *Garmon*, once the dominant means of resolving labor preemption questions, created a strong presumption in favor of federal preemption.[58]

When faced with a federal preemption question in state-law wrongful discharge actions, courts have moved away from a *Garmon* analysis and toward an analysis of preemption under Section 301 of the Labor Management Relations Act ("LMRA").[59] Section 301 of the LMRA provides as follows:

> Suits for violation of contracts between an employer and a labor organization representing employees in an industry affecting commerce as defined in this chapter, or between any such labor organizations, may be brought in any district court of the United States having jurisdiction of the parties, without respect to the amount in controversy or without regard to the citizenship of the parties.[60]

The Supreme Court definitively interpreted Section 301 as both granting federal jurisdiction and also as authorizing federal courts to develop a body of federal common law for the enforcement of collective bargaining agreements.[61] In discussing the preemptive effect of Section 301, the Court in *Teamsters, Chauffeurs, Warehousemen & Helpers v. Lucas Flour Co.*[62] stated that "federal labor law must be paramount in the area covered by the statute [so that] issues raised in suits of a kind covered by section 301 [are] to be decided according to the precepts of federal labor policy."[63] The Court concluded "that in enacting section 301, Congress intended doctrines of federal labor law uniformly to prevail over inconsistent local rules,"[64] and called for a uniform interpretation of the terms of contracts to ensure the smooth administration of the labor agreement and peaceful labor relations.[65]

Therefore, before bringing claims in state or federal court under Section 301 for a violation of a collective bargaining agreement, parties to a labor agreement are compelled by federal law to attempt to exhaust the grievance and arbitration procedures established in the collective bargaining agreement.[66] In rare circumstances, a party is not required to exhaust the remedies set forth in the labor agreement, such as when the union breaches its duty of fair representation.[67]

[2]—Section 301 Preemption of State-Law Wrongful Discharge Actions: Pre-*Allis-Chalmers* and *Lingle*

Prior to the Supreme Court's 1985 decision in *Allis-Chalmers Corp. v. Lueck*,[68] federal labor preemption analysis under Section 301 produced ad hoc judicial perceptions about whether there was actual conflict between state-law wrongful discharge actions and federal law, notwithstanding the generally broad preemptive effect given to Section 301 of the LMRA. Courts engaged in a sometimes murky inquiry as to whether allegations concerning a wrongful or retaliatory discharge conflicted with the perceived purposes and objectives of federal labor policy, resulting in significant splits in judicial authority and an evisceration of federal labor policy in favor of the arbitration of labor-management disputes.

Some courts quite properly took a broad view of the preemptive effect of Section 301. In *Olguin v. Inspiration Consolidated Copper Company*,[69] for example, the Ninth Circuit held that union employees could not rely on the terms of a preexisting personnel manual when a collective bargaining agreement included provisions inconsistent with it. The court found that any state-law action for wrongful discharge based on an express contract would arise *not* from the personnel manual but rather from the labor agreement's provision for dismissal for just cause and therefore would be preempted under Section 301 of the LMRA.[70] Plaintiff also claimed that he had been discharged in retaliation for safety complaints, thus violating public policy. Although noting that some states recognize the tort of wrongful discharge, the court held that plaintiff could not sustain such a claim since the plaintiff's complaints about mine safety were governed by the Federal Mine Safety & Health Act and the action was therefore preempted by federal law, including Section 301.[71]

The Ninth Circuit in *Buscemi v. McDonnell Douglas Corp.*[72] also found a state-law wrongful discharge action preempted by federal law, thereby reaffirming federal labor policy in favor of agreements to arbitrate. In that case, plaintiff brought an action in state court claiming he was discharged by McDonnell Douglas in retaliation for circulating petitions and voicing employees' concerns about practices at McDonnell Douglas. He sought relief under California law for retaliatory discharge, wrongful termination and intentional infliction of emotional distress.[73] Because plaintiff was covered by a collective bargaining agreement which provided for binding arbitration, and since he did not allege his discharge contravened a state statute or an independent public policy, the court held that he could not state a cause of action for common law wrongful or tortious discharge.[74] Plaintiff had to look to the grievance and arbitration procedure in the collective bargaining agreement as the exclusive remedy.

Other courts refused to extend the reach of federal preemption to all wrongful or retaliatory discharge actions. For example, the Illinois Supreme Court in *Midgett v. Sackett-Chicago, Inc.*,[75] construing Illinois state law, found that Illinois has a strong public policy in favor of protecting employees who exercise their rights under the state workers' compensation law, whether or not the employee is a member of a union. The court reasoned that it was necessary to provide the victim of a retaliatory discharge with a complete remedy, independent of any contractual remedy the employee may have had under the labor agreement.[76] The court pointed out the importance of permitting punitive damages as a remedy for the tort of retaliatory discharge.[77] Noting that arbitration remedies are generally limited to reinstatement and back pay, the court stated that

> [i]f there is no possibility that an employer can be liable in punitive damages, not only has the employee been afforded an incomplete remedy, but there is no available sanction against a violator of an important public policy of this State. It would be unreasonable to immunize from punitive damages an employer who unjustly discharges a union employee, while allowing the imposition of punitive damages against an employer who unfairly terminates a nonunion employee. The public policy against retaliatory discharges applies with equal force in both situations.[78]

The *Midgett* court disposed of the employer's argument regarding federal policy favoring arbitration, observing that the employees covered by collective bargaining agreements have been permitted to proceed against employers on claims based upon violations of civil rights.[79]

[3]—*Allis-Chalmers Corp. v. Lueck*

In 1985, the Supreme Court decided the case of *Allis-Chalmers Corp. v. Lueck*.[80] In *Allis-Chalmers*, the Court appeared to reinforce a more-sweeping federal preemption doctrine under Section 301, which raised questions about the fundamental rationale of the decisions recognizing a cause of action by a union employee for wrongful or retaliatory discharge. The Court seemed to be returning to a broad approach to preemption under Section 301 that is demanded by federal labor policy, although the Court stopped short of advancing a complete preemption doctrine.[81]

Allis-Chalmers involved an employee who claimed that his employer, Allis-Chalmers Corporation, had delayed disability payments under a union health plan in bad faith. Allis-Chalmers and the employee's union had entered into a collective bargaining agreement which provided a group health and disability plan for Allis-Chalmers' employees. In 1981, plaintiff Lueck sought disability benefits for a nonoccupational injury by filing a claim with the insurance carrier, Aetna. Aetna approved the claim and eventually paid all of plaintiff's benefits, but allegedly in an untimely manner. Rather than filing a grievance as required in the labor agreement between his union and employer, plaintiff commenced a state court action claiming tort damages under Wisconsin law for bad faith administration of the insurance plan.

A lower Wisconsin state court dismissed the complaint as preempted by federal labor law, reasoning that the employee's claim concerned a violation of a collective bargaining agreement and thus could only be raised in a suit to enforce the agreement under federal law.[82] In the alternative, the court ruled that the employee's action was preempted under *Garmon* because the employer's alleged conduct constituted arguably prohibited activity under Section 8 of the NLRA.[83] The Wisconsin Supreme Court reversed, holding that the employee's bad faith tort claim was distinct from an action to enforce the labor agreement and fell within the *Garmon* exceptions.[84]

The U.S. Supreme Court reversed on grounds of Section 301 preemption. The Court found *Garmon* inapposite because Wisconsin law presented a direct conflict with the federal law of collective bargaining under Section 301.[85] The Court rejected the Wisconsin Supreme Court's conclusion that the bad faith claim only indirectly affected the collective bargaining agreement because the claim technically involved a tort, not a contract violation. Regardless of how the employee characterized his claim, the "duties imposed and rights established through the state tort . . . derive from the rights and obligations established by the contract."[86] Applying these principles, the Court ruled that where state contract or tort claims are "substantially dependent upon analysis of the terms of an agreement made between the parties in a labor contract, that claim must either be treated as a § 301 claim . . . or dismissed as pre-empted by federal labor-contract law."[87]

The unanimous Court also went to great lengths to reaffirm a broad approach to federal preemption based upon the federal labor policy of resolving labor-management disputes through arbitration:

> Since nearly any alleged willful breach of contract can be restated as a tort claim for breach of a good-faith obligation under a contract, the arbitrator's role in every case could be bypassed easily if § 301 is not understood to pre-empt such claims. Claims involving vacation or overtime pay, work assignment, *unfair discharge*—in short, the whole range of disputes traditionally resolved through arbitration—could be brought in the first instance in state court by a complaint in tort rather than in contract. . . .

. . .

> A rule that permitted an individual to sidestep available grievance procedures would cause arbitration to lose most of its effectiveness . . . as well as eviscerate a central tenet of federal labor-contract law under § 301 that it is the arbitrator, not the court, who has the responsibility to interpret the labor contract in the first instance.[88]

The Court's reference to "unfair discharge" as disputes traditionally relegated to arbitration and therefore preempted was particularly noteworthy. *Allis-Chalmers* seemed to be suggesting that the strong federal labor policy favoring arbitration over state-court litigation should work in favor of preempting state-law wrongful discharge actions where a labor agreement governed the parties' employment relationship. The Court, however, left open the possibility that certain limited state-law rights may exist independent of any right established by a labor agreement. As the Court observed.

> [n]or do we hold that every state-law suit asserting a right that relates in some way to a provision in a collective-bargaining agreement, or more generally to the parties to such an agreement, necessarily is preempted by § 301. The full scope of the pre-emptive effect of federal labor-contract law remains to be fleshed out on a case-by-case basis.[89]

[4]—Post-*Allis-Chalmers* and Pre-*Lingle*

After *Allis-Chalmers*, many courts broadly followed the Supreme Court's reasoning and barred state-law tort claims brought by discharged union-represented employees. When an action was brought under state law seeking to protect interests that were the subject of collective bargaining, such as job security, pensions or wages, courts found that the enforcement of state law was generally preempted by the federal system of arbitration.[90] Courts also held preempted claims alleging an implied covenant of good faith and fair dealing,[91] tortious interference with employment contract,[92] intentional and tortious refusal to pay employment benefits and conspiracy to injure reputation,[93] and discharge for complaints about the handling of unsafe chemicals.[94]

Courts disagreed, however, on the extent to which tortious discharge claims based on public policy—one of the three exceptions to the at-will rule—were preempted by federal labor law. Some courts refused to recognize such claims by union employees, deferring instead to the parties' labor agreement which provided for binding arbitration of all discharge disputes. Other courts, in contrast, permitted these claims to go forward in state court, after struggling with whether the principles protected by public policy should be recognized as creating rights *independent* of those expressed in the parties' labor agreement.

In *De Soto v. Yellow Freight Systems, Inc.*,[95] for example, plaintiff brought a state-court action against his employer for tortious discharge claiming that he refused to commit a violation of the law and was fired for doing so. The case was removed to federal court. The Ninth Circuit ruled that plaintiff's claim was preempted because plaintiff was fired not because of obedience to a state *statute* but rather because he had a good faith belief that it was illegal for him to drive a trailer without the requisite permits.[96] Plaintiff's belief was mistaken, however, and the court concluded that he was not acting in defense of any state policy.[97]

In *Snow v. Bechtel Construction, Inc.*,[98] the court also considered a tortious discharge claim arising out of broad notions of public policy. Plaintiff alleged that he was discharged in retaliation for his notifying his superiors about drug use by fellow employees at the nuclear facility where he worked and because of his complaints about safety violations at the facility. The court held that the state claim was preempted, in part, by Section 301 of the LMRA, the Atomic Energy Act and the Energy Reorganization Act. The fact that the plaintiff had used the grievance procedures after he reported the drug use led the court to conclude that the plaintiff was pursuing an employment-related claim involving rights provided in the collective bargaining agreement.[99]

On the other hand, a Minnesota court, in *Brevik v. Kite Painting, Inc.*,[100] distinguished *Allis-Chalmers* and allowed plaintiffs to sue their employer for being discharged from employment in retaliation for exercising their rights under the Minnesota Occupational Safety & Health Act. The court stated that Congress did not intend to preempt the power of the state to create and enforce a statute protecting health and safety in the workplace. The court concluded that the state-law tortious discharge claim did not require an interpretation of the collective bargaining agreement between the parties and therefore survived a federal preemption defense.[101]

In *Baldracchi v. Pratt & Whitney Aircraft Division*,[102] the Second Circuit also held that Section 301 did not preempt an action by a union employee under a state statute prohibiting the discharge of an employee for filing a workers' compensation claim. The court distinguished *Allis-Chalmers* on the ground that plaintiff's claim did not turn on the substantive terms of the labor agreement.[103] The court reasoned that plaintiff's prima facie case at trial would consist of the fact that she was fired for filing a workers' compensation claim. In its defense, the employer would have to demonstrate that plaintiff was fired for another non-pretextual reason. The Second Circuit concluded that such an analysis would not require a court to interpret the parties' labor agreement.[104]

The Seventh Circuit, however, reached the opposite conclusion in *Lingle v. Norge Division of Magic Chef, Inc.*[105] The court adopted a broad approach to Section 301 preemption and concluded that purportedly "independent" claims for retaliatory discharge by employees covered by labor agreements prohibiting discharge without just cause were actually claims for wrongful discharge under the existing labor agreement.[106] As such, it found that plaintiff's claims arose under federal law and that removal was proper.[107] The Seventh Circuit observed that Section 301 required that state law give way to federal law since plaintiff's claims involved a breach of the just cause provision of the collective bargaining agreement.[108]

[5]—*Lingle v. Norge Division of Magic Chef, Inc.*

To resolve the division which had developed among the courts after *Allis-Chalmers*, the Supreme Court granted certiorari in *Lingle*. On June 6, 1988, the Court reversed the Seventh Circuit holding that plaintiff's state-law tort remedy for retaliatory discharge under the Illinois Worker's Compensation Act was not preempted by Section 301.[109]

Plaintiff Lingle was employed by defendent under an agreement protecting employees from discharge except for proper or just cause. Plaintiff had grieved her discharge under the grievance and arbitration provision of the labor agreement. Prior to receiving the arbitrator's ruling, plaintiff commenced an action in Illinois state court alleging that she had been discharged for exercising her rights under the Illinois workers' compensation law.[110] The defendant employer removed the case to federal court and then filed a motion to dismiss on preemption grounds or to stay further proceedings pending completion of the arbitration.[111]

Relying on *Allis-Chalmers*, the district court dismissed the complaint concluding that plaintiff's claim for retaliatory discharge was "inextricably intertwined" with the just cause provision of the labor agreement.[112] The Seventh Circuit agreed. While the parties were litigating these issues in federal court, the arbitrator had ruled in favor of plaintiff and ordered the employer to reinstate her with back pay.[113]

The Supreme Court unanimously reversed the Seventh Circuit. The Court began its analysis by reaffirming the importance of Section 301 in authorizing federal courts to "fashion a body of federal law for the enforcement of these collective bargaining agreements."[114] The Court emphasized, however, that Section 301 does *not* preempt a state-law claim which can be resolved without interpreting the collective bargaining agreement itself.[115] In upholding plaintiff's state-law retaliatory discharge claim, the Court reasoned that the factual questions pertaining to the conduct and motivation of the parties would not require a court to interpret any term of the parties' labor agreement. Thus, the state-law remedy was independent of the labor agreement for Section 301 preemption purposes.[116]

The Supreme Court also rejected the Seventh Circuit's reasoning that the just-cause provision of the labor agreement might prohibit the retaliatory discharge at issue and therefore both the court and the arbitrator would be deciding the same issue and analyzing the same set of facts.[117] The Court acknowledged that the state-law claim might involve the same factual determination as that made in the arbitration proceeding, but disagreed that such factual parallelism rendered the state-law claim dependent upon the contractual analysis of the labor agreement.[118] The Court noted that

> § 301 pre-emption merely ensures that federal law will be the basis for interpreting collective bargaining agreements, and says nothing about the substantive rights a State may provide to workers when adjudication of those rights does not depend upon the interpretation of such agreements. . . . [E]ven if dispute resolution pursuant to a collective-bargaining agreement, on the one hand, and state law, on the other, would require addressing precisely the same set of facts, as long as the state-law claim can be resolved without interpreting the agreement itself, the claim is "independent" of the agreement for § 301 purposes.[119]

The Court also observed that its holding was consistent with those cases that have permitted certain substantive rights to remain unpreempted by other labor-law statutes, such as federal discrimination laws and laws that fall within the traditional police power of the states.[120] The Court reasoned that these claims do not intrude upon the interpretation of the labor agreement nor the collective bargaining process.[121] The Court concluded that

> if an arbitrator should ever conclude that the contract does not prohibit a particular discriminatory or retaliatory discharge, that conclusion might or might not be consistent with a proper interpretation of state law. *In the typical case a state tribunal could resolve either a discriminatory or retaliatory discharge claim without interpreting the "just cause" language of a collective bargaining agreement.*[122]

[6]—The Impact of *Lingle*

After *Lingle*, parties to a labor agreement can no longer be sure that the grievance and arbitration provisions of their labor agreement will be the exclusive and final procedure for resolving *all* wrongful or retaliatory discharge disputes. Despite a long-standing federal labor policy of deferring to arbitration to resolve disputes between labor and management, including discharge disputes, the Court recognized in *Lingle* that certain types of state-law tortious discharge actions may be brought by union employees both in arbitration *and* in court. The Court's holding undoubtedly will have a significant impact on the future direction of labor-management relations in connection with agreements to arbitrate.

First, *Lingle* will create a two-tiered system of resolution of discharge disputes, because a discharge decision may be challenged both in arbitration and in court under a state-law cause of action which is deemed "independent" of the parties' labor agreement. Under *Lingle*, a discharged union employee, under certain circumstances, may bring an "independent" tortious discharge action (a) without first attempting to utilize the agreement's grievance and arbitration procedure; (b) after commencing the grievance and arbitration procedure under the labor agreement by filing a lawsuit during a step of a multilevel grievance procedure; or (c) after receiving an adverse or even favorable arbitration award. At whatever stage of the proceeding a lawsuit is filed, the parties contractual agreement to arbitrate disputes is undeniably affected.

Second, employers who do business in two or more states may find themselves under the same labor agreement defending a tortious discharge claim in arbitration in one state and defending a similar tortious discharge claim in state court in another state. Employers also may find themselves litigating a discharge dispute in two separate forums in the same state. The potential for possibly conflicting substantive outcomes among the competing legal systems could impede the parties' willingness to agree to a uniform system of private dispute resolution.

Indeed, this bifurcated approach to dispute resolution within the same company and under the same collective bargaining agreement raises the ultimate question whether arbitration provisions should be removed from labor agreements. If parties to a labor agreement cannot be assured that discharge disputes will be resolved finally and fully by arbitration, they may begin to question the benefits of having a grievance and arbitration procedure for resolving disputes over the discharge of employees. Parties to a labor agreement also may wish to consider ways in which they can be assured that the arbitration mechanism is the exclusive remedy for the resolution of a discharge dispute.[123]

The Supreme Court has elevated the importance of arbitration in federal labor law and federal labor policy.[124] The policy of deferring to the role of the arbitrator was apparent in *Republic Steel Corp. v. Maddox*,[125] where an individual employee brought a lawsuit for severance pay in state court without first availing himself of the binding grievance procedure. Reasoning that contract grievance and arbitration procedures are the preferred method for settling disputes, the Court found that the binding arbitration agreement prevented the employee from bypassing the grievance procedure and seeking relief in state court.[126] The Court observed that

> [a] contrary rule which would permit an individual employee to completely sidestep available grievance procedures in favor of a lawsuit has little to commend it. . . . If a grievance procedure cannot be made exclusive, it loses much of its desirability as a method of settlement.[127]

The rationale underlying this policy applies with great force when the dispute concerns the legitimacy of an employer's reasons for terminating an employee covered by a contractual just-cause provision. To the extent that state law purports to give discharged unionized employees independent claims for wrongful or retaliatory termination, the traditional federal labor policy associated with private dispute resolution mechanisms is undermined. Federal preemption of wrongful discharge actions should therefore be viewed in the context of the fundamental role of agreements to arbitrate in industrial and labor relations. The *Lingle* decision failed to do this.

Third, the Court has not indicated what types of wrongful or retaliatory discharge actions require an interpretation of the parties' labor agreement and therefore are preempted. This may lead to further divisions among the courts as to whether claims are truly "independent" of the labor agreement.

After *Lingle*, it seems clear that a state law claim under the "implied or express promise of job security" exception to the at-will rule *should* be preempted by Section 301. This claim is tantamount to a claim that employment has been terminated without "cause." Because rights and obligations to discharge for cause are derived from the parties' collective bargaining agreement, the evaluation of state-law claims based upon this exception requires extensive interpretation of the parties' labor agreement and therefore should be preempted by federal law.[128]

Claims based upon promises of job security made by employers *prior* to employees joining a union may survive a federal preemption defense after *Lingle*, however. Courts have considered these promises as raising claims independent of the parties' labor agreement and therefore not preempted by federal law.[129]

A state-law action for breach of an implied covenant of good faith and fair dealing also *should* be preempted by Section 301 after *Lingle*.[130] The implied covenant is derived from the parties' employment relationship or contract, which in a union setting is the parties' collective bargaining agreement. Thus, at least with respect to these two judicial exceptions to the employment-at-will rule, courts should treat state-law actions as preempted by federal law thereby preserving the parties' agreement to arbitrate disputes arising from a discharge decision.

The exception to the at-will rule of a tortious discharge in violation of public policy will give courts the most difficulty after *Lingle*. Courts will have to decide first whether the discharge is prohibited by some "public policy"—an issue which has not produced uniformity in the courts[131]—and second whether the tortious discharge claim requires an intepretation of the parties' labor agreement. The extent to which tortious discharge claims are recognized by state law and, if so, whether the particular claim at issue requires an interpretation of the collective bargaining agreement will vary from state to state and is certain to create divisions among the courts, thereby disrupting labor-management relations and the federal labor policy of resolving disputes through arbitration.

§ 9.04 Effect of a Grievance and Arbitration Procedure for Nonunion Employees on Wrongful Discharge Actions

It is not unusual today to find grievance and arbitration procedures employed by companies for nonunion employees. Faced with an unprecedented volume of litigation by former employees claiming that employment terminations were unlawful, employers have begun to use alternative dispute resolution mechanisms, including grievance and arbitration procedures, in an attempt to promote practices designed to further sound relations between management and employees not represented by a union. Just as the arbitration remedy promotes industrial peace in a unionized company through a private contractual system of dispute resolution, so too in a nonunion company a binding arbitration system can be a stabilizing force in the workplace. An alternative solution to nonunion termination problems can help to ensure that employment termination decisions are not made arbitrarily.

Fueling the desire of companies to adopt such a system in a nonunion setting is a growing perception that the courts may not be the best forum for resolution of employment disputes. In an action for wrongful discharge, the parties are usually subject to extensive delays associated with discovery and trial preparation, a prolonged appeal procedure and the high costs inherent in litigation. In some states it could take as long as five years to go to trial. By the time a case gets to trial the parties may be more interested in avenging themselves than in reaching a mutually acceptable resolution to their respective differences. Therefore, the adversarial nature of litigation, particularly in the labor setting, detracts from the effectiveness of litigation as a response to the problem of disputed discharges. Grievance and arbitration procedures, in contrast, are designed to avoid the costs and delays associated with litigation and are useful in preserving the employment relationship.

The extent to which such procedures in a nonunion setting must be deemed exclusive thereby requiring the employee to submit his or her claim to arbitration rather than to a court has not yet been definitively decided. However, assuming a fair procedure, the courts should treat an arbitration mechanism in the nonunion sector as broadly preempting state-law wrongful or retaliatory discharge actions.[132]

The exclusivity and finality of private arbitration agreements is supported by federal and state-law policy favoring arbitration of disputes. The Federal Arbitration Act (''FAA'')[133] flatly declares that an arbitration provision ''shall be valid, irrevocable and enforceable. . . .''[134] The Supreme Court stated in *Southland Corporation v. Keating*[135] that ''[i]n enacting § 2 of the [FAA], Congress declared a national policy favoring arbitration and withdrew the power of the states to require a judicial forum for the resolution of claims which the contracting parties agreed to resolve by arbitration."[136] The FAA's policy favoring arbitration is carried out by a rigorous enforcement of arbitration agreements through orders compelling arbitration and orders staying litigation of arbitrable issues,[137] and by limiting the scope of judicial review of arbitration awards.[138]

In two recent decisions construing the FAA, the Supreme Court has held that state laws which would operate to defeat enforcement of arbitration agreements by allowing a judicial forum for claims subject to arbitration are preempted by the FAA. In *Perry v. Thomas*,[139] the Court held that California Labor Code § 229, which specifically provides for a judicial forum for the collection of unpaid wages despite any arbitration agreement, was preempted by the FAA. Thus the employee's state-court suit against his employer for breach of contract, conversion, conspiracy and breach of fiduciary duty arising out of a commissions dispute was subject to the arbitration agreement in the plaintiff's employment contract.[140] Similarly, the Supreme Court held a few years earlier in *Southland Corporation v. Keating*[141] that a provision of the California franchise investment law that purported to require judicial resolution of claims notwithstanding an agreement to arbitrate was preempted by the FAA.[142] Therefore, federal law in favor of agreements to arbitrate arguably preempts state law wrongful discharge actions when the parties have agreed to arbitrate in a nonunion setting.

To fall within the ambit of the FAA, an arbitration system in a nonunion setting must meet two threshold requirements. First, there must be a written agreement to arbitrate. Second, the arbitration agreement must be in a contract involving "commerce."

An arbitration procedure, if properly adopted in a nonunion setting, may be an enforceable written agreement to arbitrate and therefore legally bind an employee to resolve a discharge dispute through arbitration. Courts have repeatedly held that written and unwritten policies or procedures adopted by an employer, particularly those relating to the termination of employees, become enforceable terms of a contract of employment between the employer and its employees.[143] The employee's acceptance of those policies is manifested in his continuing performance, thus creating a unilateral contract binding on both employer and employee and bringing the agreement within the scope of the FAA.[144]

The arbitration provision must also be in a contract "involving commerce." Congress enacted the FAA pursuant to its authority under the commerce clause of the Constitution.[145] The U.S. Supreme Court has routinely held that Congress's powers pursuant to the commerce clause extend to transactions and activities having only the slightest relationship to interstate commerce.[146] Thus, under the FAA courts have not hesitated to enforce arbitration provisions in contracts of employment where the job duties of employees involved only the slightest nexus to commerce.[147] Consequently, many employees are involved in commerce within the meaning of Section 2 of the FAA and should therefore be bound by agreements to arbitrate.

A court's inquiry when presented with a petition to compel arbitration pursuant to the FAA is therefore simply to determine whether there is a written agreement to arbitrate in a contract involving interstate commerce. Upon finding such an agreement to arbitrate, the FAA requires that a petition by a party to compel arbitration be granted, and any litigation concerning the arbitrable dispute be stayed.[148] The Supreme Court has held that when the requirements of the FAA are satisfied, courts have no discretion to deny an order to arbitrate.[149]

One commentator, Professor Charles J. Morris, has argued that nonunion grievance-arbitration procedures unilaterally adopted by companies violate Section 8(a)(2) of the NLRA.[150] Professor Morris reasons that an arbitration plan in a nonunion setting is a "labor organization" under Section 2(5) of the NLRA and therefore an employer would violate Section 8(a)(2) if it implemented this mechanism without first bargaining with representatives selected by the employees.[151] Morris argues that the Supreme Court's decision in *NLRB v. Cabot Carbon Co.*[152] supports a broad reading of Section 2(5) and compels the conclusion that any plan in which employees participate for the limited purpose of dealing with the employer concerning grievances is a labor organization.[153]

This view is based on a strained reading of the definition of "labor organization." Section 2(5) defines "labor organization" as any "organization of any kind, or any agency or *employee representation* committee or plan, in which employees participate and which . . . *deal[s] with* employers concerning grievances, labor disputes, wages, rates of pay, hours of employment, or conditions of work."[154]

Grievance and arbitration procedures in a nonunion setting, if designed properly are mechanisms by which *individual* employees can resolve their *individual* grievances with an employer. Such grievance and arbitration systems are *adjudicatory* bodies for invididual, not collective disputes, and are not means through which employees discuss or negotiate (i.e., "deal with") terms and conditions of their employment with their employer. Indeed, Section 9(a) of the NLRA recognizes the validity of individual contracts employers may elect to make directly with individual employees. Section 9(a) provides, in substance, that any individual employee shall have the right personally to present his or her own grievances to the employer without the intervention of the bargaining representative.[155]

Cabot Carbon and its progeny are consistent with this view. In *Cabot Carbon*, the employee committees were established and supported by the company for the stated purposes of meeting regularly with management to consider and discuss problems of mutual interest. These committees not only handled grievances on behalf of employees but also considered seniority, job classifications, job bidding, work schedules, holidays, vacations, sick leave and the improvement of working facilities and conditions.[156] The Supreme Court rejected the distinction made by the lower court that the broad term "dealing with" in the definition of a labor organization was intended to be read as synonymous with the more limited term "bargaining with."[157] The Court found that the employee committees were set up for the very purpose of "dealing with" the employer concerning workplace issues, including acting affirmatively and on behalf of employees with regard to grievances. Therefore, the employee committee fell within the statutory definition of "labor organization" under Section 2(5) of the NLRA.[158] However, *Cabot Carbon* never answered the question of how much interaction between labor and management was necessary before an employer could be deemed to be "dealing with" its employees.

Since *Cabot Carbon*, the Board has examined the "purpose" of the organization in determining whether it is a labor organization. However, in each of the cases where the Board has found a labor organization to exist, there has generally been evidence of negotiations or discussions between employees and employers over terms and conditions of employment. For example, in *American Automobile Association*,[159] the Board held that an association of sales representatives was a labor organization where the members had elected a slate of officers, discussed their common grievances and "evidenced an unequivocal intention to bargain collectively with the employer over their wages, hours and other terms and conditions of employment."[160] Similarly, in *South Nassau Communities Hospital*,[161] a "Nursing Advisory Committee" was held to be a labor organization where the participants discussed such items as wages, overtime pay, call-in pay, work shifts and weekend work.[162] And in *Ona Corporation*,[163] an "Employee Action Committee" formed to address with the employer various labor issues and to make proposals to the employer regarding terms and conditions of employment was held to be a labor organization.[164]

In contrast, the Board has never held an employer-employee committee to be a labor organization where its sole purpose was to adjust grievances, and not to negotiate or discuss terms and conditions of employment. The leading case is *Sparks Nugget Inc.*,[165] where the Board found that a joint employer-employee grievance council structured by management did not "deal with" the employer and thus did not come within the coverage of Section 2(5) of the NLRA.[166] The "Employees' Council" was composed of the employer's director of employee relations, an elected representative from grievant's department and a third neutral member. Despite substantial employer influence, the Board found that the council served a legitimate "adjudicatory function" unrelated to the *initiation* of grievances, the recommendation to management of changes in terms and conditions of employment or the advocacy of employee interests.[167] The Board concluded that

> the Employees' Council performs a purely adjudicatory function and does not interact with management for any purpose or in any manner other than to render a final decision on the grievance. Therefore, it cannot be said that the Employees' Council herein "deals with" management. Rather, it appears to perform a function for management; i.e., resolving employee grievances.[168]

In *Mercy-Memorial Hospital Corp.*,[169] the Board carried the reasoning of *Sparks Nugget* even further. There a grievance committee was created to give employees a voice in resolving the grievances of their fellow employees by deciding the validity of employees' complaints. While the committee did not negotiate with management, it did have the right to recommend changes in rules, regulations and standards for the committee.[170] The Board accepted the argument that the committee existed not to deal with management but to give employees a voice in resolving the grievances of their fellow employees.

Therefore, the overtly broad construction of "labor organization" proposed by Professor Morris is not supported by *Cabot Carbon* and subsequent Board decisions. Congress could not have intended the term "labor organization" to be construed to encompass an alternative dispute resolution system between nonunion employees and their employers. Employees who participate in nonunion alternative dispute resolution systems do not deal with employers other than to be involved in rendering a final decision on a grievance.

§ 9.05 Conclusion

The system of industrial self-government envisioned by federal law is in danger of being bypassed in favor of state law actions for wrongful or retaliatory discharge. State law provides, in its present form, generous remedies for tortious discharge that employees would ordinarily not obtain through grievance and arbitration procedures under collective bargaining agreements, such as punitive damages. Employees have more incentive to pursue state remedies leading to the further undermining of the exclusivity and finality of private arbitration of labor disputes.

Faced with an unprecedented number of lawsuits for wrongful or retaliatory discharge, there is a clear need for courts to reaffirm the federal policy in favor of agreements to arbitrate. The grievance and arbitration system remedy has traditionally promoted stability in industrial relations and should not be undermined by creative pleading to avoid its jurisdictional reach. In the nonunion sector, employers should consider implementing an exclusive alternative dispute resolution system which has the potential to prevent long and costly wrongful discharge litigation and to further sound relations between companies and their work force.

Notes

1. For a general overview of this constantly changing area of employment law, see C. Bakaly, Jr., & J. Grossman, *Modern Law of Employment Contracts: Formation, Operation & Remedies for Breach* (Harcourt Brace Jovanovich, 1984). Many other scholarly works address the erosion of the employment-at-will rule. See, e.g., DeGiuseppe, *The Effect of the Employment-at-Will Rule on Employee Rights to Job Security and Fringe Benefits*, 10 Fordham Urb. L.J. 1 (1981); Peck, *Unjust Discharges from Employment: A Necessary Change in the Law*, 48 Ohio St. L.J. 1 (1979); Summers, *Individual Protection Against Unjust Dismissal: The Time for a Statute*, 62 Va. L. Rev. 481 (1976); Note, *Protecting at Will Employees Against Wrongful Discharge: The Duty to Terminate Only in Good Faith*, 93 Harv. L. Rev. 1816 (1980). For a practical new treatise in this area of the law, see S. Pepe and S. Dunham, *Avoiding and Defending Wrongful Discharge Claims: Prevention, Pre-Litigation Strategy, Litigation Tactics* (Callaghan, 1988).
2. The employment-at-will rule was first recognized in the United States in *Hathaway v. Bennett*, 10 N.Y. 108 (1854). Relying on British precedent, the New York Court of Appeals held that a newspaper carrier was properly terminated without advance notice. In 1872, the at-will rule began to be codified, beginning in California, and in some states the at-will rule remains codified today. See, e.g., Cal. Lab. Code § 2922. Many states, however, still treat the rule only as a product of the common law. For a general overview and breakdown of each state's approach to the employment-at-will rule and the recognized exceptions thereto, see C. Bakaly, Jr., & J. Grossman, *supra* note 1 at 207–270.7, Appendix A.
3. Many commentators view actions for wrongful termination as a necessary weapon for employees whose job security is otherwise not legally protected by contract and propose limiting or doing away with the at-will rule. See, e.g., Peck, *supra* note 1.
4. 56 U.S.L.W. 4512 (June 6, 1988).
5. *Id.* at 4515.
6. The underpinning of the employment-at-will rule is the principle of "mutuality of obligation," which means that if one party is not bound to a particular contractual provision, neither is the other. See *Hathaway v. Bennett*, 10 N.Y. at 112. Since employees could not be required to serve against their will, courts refused to impose an analogous obligation on employers.
7. See generally A. Chandler, Jr., *The Visible Hand: The Managerial Revolution in American Business* (Harvard University Press, 1977); Note, *supra* note 1, at 1824–1826; Note, *Implied Contract Rights to Job Security*, 26 Stan. L. Rev. 335, 343 (1974).
8. 29 U.S.C. § 151 *et seq.*
9. 301 U.S. 1 (1937).
10. *Id.* at 30, 33.
11. See, e.g., 42 U.S.C. §§ 2000e *et seq.* (Title VII); N.Y. Exec. L. §§ 290–298.
12. See, e.g., 29 U.S.C. §§ 621 *et seq*,; Cal. Gov't Code § 12941; N.Y. Exec. Law § 296.
13. See, e.g., Cal. Labor Code § 132a; N.Y. Work. Comp. Law § 120.
14. See, e.g., Cal. Gov't Code § 12940; N.Y. Exec. Law § 296.
15. See, e.g., N.Y. Lab. Law § 740. "Whistleblowing"—the disclosure by an employee of an employer's or fellow employee's wrongful activity—may result in the discharge of an employee by an employer. Both federal and state laws under certain circumstances offer statutory protection from this form of retaliatory discharge. See, e.g., Fair Labor Standards Act, 29 U.S.C. §§ 215(a)(3), 216(b) (protection against reprisals for calling

attention to violations of law dealing with labor standards); N.Y. Lab. Law § 740 ("Whistleblowing" law).

16. See, e.g., Cal. Lab. Code § 230; N.Y. Jud. Law § 519.
17. Some states are now considering legislation which would impose uniform standards for the protection of most at-will employees from wrongful termination. See C. Bakaly, Jr., & J. Grossman, *supra*, note 1, at 206.9.
18. 174 Cal. App. 2d 184, 344 P.2d 25 (1959).
19. 174 Cal. App. 2d at 188.
20. 114 N.H. 130, 316 A.2d 549 (1974).
21. *Id.* at 133, 316 A.2d at 551.
22. See, e.g., *Tameny v. Atlantic Richfield Co.*, 27 Cal. 3d 167, 164 Cal. Rptr. 839 (1980).
23. See, e.g., *Weiner v. McGraw-Hill, Inc.*, 57 N.Y.2d 458, 457 N.Y.S.2d 193 (1982).
24. See, e.g., *Fortune v. National Cash Register Co.*, 373 Mass. 96, 364 N.E.2d 1251 (1977).
25. See, e.g., *Nees v. Hocks*, 272 Or. 210, 536 P.2d 512 (1975).
26. See, e.g., *Harless v. First National Bank of Fairmont*, 162 W. Va. 116, 246 S.E.2d 270 (1978).
27. See, e.g., *Petermann v. International Brotherhood of Teamsters*, 174 Cal. App. 2d 184, 344 P.2d 25 (1959). But see *Murphy v. American Home Products Corp.*, 58 N.Y.2d 293, 461 N.Y.S.2d 232 (1983) (declining to recognize a cause of action based on public policy).
28. *Tameny v. Atlantic Richfield Co.*, 27 Cal. 3d 172, 164 Cal. Rptr. 839 (1980) (employee refused to engage in price-fixing in violation of antitrust law); *Petermann v. International Brotherhood of Teamsters*, 174 Cal. App. 2d 184, 164 Cal. Rptr. 839 (1959) (employee refused to commit perjury).
29. *Sventko v. Kroger Co.*, 69 Mich. App. 644, 245 N.W.2d 151 (1976).
30. *Sheets v. Teddy's Frosted Foods, Inc.*, 179 Conn. 471, 427 A.2d 385 (1980).
31. See generally *Hinrichs v. Tranquilaire Hospital*, 352 So. 2d 1130 (Ala. 1977) (public policy is "too vague" a concept on which to ground a cause of action); *Petermann v. International Brotherhood of Teamsters*, 174 Cal. App. 2d 184, 344 P.2d 25 (1959) (recognizing that "[t]he term 'public policy' is inherently not subject to precise definition"); *Martin v. Platt*, 179 Ind. App. 688, 386 N.E.2d 1026 (1979) ("[B]road determinations [of public policy] should be left for the legislature."); *Pierce v. Ortho Pharmaceutical Corp.*, 84 N.J. 58, 417 A.2d 505 (1980) (public policy must be based on a "clear mandate"). Although this question is presently unresolved in California, the California Supreme Court is expected to rule shortly on whether public policy can only arise out of a legislative enactment. See *Foley v. Interactive Data Corp.*, 184 Cal. App. 3d 241, 219 Cal. Rptr. 866 (1985), review granted, 222 Cal. Rptr. 740 (1986).
32. *Novosel v. Nationwide Ins. Co.*, 721 F.2d 894 (3d Cir. 1983).
33. See, e.g., *Pugh v. See's Candies, Inc.*, 116 Cal. App. 3d 311, 171 Cal. Rptr. 917 (1981) (oral promises of job security made to a 32-year employee); *Martin v. Federal Life Insurance Co.*, 109 Ill. App. 3d 596, 440 N.E.2d 998 (1982) (employer promised employee he would not be discharged for cause, taking the relationship out of the employment-at-will rule); *Weiner v. McGraw-Hill, Inc.*, 57 N.Y.2d 458, 457 N.Y.S.2d 193 (1982) (oral and written assurances of job security made to employee who relied upon same in relocating).
34. See, e.g., *Pugh v. See's Candies, Inc.*, 116 Cal. App. 3d 311, 171 Cal. Rptr. 917 (1981).
35. See, e.g., *Toussaint v. Blue Cross & Blue Shield of Michigan*, 408 Mich. 579, 292 N.W.2d 880 (1980).
36. See, e.g., *Hepp v. Lockheed-California Co.*, 86 Cal. App. 3d 714, 150 Cal. Rptr. 408 (1978); *Toussaint v. Blue Cross & Blue Shield of Michigan*, 408 Mich. 579, 292 N.W. 2d 880 (1980); cf. *Weiner v. McGraw-Hill Inc.*, 57 N.Y.2d 458, 457 N.Y.S.2d 193 (1982) (statements in manual along with oral promises at time of employment can create binding contract).
37. See, e.g., *Cleary v. American Airlines, Inc.*, 111 Cal. App. 3d 443, 168 Cal. Rptr. 722 (1980). But see *Murphy v. American Home Products Corp.*, 58 N.Y.2d 293, 461 N.Y.S.2d 232 (1983) (refusing to recognize a cause of action in tort for breach of the implied covenant of good faith and fair dealing).
38. See *Kirke La Shelle Co. v. Paul Armstrong Co.*, 263 N.Y. 79, 87 (1933).
39. 373 Mass. 96, 364 N.E.2d 1251 (1977).

40. 364 N.E.2d at 1256.
41. *Id.* at 1254.
42. 181 Cal. App. 3d 1155, 226 Cal. Rptr. 820 (1986).
43. *Id.* at 1171, 226 Cal. Rptr. at 829.
44. *Foley v. Interactive Data Corp.*, 184 Cal. App. 3d 241, 219 Cal. Rptr. 866 (1985), review granted, 222 Cal. Rptr. 740 (1986).
45. 219 Cal. Rptr. at 871.
46. See, e.g., *Sabetay v. Sterling Drug, Inc.*, 69 N.Y.2d 329, 514 N.Y.S.2d 209 (1987).
47. *Magnan v. Anaconda Indus. Inc.*, 193 Conn. 558, 479 A.2d 781 (1984).
48. *Id.* at 571, 479 A.2d at 788.
49. U.S. Const. Art. VI, § 32, Cl. 2. The supremacy clause reads as follows: "This Constitution, and the Laws of the United States which shall be made in Pursuance thereof; and all Treaties made, or which shall be made, under the Authority of the United States, shall be the supreme Law of the Land; and the Judges in every State shall be bound thereby; anything in the Constitution or laws of the State to the contrary notwithstanding."
50. *Gibbons v. Ogden*, 22 U.S. (9 Wheat) 1 (1824).
51. See *Jones v. Rath Packing Co.*, 430 U.S. 519, 525 (1977).
52. See *Malone v. White Motor Corp.*, 435 U.S. 497, 504 (1978).
53. See *Hines v. Davidowitz*, 312 U.S. 52, 67 (1941).
54. 346 U.S. 485 (1953).
55. *Id.* at 488.
56. 359 U.S. 236 (1959).
57. *Id.* at 245.
58. Garmon recognized two limitations on its broad holding. First, federal labor law will not preempt state law which only remotely affects the NLRA. Second, courts should not preempt state regulation of activity "touch[ing] interests . . . deeply rooted in local feeling and responsibility." *Id.* at 243–244, see, e.g., *Farmer v. United Brotherhood of Carpenters & Joiners*, 430 U.S. 290 (1977) (intentional infliction of emotional distress); *Linn v. United Plant Guard Workers*, 383 U.S. 53 (1966) (libel); *Youngdahl v. Rainfair, Inc.*, 355 U.S. 131 (1957) (violence).
59. 29 U.S.C. § 185(a).
60. *Id.*
61. *Textile Workers Union v. Lincoln Mills of Alabama*, 353 U.S. 448 (1957); see also *Republic Steel Corp. v. Maddox*, 376 U.S. 650 (1965); *United Steelworkers of America v. Enterprise Wheel & Car Corp.*, 363 U.S. 593 (1960); *United Steelworkers of America v. Warrior & Gulf Navigation Co.*, 363 U.S. 574 (1960); *United Steelworkers of America v. American Manufacturing Co.*, 363 U.S. 564 (1960).
62. 369 U.S. 95 (1962).
63. *Id.* at 103; see also *Textile Workers Union v. Lincoln Mills of Alabama*, 353 U.S. 448 (1957).
64. 369 U.S. at 104.
65. *Id.*
66. *Republic Steel Corp. v. Maddox*, 379 U.S. 650, 652 (1965).
67. See *Vaca v. Sipes*, 386 U.S. 171 (1967).
68. 471 U.S. 202 (1985).
69. 740 F.2d 1468 (9th Cir. 1984).
70. *Id.* at 1474.
71. *Id.* at 1475.
72. 736 F.2d 1348 (9th Cir. 1984).
73. *Id.* at 1349.
74. *Id.* at 1350-1351; see also *Lamb v. Briggs Manufacturing Corp.*, 700 F.2d 1092 (7th Cir. 1983) (retaliatory discharge for filing a workers' compensation claim was subsumed within the just cause standard of the parties' labor agreement).
75. 105 Ill. 2d 143, 473 N.E.2d 1280 (1984), cert. denied, 474 U.S. 909 (1985).
76. *Id.* at 150, 473 N.E.2d at 1284.
77. *Id.*

78. *Id.*
79. *Id.* (citing *Alexander v. Gardner-Denver Co.*, 415 U.S. 36 (1974)); see also *Messenger v. Volkswagen of America, Inc.* 585 F. Supp. 565 (D. W. Va. 1984) (noting that a state-law retaliatory discharge claim under West Virginia's workers' compensation law presented a "distinctly separate" claim).
80. 471 U.S. at 202.
81. See *id.* at 220.
82. See *id.* at 206.
83. See *id.*
84. *Lueck v. Aetna Live & Casualty Co.*, 116 Wis. 2d 559, 566, 342 N.W.2d 699, 703 (1984), *rev'd, Allis-Chalmers Corp. v. Lueck*, 471 U.S. 202 (1985). The Wisconsin Supreme Court's analysis closely followed *Farmer v. United Brotherhood of Carpenters & Joiners*, 430 U.S. 290 (1977).
85. 471 U.S. at 212 n.6.
86. *Id.* at 217.
87. *Id.* at 220 (citing *Avco Corp. v. Aero Lodge 735*, 390 U.S. 557 (1968)). The Court stated that the relevant analysis is whether the state-law action "confers non-negotiable state-law rights on employers or employees independent of any right established by contract, or, instead whether evaluation of the tort claim is inextricably intertwined with consideration of the terms of the labor contract." 471 U.S. at 213.
88. 471 U.S. at 219-220 (emphasis added) (citing *Republic Steel Corp. v. Maddox*, 379 U.S. 650, 653 (1965)); see also *International Brotherhood of Electrical Workers v. Hechler*, 107 S. Ct. 2161 (1987) (holding that a union employee's state tort claim that her union breached its duty of care to provide her with a safe working place was sufficiently dependent on the collective bargaining agreement and therefore was preempted).
89. 471 U.S. at 220.
90. See, e.g., *Harper v. San Diego Transit Corp.*, 764 F.2d 663, 668 (9th Cir. 1985) (holding preempted plaintiff's claims for breach of contract and breach of the implied covenant of good faith and fair dealing).
91. See *id.*
92. See *Hillard v. Dobelman*, 774 F.2d 886, 887 (8th Cir. 1985); see also *Dougherty v. Parsec, Inc.*, 824 F.2d 1477, 1478 (6th Cir. 1987).
93. See *Cavins v. Aetna Life Ins. Co.*, 609 F. Supp. 309, 313-314 (E.D. Wis. 1985).
94. See *Friday v. Hughes Aircraft Co.*, 188 Cal. App. 3d 117, 123-124, 225 Cal. Rptr. 89, 93-94 (1985).
95. 811 F.2d 1333 (9th Cir. 1987), *vacated*, 56 U.S.L.W. 3847 (June 13, 1988).
96. *Id.* at 1335.
97. *Id.* at 1336.
98. 647 F. Supp. 1514 (C.D. Cal. 1986).
99. *Id.* at 1519-1520.
100. 2 I.E.R. Cases (BNA) 1284 (Minn. 1987).
101. *Id.* at 1286-1287; see also *Paige v. Henry J. Kaiser Co.*, 826 F.2d 857, 863 (9th Cir. 1987) (terminated plaintiffs' claims of tortious discharge based on state health and safety regulations were not preempted by federal law), cert. denied, 56 U.S.L.W. 3848 (June 13, 1988).
102. 814 F.2d 102 (2d Cir.), *cert. denied*, 108 S. Ct. 224 (1987).
103. *Id.* at 105; see also *Herring v. Prince Macaroni of New Jersey, Inc.*, 799 F.2d 120 (3d Cir. 1986) (Section 301 did not preempt a retaliatory discharge claim because workers' compensation rights were deeply rooted in state law rather than derived from the parties' labor agreement).
104. 814 F.2d at 105. The court acknowledged that a state court might have to examine the labor contract in determining what relief plaintiff might be entitled to if she prevailed on the merits. The court noted, however, that "not every question 'tangentially involving a provision of a collective bargaining agreement [ ] is pre-empted by § 301.' " *Id.* at 106 (citing *Allis-Chalmers*, 471 U.S. at 211).
105. 823 F.2d 1031 (7th Cir. 1987), *rev'd*, 56 U.S.L.W. 4512 (June 6, 1988).

106. 823 F.2d at 1039-1041.
107. *Id.* at 1041–1042.
108. *Id.* at 1050–1051.
109. 56 U.S.L.W. 4512 (1988).
110. *Id.*
111. *Id.* at 4512–4513.
112. *Id.* at 4513.
113. *Id.* at 4512.
114. *Id.* at 4513 (quoting *Textile Workers v. Lincoln Mills of Alabama*, 353 U.S. 448, 451 (1957)). The Court also quoted extensively from *Teamsters v. Lucas Flour Co.*, 369 U.S. 95 (1962), where the Court reaffirmed the importance of uniformity of federal law for the enforcement of labor agreements:
"The possibility that individual contract terms might have different meanings under state and federal law would inevitably exert a disruptive influence upon both the negotiation and administration of collective agreements. Because neither party could be certain of the rights which it had obtained or conceded, the process of negotiating an agreement would be made immeasurably more difficult by the necessity of trying to formulate contract provisions in such a way as to contain the same meaning under two or more systems of law which might someday be involved in enforcing the contract. Once the collective bargain was made, the possibility of conflicting substantive interpretation under competing legal systems would tend to stimulate and prolong disputes as to interpretation. Indeed, the existence of possibly conflicting legal concepts might substantially impede the parties' willingness to agree to contract terms providing for final arbitral or judicial resolution of disputes." *Id.* at 103–104 (quoted in *Lingle*, 56 U.S.L.W. at 4513 n.3).
115. 56 U.S.L.W. at 4514.
116. *Id.* at 4514–4515.
117. *Id.* at 4514.
118. *Id.*
119. *Id.* (citations omitted).
120. *Id.* at 4515 (citing *Alexander v. Gardner-Denver Co.*, 415 U.S. 36 (1974) (Title VII)).
121. 56 U.S.L.W. at 4515 (citing *Fort Halifax Packing Co. v. Coyne*, 107 S. Ct. 2211 (1987), (rejecting a claim that federal labor law preempted a state statute providing severance benefits to employees in the event of a plant closing).
122. 56 U.S.L.W. at 4515 (emphasis added). After *Allis-Chalmers* and prior to *Lingle*, some courts addressed the federal preemption defense in the context of removal jurisdiction. The question of removal jurisdiction is governed by the "well-pleaded complaint rule" which provides that federal jurisdiction exists only when the federal issue appears on the face of the complaint. Thus, when preemption is raised only as a defense, federal jurisdiction is not conferred. The Supreme Court in *Caterpillar Inc. v. Williams*, 107 S. Ct. 2425 (1987), held that state court actions for breach of individual employment agreements were not removable notwithstanding the fact that plaintiffs were subject to a collective bargaining agreement. See also *Garibaldi v. Lucky Food Stores, Inc.*, 726 F.2d 1367 (9th Cir. 1984), *cert. denied*, 471 U.S. 1099 (1985). The *Caterpillar* Court rejected a "complete preemption" doctrine and thus found that there was no removal jurisdiction. The Court in *Lingle* seemed to suggest that *Caterpillar* was decided under a *preemption* analysis as well as under removal jurisdiction. Referring to the analysis in *Caterpillar*, the Court in *Lingle* stated that "as long as the state-law claim can be resolved without interpreting the agreement itself, the claim is 'independent' of the agreement for § 301 preemption purposes." 56 U.S.L.W. at 4515.
123. After *Lingle*, employers may want to reevaluate the arbitration provisions in their collective bargaining agreements. Because employers can no longer be sure whether they will be forced to relitigate a discharge issue in state court, employers may want to consider ways to avoid a two-tiered proceeding before agreeing to arbitration, such as requiring the employee to choose one forum over the other to resolve the discharge dispute. Of course, any agreement requiring employees to elect arbitration over state-law remedies will have to be negotiated with the union. The *Lingle* Court did not resolve the

question of whether such an election of remedies would be a bar to a state-court action for wrongful or tortious discharge. 56 U.S.L.W. at 4515 n.9. The enforceability of an employee's election of remedies is beyond the scope of this Article.

124. See *Republic Steel Corp. v. Maddox*, 376 U.S. 650 (1965); *United Steelworkers of America v. Enterprise Wheel & Car Corp.*, 363 U.S. 593 (1960); *United Steelworkers of America v. Warrior & Gulf Navigation Co.*, 363 U.S. 574 (1960); *United Steelworkers of America v. American Manufacturing Co.*, 363 U.S. 564 (1960).
125. 376 U.S. 650 (1965).
126. *Id.* at 653.
127. *Id.*; see also *Allis-Chalmers*, 471 U.S. at 219 (preemption of derivative tort claims "preserves the central role of arbitration" as an essential component in labor law).
128. See, e.g., *Olguin v. Inspiration Consolidated Copper Co.*, 740 F.2d 1468 (9th Cir. 1984) (any independent agreement, such as those which may be contained in personnel manuals, is preempted by the parties' collective bargaining agreement); *Childers v. Chesapeake & Potomac Telephone Co.*, 670 F. Supp. 624 (D. Md. 1987) (state law wrongful discharge claims were preempted because they were inextricably intertwined in the parties' labor agreement); *Seid v. Pacific Bell, Inc.*, 635 F. Supp. 906 (S.D. Cal. 1985) (where a relationship is otherwise governed by a collective bargaining agreement, a claim for breach of implied contract is preempted by federal law).
129. *Anderson v. Ford Motor Co.*, 803 F.2d 953 (8th Cir. 1986) (claim for breach of contract could be maintained because the promises were made *before* the plaintiffs were hired or covered by the collective bargaining agreement), *cert. denied*, 107 S. Ct. 3242 (1987); see also *Caterpillar, Inc. v. Williams*, 107 S. Ct. 2425 (1987) (no removal jurisdiction where independent promises were made to employees outside of the bargaining unit); *Malia v. RCA Corp.*, 794 F.2d 909 (3d Cir. 1986) (no preemption of state law breach of contract claim based on oral promises made after employee left bargaining unit).
130. See, e.g., *Carter v. Smith Food King*, 765 F.2d 916 (9th Cir. 1985); *Harper v. San Diego Transit Corp.*, 764 F.2d 663 (9th Cir. 1985).
131. See *supra* notes 27–32 and accompanying text.
132. The Center for Public Resources' Employment Disputes Committee has published the CPR Model Procedure for Mediation of Termination and Other Employment Disputes. This Committee was established to develop and promote the use of alternative dispute resolution procedures in the private sector. The Committee is located at 680 Fifth Avenue, New York, New York 10019.
133. 9 U.S.C. § 1 *et seq.*
134. *Id.* § 2; accord N.Y. Civ. Prac. L. & R. § 7501 *et seq.*
135. 465 U.S. 1 (1984).
136. *Id.* at 10.
137. 9 U.S.C. §§ 3, 4.
138. *Id.* § 10.
139. 107 S. Ct. 2520 (1987).
140. *Id.* at 2526. Since *Perry* is an FAA case, *Lingle*, a Section 301 case, should not be read as overruling or even narrowing the *Perry* decision.
141. 465 U.S. 1 (1984).
142. *Id.* at 7–8.
143. Courts in California, for example, have uniformly recognized that such procedures may become enforceable terms of an employment contract. See, e.g., *Gray v. Superior Court*, 181 Cal. App. 3d 813, 226 Cal. Rptr. 570 (1986) (written employer policy regarding termination and discipline); *Walker v. Northern San Diego County Hospital District*, 135 Cal. App. 3d 396, 185 Cal. Rptr. 617 (1982) (statements in employee handbook implicitly precluding termination without cause after the completion by employees of a probationary period); *Hepp v. Lockheed-California Co.*, 86 Cal. App. 3d 714, 150 Cal. Rptr. 408 (1978) (employer policy regarding recall of laid-off employees).
144. 9 U.S.C. § 2. Although the courts have not yet resolved the issue, a written arbitration agreement governing claims of nonunion employees may be deemed to create a binding unilateral written arbitration agreement under the FAA even if the employee has not signed the agreement. Cf. *Wiley v. California Hosiery Co.*, 32 P. 522 (1883) (written

proposal for sales commissions given to employee by employer was binding on employee even though not signed by him; court would not accept parol evidence to modify terms of the written contract); *Nelkin v. Marvin Hime & Co.*, 39 Cal. Rptr. 701, 704 (1964) (consignee's acceptance of a memorandum containing provision that consignee would be responsible in the event goods were stolen resulted in a contract between the parties even though consignee failed to sign agreement; acceptance of memorandum with knowledge of its contents and continued possession of goods were deemed to create a binding written contract).

145. See *Southland*, 465 U.S. at 11.
146. See, e.g., *United States v. Wrightwood Dairy Co.*, 315 U.S. 110 (1942) (price of milk sold entirely within one state regulated pursuant to the commerce clause); *Wickard v. Filburn*, 317 U.S. 111 (1942) (Congress's commerce power covers wheat consumed wholly on the farms where grown). Employees who have even an attenuated connection with merchandise shipped in interstate commerce have been held to be involved in commerce. See, e.g., *Walton v. Southern Package Corp.*, 320 U.S. 540 (1944) (night watchman in wood veneer plant involved in commerce because the veneer was shipped in interstate commerce, even though the plant was not operated at night while the watchman worked and he did not assist in manufacture and shipment of goods); *Martino v. Michigan Window Cleaning Co.*, 327 U.S. 173 (1946) (employees of company providing commercial window washing services wholly within the state of Michigan involved in commerce).
147. See, e.g., *Perry*, 107 S. Ct. 2520 (arbitration provision in contract of employment of stock broker); *Tonetti v. Shirley*, 173 Cal. App. 3d 1144, 219 Cal. Rptr. 616 (1985) (same); *Erving v. Virginia Squires Basketball Club*, 468 F.2d 1064, 1068-1069 (2d Cir. 1972) (arbitration provision in contract of employment of professional basketball player); *Swenson v. CDI Corp.*, 670 F. Supp. 1438 (D. Minn. 1987) (managerial employee's contract with arbitration clause).
148. *Dean Witter Reynolds, Inc. v. Byrd*, 470 U.S. 213, 218 (1985).
149. *Id.*
150. Morris, *EGAPs - Arbitration Plans for Nonunion Employees*, 14 Pepperdine L. Rev. 827, 834 (1987).
151. *Id.* at 830–31.
152. 360 U.S. 203 (1959).
153. Morris, *supra* note 150, at 831.
154. 29 U.S.C. § 152(5) (emphasis added).
155. *Id.* § 159(a).
156. 360 U.S. at 205–208.
157. *Id.* at 210–211.
158. *Id.*
159. 242 NLRB 722, 101 LRRM 1440 (1970).
160. 101 LRRM at 1442.
161. 247 NLRB 527, 103 LRRM 1175 (1980).
162. *Id.*
163. 285 NLRB No. 77, 128 LRRM 1013 (1987).
164. 128 LRRM at 1013–1014.
165. 230 NLRB 275, 95 LRRM 1298 (1977), *modified*, 623 F.2d 571 (9th Cir. 1980).
166. 95 LRRM at 1300.
167. *Id.*
168. *Id.* at 1300–1301.
169. 231 NLRB 1108, 96 LRRM 1239 (1977).
170. 96 LRRM at 1240.

Report on the Labor Arbitrator's Role in Cases Involving External Law*

Report of the Committee on Labor and Employment Law of the Association of the Bar of the City of New York

Introduction

Labor lawyers who represent clients in arbitrations are faced with an ever-present problem to which there is no absolute answer, namely, should issues of external law be litigated before an arbitrator. Correspondingly, labor arbitrators are presented with the same problem of how much, if at all, should an arbitrator's decision be influenced by external law. The purpose of this report is to set forth the current state of the law affecting the arbitrator's use or non-use of external law, *i.e.*, statutory and decisional law. Thus, we will examine the decisional standards of the NLRB and courts used in reviewing arbitrators' decisions, on the positions of management and union representative and arbitrators on the use of external law, and, finally, attempt to evolve an approach for parties in arbitrations which would meet the standards of the NLRB and courts while preserving the essential nature of the arbitral process.

I. The Board's Deferral Doctrine

The problems raised by external law in arbitrations were highlighted when the NLRB promulgated the *Spielberg* doctrine[1] in 1955. There the Board set forth three conditions which, if met, would cause the Board to defer to the decision of an arbitrator: (1) the arbitration appears to have been fair and regular, (2) the parties agreed to accept the award as final and binding, and (3) the decision of the arbitrator was not "clearly repugnant" to the purposes and policies of the NLRA. A fourth proviso was added in 1963 by *Raytheon*,[2] namely, that the arbitrator had considered the unfair labor practice issue.

In the years following *Spielberg*, the NLRB has, through a series of cases, developed a policy of deferring to arbitration. Starting with *Collyer Insulated Wire*,[3] the Board's deferral policy has expanded, then contracted and now, since 1984, is at its most expansive state. In *Olin Corp.*, 268 NLRB 573 (1984), the Board returned to the *Spielberg* criteria with the addition of a

* This article is reprinted in its entirety with permission from the Committee on Labor and Employment Law of the Association of the Bar of the City of New York.

two-prong test. In *Olin*, the Board adopted the following standard for deferral to arbitration awards:

> We would find that an arbitrator has adequately considered the unfair labor practice if (1) the contractual issue is factually parallel to the unfair labor practice issue, and (2) the arbitrator was presented generally with the facts relevant to resolving the unfair labor practice.

In its application of the *Spielberg* standard of "clearly repugnant" to the NLRA, the award need not be totally consistent with Board precedent. "Unless the arbitrator's decision is not susceptible to an interpretation consistent with the Act, we will defer." The Board also placed the affirmative burden of demonstrating the defects in the arbitral process or award on the party advocating non-deferral.

II. The Board's Deferral Doctrine In Operation

Initially it should be noted that the Board will not defer to arbitration awards involving (a) violations of section 8(a)(4) (discrimination for filing NLRB charges) of the Act,[4] (b) compliance with a Board order,[5] representation issues,[6] and violations of section 8(a)(2) (unlawful assistance to a union).[7]

A sampling of recent Board decisions involving the *Olin* standards discloses fairly strict application. Thus, in *Trustees of Columbia University*, 279 NLRB No. 19 (1986), the Board held that it would defer if *Olin* standards are present even where the arbitrator is specifically advised that only the contractual question is before him and neither party introduces any evidence as to the statutory violation.

However, where the arbitrator stated in the award that he did not have the authority to decide the statutory issue or declined to consider the unfair labor practice question, the Board will not defer. *Cotter & Co.*, 276 NLRB No. 75 (1985); *Laborers Local Union No. 380*, 275 NLRB No. 147 (1985). An illustration of non-deferral because of a "repugnant" arbitral decision is the award reducing a discharge to a three-week suspension for an employee who engaged in activities protected under the NLRA. *Garland Coal and Mining Co.*, 276 NLRB No. 102 (1985). *Aces Mechanical Corp.*, 282 NLRB No. 137 (1987), is a case in which not only was the contractual issue not factually parallel to the unfair labor practice issues but the arbitrator permitted an employee's reinstatement to be conditioned on his relinquishing his shop steward's position. It should be noted that the Second Circuit refused to enforce the Board order. See discussion *infra*.

In *United Technologies Corp.*, 268 NLRB 557 (1984), the Board enunciated its current policy of staying the Board's processes where contractual grievance-arbitration procedures have been invoked voluntarily, in order to permit the parties to give full effect to those procedures. Applying this concept, the Board dismissed a complaint issued by the General Counsel because it found that the union had invoked the contractual grievance and arbitration procedures and that the process had not been completed. The Board, however, retained jurisdiction over the matter for the limited purpose of entertaining any subsequent motion for further consideration upon a showing that (1) the employer is resisting or impeding prompt processing of the grievance, or (2) the grievance or arbitration procedures have not been fair or regular or have reached a result that is repugnant to the NLRA. The Eighth Circuit approved this policy in *Lewis v. NLRB*, — F.2d — (CA 8 1986) 123 LRRM 2469.

The terms of the Board's reservation of jurisdiction pose the question of what the Board would do if either one or both of the parties declined to present or litigate the unfair labor practice issue before the arbitrator. Would such a failure or refusal constitute resisting or impeding the processing of the grievance? The answer in part depends upon what action is taken by the union when the employer refuses to litigate the unfair labor practice before the arbitrator. If the union moves the Board to revoke its dismissal on the ground that the employer is impeding the arbitral process, the Board, depending upon the nature of the case, may indeed reverse its dismissal. On the other hand, the Board may deem the motion premature, preferring to let the arbitration run its course and then to determine whether the contract issue was factually parallel to the unfair labor practice issue and whether the arbitrator was generally presented with the facts relevant to resolving the unfair labor practice, despite the ostensible refusal to litigate the unfair labor practice issues.

An illustration of the thinking of the General Counsel is seen in *Delman Shoe Salon*, Case No. 2-CA-19585, Advice Memorandum May 22, 1985. There, the General Counsel declined to issue a complaint and deferred to the arbitration decision where the charging union refused to present evidence of an unfair labor practice motive to the arbitrator but where the employer solicited such a contention on cross-examination at the arbitration and the arbitrator found that there was insufficient evidence of an unfair labor practice.

The *Delman* Advice Memorandum noted that "the Board does not require that all, or even substantially all, of the 'ULP' evidence be presented to the arbitrator. It requires only that the arbitrator be 'presented generally with the facts relevant to the unfair labor practice.' " The Memorandum in footnote 2 stated:

> The fact that the arbitrator did not consider more Section 8(a)(3) evidence was attributed to the Union's position that the arbitrator should avoid the statutory issue. If the arbitrator had agreed with the Union and had avoided the statutory issue, the mere fact that the Union

had the opportunity to present the statutory issue would not be sufficient to warrant deferral. See *Olin Corp., supra* at n.10.

The Advice Memorandum provides, to a certain extent, the General Counsel's answer to the above questions posed by this report. Thus, the General Counsel notes that the board holds that "it is not necessary for the arbitral opinion to expressly state that the statutory issue was considered," citing *Martin Redi-Mix*, 274 NLRB No. 79. Where the arbitral opinion does not so state, it is permissible to look at the underlying record in the arbitration hearing and to infer that the arbitrator considered the statutory issue.

III. Court Acceptance of NLRB Decisions on Deferral

In a review of the Board application of the *Olin* standard by eight federal circuit courts, seven circuits limited their review to whether the Board abused its discretion in its deferral decision. The Eleventh Circuit, on the other hand, rejected the *Olin* standard and has adopted its own guidelines. *Taylor v. NLRB*, 785 F.2d 1516 (1985).

Set forth below are recent court decisions reviewing the Board's *Olin* decisions, with particular regard to external law issues:

In *NLRB v. Aces Mechanical Corp., slip op.*, Jan. 22, 1988, the Second Circuit found that the Board should have deferred to the arbitrator's award. Holding that the contractual and statutory issues are "factually parallel" if the arbitrator's decision on the threshold issue is such that the statutory claim cannot survive, the court rules that the arbitrator's finding of just cause blunts the claim of discharge for union activity. It should be recalled that the Board refused to defer because not only was the "factually parallel" test not met but the arbitrator permitted the employee's reinstatement to be conditioned on the relinquishment of his shop steward's position. In *Nevins v. NLRB*, 796 F.2d 14 (1986), the Second Circuit held that deferral was not proper because the arbitrator was not presented with enough evidence to resolve the unfair labor practice claim that an offer of employment was conditioned on acceptance of sub-scale wages.

Deferral was upheld by the Third Circuit when the arbitrator found the grievant to be a supervisor under the Act and therefore not protected. By this finding, the arbitrator merged the contractual and statutory issues.

The Fifth Circuit in *NLRB v. Ryder/P.I.E. Nationwide, Inc.*, 810 F.2d 502 (1987), ruled against deferral by finding that the arbitrator was not presented with "crucial evidence" concerning the employer's motivation to rebut the just cause evidence. Thus, the arbitrator did not have the facts relevant to resolving the unfair labor practice.

In *Wheeling-Pittsburgh Steel Corp. v. NLRB*, 821 F.2d 342 (1987), the Sixth Circuit supported non-deferral, holding that although the unfair labor practice claim was "factually parallel" to the contract issue, the evidence *necessary* to resolve the unfair labor practice must be before the arbitrator. It is not enough that the ALJ found that additional evidence considered to be critical to a fair resolution of the dispute was not before the arbitrator.

The Ninth Circuit in *Garcia v. NLRB*, 785 F.2d 807 (1986), found the deferral to be a violation of public policy and a departure from the Board's standards. The Board had deferred to an arbitrator's decision upholding discipline of an employee who refused to carry out his employer's orders which were in violation of the state vehicle and traffic law. The court also held that to permit the discipline is to punish for engaging in protected concerted activity.

In *Harberson v. NLRB*, 810 F.2d 977 (1987), the Tenth Circuit gave as reason for non-defferal the fact that the arbitrator did not resolve the crucial factual question. The court held that if the ALJ believes this question to be dispositive to the case, he may not defer. The court also stated that if the factual issue is "dissimilar" to the unfair labor practice claim, the decision of the arbitrator was not based on "facts relevant to the statutory claim."

The Eleventh Circuit, in *Taylor v. NLRB*, 786 F.2d 1516 (1986), rejected *Olin* because "factual parallelism does not always guarantee legal parallelism" and, as a result, many unfair labor practice issues will be inadequately litigated or not reached at all. The court commented that deferral is appropriate when arbitral proceedings are adequate to protect an employee's statutory rights; the arbitral proceeding must "inspire confidence in the fairness of the process or the accuracy of the result." This rejection of *Olin* appears to be more of form than of substance because this circuit, as do other circuits, examines each case for the application of the NLRA.

A decision of the District of Columbia Circuit remanding to the Board its decision to defer for further explanation is instructive because the Circuit Court developed reasons for deferral that the Board should give depending upon which *Spielberg/Olin* ground it chose to assert. See *Darr v. NLRB*, 801 F.2d 1404 (1986). The *Darr* court advised that if the Board were to decide to defer on the ground that the NLRA rights were litigated before the arbitrator, then the Board "must explain how the statutory claim merged into the contract claim when the arbitrator himself treated the claim as outside his jurisdiction." *Id*. at 1409. If the NLRB were to offer as a reason to defer that all the parties had agreed to be bound by the arbitration proceeding, then the Board must, at a minimum, determine whether the arbitrator has found that the parties agreed to incorporate the NLRA into the collective bargaining agreement by reference. *Id*. Where the NLRB has deferred because the arbitrator's award was "not clearly repugnant to the Act," the *Darr* court asks the Board to explain whether its level of scrutiny is higher when the arbitration award is based on an application of the NLRA as opposed to when the award is based on a conclusion that the union has waived its member's NLRA rights. *Id.* Finally, if it is found that the parties to the collective bargaining agreement have waived statutory rights over which the NLRB has authority, then the board must "set forth a waiver theory" if it determines that the particular rights in issue are waivable.

The tests set forth by the *Darr* court reflect the general approach of most circuit courts, i.e., that the NLRB's deferral decisions should be examined closely to see if the Board is giving away too much of its responsibility to enforce employee rights under the Act.

IV. The Nature of the Arbitral Process

Thus far, this report has examined what the Board and courts expect of the arbitral process in order for the award to be given deference under *Olin*. Inherent in the Board's approach under *Olin* is the fact that the arbitrator will consider, at least to some extent, external law. However, the theory of the arbitration process as expounded by many arbitrators is at odds with the Board's (and courts') expectations in the *Olin* area.

Significantly, the Supreme Court has not looked to arbitration as a means of upholding or enforcing statutory rights. Thus in *Carey v. Westinghouse Electric Corp.*, 375 U.S. 261 at 272, the Court stated:

> Should the [National Labor Relations] Board disagree with the arbiter . . . the Board's ruling would, of course, take precedence. . . .

In *NLRB v. Acme Industrial Co.*, 385 U.S. 432, based upon its construction of the arbitration provisions of the contract, the Seventh Circuit refused to enforce a Board order requiring the employer to furnish information to the union. The Supreme Court reversed the Seventh Circuit and enforced the Board's order requiring the employer to provide information in aid of the arbitral process. The Supreme Court noted that the Board is not "automatically" required "to defer to the primary determination of an arbitrator."

McDonald v. City of West Branch, Michigan, 466 U.S. 284 (1984) provides an explicit explanation of why the Supreme Court does not view arbitration as an appropriate vehicle for the enforcement of statutory rights. In that case, a discharged City policeman instituted arbitration under the contract between his union and the City. The arbitrator ruled against the officer. No review of the award was sought. However, when the officer instituted a Federal Civil Rights Act suit under Section 1983, the City defended on the ground that the arbitrator had decided the issues. Writing for the Court, Justice Brennan held that the Federal full faith and credit statute did not require that preclusive effect be given to an arbitration award. Nor was there a need to create judicially a rule that preclusive effect be given to labor arbitration awards in civil rights suits. Citing *Alexander v.*

Gardner-Denver, 415 U.S. 36 (1974) and *Barrentine v. Arkansas Best-Freight System*, 450 U.S. 728 (1981), the Court noted that claims under Title VII of the Civil Rights Act of 1964 and the Fair Labor Standards Act are not foreclosed by arbitral decisions. Analyzing the arbitral process, Justice Brennan noted that an arbitrator's expertise pertains to the law of the shop—not the law of the land; and that an arbitrator's authority derives solely from the contract. Thus, says the Court, when rights guaranteed by Section 1983 conflict with the provisions of the contract, the arbitrator must enforce the contract. Commenting further on the arbitral process, Justice Brennan points out that the union usually has exclusive control over the manner and extent of the presentation of the grievance and that the union's interests are not always identical or compatible with those of the grievants. The decision notes that arbitral fact-finding is generally not equivalent to judicial fact-finding because the record is not as complete; the usual rules of evidence do not apply; the rights and procedures of a civil trial, such as discovery, compulsory process, cross-examination and testimony under oath, are often severely limited or unavailable; and, finally, that many arbitrators are not lawyers. In sum the Court holds that in a Section 1983 action, a Federal court should not afford *res judicata* or collateral estoppel effect to an arbitration award. However, the decision notes that an arbitration decision may be admitted into evidence in a Civil Rights Act suit.

The Supreme Court's recent decision in *United Paperworkers International Union v. Misco, Inc.*, decided December 1, 1987, provides the most up-to-date statement by that Court of its view of the arbitral process.

In *Misco*, the Supreme Court reviewed the Fifth Circuit's refusal to enforce an arbitration award ordering the reinstatement of an employee discharged for allegedly possessing marijuana on the plant premises. The Fifth Circuit set the award aside on public policy grounds and also reviewed the fact-finding aspect of the award, disagreeing with his treatment of the evidence. With respect to the public policy grounds, the Supreme Court held that a court's refusal to enforce an arbitrator's interpretation of a collective bargaining agreement is limited to situations where the contract, as interpreted by the arbitrator, would violate "some explicit public policy" that is "well defined and dominant, and is to be ascertained by reference to the laws and legal precedents and not from general considerations of supposed public interest." The Supreme Court also held that the Fifth Circuit exceeded the limited authority possessed by a court reviewing an arbitrator's award when it reached a different evaluation of the evidence and disregarded the facts found by the arbitrator.

The Supreme Court's view of the arbitral process is set forth in the following excerpt from *Misco*:

> Because the parties have contracted to have disputes settled by an arbitrator chosen by them rather than by a judge, it is the arbitrator's

> view of the facts and of the meaning of the contract that they have agreed to accept. Courts thus do not sit to hear claims of factual or legal error by an arbitrator as an appellate court does in reviewing decisions of lower courts. To resolve disputes about the application of a collective-bargaining agreement, an arbitrator must find facts and a court may not reject those findings simply because it disagrees with them. The same is true of the arbitrator's interpretation of the contract. The arbitrator may not ignore the plain language of the contract; but the parties having authorized the arbitrator to give meaning to the language of the agreement, a court should not reject an award on the ground that the arbitrator misread the contract. *Enterprise Wheel, supra*, at 599. So, too, where it is contemplated that the arbitrator will determine remedies for contract violations that he finds, courts have no authority to disagree with his honest judgment in that respect. If the courts were free to intervene on these grounds, the speedy resolution of grievances by private mechanisms would be greatly undermined. Furthermore, it must be remembered that grievance and arbitration procedures are part and parcel of the ongoing process of collective bargaining. It is through these processes that the supplementary rules of the plant are established. As the Court has said, the arbitrator's award settling a dispute with respect to the interpretation or application of a labor agreement must draw its essence from the contract and cannot simply reflect the arbitrator's own notions of industrial justice. But as long as the arbitrator is even arguably construing or applying the contract and acting within the scope of his authority, that the court is convinced he committed serious error does not suffice to overturn his decision. Of course, decisions procured by the parties through fraud or through the arbitrator's dishonesty need not be enforced. But there is nothing of that sort involved in this case.

Misco thus stresses the primacy of the arbitrator as a fact-finder and interpreter of the collective bargaining agreement. See also *Sheet Metal Workers Local 20 v. Baylor Heating and Air Conditioning, Inc.* (7 Cir., decided June 13, 1989).

At the end of its 1987–1988 term, the Supreme Court issued another decision defining the role of courts on questions of state law involving labor-management relations. In *Lingle v. Norge Division of Magic Chef, Inc.*, — U.S. — , 56 U.S.L.W. 4512, decided June 6, 1988, the Court made it "clear that the interpretation of collective-bargaining agreements remains firmly in the arbitral realm" and that the role of courts in determining such questions was only operative "if such questions do not require construing collective-bargaining agreements."

Lingle involved an employee who filed a complaint in July 1985, in the Illinois Circuit Court, alleging that she had been discharged in December 1984 for filing a worker's compensation claim. Prior to the court complaint, the union representing Lingle had filed a grievance pursuant to its collective bargaining agreement with Norge Division. The agreement protected employees from discharge except for "proper" or "just" cause, and contained a procedure for the arbitration of grievances. Following the filing of the state court action, Norge Division removed the case to the Federal District Court on the basis of diversity of citizenship, and then filed a motion praying that the Court either dismiss the case on pre-emption grounds or stay further proceedings pending the completion of the arbitration. The District Court dismissed Lingle's complaint on the basis that the claim for retaliatory discharge was "inextricably intertwined" with the collective bargaining provision prohibiting wrongful discharge or discharge without just cause and that allowing the state-law action to proceed would undermine the contractual arbitration procedures. The Seventh Circuit agreed with the District Court and rejected Lingle's argument that the disposition of the retaliatory discharge claim did not depend upon an intepretation of the collective bargaining agreement. The Seventh Circuit also concluded that the same analysis of facts was involved under both the state court procedure and the arbitration.

In its decision, the Supreme Court first reiterated the principle of Section 301 pre-emption developed in *Lucas Flour*,[8] i.e.,

> if the resolution of a state-law claim depends upon the meaning of a collective-bargaining agreement, the application of state law (which might lead to inconsistent results since there could be as many state-law principles as there are states) is pre-empted and federal labor-law principles—necessarily uniform throughout the nation—must be employed to resolve the dispute.

After analyzing the elements of proof necessary to show a retaliatory discharge the Court concluded that neither element, the discharge or the motive, required a court to interpret any term of the collective bargaining agreement. Thus, Section 301 did not pre-empt Lingle's state court action.

The Supreme Court's view should be examined in light of the three prevailing schools of thought among arbitrators. The first, propounded by David Feller and Bernard Meltzer, among others, holds that arbitrators in grievance arbitrations should not consider external law or public policy unless clearly directed otherwise by the parties or if the action complained of is clearly required by external law even in violation of the contract. The second school, of which the late Robert Howlett was a chief advocate, teaches that arbitrators should not avoid statutory or common law questions in making decisions. The middle ground, held by Richard Mittenthal, among others, is that external law and public policy can be considered under certain circumstances. Thus, where the employer seeks to justify action in violation of the contract on the ground it was required by law, external law should be applied. Where the employer complies with the contract but the claim is that he should comply with the law, the arbitrator should base his decision on the contract, where such decision does not conflict with clear decisional or statutory law. Where such a conflict occurs, some arbitrators have declined to issue an award, but have pointed out to the parties what they believe the contract means.

In a late 1988 decision, *Roadmaster Corp. v. Production & Maintenance Employees Local 504, etc.*,[9] involving a broad management rights clause, and a clause denying the arbitrator the power to add to or subtract from the terms of the contract, the Seventh Circuit laid down its rules for arbitrators on the issue of external law. The Court held that an arbitrator, when resolving a grievance under a contract, may not consider outside "positive law" in making a decision, even if the decision conflicts with federal statutory law. The Court cites *Alexander v. Gardner-Denver Co.*, where the Supreme Court held that "the arbitrator, however, has no general authority to invoke public laws that conflict with the bargain between the parties." Thus, states the Seventh Circuit, an arbitrator can use outside law only when specifically authorized by the contract. The Court notes that if an arbitrator's decision is based solely upon the arbitrator's view of the requirements of enacted legislation rather than on an interpretation of the collective bargaining agreement, the arbitrator has exceeded the scope of the submission and the award will not be enforced.

Although the Supreme Court has thus far given the labor arbitrator a very limited role in the application of external law, the Court has not similarly circumscribed commercial arbitrators. In *Mitsubishi Motors Corporation v. Soler Chrysler-Plymouth, Inc.*, 473 U.S. 614 (1985), a Japanese manufacturer sued a Puerto Rican corporation under the Federal Arbitration Act to compel an arbitration in Japan pursuant to the arbitration clause in their contract. The Puerto Rican corporation counterclaims raised various issues including violation of the Sherman Act, the anti-trust law. Reversing the First Circuit, which had held the submission of the anti-trust claims to be improper, the Supreme Court directed the arbitration sought even as to the anti-trust issues.

It may be argued that *Mitsubishi* should be viewed as applying to arbitration agreements in international transactions, because the majority opinion noted that certiorari was granted primarily to consider whether an American court should enforce an agreement to resolve anti-trust claims by arbitration when that agreement arises from an international transaction. However, several broad statements by the majority may arguably indicate a change by the majority in its limited view of the arbitrator's ability to deal with and resolve statutory issues. Thus, the majority opinion held that there was no warrant in the Arbitration Act for implying in every contract within its ken a presumption against arbitration of statutory claims; nor was there any reason to depart from the federal policy favoring arbitration where a party bound by the arbitration agreement raises claims founded on statutory rights. Regarding the arbitration process, the Court noted that the potential complexity of anti-trust matters did not suffice to ward off arbitration; nor did an arbitration panel pose too great a danger of innate hositility to the constraints on business conduct that anti-trust law imposed. Referring to *Steelworkers v. Warrior & Gulf Navigation Co.*, 363 U.S. 574 (1960), part of the *Trilogy*, the Court stated that any doubts regarding the scope of arbitration issues should be resolved in favor of arbitration, whether the problem is the construction of contract language or an allegation of waiver, delay, or a like defense to arbitrability. In language directly opposed to that of Justice Brennan in *McDonald v. City of West Branch*, discussed above, the Court states that "we are well past the time when judicial suspicion of the desirability of arbitration and of the competence of arbitral tribunals inhibited the development of arbitration as an alternative means of dispute resolution." Conceding that not all controversies implicating statutory rights are suitable for arbitration, the majority places the burden on Congress to expressly provide in statutes "any category of claims as to which agreements to arbitrate will be held unenforceable."

The significance of the majority's pronouncements must be measured against the vigorous dissent which claimed that the policy favoring arbitration should not cover alleged violations of federal law; that the Arbitration Act does not cover claims under federal law; that it was unreasonable to assume that Congress intended to give arbitrators final authority to implement federal statutory policy, citing *Alexander v. Gardner-Denver, Barrentine*, and *McDonald*; that arbitrations effectuate the intent of parties rather than the requirements of enacted legislation, the courts being the forums responsible for the resolution of statutory and constitutional issues; that arbitrators are chosen because of their knowledge and judgment in their respective areas of specialization; and that the informal procedures in arbitration are inadequate to develop a record for appellate review of constitutional and statutory questions.

In June 1987, the Supreme Court again reiterated its view that statutory claims should not bar implementation of an arbitration agreement. In *Shearson/American Express, Inc. v. McMahon*, 107 S. Ct. 2332 (1987), customers of a stockbroker started a court action against the broker claiming tort, securities fraud, and civil RICO violations. The broker claimed that the customers were bound by their agreement to arbitrate disputes. Siding with the broker, the Supreme Court held that claims under Section 10(b) of the Securities Act were arbitrable and that the customers could effectively vindicate their RICO claims against the broker in the arbitral forum. The Majority opinion echoed its *Mitsubishi* position regarding Congressional intent by placing the burden on the party opposing arbitration to show that Congress intended to preclude a waiver of judicial remedies for statutory rights at issue. Holding that the Securities Act did not manifest a Congressional intent to require claims to be resolved in a judicial forum rather than by arbitration, the Court found that the customers' agreements to submit to arbitration was not an impermissible waiver of rights under the Act. As to the RICO aspect of the claims, the Court held that the potential complexity of RICO suits did not preclude enforcement of the arbitration agreement as to these claims; nor did the overlap between the civil and criminal provisions of RICO render civil claims non-arbitrable. The dissent concurred in enforcing arbitration on the RICO claims but disagreed that the Securities Exchange Act claims were subject to arbitration.

On May 15, 1989, in *Rodriguez de Quijas et al. v. Shearson/American Express, Inc.*, No. 88-885, the Court held that disputes between investors and brokers arising under the Securities Act of 1933 must be resolved by arbitration. The majority overturned a 1953 case, calling it "inconsistent with prevailing uniformity of construction of other federal statutes governing arbitration agreements in the setting of *business transactions* [emphasis added]."

Thus, in commercial arbitrations the latest Supreme Court position is that arbitrators are capable of dealing with anti-trust issues, civil RICO violations, and claims under the Securities Act. Significantly, the majority decisions did not overrule or directly undercut the decisions in which the statutory protections afforded to individuals by the Civil Rights Act and the FLSA are kept from adjudication by arbitrators. An obvious explanation for the Court's non-action in the latter areas is that the *Mitsubishi* and *Shearson* cases were commercial arbitration cases involving sophisticated parties or parties with substantial economic power, who did not require the degree of protection which persons subject to civil rights discrimination or FLSA violations require. Nonetheless the enhanced role which the Court has given to the arbitral process in dealing with claims of anti-trust, RICO, and Securities Act violations may be the harbinger of change in the Court's treatment of statutory claims in the labor arbitral process.

V. The Arbitral Process in Operation

The varying philosophies of arbitrators and the standards of the courts and the NLRB pose very concrete problems for the arbitrator and the parties. The views of two very experienced arbitrators on the issue of dealing with external law in arbitrations are pertinent and enlightening.

The first arbitrator minced no words: "Arbitrators should not entertain questions of external law." Her usual experience has been that parties do not present testimony or evidence adequate to enable the arbitrator to handle issues of external law. Nor do parties properly brief the issues. As a result the arbitrator is left on her own. This arbitrator believes that the parties want the arbitrator to take the narrowest approach possible; that in selecting the arbitrator, they want the arbitrator's expertise. Thus, the arbitrator should not rely on or use decisions of other arbitrators. Further, if the arbitrator deals with all questions, an appeal is virtually certain. However, if the case is Collyered *and* the parties prepare the case properly *and* request the arbitrator to decide the issues, she will deal with the external law questions. This arbitrator notes that in the Federal sector, appeals of arbitrators' decisions are often based upon the arbitrator's failure to consider outside laws.

The other veteran arbitrator, a member of this committee, sets forth in detail his thinking on the issue of dealing with external law:

These standards place a responsibility upon the parties as well as the arbitrator. And it is a responsibility which one or the other party may be unwilling to meet. The parties must present not only the contractual allegations and defenses to the arbitrator, but also those relevant to the ULP. Suppose that the charging party desires to have the opportunity for a Board review decision if the arbitration award is unfavorable. That party may refuse to litigate issues which are raised in the charge but which are not considered to be crucial in the proceedings under the contract. How does the arbitrator compel the submission of matters which one or the other party eliminates from the case it wishes to litigate before him?

In NLRB cases, the arbitrator may have a clear idea of what the alleged statutory issues are. The Board charge involved in the case deferred to arbitration will set forth the alleged violations of the Act. Often, in a disciplinary matter, the charge will allege that the employer's reason for imposing the discipline at issue is a subterfuge and that the real reasons involve actions prohibited by the Act.

Can the arbitrator direct the parties to set forth evidence on all the matters covered by the charge? Does a deferral confer upon the arbitrator the authority to compel a presentation which at least one party is unwilling to undertake? How does the arbitrator enforce such a requirement if one of the parties is willing—or eager—to return to the Board in the event of an unfavorable outcome?

Another equally interesting question is what the arbitrator is to do if both parties *do* meet the standards for deferral. Where the issues to be decided are entirely factual, no problem is presented. The issues of fact are determined on the basis of evidence or credibility, or both.

But what if issues of law are presented? Does the arbitrator decide within the "four corners of the contract"? As noted above, many practitioners and parties have argued over the years that this is the proper standard. Other arbitrators and advocates have argued that the arbitrator must apply the principles of the statutory and decisional law and should not promulgate an award which is *ultra vires*. What if the arbitrator misinterprets the law in such a case?[10] Zimny, interpreting a Supreme Court decision on another issue, i.e., *Alexander v. Gardner-Denver*, contends that an

> arbitral decision must be based on contractual rights not the requirements of enacted legislation, regardless of whether certain of these contractual rights are duplicative of statutory ones.

But, at least as far as NLRA law is concerned, Judge Posner wrote that an arbitration award should not be vacated because of an error of law. *Jones Dairy Farm v. Local P-1236, United Food and Chemical Workers*, 760 F.2d 173 (7th Cir. 1985) *revising* 755 F.2d 583 (7th Cir. 1985).

An even broader protection of an award based on the contract arises from the decision in *W.R. Grace & Co. v. Local Union 759*, 461 U.S. 757 (1983), and its progeny. In *Grace*, the Court ruled:

> If the contract as interpreted by Barrett violates some explicit public policy, we are obliged to refrain from enforcing it. Such a public policy, however, must be well defined and dominant, and is to be ascertained "by reference to the laws and legal precedents and not from general considerations of supposed public interest."

This position was further elucidated in *Misco, supra*. This analyst insists that it is for the court and not for the arbitrator to interpret and apply law and public policy.

The problem becomes more difficult when the overlapping issue involves questions of contract interpretation and also involves allegation that a statute other than the NLRA has been violated. In these cases, unless the contract incorporates the external law, the statutory issue has not been placed before the arbitrator by some deferral of an administrative agency. The issues which may arise in this way encompass many of the questions which arbitrators face.

Was a failure to hire or a discharge a violation of the protections of equal employment statutes as well as of contract prohibitions against discrimination on the basis of race, nationality, age, and sex? Was a condition in the workplace violative of a contractual safety provision as well as of various state and federal enactments concerning occupational safety and work conditions? Did a discipline go beyond contractual questions concerning the right to refuse orders on the basis of an imminent danger of health or safety and involve rights under occupational safety enactments? Was an alleged failure to make overtime payments or a direction to work certain hours not only an alleged violation of contract provisions but also an alleged violation of statutes such as the Fair Labor Standards Act?

Parties have urged arbitrators to consider the statutory as well as the contract questions. Where the contract incorporates external law, the arbitrator must consider such issues. In these cases, the parties must assume the responsibility of selecting an arbitrator competent to decide the statutory as well as the contractual issues. They well may be bound by the award even where a misinterpretation of the statutory requirements arises.[11]

Even where the contract deals with matters covered by external law, court decisions have provided that further proceedings may occur in administrative agencies and in the courts. Such was the result in the equal employment dispute adjudicated in *Alexander v. Gardner-Denver.*[12] A similar result was reached in a FLSA decision, *Barrentine v. Arkansas Best-Freight System.*[13]

It is suggested that the parties may not avoid other forums with concurrent jurisdiction by proceeding to arbitration. The arbitrator's authority and expertise is based upon an understanding of contracts and their application. Nothing prevents the parties from entering into a separate stipulation that they will accept an award as dispositive of the issues arising in other forums if the law allows such stipulation. On the other hand, as Zimny has written, if a contract "specifically incorporates external law, an arbitrator must construe external law."[14]

Unless the grievants freely enter into such a stipulation, the parties cannot take the right to further proceedings from individuals in any case. Such is the message of the courts' rulings in EEO, FLSA, and other matters.

There are examples of situations where the contract has replaced other law. The State of New York and the Public Employees Federation have agreed in their 1985–1988 agreement (and in a number of predecessor contracts) that[15]

> The disciplinary procedure set forth in this Article shall be in lieu of the procedure specified in Section 75 and 76 of the Civil Service Law and shall apply to all persons currently subject to Section 75 and 76 of the Civil Service Law.

By this provision the parties substituted a contract procedure leading to final and binding arbitration for a hearing officer process whose result could be appealed to the courts.

On the other hand, this same agreement, in the article on contract interpretation as opposed to disciplinary grievances, excludes from the process and hence from arbitration[16]

> . . . Other disputes for which other means of resolution are provided or foreclosed by this Agreement, or by statute or administrative procedures applicable to the State. . . .

VI. Litigators' Views

When a grievance reaches the arbitration stage, it usually has gone through the various steps of the grievance procedure during which processing the issues have been framed without the guidance of the litigator. There are, of course, exceptions to this rule. Therefore, when faced with the arbitration hearing, the litigator must appraise the case to determine whether contractual and/or statutory issues are involved and what approach to take in placing the issues before the arbitrator. In coming to a decision, the litigator must perforce keep in mind the Supreme Court's views, discussed above, on the role of the arbitrator in handling issues of external law.

To aid in reaching this decision, the litigator has available educational courses and materials covering the theory and practice of the arbitral process. With respect to the performance and thinking of individual arbitrators, as well as evaluations of arbitrators by parties, there are several services which may be consulted. In addition, of course, a litigator can research the past opinions of arbitrators.

Two schools of thought are apparent among litigators. The first seeks to have the arbitrator dispose of all issues and avoid multiple litigation. Thus, followers of this first school would place all issues specifically before the arbitrator and urge disposition of them under the contract and/or applicable external law. Those arbitrators who decline to apply external law might not be chosen for future cases. These litigators recognize that their position may make arbitrations more complex and legalistic, thus negating some of the positive factors of the arbitral process. However, they argue, this is the inevitable result of pressures by regulatory agencies, particularly the NLRB, and by the courts to use arbitrations as a way to reduce their caseloads. Even if the arbitrator's resolution of the external law issue is not binding on the court or agency, the arbitral decision may have great weight before the agency or court.[17]

Reflecting Justice Brennan's remarks about the arbitral process in the *McDonald* case, the second school of litigators seeks to keep issues of external law away from arbitrators for the reason that arbitrators are either not trained to, or are reluctant to, deal with statutory issues. Further, a full exposition of the statutory issue cannot be had in an arbitration because of the absence of pre-trial discovery and the limited subpoena procedures. Many unions and individual complainants desire the full protection of the agencies which adminster the external law, e.g., the NLRB, EEOC, OSHA, or the Department of Labor. In *Taylor v. NLRB*, discussed above, the Eleventh Circuit found that the NLRB's *Olin* standards did not sufficiently protect the employee's rights because although contractual and statutory issues may be factually parallel, different elements of proof and factual relevance are involved. Of course, an answer to the latter arguments is to make arbitral procedures more legalistic. However, as noted above, the *McDonald* and *Misco* decisions may well retard any trend toward more legalistic procedures.

VII. Conclusions

Central to any consideration of the arbitrator's role in cases involving external law must be the understanding that arbitration is a voluntary process, that the arbitrator is a creature of that process and that the arbitrator's authority is largely circumscribed by the contract between the parties. Thus, in *Misco* the Supreme Court stressed that "the grievance and arbitration procedures are part and parcel of the ongoing process of collective bargaining" and that "the arbitrator's award settling a dispute with respect to the interpretation or application of a labor agreement must draw its essence from the contract and cannot simply reflect the arbitrator's own notions of industrial justice." Although the arbitrator "may not ignore the plain language of the contract," his award cannot be rejected because he "misread the contract." Given the voluntary nature of the arbitration, the parties have wide latitude to make of the process what they wish, i.e., to determine its scope and direction. Another important element in the process is supplied by the varying philosophies of the arbitrators regarding the application of external law.

The potential of the arbitral process as a means of resolving disputes between employers, labor organizations, and employees has, as the Supreme Court noted in *Lingle*, certain limitations:

> This Court has, on numerous occasions, declined to hold that individual employees are, because of the availability of arbitration, barred from bringing claims under federal statutes. See, e.g., *McDonald v. West Branch*, 466 U.S 284 (1984); *Barrentine v. Arkansas-Best Freight System, Inc.*, 450 U.S. 728 (1981); *Alexander v. Gardner-Denver Co.*, 415 U.S. 36 (1974). Although the analysis of the question under each statute is quite distinct, the theory running through these cases is that notwithstanding the strong policies encouraging arbitration, "different considerations apply *where the employee's claim is based on rights arising out of a statute designed to provide minimum substantive guarantees to individual workers.*" *Barrentine, supra*, 450 U.S., at 737. *Atchison, T. & S.F.R. Co. v. Buell*, 480 U.S. __ , (1987) [emphasis added].

With *Lingle*, the Supreme Court has further narrowed the potential scope of arbitration by declining to impose a section 301 preemption on claims made under state law which do not require the interpretation of a collective bargaining agreement.

It is against this background that the NLRB's deferral doctrine should be examined. The principle of that doctrine is that the Board will stay its processes with regard to an alleged unfair labor practice where the subject matter of the unfair labor practice charge is involved in or related to a grievance which is subject to the grievance-arbitration procedure of a contract. The Board does not refer the alleged unfair labor practice to the arbitral process for adjudication; the Board only states that after the grievance-arbitration machinery has done its work, the resulting disposition and its effect on the alleged unfair labor practice will be examined under the *Olin* standards: (1) Was the contractual issue factually parallel to the unfair labor practice issue? (2) Was the arbitrator presented generally with the facts relevant to resolving the unfair labor practice? and (3) Was the arbitrator's award not susceptible to an interpretation consistent with the Act?

At this point, it may be appropriate to speculate how the Board's deferral doctrine might fare in the Supreme Court, particularly in view of the Court's reaffirmation of the principle that arbitration does not bar claims of employees alleging violations of rights under federal statutes, and the Court's decision in *Lingle*. If the Court takes a pro-employee viewpoint, it might hold that the Board has impermissibly delegated to the arbitrator the Board's remedial powers under the NLRA. Or, the Court might find that the *Olin* standards are too loose and substantially undermine employee rights under the NLRA. Still another possibility is that the Court will accept the *Olin* standards as a permissible exercise of the Board's discretion in its administration of the Act, noting that the Board reserves the right and power not to defer to the arbitrator's award.

The last mentioned position appears the most probable in view of the Supreme Court's pronouncement in *N.L.R.B. v. Acme Industrial Co.*[18] that the Board is not "automatically" required "to defer to the primary determination of an arbitrator," and its earlier position in *Carey v. Westinghouse Electric Corp.*,[19] that if the Board disagrees with the arbiter, "the Board's ruling would, of course, take precedence. . . ."

Given the above background, of which it must be assumed that knowledgeable parties are aware, it is clear that the parties themselves largely hold the key to whether and to what extent the unfair labor practice will be presented to the arbitrator. The arbitrator supplies the other part of that equation, i.e., the willingness to hear and determine the unfair labor practice. The Board's deferral action may also influence the parties in their case presentations to the arbitrator.

In examining the motives of parties for presenting or not presenting issues of external law to arbitrators, it must be kept in mind that arbitration is in a very large sense a part of the collective bargaining process and a substitute for industrial warfare. The Supreme Court in footnote 11 of *Lingle* noted that, "Arbitrators are delegated by nearly all collective-bargaining agreements as the adjudicators of contract disputes."

The preparation and presentation of cases by litigators is usually determined by the wishes of the client, influenced to a certain degree by the advice and counsel of the litigator. This process produces a variety of motives for and against presenting issues of external law to arbitrators.

Most of these views have already been discussed above. To these must be added a motive for not presenting external law issues to an arbitrator, which is prevalent in a substantial number of bargaining relationships; namely, the exhaustion of the resources of the opposite side by multiple litigations. Although this tactic may achieve the desired goal, the failure promptly to resolve disputes may produce other, and undesirable, results. Thus, the basic grievance persists and festers and can give rise to more grievances. Unresolved grievances tend to undermine the relationship of the parties and to affect employee morale and production, thus producing a modified form of industrial strife. Clearly, the use of this tactic conflicts directly with arbitration's avowed objective of being a substitute for industrial warfare.

The multiplicity of factors in the arbitral process and the nature of the process itself, in the opinion of the Committee, preclude a recommendation for a course of actions which all participants in the process should follow. The thrust of the Supreme Court decisions discussed above is to confine arbitrators to the resolution of contractual disputes and to undermine if not vitiate arbitrators' decisions on external law. However, the Board's *Olin* doctrine and the courts' willingness to give weight to arbitral decisions dealing with external law will lead a substantial number of litigators to present such issues to arbitrators. For these practitioners, the following may serve as a guide to handling issues of external law in arbitrations:

1. Where both parties wish to present the unfair labor practice or other issue of external law to the arbitrator, the arbitrator should be explicitly directed by the parties to consider and rule on the questions of external law. If the parties wish to have external law questions handled in all their arbitrations, the collective bargaining agreement should provide so explicitly. Parties should also consider stipulating that they will accept awards dispositive of external law issues which can be used in other forums.

The parties should also make all efforts to present the witnesses and other evidence bearing on these questions. Particular attention should be paid to the procedures at the arbitration to ensure that they are "fair and regular." Experience has shown that occasionally the parties' intentions can be frustrated by an arbitrator who will decline to consider the questions of external law, regardless of the wishes of the parties. Where the arbitrator's position is known to the parties before the hearing, they may wish to reconsider their choice of arbitrator. If the arbitrator makes his/her position known during the hearing, the parties will have several courses of action, depending on whether the arbitrator is declining to rule on matters of external law but will consider the evidence and find facts or whether the arbitrator is refusing to consider any evidence on such matters. In the former case, the parties may conclude that the admission of the evidence and fact-finding will satisfy the NLRB or other reviewing agency, whereas the latter course taken by the arbitrator would totally frustrate the parties' intentions and may impel them to seek another arbitrator.

2. When one party desires to present the external law issue to the arbitrator and the other party resists such presentation, complications arise. First, the arbitrator may decline to hear any evidence on the external law issue unless both parties so direct the arbitrator or the contract requires such consideration. If the objecting party declines to join in such a direction, that may close the matter for the particular arbitration. In some situations, the objecting party may only decline to present its evidence on the external law issue while specifically not objecting to the arbitrator's consideration of whatever evidence the other side adduces on that issue. In this latter case, the use of subpoenas should be considered to obtain from the opposing party the evidence needed for the external law presentation. The arbitrator also should be requested to require production of necessary evidence on the external law issue by the non-cooperating party.

The Committee recognizes that placing all issues in front of the arbitrator, whether they relate to contractual interpretation or external law, could result in expeditious dispute resolution and the avoidance of duplicative litigation, goals which judicial authorities and the industrial community, including many unions, have sought to achieve. The high cost and slowness of civil litigation, coupled with the decline in effectiveness and speed of regulatory agencies as contrasted with the relatively low cost and faster arbitral process, point to arbitration as the more effective and efficient method of dispute resolution. Although on issues of external law not involving the NLRA, e.g., race and sex discrimination or OSHA, there are no deferral doctrines, and these issues may be carried to administrative agencies and courts, experience has demonstrated that arbitrators' decisions on these issues of external law are accorded great weight by courts and administrative agencies. Further, in the majority of cases with external law issues, the parties do not go further than the arbitration award.

Notwithstanding the apparent advantages of arbitral treatment of external law issues, the Committee notes that the views of the Supreme Court and Circuit Courts concerning the handling of external law by arbitrators strongly negates such a role. In an unbroken line of cases starting with *Gardner-Denver*, the Court has defined the arbitrator's authority as being derived from the collective bargaining agreement and the arbitrator's role as interpreting that agreement. The *McDonald* case detailed the disabilities of the arbitral process in dealing with statutory rights and attributed to the arbitrator's decision only a peripheral value.

Complementing the Supreme Court's view is that of many arbitrators, set forth above in detail, that an arbitrator should not consider external law or public policy unless clearly directed otherwise by the parties or if the action complained of is clearly required by external law even in violation of the collective bargaining agreement. As noted, this is the view of David Feller. Significantly, Mr. Feller was the principal author of the brief filed in *Misco* on behalf of the National Academy of Arbitrators.

In practice, the dual forces of the Supreme Court's decisions and the parallel arbitral theory (Feller's) have influenced a substantial number, if not the majority, of arbitrators to avoid dealing with issues of external law. As a result, the litigator desiring to present external law issues to an arbitrator is faced with so many obstacles both in the arbitration and in subsequent court or agency review, as to cause second and even third thoughts about the proposed course of action.

This reluctance by arbitrators to deal with issues of external law may affect the NLRB's administration of the cases deferred under *Olin*. Where the arbitrator has not applied or considered Board law or has not gone into the evidence regarding the alleged statutory violations sufficiently, the Board will not have a valid basis for deferring to the award and will be required to consider the case *de novo*.

In conclusion, the Committee notes that this report makes no recommendations; its purpose is to set forth the status of the law, the various theories and practices regarding arbitral treatment of external law so that the litigator may make an informed choice when planning and trying an arbitration case.

Respectfully submitted,
June, 1989

Eugene S. Friedman
Chair

Lawrence H. Ross
Stanley M. Berman
Richard Michael Betheil
Jane Denkensohn
Marvin Dicker
David Lawrence Gregory
John T. Rose II
David I. Rosen
Robert Bruce Stulberg
Roy N. Watanabe
Albert X. Bader, Jr.
Linda Gail Bartlett
Joseph M. Bress
Sheldon Engelhard
Michael F. Hoellering
Evan J. Spelfogel
Katherine Van Wezel Stone
Jay W. Waks
Leona Lynn Barsky
Richard Harris Block
Leonard Leibowitz
Frances Milberg
Bertrand B. Pogrebin
James R. Sandner
Shailah Taylor Stewart
Dr. Maurice Benewitz
Daniel Silverman

The Committee wishes to thank former member Harold Richman for his substantial contribution in preparing this report.

The Committee also wishes to thank the following interns for their assistance in preparing this report: Regina Flaherty, John Bello, Joan Sullivan, and Thomas Saitta, all of St. John's University School of Law.

Notes

1. *Spielberg Manufacturing Company*, 112 NLRB 1080 (1955).
2. *Raytheon Company*, 140 NLRB 883 (1963).
3. 192 NLRB 837 (1971).
4. *Filmation Associates*, 227 NLRB 1721 (1977).
5. *Ernst Steel Corp.*, 217 NLRB 1069, fn. 1; *Lockheed Shipbuilding Co.*, 282 NLRB #41 (1986).
6. *Long Island College Hospital v. NLRB*, 566 F.2d 833, 845; *Commonwealth Gas Co.*, 218 NLRB 857, 858.
7. *Servair, Inc.*, 236 NLRB 1278 (1978).
8. *Teamsters v. Lucas Flour Co.*, 369 U.S. 95 (1962).
9. __ F.2d __ , 129 LRRM 2449 (7 Cir. 1988).
10. Max Zimny, "External Law: The Albatross of Arbitrators," in *Second Annual Labor and Employment Law Institute*, School of Law, University of Louisville (Fred Rothman & Co., 1986) 259.
11. *Wilko v. Swan*, 346 U.S. 427, 436 (1953).
12. 415 U.S. 36 (1974).
13. 450 U.S. 728 (1981).
14. Zimny, *op. cit.* 371.
15. Article 33, Section 33.1.
16. Article 34, Section 34.1(a).
17. *Owens v. Texaco, Inc.*, 48 FEP Cases 147 (5 Cir. 1988).
18. 385 U.S. 432, 436.
19. 375 U.S. 261, 272.

3

International Arbitration

A. SURVEY OF CASES

CASE DIGESTS

EMINENT DOMAIN—CONSTITUTIONALITY—FIFTH AMENDMENT—IRAN-U.S. CLAIMS TRIBUNAL

A federal statute authorizing a deduction from an Iran-U.S. Claims Tribunal award to reimburse the federal government for its arbitration costs was held by the U.S. Supreme Court to be constitutional and not in violation of the Fifth Amendment.

Following the seizure of the U.S. embassy in Tehran by Iranian nationals, Sperry filed suit in the U.S. district court against Iran and fifteen of its instrumentalities for breach of contract, conversion of property, and interference with business relations. Sperry successfully obtained a prejudgment attachment against Iranian assets in the United States. Subsequently, the United States and Iran entered into the Algiers Accords, which established the Claims Tribunal to hear claims against Iran by U.S. nationals.

Sperry filed a claim with the Claims Tribunal and entered into settlement negotiations with the Iranian government. An award reflecting the agreement reached in those negotiations was entered in favor of Sperry. Pursuant to a directive of the Secretary of the U.S. Treasury, the United States deducted 2 percent from the award as reimbursement for costs incurred in connection with actions before the Claims Tribunal.

An action was filed in the U.S. Court of Claims by Sperry, which alleged that the fees were "illegally exacted" and requested that the directive license be invalidated. In a bench ruling, the court held that the directive was unlawful and ordered the return of the deduction. On appeal, the court ruled that the deduction without compensation was unconstitutional because it amounted to a taking of property.

The United States appealed the decision, and the U.S. Supreme Court reversed. The Court found that the section of the statute authorizing the deduction is a "specific declaration by Congress that the deductions are intended to reimburse costs incurred by the United States." It agreed with the United States that the deduction was not a taking but rather a reasonable "user fee" assessed against claims before the Claims Tribunal to reimburse the U.S. for arbitration costs. The Court specifically noted that it "was never held that the amount of the user fee must be precisely calibrated to the use that a party makes of government services." It also distinguished *Sperry* from other cases because *Sperry* was "not a situation where the government has appropriated all, or most, of the award to itself and labelled the booty as a user fee." ***United States v. Sperry,*** ____ U.S. ____, 110 S. Ct. 387 (1989).

TERMINATION OF DISTRIBUTORSHIP AGREEMENT—ENFORCEMENT OF ARBITRATION AGREEMENT—ARBITRABILITY—ASSIGNMENT

Parties who agree to have all disputes arising out of or in connection with the distributorship agreement submitted to arbitration for resolution have agreed to submit issues of arbitrability to the arbitrator.

Apollo and Dicoscan entered into an agreement granting Dicoscan the right to distribute Apollo's computers in four Scandinavian countries. Helge Berg and Lars Arvid Skoog, chairman and president, signed the agreement on behalf of Dicoscan. The agreement also contained an arbitration agreement providing for the arbitration of disputes under the Rules of Arbitration of the International Chamber of Commerce (ICC), a clause stating that Massachusetts law would govern, and a nonassignment provision.

Apollo terminated the agreement after several disputes arose. Thereafter, Dicoscan filed for protection under Swedish bankruptcy law. The trustee assigned Dicoscan's right to bring claims against Apollo to Berg and Skoog, who filed a complaint and a request for arbitration with the ICC. Apollo rejected arbitration on the ground that there was no agreement to arbitrate and that arbitration was precluded by the nonassignment provision. The ICC ruled that the issues should be resolved by the arbitrator and directed the parties to proceed to arbitration. Apollo filed an action in federal court seeking a stay of arbitration. The court denied the request, and Apollo appealed.

The appellate court found that it had jurisdiction because the lower court's order resolved the only issue before it—Berg's and Skoog's right to compel arbitration—in its entirety. As for the arbitrability issue, the court first reviewed the lower court's opinion. It found that the lower court had determined that the "parties had explicitly agreed to have the issue of arbitrability decided by the arbitrator." On the issue of whether "the agreement's nonassignment clause prevented [Berg and Skoog] from asserting [Dicoscan's] right to arbitrate," the lower court ruled that "it did not because under Massachusetts law, a general nonassignment clause will be construed as barring only the delegation of duties, not the assignment of rights."

Agreeing with the lower court's reasoning, the appellate court declined to consider Apollo's arguments that the right to compel arbitration did not survive the termination of the agreement and that the nonassignment clause rendered the purported assignment unenforceable against Apollo. It found that the lower court was correct in finding that the parties had contracted to submit issues of arbitrability to the arbitrator. The court further stated that whether the right to compel arbitration survived the termination of the agreement and whether that right was validly assigned were issues of arbitrability relating to the continued existence and validity of the agreement which the parties had delegated to the arbitrator for resolution. In accordance with its findings, the court affirmed the lower court's order denying a permanent stay of arbitration. ***Apollo Computer, Inc. v. Berg,*** 886 F.2d 469 (1st Cir. 1989).

IRAN–U.S. CLAIMS TRIBUNAL—PROPER PARTY TO ARBITRATION

The court affirmed a lower court's determination that a party who had executed and entered into a contract containing an arbitration agreement as a joint obligor and on behalf of a joint venture may be required to arbitrate claims pursuant to that agreement.

TAMS, a New York consulting partnership, and AFFA, an Iranian engineering firm, created an Iranian entity (TAMS-AFFA) to perform services on the Tehran International Airport (TIA). In August 1975, the principals of TAMS and AFFA entered into a contract with Tehran-Berkeley, which agreed to perform soil exploration for the TIA project. A dispute arose and Tehran-Berkeley demanded arbitration, seeking payment from TAMS for work performed. TAMS refused to arbitrate and Tehran-Berkeley petitioned to compel arbitration. The federal district court dismissed the petition, ruling that TAMS was not a party to the contract on the basis that the contact was between Tehran-Berkeley and a "single counter-contracting 'party,' TAMS-AFFA."

On appeal, the court reversed and remanded, finding that where it was unclear whether a party had signed the agreement in an individual capacity, the district court erred in dismissing a petition to compel arbitration without conducting an evidentiary hearing. On remand, the district court concluded that "TAMS/AFFA as a joint venture . . . entered into this contract with Tehran-Berkeley" and that "TAMS, as a partner, is properly a party to arbitration, and such arbitration should be compelled." TAMS appealed, contending that the determination of the district court that TAMS-AFFA contracted as a joint venture with Tehran-Berkeley barred compelling TAMS to arbitrate Tehran-Berkeley's claim.

The appellate court disagreed and affirmed the district court's decision. It noted that TAMS and AFFA, rather than TAMS-AFFA, had executed and entered into the Tehran-Berkeley contract, leading the court to interpret the district court's ruling to mean that TAMS and AFFA executed the contract as joint obligors and on behalf of the TAMS-AFFA joint venture. Because TAMS and AFFA did execute the Tehran-Berkeley contract—which contained an arbitration agreement—as joint ventures, the court concluded that an arbitration agreement was established under section 4 of the Federal Arbitration Act. Consequently, Tehran-Berkeley could require TAMS to arbitrate its claims pursuant to the arbitration agreement. ***Tehran-Berkeley Civil and Environmental Engineers v. Tippetts-Abbett-McCarthy-Stratton,*** 888 F.2d 239 (2d Cir. 1989).

MARITIME—PRE-ARBITRAL ATTACHMENT—U.N. CONVENTION—IN PERSONAM JURISDICTION—FEDERAL ARBITRATION ACT

The court held that an arbitration agreement may be subject to the United Nations Convention on the Recognition and Enforcement of Foreign Arbitral Awards (U.N. Convention) even if one of the parties is from a nonsignatory nation so long as the agreement provides that arbitration will take place in a country that is a signatory nation. In addition, pre-arbitral arrest of a vessel is not inconsistent with the U.N. Convention, and an owner's appearance in personam gave the court jurisdiction to order arbitration.

E.A.S.T. time chartered a vessel, the *M/V Alaia*, from Advance. The charter party contained an arbitration clause. E.A.S.T. subsequently brought an action against Advance for breach of warranty of seaworthiness, claiming also that it was entitled to a maritime lien on the vessel. Pursuant to a warrant, the U.S. deputy marshall arrested the vessel. Two days later, Advance filed a notice of appearance in personam and moved to vacate the arrest. The district court found that the seizure was proper and that E.A.S.T.'s earlier filing of an in rem action under the Federal Arbitration Act (FAA) to compel arbitration provided a sufficient basis to refer the parties to arbitration. The court also stated that if there was any defect in its jurisdiction, it was cured by Advance's appearance in personam to defend E.A.S.T.'s action. Advance appealed, arguing that the court had erred in finding in rem jurisdiction a sufficient basis on which to refer the parties to arbitration and that pre-arbitral attachment is inconsistent with the U.N. Convention.

Noting at the outset that the order upholding the pre-arbitration arrest of the vessel is appealable, the appellate court went on to consider whether pre-arbitration arrest of a vessel is available under the U.N. Convention. It rejected E.A.S.T.'s argument that Advance could not avail itself of any defenses under the U.N. Convention because Liberia, the country where Advance is incorporated, is not a signatory to the U.N. Convention. The court, citing *La Société Nationale pour la Recherche, la Production, le Transport, la Transformation et la Commercialisation des Hydrocarbures v. Shaheen Natural Resources, Inc.*, 585 F. Supp. 57, 64 (S.D.N.Y. 1983), *aff'd*, 733 F.2d 260 (2d Cir. 1984), *cert. denied*, 469 U.S. 883 (1984), stated that the principle of reciprocity in the application of the U.N. Convention is "concerned with the forum in which arbitration will occur and whether that forum state is a signatory to the Convention—not with whether both parties to the dispute are nationals of signatory states." Because the parties provided for arbitration to take place in London, and Great Britain is a signatory, the court ruled that it "cannot conclude that Advance's Liberian nationality removes the arbitration provision in this charter party from the purview of the Convention."

The court went on to rule that pre-arbitral attachment of the vessel was not inconsistent with the U.N. Convention because section 8 of the FAA reserves the right of an aggrieved party in an admiralty case to employ traditional admiralty law procedures, including the arrest of a vessel. Since the U.N. Convention does not expressly forbid pre-arbitral attachment, the court found that such attachment may "serve [] as a security device in aid of arbitration."

As to the other issue raised by Advance, the court determined that the breach of a time charter may create a maritime lien and concluded that it need not rule on whether in rem jurisdiction is an adequate basis on which to refer the parties to arbitration because Advance had submitted to the court's in personam jurisdiction. ***E.A.S.T., Inc. of Stamford, Connecticut v. M/V Alaia,*** 876 F.2d 1168 (5th Cir. 1989).

IRAN–U.S. CLAIMS TRIBUNAL—SUBJECT-MATTER JURISDICTION—U.N. CONVENTION

The court affirmed the lower court's decision that under the U.N. Convention, federal courts have enforcement jurisdiction for arbitral awards issued by the Iran–U.S. Claims Tribunal.

Hoffman filed a claim before the Iran–U.S. Claims Tribunal, and Iran filed counterclaims. The tribunal issued its award in favor of Iran, which moved to confirm the award. Hoffman, in turn, moved to dismiss Iran's petition. The district court determined that although federal courts do not have enforcement jurisdiction under 28 U.S.C. § 1331, jurisdiction was obtainable under the U.N. Convention on the Recognition and Enforcement of Foreign Arbitral Awards (*Iran v. Gould*, No. CV 87-03673 RG (C.D. Cal. 1988)). Gould, which the tribunal substituted as claimant in lieu of Hoffman, appealed.

Gould argued that the district court lacked jurisdiction over the award's enforcement under the U.N. Convention because certain requirements were not met. The court, however, disagreed with Gould's contention that the U.S. government lacked the authority to enter into the written arbitration agreement as required under the U.N. Convention. It found that even if the U.S. government lacked such authority, the actions of the United States were ratified by Gould when Gould filed its claim and arbitrated it before the tribunal.

The court also disagreed with Gould's contention that because the tribunal's award "was a creature of international law, and not national law, it [did] not 'fall under' the U.N. Convention." The court found that there was no jurisdictional requirement that the arbitration award be rendered subject to a "national law." Consequently, it concluded that "an award need not be made 'under a national law' for a court to entertain jurisdiction over its enforcement pursuant to the [U.N.] Convention."

In accordance with its findings, the court concluded that enforcement jurisdiction existed under the U.N. Convention and affirmed the district court's decision. ***Ministry of Defense of the Islamic Republic of Iran v. Gould, Inc.,*** Nos. 88-5879, 88-5881 (9th Cir. Oct. 23, 1989).

FEDERAL ARBITRATION ACT—APPEALS—RETROACTIVE APPLICATION—MANIFEST INJUSTICE

The court held that retroactive application of an amendment to the Federal Arbitration Act was allowed because such retroactive application did not result in any manifest injustice to the parties.

Delta filed an action for an alleged breach of a distribution contract against Samsung. The district court directed the parties to proceed to arbitration in Seoul, Korea. Delta appealed.

The appellate court dismissed Delta's action. During the interim between Delta's filing of its Notice of Appeal and the date on which the case was ordered to be submitted, the Federal Arbitration Act (FAA) was amended to provide for a new section regarding appeals. The appellate court found that there was nothing in the text of the act amending the FAA, nor in its legislative history, that indicated an intent to preclude retroactive application of the amendment. It also found that retroactive application is not allowed when it would result in manifest injustice to the parties. The court concluded that the three factors used in determining whether manifest injustice exists—the nature and identities of the parties, the nature of their rights, and the nature of the impact of the change in law upon those rights—did not point toward such a finding. Consequently, the court applied the amendment "retroactively without hesitation in this case."

In addition, the court rejected Delta's argument that the district court's order was final, rather than interlocutory. The court also noted that the new amendment's exception for appeals pursuant to 28 U.S.C. § 1292(b) was inapplicable because there was no certification by the district court that the order "involve[d] a controlling question of law as to which there is substantial ground for difference of opinion and that an immediate appeal from the order may materially advance the ultimate termination of the litigation." It did, however, remand the case to the district court with instructions to permit Delta to apply for a section 1292(b) certification. ***Delta Computer Corp. v. Samsung Semiconductor & Telecommunications Co.***, 879 F.2d 662 (9th Cir. 1989).

MOTION TO CONFIRM—PERSONAL JURISDICTION—SUBJECT-MATTER JURISDICTION—WAIVER OF SOVEREIGN IMMUNITY—FOREIGN SOVEREIGN IMMUNITIES ACT

The court ruled that the Republic of Trinidad and Tobago implicitly waived its sovereign immunity, finding that the Republic's selection of its own law as the governing law for the dispute was not the same as providing that the Republic's courts had sole jurisdiction to enforce the arbitration award and that there was a waiver of immunity under the U.N. Convention. The court also ruled that the Republic could not assert the defense of lack of personal jurisdiction.

M.B.L. and the Republic of Trinidad and Tobago entered into a contract for the repair of airfield pavements by M.B.L. Disputes arose in the course of the performance of the contract. The parties agreed to submit the disputes to arbitration, and an award was rendered in favor of M.B.L. M.B.L. moved to confirm the award pursuant to the U.N. Convention on the Recognition and Enforcement of Foreign Arbitral Awards. The Republic moved to dismiss the motion on the ground that sovereign immunity precludes the court from exercising subject-matter and personal jurisdiction.

The issue before the court was whether the Republic had waived its sovereign immunity. The Republic argued that there was no waiver because the arbitration agreement provided that the law of Trinidad and Tobago governed the arbitration of the dispute. The court found that the agreement stated that the Republic's law would apply to the dispute, not that the Republic was willing to have the dispute settled only in its own courts. It further found that the Republic's "selection of its own law for the underlying dispute [was] not tantamount to providing that only [the Republic's] courts can enforce the arbitration award."

In addition, the court declined to accept the Republic's "contention that it did not waive its sovereign immunity by agreeing to arbitrate this dispute under the terms of the [U.N.] Convention," because to do otherwise "would defeat the very purpose of the [U.N.] Convention which is to provide for the enforcement of foreign arbitration awards."

The court also rejected the Republic's argument that the court lacked personal jurisdiction because of the Republic's insufficient contacts with the United States. It ruled that the Foreign Sovereign Immunities Act governed both personal and subject-matter jurisdiction, and that the Republic's implicit waiver of immunity constituted a waiver of the defense of lack of personal jurisdiction. ***M.B.L. International Contractors, Inc. v. Republic of Trinidad and Tobago,*** No. 89-1003 (D.C. Oct. 30, 1989).

U.N. CONVENTION—ENFORCEMENT OF ARBITRATION AGREEMENT—TORT CLAIMS—FEDERAL ARBITRATION ACT

The court held that the possibility that Italian law could divest a panel of Italian arbitrators of jurisdiction was not determinative of an American court's duty to enforce the arbitration agreement and that tort claims against nonparties to the arbitration agreement could be arbitrated.

DeKalb Agricultural Association and Antonio and Sergio Marchetto entered into a joint venture agreement to form DeKalb Italiana. The shareholder agreement contained a provision restricting the transfer of stock of DeKalb Italiana and was later amended to provide for arbitration of any shareholder disputes in Italy. Through a series of stock transfers, DeKalb Italiana was reorganized into three publicly traded companies, one of which was DeKalb Genetics. The Marchettos filed an action against all three publicly traded companies, alleging that the transfers of DeKalb Italiana stock violated the shareholder agreement. DeKalb Genetics moved to dismiss on the basis of the arbitration clause.

The court noted that courts must vigorously enforce arbitration agreements, that doubts over the agreement's validity must be resolved in favor of arbitration, and that the "strong presumption favoring enforcement of the arbitration clauses in international commercial agreements divests this court of substantial discretion in deciding whether to order arbitration." Finding that a written arbitration agreement existed, the agreement provided for arbitration in a signatory country, the agreement arose out of a commercial legal relationship, and the commercial transaction had a reasonable relationship to a foreign state, the court ruled that arbitration was mandatory under the U.N. Convention. In so ruling, the court rejected the claim by the Marchettos that per Italian law, the arbitration clause would not be enforceable since the three publicly traded companies were not parties to the arbitration agreement. It reasoned that the validity of an arbitration agreement is determined by reference to the Federal Arbitration Act and the federal substantive law of arbitrability, not by the possibility that a foreign country's law might divest a panel of that country's arbitrators of jurisdiction.

The court also ruled that federal law permits nonparties to an arbitration agreement to participate in the arbitration proceedings. Specifically, because one of the publicly traded companies was the successor corporation to DeKalb Agricultural, which was a party to the arbitration clause with the Marchettos, the other two companies may be jointed in the arbitration proceeding. The court was unpersuaded by the Marchettos' reliance on *Volt Information Sciences, Inc. v. Board of Trustees of Leland Stanford Junior University,* 489 U.S. ___, 109 S. Ct. 1248 (1989). It distinguished *Volt* on the ground that *Volt* was not a preemption case but instead involved a special incorporation clause providing for California law to apply. Because of this provision, the court determined that "*Volt* is restricted to its facts and has no bearing on this dispute." In accordance with its findings, the court concluded that the arbitration clause was valid and enforceable. ***Marchetto v. DeKalb Genetics Corporation,*** 711 F. Supp. 936 (N.D. Ill. 1989).

MARITIME—U.N. CONVENTION—CONFIRMATION OF AWARD—NOTICE—IMMUNITY—FOREIGN SOVEREIGN IMMUNITIES ACT—PREJUDGMENT ARREST OR ATTACHMENT

An arbitral award may be refused confirmation for failure to provide adequate notice of the arbitration proceedings. In addition, a mortgagee was not entitled to immunity under the Foreign Sovereign Immunities Act (FSIA).

Sesostris chartered two ships from Transportes under two separate charter party agreements. A dispute arose over the payment of subsidies, and Sesostris arrested and attached one of the vessels. Banco de Credito Industrial, S.A. (BCI) appeared in the court action, seeking release of the vessel as the mortgagee in possession. Pursuant to a stipulation, Sesostris agreed to the vessel's release on the condition that BCI post substitute security for Sesostris's claims, which BCI did. Several motions were filed by both sides, resulting in a stay of the court proceeding pending foreign arbitration under the charter parties. Communication between the parties was minimal, and shortly after BCI sought information regarding when and where arbitration was to proceed, it received notification from Sesostris that the arbitration proceeding had been concluded. On the basis of stipulated facts, a panel of three Spanish arbitrators rendered an award in favor of Sesostris, which moved for confirmation in an American federal court.

The court agreed with BCI's contention that it had not received proper notice of the foreign proceedings and rejected Sesostris's position that BCI had not received notice of the arbitration because BCI was not a proper party to the arbitration proceedings. The court recognized BCI as the proper party to the action because BCI claimed interest in the arrested vessel as mortgagee, maintained possession of the vessel ever since its release, and tendered substitute security from which Sesostris is seeking satisfaction. It concluded from the record of correspondence between the parties that BCI had not received adequate notice.

The court also declined to grant BCI immunity from prejudgment arrest or attachment per the FSIA. It found that BCI had failed to provide either sufficient proof of ownership of the vessel in question or that it was an agent of a foreign state. In addition, the court concluded that even if BCI had successfully proved otherwise, immunity would still have been inappropriate because there is no immunity from arrest or attachment where the property was "used for commercial activity" and that activity is the basis for the claim. Accordingly, the court refused to confirm the arbitration award and declined to grant BCI immunity under the FSIA. ***Sesostris, S.A.E. v. Transportes Navales, S.A.,*** 727 F. Supp. 737 (D. Mass. 1989).

CONSTRUCTION—ARBITRABILITY

The court held that claims against the prime contractor were arbitrable except those for tortious interference with fiduciary duties owed by the late President Marcos to the Philippine people. In addition, although claims against the subcontractor were not arbitrable, those claims that were similar to the arbitrable claims against the prime contractor would be stayed pending the outcome of arbitration between the government and the prime contractor.

National Power Corporation, the Philippine government agency responsible for electric power generation, entered into a contract with Westinghouse for the construction of a nuclear power plant. Prior to Westinghouse's being awarded the contract, a series of meetings and negotiations took place between Westinghouse and an intermediary to the government. After Marcos declared a state of martial law, he directed National to award the architect/engineering contract to Burns & Roe, which would work as subcontractors of Westinghouse. Finalization of the contract between National and Westinghouse took some time because National objected to many of the provisions proposed by Westinghouse, including one for arbitration. After all the issues were resolved, and the contract signed, several disputes arose. National then filed suit against Westinghouse, alleging breach of contract, fraud, conspiracy, and RICO and antitrust violations. Westinghouse moved to stay the action pending arbitration.

The court determined that all of the claims raised by National, except those of tortious interference with fiduciary duties, were arbitrable. It noted that the bribery charges should not be treated as fraud in the inducement nor, as National argued, as fraud in factum. The court determined that National could not use a fraud in factum claim to vitiate its assent to the agreement, thereby making the contract *void ab initio*, because "[t]here is no question but that the [National] officials negotiating the contract were fully aware of the nature of [the contract's] terms." Furthermore, because the arbitration clause used in the parties' contract was broadly worded, the court ruled that arbitration of the disputes was warranted.

The court did find, however, that claims for tortious interference with the fiduciary duties owed by Marcos to the people was not a matter for submission to arbitration because the Republic of the Philippines is not a party to the contract and, therefore, not bound directly by the arbitration clause. Accordingly, these claims were ordered stayed pending the outcome of arbitration. In addition, the court also ruled that National could not arbitrate its claims against Burns and Roe because they did not intend to arbitrate such claims. Where there was a similarity of claims between those against Burns and Roe and those against Westinghouse, the court ruled that those claims would be stayed pending the outcome of arbitration. ***Republic of the Philippines v. Westinghouse Electric Corporation,*** 714 F. Supp. 1362 (D.N.J. 1989).

FEDERAL RULES OF CIVIL PROCEDURE—U.N. CONVENTION—FEDERAL ARBITRATION ACT—STATE LAW—NEW YORK—UNILATERAL ADDITION

The court ruled that under New York law, an arbitration agreement that was unilaterally added to the parties' agreement became part of that agree-

ment. In addition, the action before the court was dismissed for lack of jurisdiction because the U.N. Convention on the Recognition and Enforcement of Foreign Arbitral Awards (U.N. Convention) applied.

Astor placed a verbal order with Mikroverk for the design, manufacture, and installation of a chocolate molding machine. Mikroverk confirmed the verbal order by a letter setting forth the specifications for the equipment, the purchase price, and other terms. The parties subsequently entered into an oral contract of sale, which was later confirmed by a letter containing a reference to arbitration. A problem arose over the molding machine's alleged failure to function according to Astor's requirements. Astor subsequently filed a breach of contract and breach of warranty action against Mikroverk, which moved for a dismissal pursuant to the Federal Rules of Civil Procedure 12(b)(1) or, in the alternative, a stay of the action pending arbitration.

The court noted at the outset Mikroverk's reliance on the Federal Arbitration Act (FAA) and the U.N. Convention for the enforcement of the arbitration agreement. It stated that because the scope of the arbitration agreement was not at issue, state and not federal law would govern since the issue before the court was whether or not the clause was part of the contract. Since New York law applied because it was the "state with the most contacts with the sales transaction," the court remarked that the arbitration agreement would be considered a part of the agreement if the arbitration agreement was explicit and unequivocal. The court found that these requirements were met and that Astor had had knowledge of the arbitration agreement. Because of such knowledge, the court deemed that the arbitration agreement was a unilateral addition by Mikroverk that became part of the parties' agreement. In addition, because there was a valid arbitration agreement, the court determined that the U.N. Convention mandated that Mikroverk's motion to dismiss for lack of jurisdiction must be granted. ***Astor Chocolate Corp. v. Mikroverk Ltd.***, 704 F. Supp. 30 (E.D.N.Y. 1989).

MOTION TO COMPEL ARBITRATION—ARBITRABILITY—FEDERAL ARBITRATION ACT—SCOPE OF ARBITRATION AGREEMENT

The Federal Arbitration Act mandates enforcement of arbitration agreements where the making of the agreement is not in question. In addition, the use of a broad arbitration clause rendered arbitrable a dispute over the contamination of cargo.

Mobil Petrochemical Sales and Supply entered into a contract of affreightment of ethylene glycol. The contract incorporated a charter party containing a broad arbitration clause. Mobil also entered into a sales contract with Nisso Petrochemicals Industries for the manufacture of ethylene glycol. The cargo was on board the M/T Brimanger when, en route from Saudi Arabia to Japan, it became contaminated by salt water. Other tanks on board—some owned by Dow Chemical—were also contaminated. Mobil filed suit against Brimanger and Odfjell (collectively, "Brimanger") seeking damages. It subsequently moved to compel arbitration pursuant to the Federal Arbitration Act (FAA) and the parties' contract. Brimanger argued that Mobil was actually seeking to arbitrate a claim against Dow Chemical, which was not a party to the contract of affreightment.

The court noted at the outset that the FAA mandates enforcement of arbitration agreements unless the making of the agreement is put into question. Because neither party contested the validity of the arbitration agreement, the court ordered arbitration to proceed. Finding that doubts concerning arbitrability are decided in favor of arbitration, the court held that the dispute regarding the contamination of Mobil's cargo was arbitrable, because it fell within the scope of a broad arbitration clause. ***Mobil Petrochemical Sales and Supply Corp. v. M/T Brimanger,*** 711 F. Supp. 131 (S.D.N.Y. 1989).

ARBITRATION AWARD—PREJUDGMENT INTEREST—EXCEPTIONAL CIRCUMSTANCES

Currency control problems experienced by a foreign government do not constitute "exceptional circumstances" so as to preclude prejudgment interest on an arbitration award.

Reefer Express Lines and the General Authority for Supply Commodities (GASC) were parties to an arbitration proceeding. The GASC is a department in the Ministry of Supply of the Government of Egypt. An award was rendered in favor of Reefer, which then moved for a court order for prejudgment interest. The GASC opposed, arguing that existing currency control problems experienced by the government constituted exceptional circumstances so as to preclude prejudgment interest on the award.

The court stated that the general rule is that "[p]rejudgment interest on an arbitration award is at the discretion of the district court" and that it "is usually permitted and should be granted 'in the absence of exceptional circumstances.'" As for the definition of "exceptional circumstances," the court found that case law shows that such circumstances exist where the "party *requesting* interest had delayed the proceedings or has made a bad faith estimate of damages. . . ." Because there was no charge of bad faith on the part of Reefer, and because the court found that the currency control problems do not constitute exceptional circumstances, the court ordered prejudgment interest on the arbitration award. ***Reefer Express Lines Pty., Ltd. v. General Authority for Supply Commodities,*** 714 F. Supp. 699 (S.D.N.Y. 1989).

MARITIME—EVIDENT PARTIALITY—
VACATUR OF AWARD—MANIFEST DISREGARD OF THE LAW—
CARRIAGE OF GOODS BY SEA ACT

The court refused to vacate an arbitration award because there was no evidence of evident partiality or manifest disregard of the law.

Southwind Shipping entered into a contract of affreightment with Nippon Steel & C. Itoh & Co., Ltd., for the transportation of cargo on a vessel that subsequently stranded and sank off an islet. Nippon and others filed a claim against Southwind in federal court. The parties were directed to proceed to arbitration pursuant to an arbitration clause in their affreightment contract that provided for arbitration in New York. Arbitration was held, and the panel rendered an award against Southwind. Southwind moved to vacate the award while Nippon cross-moved to confirm the award.

The court denied the motion to vacate the award. It disagreed with Southwind's contention that the award should be vacated because it improperly included awards to parties who, although named in the bills of lading, were not parties to the affreightment contract. The court, citing *Son Shipping v. De Fosse & Tanghe*, 199 F.2d 687 (2d Cir. 1952) and *Siderius, Inc. v. M.V. Ida Prima*, 613 F. Supp. 916, 919 (S.D.N.Y. 1985), found that "[a]n arbitration clause in a contract of affreightment is deemed incorporated in the bill of lading, and binding on the parties to the bill of lading if the bill of lading states that it is governed by the contract." In this case, the bill of lading had incorporated the terms of the affreightment contract.

In addition, the court rejected the arguments that the panel's decision was unsupported by the evidence and that the arbitrators were evidently partial and had manifestly disregarded the law. It ruled that there was no basis for finding either evident partiality or manifest disregard of the law because there was substantial evidence in the record to support the arbitrators' conclusions.

The court also rejected Southwind's argument that it was protected from liability by the "negligent navigation" exception in the Carriage of Goods by Sea Act on the ground that Southwind had had knowledge of the causative faults that contributed to the unseaworthiness of the vessel. It concluded that the findings of the arbitrators supported a conclusion of such knowledge. Consequently, the award was confirmed by the court. ***Complaint of Southwind Shipping Co., S.A.,*** 709 F. Supp. 79 (S.D.N.Y. 1989).

MARITIME—PERSONAL JURISDICTION—AGENCY—SERVICE

The court determined that a New York corporation was acting as a foreign corporation's agent, thereby subjecting the foreign corporation to the jurisdiction of a New York court. In addition, service on a foreign corporation's New York agent constituted proper service on the foreign corporation.

Ektrans is a Turkish corporation that is part of a group of closely held corporations owned and controlled by the Ekinci family. One of these other corporations, Ekco, has offices in New York, which Ektrans used as an American collection and disbursement office. Because of the quality of the firm's contracts with the forum state, as well as the continuous, permanent, and substantial activity in the state, the court found that the facts and circumstances in this case indicated that personal jurisdiction was proper over Ektrans. It also found that service on the New York offices of Ekco constituted proper service on Ektrans because Ekco served as agent for Ektrans. Finally, the court rejected the other claims of lack of venue and *forum non conveniens* argued by Ektrans on the ground that Ektrans had failed to sustain its burden of proof. Because Ektrans had failed to show that New York Marine Managers or its subrogor Orban had actual or constructive notice of a governing charter party, the arbitration clause in the charter party was not binding on them. ***New York Marine Managers, Inc. v. M.N. Topor-1***, 716 F. Supp. 783 (S.D.N.Y. 1989).

DEALERSHIP AGREEMENTS—PREEMPTION—FEDERAL ARBITRATION ACT—ANTITRUST—PUERTO RICO

The Federal Arbitration Act (FAA) requires enforcement of an arbitration clause in a distributorship agreement, despite local antitrust law prohibiting the arbitration of disputes arising under such agreements.

GKG Caribe, Inc., a Puerto Rican corporation doing business as Cellular One, entered into an exclusive distributor agreement with Nokia-Mobira, Inc., a Florida corporation, for the exclusive distribution of Nokia-Mobira's products in Puerto Rico. The agreement provided for arbitration of disputes in Florida in accordance with the American Arbitration Association's rules. GKG filed an action seeking damages for an alleged breach of the parties' agreement. Nokia-Mobira moved to compel arbitration pursuant to section 3 of the FAA.

The issue before the court was whether it "should enforce an agreement to arbitrate [that] involves a domestic transaction covered by local antitrust law [10 L.P.R.A. § 278–278d] which forecloses the intended arbitration." The court noted that the FAA establishes a federal policy favoring arbitration and "creates a body of federal substantive law establishing and regulating the duty to honor an agreement to arbitrate." Because of this, the court considered whether the parties had intended to arbitrate their dispute and intended to apply the federal substantive law of arbitrability. Finding the recent Supreme Court decisions in *Mitsubishi Motors v. Soler Chrysler-Plymouth*, 473 U.S. 614 (1985), and *Shearson/American Express v. McMahon*, 482 U.S. 220 (1987), persuasive and controlling, and the mistrust of arbitration that formed the basis for the *American Safety Equipment Corp. v. J.P. Maguire & Co.*, 391 F.2d 821 (2d Cir. 1968), not in conformity with the current assessment of arbitration, the court concluded that the FAA compels the enforcement of the parties' arbitration clause in their distributorship agreement. It also stated that the "antitrust laws of the Commonwealth of Puerto Rico cannot dictate a different result." ***GKG Caribe, Inc. v. Nokia-Mobira, Inc.***, 725 F. Supp. 109 (D.P.R. 1989).

INSURANCE—FEDERAL ARBITRATION ACT—SUPREMACY CLAUSE—COMMERCE CLAUSE

The arbitration provision in the maritime insurance contract was enforceable, thereby requiring the insured to submit its claim to arbitration.

Triton Lines and Triton Transworld Navigation were the owners of M.V. Triton Trader. They obtained insurance from Steamship Mutual Underwriting, an association of shipowners referred to as a club, of which Triton was a member. The insurance contract incorporated the rules of the club, which included a choice of English law and an arbitration requirement. Triton subsequently sued Steamship, seeking payment for the loss of the M.V. Triton Trader. Triton refused to abide by the arbitration provision, and Steamship moved for stay pending arbitration. The primary issue before the court was whether Triton was bound by the rules of the club.

The court noted at the outset that the Federal Arbitration Act (FAA) mandates enforcement of an arbitration clause that is part of a maritime contract. It then went on to reject Triton's argument that the FAA did not apply, reasoning that under *Southland Corporation v. Keating*, 465 U.S. 1 (1984), "[w]hen an action involving interstate, foreign or maritime commerce pends in federal court, the supremacy clause allows the exercised commerce clause power of the arbitration act to force arbitration." The court found that Triton's reliance on the McCarran-Ferguson Act, 15 U.S.C.A. § 1011 (1982), to bar the enforcement of arbitration clauses in insurance contracts was misplaced because Triton's contract with Steamship involved a foreign insurer, whereas existing case law interpreting McCarran-Ferguson involved conflicts among the states over the requirements an insurance company must meet to do business in a particular state. Consequently, Triton was required to submit its dispute to arbitration. ***Triton Lines, Inc. v. Steamship Mutual Underwriting Association (Bermuda) Ltd.***, 707 F. Supp. 277 (S.D. Tex. 1989).

INSURANCE—REINSURANCE—U.N. CONVENTION—FEDERAL ARBITRATION ACT—MCCARRAN-FERGUSON ACT—NEW YORK INSURANCE LAW—BANKRUPTCY—LIQUIDATION

Dispute between an insurer and a foreign reinsurer over the right to reimbursement could not be subject to arbitration under either the Federal Arbitration Act (FAA) or the United Nations Convention on the Recognition and Enforcement of Foreign Arbitral Awards (U.N. Convention).

Nassau entered into three reinsurance contracts with Ardra. Each contract contained a broad arbitration clause. Nassau subsequently became insolvent and James P. Corcoran, as superintendent of insurance and liquidator of Nassau, filed an action against Ardra in state court for the recovery of reinsurance balances allegedly owed by Ardra. Ardra removed the action to federal court to compel arbitration under the U.N. Convention, but the court remanded the action on federal abstention grounds. Ardra then moved in state court to dismiss the action on the ground that arbitration was required.

The court stated that the issue before it was whether the U.N. Convention mandates arbitration, thereby precluding application of the liquidation provisions of New York's Insurance Law. It found that case law holds that the Insurance Law gives the court exclusive jurisdiction of all claims involving insolvent insurers. The court also found that there was no invalidation of the Insurance Law by the FAA under the McCarran-Ferguson Act because the law in question was enacted for the purpose of regulating the business of insurance.

As to the application of the U.N. Convention, the court found several reasons as to why it would not mandate arbitration in this instance. Specifically, the U.N. Convention does not apply when the agreement to arbitrate is null and void. In the case before it, the court determined that the agreement to arbitrate became null and void when the Insurance Law became operative, which occurred when Nassau became insolvent. In addition, the U.N. Convention applies only to commercial matters. The court concluded that it did not apply to the Nassau/Ardra contracts because their relationship was transformed from "one of a commercial nature to one of a regulatory nature" since their contracts contained provisions requiring Ardra to pay reinsurance proceeds to Nassau's liquidator if Nassau became insolvent. Moreover, the court noted that the present action by Ardra was not against Nassau but against the superintendent as liquidator of Nassau. Consequently, the court noted, the matter was not commercial in nature.

The court also concluded that the U.N. Convention provides that an arbitration award will be refused recognition and enforcement if it deals with an issue not contemplated and not capable of settlement. Because a dispute with the liquidator of an insolvent insurer under New York law is not "contemplated" as within an agreement to arbitrate, the court found that such a dispute is not "capable of settlement" by arbitration. As a final point, the court stated that article V(1)(a) of the U.N. Convention also provides for unenforcement if the parties "were under the law applicable to them, under some incapacity." It concluded that the "incapacity" applied in the action before it because Nassau was incapacitated when it became bankrupt. In accordance with its findings, the court refused to order the parties to proceed to arbitration. ***Corcoran v. Ardra Insurance Company, Ltd.,*** No. 38597-98 (N.Y. App. Div, 1st Dep't 1990).

INSURANCE—REINSURANCE—U.N. CONVENTION—FEDERAL ARBITRATION ACT—MCCARRAN-FERGUSON ACT—NEW YORK INSURANCE LAW—BANKRUPTCY—LIQUIDATION—COMITY

Although arbitration of a dispute between an insurer and a foreign reinsurer over the right to reimbursement was not required under the Federal Arbitration Act (FAA), arbitration of a dispute was mandated under the United Nations Convention on the Recognition and Enforcement of Foreign Arbitral Awards (U.N. Convention).

Union Indemnity Insurance Company of New York entered into a series of reinsurance agreements with AIG and other reinsurers. The agreements contained arbitration provisions. Under the contracts, the reinsurers agreed to indemnify Union for a portion of the liability incurred by them as a result of losses sustained by third parties covered under certain insurance policies issued by Union. An action was filed to recover money owed as reimbursement under the reinsurance contracts. Union subsequently became insolvent and James P. Corcoran, as Superintendent of Insurance, became Union's liquidator. The reinsurers moved to compel arbitration, arguing that the FAA and the U.N. Convention mandated arbitration of the dispute.

The court found that the FAA was not implicated because under the McCarran-Ferguson Act the state is vested with the authority to regulate insurance matters, and that exclusive jurisdiction was vested in the court supervising the liquidation so as to preclude arbitration. However, because several of the reinsurers were foreign corporations, the court also considered whether the U.N. Convention controlled the issue of arbitration. It concluded that the U.N. Convention applied because there were definite agreements in writing, the arbitration agreements provided for arbitration in the territory of a signatory of the U.N. Convention, the agreements arose out of a legal relationship considered commercial, and there was sufficient foreign involvement in the proceedings to require recourse to the U.N. Convention. In ruling in favor of arbitration, the court stated that the U.N. Convention, as implemented at 9 U.S.C. § 201 *et seq.*, is the supreme law of the land and takes precedence over local statutes. It also found that public policy arguments do not render the arbitration agreements null and void because the "interests of international comity outweigh such local statutory policy claims as . . . regulation of bankruptcy proceedings, even where a different result might occur in a purely domestic dispute." The court further determined that "incapacity rendering an award null and void [under article V(1)(a) of the U.N. Convention] is also to be narrowly read and refers to 'internationally recognized defense[s] such as duress, mistake, fraud, or waiver.'" Because "incapacity, as the [U.N. Convention] indicates by use of the past tense, must relate back to the contract [, the court concluded that i]ntervening liquidation could not . . . support a claim of incapacity." In addition to ordering arbitration, the court ruled that a consolidated arbitration of all claims would be the most expeditious means of resolving the controversy. ***Corcoran v. AIG Multi-Line Syndicate, Inc.***, 539 N.Y.S.2d 630 (S. Ct. N.Y. Cty. 1989).

COMMENTARY

International Commercial Arbitration in the United States*

Michael F. Hoellering

The United States provides a most hospitable climate for the arbitral resolution of disputes. Modern legislation at both federal and state levels provides an orderly and predictable legal framework for the enforcement of arbitral agreements and awards, and for judicial assistance without undue interference from the courts.

---

* Michael F. Hoellering is General Counsel of the American Arbitration Association. The assistance of Vicki M. Young, Editor of Court Decisions, American Arbitration Association, in the preparation of this article is gratefully acknowledged.

I. The United States Arbitration Act

The United States Arbitration Act (FAA)[1] was enacted to foster the use of arbitration and to end judicial hostility toward this form of private dispute resolution. It applies to international and maritime transactions, as well as to those arising in commerce between states. Section 2 of the FAA provides that arbitration agreements "shall be valid, irrevocable, and enforceable, save upon such grounds as exist at law or in equity for the revocation of any contract."[2] The act further provides for a stay of judicial proceedings where the contested issue is arbitrable under the agreement, and directs the courts to order arbitration if a party fails to honor an agreement to arbitrate. Chapter 2 of the FAA serves to implement the United Nations Convention on the Recognition and Enforcement of Foreign Arbitral Awards[3] in the United States. It sets forth the conditions under which international commercial disputes may be subject to the FAA's reach, establishes which courts have proper jurisdiction, and delineates their role in compelling arbitration and confirming awards. All but two states have their own arbitration laws governing the form and substance of arbitration within their borders.[4] These statutes closely resemble the FAA, although some are more detailed in certain procedural aspects.[5]

II. U.S. Law and Arbitrators

U.S. arbitration law sets no formal qualification requirements for arbitrators. Arbitrators need not be citizens or residents of the United States, and many nonnationals are appointed as arbitrators. Under United States law, arbitrators possess powers that may even be broader than the judiciary's if the parties so provide in their agreement.[6] Arbitrators must disclose any potentially disqualifying relationship, and one of the grounds for setting aside an arbitral award under the FAA is arbitrator bias. While impartiality is a fundamental and indispensable attribute of a neutral arbitrator, a different standard has been applied to party appointees, especially in domestic cases.[7] This difference is reflected in the legislative enactments of several states and in the Code of Ethics for Commercial Arbitrators in Commercial Disputes.[8] The Code acknowledges the frequently partisan predisposition of a party-appointed arbitrator and limits partiality as a ground for *vacatur* of an award to the bias of a neutral arbitrator. However, in international cases under the administration of the American Arbitration Association (AAA), any arbitrator, including one appointed by a party, may be challenged "if circumstances exist that give rise to justifiable doubts as to the arbitrator's impartiality or independence."[9]

III. Arbitration and the U.S. Judiciary

A. Judicial Support for Arbitration

In addition to the efforts of state legislatures, the U.S. judiciary, in fashioning U.S. arbitration law, has also been highly supportive of the arbitral process. The scope of arbitrable subject matter is defined in the broadest of terms, and almost any type of dispute—including claims under federal antitrust,[10] fraud,[11] securities,[12] and patent laws[13]—may be submitted to arbitration. In its implementation of liberal federal policy favoring arbitration, the U.S. Supreme Court interpreted the FAA as "a body of federal substantive law of arbitrability, applicable to any arbitration agreement within the coverage of the Act,"[14] An unbroken line of decisions by the high court has established that arbitration clauses in commercial contracts must be vigorously enforced, and that "as a matter of federal law, any doubts regarding the scope of arbitrable issues should be resolved in favor of arbitration, whether the problem at hand is the construction of the contract language itself or an allegation of waiver, delay, or like defense to arbitrability."[15]

B. Limited Judicial Intervention

U.S. courts rarely issue orders for prehearing discovery, leaving to the arbitrators, who have the power to direct the production of evidence, the task of deciding what information needs to be exchanged between the parties during arbitration.[16] Thus, the concern of some foreign parties that by arbitrating in the United States they will subject themselves to prehearing discovery of the type traditionally employed in litigation is wholly unjustified, for "[d]iscovery [in aid of arbitration] under court supervision will not be granted except under extraordinary circumstances and then only where it is shown to be absolutely necessary for the protection of the rights of a party."[17]

Judicial review of arbitral awards in the United States is limited. Only proof that an award was procured by fraud or undue means, or that the arbitrator was biased, exceeded his or her jurisdiction, or denied fundamental due process to one or more parties can serve as grounds for *vacatur*.[18] The enforcement of both arbitration agreements and awards is achieved through expedited summary proceedings in either federal or state courts, with only restricted inquiry into factual issues. When frivolous litigation in contravention of the arbitration agreement is interposed, the federal courts have not hesitated to impose sanctions on the offending party, especially when established principles of arbitration law are disregarded.[19]

C. Judicial Precedents

The guiding principles that should emerge from a well-developed body of judicial precedents include recognition of the need for speedy enforcement of arbitration agreements and awards, limited but effective judicial intervention to safeguard the integrity of the proceedings and advance the arbitral process, support for party autonomy in fashioning the arbitral forum, and the liberation of international arbitration from parochial concepts of domestic law.

Mindful that "we cannot have trade and commerce in world markets and international waters exclusively on our terms, governed by our laws, and resolved in our courts,"[20] the U.S. Supreme Court has applied different standards to international arbitration than to domestic arbitration. Thus, in both *Scherk v. Alberto-Culver Co.*[21] and *Mitsubishi Motors Corp. v. Soler Chrysler-Plymouth, Inc.*,[22] the Court called for the arbitration of securities and antitrust claims arising in an international context at a time when such claims were, in the domestic context, still considered nonarbitrable for public policy reasons.[23] The same rule of arbitrability now applies to domestic cases as a result of the Court's decisions in *Shearson/American Express, Inc. v. McMahon*[24] and *Rodriguez de Quijas v. Shearson/American Express, Inc.*[25] The obvious advantage of a uniform rule is that it prevents arbitration from being categorized as international or domestic, a practice that generally works to the disadvantage of arbitration.

This supportive attitude toward international arbitration is also apparent in judicial decisions in cases governed by the New York Convention, which the United States ratified in 1970.[26] The Court noted that "[t]he goal of the [New York] Convention, and the principal purpose underlying American adoption and implementation of it, was to encourage the recognition and enforcement of commercial arbitration agreements in international contracts and to unify the standards by which agreements to arbitrate are observed and arbitral awards are enforced in the signatory countries."[27] Guided by the pro-enforcement bias of the New York Convention, the courts have construed narrowly the "public policy" exception of the New York Convention: enforcement of awards may be denied "only where enforcement would violate the forum State's most basic notions of morality and justice."[28] The Courts have also extended application of the New York Convention to awards rendered in the United States between foreign parties,[29] but have held that the doctrine of "manifest disregard" of the law does not imply that it should violate public policy justifying the nonenforcement of an award.[30]

One of the interesting issues debated internationally in recent years has been the extent to which international arbitration can, by agreement of the parties, be delocalized, i.e., detached completely from any national system of law.[31] Because no U.S. court has yet been confronted with this issue, it is inappropriate to make categorical predictions about the outcome. To the extent that there has been a U.S. position on this subject, it is that proper, limited judicial assistance in aid of the arbitral process will always be necessary. Such assistance ultimately guarantees compliance with the contractual promise to arbitrate, ensures that basic due process is observed, and provides the order and predictability necessary in a system of dispute resolution.

IV. Institutional Support: The AAA

Under U.S. law, parties are masters of their agreement and, consistent with the principle of party autonomy, exercise a good deal of control over the bearings of the arbitral process: they may choose what to arbitrate, where to arbitrate, who the arbitrators will be and the method of their selection, the procedural rules applicable to the arbitration, and the law to be applied to the substance of the dispute.[32] To ensure the effectiveness of arbitration, contracting parties frequently provide in their agreement for the services of an established arbitral institution, such as the AAA, to administer the proceedings.

The AAA, a private, nonprofit organization, has been a major force since 1926 in advancing the use of arbitration and was in the forefront of organizations recommending that the United States accede to the New York Convention. Over the years, the AAA has also established working relationships with arbitration agencies in other countries, providing a world-wide administrative network for businesses that need reliable international arbitration services.[33] In 1988, one hundred forty-two international cases involving parties in thirty-five foreign countries, with claims spanning the gamut of international commercial transactions, were arbitrated under AAA auspices.[34] The AAA's Corporate Counsel Committee, which plays an integral part in the association's international activities, provides a practitioner's forum for the exchange of the latest information in the field.[35]

In international cases administered by the AAA, the parties may choose from a variety of rules, which are accompanied by Supplementary Procedures for International Commercial Arbitration.[36] The AAA's list system offers parties a wide choice in the selection of arbitrators with international experience and fluency in foreign languages. Under the Supplementary Procedures, parties may obtain third-country arbitrators,[37] AAA assistance in the exchange of pleadings and documentary evidence and in the channeling of communications to arbitrators,[38] arrangement for consecutive hearings,[39] and determination of the language of the proceedings when they cannot reach agreement.[40] Naturally, parties may be certain that the tribunals acting in accordance with AAA rules make reasoned awards.[41] If so desired by the parties, the AAA will also arrange for mediation of a dispute or will schedule prearbitration conferences to streamline the arbitral process.[42]

Furthermore, the AAA provides services for and administers cases under the UNCITRAL Arbitration Rules.[43] An AAA-administered arbitration can take place anywhere in the world. The AAA is also the U.S. National Section of the Inter-American Commercial Arbitration Commission (IACAC) and administers arbitrations under the IACAC Rules in the United States.[44]

Other organizations providing arbitration services in the United States include the Court of Abitration of the International Chamber of Commerce, the Society of Maritime Arbitrators, and specialized arbitration facilities of various trade associations. With respect to international investment disputes, the World Bank is a provider of arbitration services under the International Convention for the Settlement of Investment Disputes.[45]

V. Federal Legislation

The growth of U.S. arbitration law has been a continual process. Recently, several important amendments to the FAA and the Foreign Sovereign Immunities Act (FSIA)[46] were passed into law. The FAA amendments provide useful clarification in two areas—arbitration-related court appeals, and the applicability of the Act of State doctrine to arbitration.

A. *FAA Amendments*

When it was enacted, the FAA contained no provisions regarding appeals, leaving appealability open to uncertainty.[47] The new provisions add certainty to this area of arbitration law in a way that advances the purposes of arbitration: they provide for an appeal from a court's denial of an order to compel arbitration, and deny an appeal when litigation has been stayed and arbitration directed.[48]

The amendment pertaining to the Act of State doctrine serves to remove any remaining doubts in the wake of *Libyan American Oil Company v. Socialist People's Libyan Arab Jamahirya*,[49] which, under the doctrine, denied enforcement of an award in favor of the Libyan-American Oil Company for the nationalization of its assets by Libya. The decision, though vacated for purposes of precedent following a settlement between the parties, raised serious concerns: to allow any government to repudiate unilaterally an arbitral agreement or award would strike precisely at the effectiveness of arbitration involving governmental parties. The new provision meets these concerns by providing that the "[e]nforcement of arbitral agreements, confirmation of arbitral awards, and execution upon judgments based on orders confirming such awards shall not be refused on the basis of the Act of State doctrine.''[50]

B. FSIA Amendments

The FSIA amendments were designed to address an important issue that regularly arises in arbitrations involving governments: whether a given arbitration or choice-of-law clause constitutes a waiver of a government's immunity from suit. While foreign states are generally immune from the jurisdiction of U.S. courts, the FSIA, which ultimately codified U.S. law in this area, provides that a foreign state may waive its immunity either explicitly or by implication. Early court decisions found waivers of immunity when a foreign state had agreed to arbitrate in ''another country'' anywhere in the world or to be governed by the laws of any ''particular country'' with respect to a transaction occurring anywhere in the world.[51]

More recent decisions have questioned the adequacy of such broad clauses to effect consent to U.S. jurisdiction in the absence of requisite contacts in the United States.[52] In order to eliminate the ambiguity surrounding consent, the FSIA was amended to provide that foreign states and their instrumentalities may not invoke sovereign immunity whenever: (i) the agreement calls for arbitration in the United States; (ii) the agreement falls within a treaty to which the United States is a signatory calling for the recognition and enforcement of arbitral awards; and (iii) the underlying claim against a foreign state could have been brought before a United States court under the conditions in the FSIA.[53]

In addition, the FSIA now provides for another exception to immunity from attachment or execution of commercial property owned by a foreign state. Execution against the commercial property of a state is effectively no longer limited to property used only for the commercial activity on which the claim was based, but extends to all property used for commercial purposes in the United States.[54]

VI. State Enactments

Efforts in the United States to provide for the efficient arbitration of international commercial disputes have not been confined to the federal sphere. During the last three years, California, Connecticut, Florida, Georgia, Hawaii, and Texas have each adopted legislation regulating international commercial arbitration within their borders.[55] Most of these laws are patterned on the UNCITRAL Model Law. These statutes are more comprehensive than the FAA and conveniently supplement it by addressing various aspects of international arbitration practice. Many of the Model Law's provisions and basic concepts largely parallel existing United States law, and their common purpose was "to send a clear message that the jurisdiction is hospitable to international arbitration and interested in promoting it."[56]

A major departure from the Model Law, however, is the inclusion in the California and Texas statutes of a chapter on conciliation to encourage that mode of dispute resolution. The Georgia law supplements that state's new commercial arbitration code with provisions that apply concurrently to international transactions. The Hawaii law does not deal with arbitration procedure specifically, but instead structures and authorizes the creation of centers to promote international arbitration and mediation.

A. *Federal Preemption*

While most of the new state laws are designed to facilitate international arbitration in a manner that is harmonious with existing federal arbitration law, questions of federal preemption are bound to arise in the wake of the state enactments.[57] When this occurs, the preemptive effect of the FAA will depend largely on the degree to which it coincides with the particular state law provision. Where the state provision does not derogate from, but in fact supplements the FAA, it will be upheld. On the other hand, where the state provision conflicts with or departs significantly from the policy and existing interpretation of the FAA, the Supremacy Clause of the United States Constitution[58] requires that federal rather than state law provide the rule of decision.

B. *Choice of Law*

The need for practitioners to be more familiar with state arbitration laws is also illustrated by the U.S. Supreme Court's recent decision in *Volt Information Sciences, Inc. v. Board of Trustees of Leland Stanford Junior University*.[59] In that case, the court left undisturbed a California decision holding that when parties insert a routine choice-of-law clause in their contract, they thereby elect to arbitrate under state rather than federal arbitration law. Because the general impact of this ruling on arbitration and on those cases governed by the New York Convention is still uncertain, it may be advisable for anyone drafting agreements providing for arbitration to refer specifically to the FAA as a way of ensuring that a choice-of-law clause intended to govern the substance of the dispute does not unwittingly serve to substitute state for federal arbitration law.

VII. Future Developments

A. The Inter-American Convention

As recent legislative changes indicate, U.S. arbitration law is evolving continuously to respond effectively to the need for efficient and impartial transnational dispute resolution in a rapidly changing global economy. High on the agenda of unfinished business is the enactment by Congress of implementing legislation for the Inter-American Convention on International Commercial Arbitration.[60] The Convention, a timely regional initiative, creates a framework of law and practice for international arbitration in the Western Hemisphere. It has already brought several Latin American countries into the ambit of international commercial arbitration, from which they have in the past been largely absent.[61]

B. Provisional Remedies

An important but still unresolved issue concerns the availability of provisional remedies in aid of arbitration. It is fairly well established that attachment is available in international arbitrations involving the maritime industry.[62] Outside admiralty, the accessibility of attachments in cases governed by the New York Convention, however, is not established, with a majority of courts holding that an attachment contravenes the intent of the New York Convention.[63] Given the clear need of such security in certain cases, and that most signatory nations other than the United States expressly permit prearbitral attachment and other forms of provisional relief, a near consensus has emerged that the FAA should be amended to ensure the availability of provisional remedies in aid of arbitration. There is also need for clarification on the authority of the courts to determine an appropriate venue for arbitration where the parties have failed to agree on it.[64]

C. Adoption of the UNCITRAL Model Law

A much larger subject of debate is whether the entire UNCITRAL Model Law should be adopted at the federal level. At least two recent comparative studies have concluded that replacement of the FAA by the Model Law is not warranted since the FAA, supplemented by decisional authority and state arbitration codes, adequately addresses most important aspects of international arbitration.[65] While this debate has yet to run its course, such findings are not surprising, given that during the last thirty years, the United States has had a regime for international commercial arbitration that is as sophisticated and attractive as any other in the world.

Notes

1. 9 U.S.C. § 1 *et seq.* (1988).
2. 9 U.S.C. § 2 (1988).
3. Also known as the New York Convention, 21 U.S.T. 2517, T.I.A.S. No. 6997, 330 U.N.T.S. 4739 (June 10, 1958). The FAA implements the U.N. convention at 9 U.S.C. §§ 201-208 (1988).
4. The arbitration statues of Alabama and West Virginia are applicable only to existing controversies. Ala. Code § 6-6-1 (1977); W. Va. Code § 55-10-1 (1981).
5. Alaska Stat. §§ 09.43.010 *et seq.* (1983); Ariz. Rev. Stat. Ann. §§ 12-1501 *et seq.* (1982); Ark. Stat. Ann. §§ 34-511 *et seq.* (Supp. 1985); Cal. Civ. Proc. Code §§ 1280 *et seq.* (West 1982 & Supp. 1989); Colo. Rev. Stat. §§ 13-22-201 *et seq.* (1987); Conn. Gen. Stat. Ann. §§ 52-408 *et seq.* (West 1960 & Supp. 1989); Del. Code Ann. tit. 10, §§ 5701 *et seq.* (1975); D.C. Code Ann. §§ 16-4301 *et seq.* (1989); Fla. Stat. Ann. §§ 682.01 *et seq.* (Supp. 1989); Ga. Code Ann. §§ 9-9-1 *et seq.* (Supp. 1989); Haw. Rev. Stat. §§ 658-1 *et seq.* (1985); Idaho Code §§ 7-901 *et seq.* (1979); Ill. Rev. Stat. ch. 10, §§ 101 *et seq.* (1975 & Supp. 1989); Ind. Code Ann. §§ 34-4-2-1 *et seq.* (1983); Iowa Code Ann. §§ 679A.1 *et seq.* (West 1983); Kan. Stat. Ann. §§ 5-401 *et seq.* (1982 & Supp. 1987); Ky. Rev. Stat. Ann. §§ 417.045 *et seq.* (Supp. 1986); La. Rev. Stat. Ann. §§ 9:4201 *et seq.* (West 1983); Me. Rev. Stat. Ann. tit. 14, §§ 5927 *et seq.* (1980); Md. Cts. & Jud. Proc. Code Ann. §§ 3-201 *et seq.* (1984); Mass. Gen. Laws Ann. ch. 251, §§ 1 *et seq.* (West 1988); Mich. Comp. Laws Ann. §§ 600.5001 *et seq.* (West 1987); Minn. Stat. Ann. §§ 572.08 *et seq.* (West 1987); Miss. Code Ann. §§ 11-15-1 *et seq.* (Supp. 1989); Mo. Ann. Stat. §§ 435.012 *et seq.* (Supp. 1989); Mont. Code Ann. §§ 27-5-111 *et seq.* (1987); Neb. Rev. Stat. §§ 25-2601 *et seq.* (Supp. 1988); Nev. Rev. Stat. §§ 38.015 *et seq.* (1987); N.H. Rev. Stat. Ann. §§ 542:1 *et seq.* (1974); N.J. Stat. Ann. §§ 2A:24-1 *et seq.* (West 1987); N.M. Stat. Ann. §§ 44-7-1 *et seq.* (1978); N.Y. Civ. Prac. L. & R. §§ 7501 *et seq.* (McKinney 1980 & Supp. 1989); N.C. Gen. Stat. §§ 1-567.1 *et seq.* (1988); N.D. Cent. Code §§ 32-29.2-01 *et seq.* (Supp. 1989); Ohio Rev. Code Ann. §§ 2711.01 *et seq.* (Anderson 1981); Okla. Stat. Ann. tit. 15, §§ 801 *et seq.* (West Supp. 1989); Or. Rev. Stat. §§ 33.210 *et seq.* (1987); Pa. Stat. Ann. tit. 42, §§ 7301 *et seq.* (1982); P.R. Laws Ann. tit. 32, §§ 3201 *et seq.* (1968); R.I. Gen. Laws §§ 10-3-1 *et seq.* (1985); S.C. Code Ann. §§ 15-48-10 *et seq.* (Law. Co-op. Supp. 1988); S.D. Codified Laws Ann. §§ 21-25A-1 *et seq.* (1987); Tenn. Code Ann. §§ 29-5-301 *et seq.* (Supp. 1988); Tex. Rev. Civ. Stat. Ann. arts. 224 *et seq.* (1973 & Supp. 1989); Utah Code Ann. §§ 78-31a-1 *et seq.* (1987); Vt. Stat. Ann. tit. 12, §§ 5651 *et seq.* (1989); Va. Code Ann. §§ 8.01-577 *et seq.* (Supp. 1989); Wash. Rev. Code Ann. §§ 7.04.010 *et seq.* (1961 & Supp. 1989); Wis. Stat. Ann. §§ 788.01 *et seq.* (1981 & Supp. 1988); Wyo. Stat. §§ 1-36-101 *et seq.* (1989).
6. Hoellering, "Remedies in Arbitration," in *Arbitration & the Law, 1984*, at 37 (1985).
7. *Barcon Associates, Inc. v. Tri-County Asphalt Corp.*, 430 A.2d 214 (N.J. 1981); Matter of Astoria Medical Group (Health Ins. Plan of N.Y.), 11 N.Y.2d 128, 182 N.E.2d 85, 227 N.Y.S.2d 401 (1962).
8. The Code, which was jointly developed by the AAA and the American Bar Association, sets standards for acceptable arbitrator behavior. Copies of the Code may be obtained by writing to the American Arbitration Association, Publications Department, 140 West 51st Street, New York, NY 10020.
9. American Arbitration Association's Supplementary Procedures for International Commercial Arbitration, as amended and in effect February 1, 1986, § 2 [hereinafter Supplementary Procedures].
10. *Mitsubishi Motors Corp. v. Soler Chrysler-Plymouth, Inc.*, 473 U.S. 614 (1985).
11. *Prima Paint Corp. v. Flood & Conklin Mfg. Co.*, 388 U.S. 395 (1967).
12. *Shearson/American Express, Inc. v. McMahon*, 482 U.S. 220 (1987); *Rodriguez de Quijas v. Shearson/American Express, Inc.*, __ U.S. __ , 109 S. Ct. 1917 (1989).
13. 35 U.S.C. § 294 (1982).
14. *Moses H. Cone Memorial Hospital v. Mercury Construction Corp.*, 460 U.S. 1, 24 (1983).
15. *Id.* at 24–25.
16. Stein & Wotman, "The Arbitration Hearing" in *International Commercial Arbitration in*

New York 87 (J. McClendon & R. Goodman eds. 1986) [hereinafter McClendon & Goodman].

17. *Id.* at 88.
18. 9 U.S.C. §§ 10, 207 (1988); art. V(2) of the New York Convention.
19. See *Thomas C. Baer, Inc. v. Architectural and Ornamental Iron Workers Local Union No. 580 of the International Association of Bridge, Structural and Ornamental Iron Workers*, 813 F.2d 562 (2d Cir. 1987); *First Investors Corp. v. American Capital Financial Services, Inc.*, 823 F.2d 307 (9th Cir. 1987); *Hill v. Norfolk and Western Railroad*, 814 F.2d 1192 (7th Cir. 1987); *Norris v. Grosvenor Marketing Ltd.*, 803 F.2d 1281 (2d Cir. 1986); *Pallante v. Paine Webber, Jackson and Curtis*, [1985–1986 Transfer Binder] Fed. Sec. L. Rep. (CCH) Para. 92,219, at 91,613 (Aug. 7, 1985).
20. *Scherk v. Alberto-Culver Co.*, 417 U.S. 506, 519 (1973) (citing *The Bremen v. Zapata Off-Shore Co.*, 407 U.S. 1 (1972)).
21. *Id.*
22. 473 U.S. 614 (1985).
23. *Id.* at 629. The court reasoned in *Mitsubishi* : "[w]e conclude that concerns of international comity, respect for the capacities of foreign and transnational tribunals, and sensitivity to the need of the international commercial system for predictability in the resolution of disputes require that we enforce the parties' agreement, even assuming that a contrary result would be forthcoming in a domestic context."
24. 482 U.S. 220 (1987). The Court held that agreements to arbitrate future disputes raising statutory claims, such as those under the Securities Exchange Act of 1934 and the Racketeer Influenced and Corrupt Organizations Act, are enforceable under the Federal Arbitration Act, absent clear expression of congressional intent to the contrary.
25. __ U.S. __ , 109 S. Ct. 1917 (1989). The Court held that an agreement to arbitrate claims arising under the Securities Act of 1933 is enforceable, thereby overruling *Wilko v. Swan*, 346 U.S. 427 (1953), which it deemed incorrectly decided and inconsistent with the prevailing uniform construction of other federal statutes governing arbitration agreements in business transactions. By overruling *Wilko*, the Court has discarded the last remaining remnant of judicial suspicion of arbitration that Congress intended to eliminate through its enactment of the FAA.
26. For a current list of other signatures, ratifications, accessions, and extensions, contact AAA's Eastman Arbitration Library, 140 W. 51st, New York, NY 10020.
27. 417 U.S. at 520 (footnote 15), *supra* note 20.
28. *Parsons & Whittemore Overseas Co., Inc. v. Société Génerale de L'Industrie du Papier (RAKTA)*, 508 F.2d 969, 974 (2d Cir. 1974).
29. *Bergesen v. Joseph Muller Corporation*, 710 F.2d 928 (2d Cir. 1983).
30. *Brandeis Intsel, Ltd. v. Calabrian Chemicals Corp.*, 656 F. Supp. 160 (S.D.N.Y. 1987).
31. Law Committee of the American Arbitration Association, "Report on Delocalized Arbitration," 39 *Arb. J.* 58 (Sept., 1984).
32. M. Domke, *Commercial Arbitration*, rev. ed. (G. Wilner, 1989).
33. The agencies with which the AAA has working relationships include: the Arbitration Centre of the Federal Economic Chamber in Vienna; the Arbitration Institute of the Stockholm Chamber of Commerce in Stockholm; the Australian Commercial Disputes Centre Limited in Sydney; the British Columbia International Commercial Arbitration Centre in British Columbia; the Court of Arbitration of the International Chamber of Commerce in Paris; the Greek Arbitration Association in Athens; the Japan Commercial Arbitration Association in Tokyo; the Korean Commercial Arbitration Board in Seoul; the London Court of International Arbitration in London; the Netherlands Arbitration Institute in Rotterdam; and the Quebec National and International Commercial Arbitration Center in Quebec.
34. Information based on statistics compiled by the American Arbitration Association.
35. For further information on the activities of the Corporate Counsel Committee, contact the author or Richard E. Lerner, AAA Associate General Counsel.
36. *Supra* note 9.
37. Supplementary Procedures § 1.
38. *Id.* §§ 3 and 4.

39. *Id.* § 5.
40. *Id.* § 6.
41. *Id.* § 7.
42. American Arbitration Association's Commercial Arbitration Rules, as amended and in effect September 1, 1988, § 10.
43. American Arbitration Association's Procedures for cases under the UNCITRAL Arbitration Rules, as amended and in effect May 1, 1988.
44. McClendon & Goodman, *supra* note 16, at 45.
45. See *id.* at 40.
46. Pub. L. No. 94-583, 90 Stat. 2891 (1976) (codified at 28 U.S.C. §§ 1330, 1332 (a)(2)-(4), 1391(f), 1441(d), and 1602-1611) (1982).
47. Uncertainty as to whether arbitration-related actions were appealable resulted also from outdated distinctions between legal and equitable proceedings that had no relevance in modern litigation practice. See Enelow-Ettelson rule based on *Enelow v. New York Life Ins. Co.*, 293 U.S. 379 (1935), and *Ettelson v. Metropolitan Life Ins. Co.*, 317 U.S. 188 (1942).
48. Pub. L. No. 100-702, Title X, § 1019(a), 102 Stat. 4671 (1988) (codified at 9 U.S.C. § 15 (1988)).
49. 482 F. Supp. 1175 (D.D.C. 1980), *vacated after settlement*, 684 F.2d 1032 (D.C. Cir. 1981).
50. Pub. L. No. 100-669, § 1, 102 Stat. 3969 (1988) (codified at 9 U.S.C. § 15 (1988)).
51. *Victory Transport Inc. v. Comisaria General de Abastecimientos y Transportes*, 336 F.2d 354 (2d Cir. 1964).
52. *Maritime International Nominees Establishment v. Republic of Guinea*, 693 F.2d 1094 (D.C. Cir. 1982); *Chicago Bridge & Iron Co. v. The Islamic Republic of Iran*, 506 F. Supp. 981 (N.D. Ill. 1980); *Yessenin-Volpin v. Novosti Press Agency*, 443 F. Supp. 849 (S.D.N.Y. 1978); *Ipitrade International, S.A. v. Federal Republic of Nigeria*, 465 F. Supp. 824 (D.D.C. 1978).
53. Pub. L. No. 100-669, § 2, 102 Stat. 3969 (1988) (28 U.S.C.A. § 1605(a) (West Supp. 1989)).
54. Pub. L. No. 100-669, § 3, 102 Stat. 3969 (1988) (28 U.S.C.A. § 1610(a) (West supp. 1989)).
55. Cal. Civ. Proc. Code §§ 1297.11-1297.432 (Supp. 1989); 1989 Conn. Acts 89-179 (Reg. Sess.); Fla. Stat. Ann. §§ 684.01-684.35 (Supp. 1989); Ga. Code Ann. §§ 9-9-30 to 9-9-43 (1989); Haw. Rev. Stat. §§ 658D-1 to 658D-9 (Supp. 1989); Tex Rev. Civ. Stat. Ann. arts. 249-1 to 249-43 (Vernon Supp. 1990) (see Acts of 71st Leg., Reg. Sess., 1989, ch. 309, (S.B. 391, 1989) Tex. Sess. Law Serv.).
56. "Select Committee in Washington Finds That Federal Law Strongly Supports Arbitration Agreements," 3 *News & Notes Inst. Transnat'l Arb.* 1, 3 (Jan., 1988).
57. *Southland Corp. v. Keating*, 465 U.S. 1 (1984); *Securities Industry Asso. v. Connolly*, No. 89-1022 (1st Cir. Aug. 31, 1989), *aff'g* 703 F. Supp. 146 (D. Mass. 1988); *New England Energy, Inc. v. Keystone Shipping Co.*, 855 F.2d 1 (1st Cir. 1988); *Drexel Burnham Lambert Inc. v. Ruebsamen*, *N.Y.L.J.*, July 28, 1988, at 17, col. 3 (App. Div. 1st Dept July 21, 1988).
58. U.S. Const. art. VI, cl. 2.
59. __ U.S. __, 109 S. Ct. 1248 (1989). The Court declined to set aside a ruling by the California Court of Appeals that raised the question of whether the state arbitration law was preempted by the FAA. Note that *Volt* involved a contract that contained a choice-of-law clause.
60. This was signed in 1976. The AAA testified in support of ratification, and while the Senate Foreign Relations Committee gave its advice and consent to ratification, the process was not completed by the passage of implementing legislation by the House of Representatives. The ratification process has been reactivated during this last congressional session.
61. See statement of Michael F. Hoellering, General Counsel of the American Arbitration Association, in support of United States' Ratification of the Inter-American Convention on International Commercial Arbitration, before the Senate Foreign Relations Committee (June 11, 1986) (available at the AAA Eastman Arbitration Library, 140 West 51st Street, New York, NY 10020). At present, Chile, Colombia, Costa Rica, El Salvador, Guatemala,

Honduras, Mexico, Panama, Paraguay, Peru, Uruguay, and Venezuela have ratified the Inter-American Convention.

62. *Atlas Chartering Services, Inc. v. World Trade Group, Inc.*, 453 F.Supp. 861 (S.D.N.Y. 1978); *Andros Compania Maritima, S.A. v. Andre & Cie, S.A.*, 430 F. Supp. 88 (S.D.N.Y. 1977).
63. *Drexel Burnham Lambert Inc. v. Ruebsamen, N.Y. L.J.*, July 28, 1988, at 17, col. 3 (App. Div. 1st Dept July 21, 1988); *McCreary Tire & Rubber Co. v. CEAT S.p.A.*, 501 F.2d 1032 (3d Cir. 1974); *Carolina Power & Light Co. v. Uranexs*, 451 F. Supp. 1044 (N.D. Cal. 1977); *Cooper v. Ateliers de la Motobecane, S.A.*, 57 N.Y.2d 408, 442 N.E.2d 1239, 456 N.Y.S.2d 728 (1982).
64. 9 U.S.C. § 204 (1988); *Bauhinia Corp. v. China National Machinery & Equipment Import & Export Corp.*, 819 F.2d 247 (9th Cir. 1987); *Econo-Car International Inc. v. Antilles Car Rentals, Inc.*, 499 F.2d 1391 (3d Cir. 1974); *Merrill Lynch, Pierce, Fenner & Smith, Inc. v. De Caro*, 577 F. Supp. 616 (W.D. Mo. 1983).
65. Report to the Washington Foreign Law Society on the UNCITRAL Model Law on International Commercial Arbitration, prepared by the Society's Committee on the UNCITRAL Model Law on International Commercial Arbitration; Adoption of the UNCITRAL Model Law on International Commercial Arbitration as Federal or State Legislation, Report of the Committee on Arbitration and Alternative Dispute Resolution of the City Bar of New York.

Arbitrability Revisited*

Michael F. Hoellering

Introduction

Since the last time we addressed the topic of arbitrability in 1984, there have been a number of developments and landmark decisions from the U.S. Supreme Court, which have expanded significantly the domain of arbitration. Specifically, the recent decisions have extended the scope of arbitrable subject matter to a broad range of claims including those based on statutory rights and have reaffirmed the suitability of arbitration as a fair and effective means of resolving commercial disputes.

Broad Clause Presumption

Early decisions of the United States Supreme Court have established that when courts are called upon to compel arbitration under a broad arbitration clause, arbitration is to proceed unless there is clear evidence that the parties did not intend the matter of the dispute to be arbitrable. See, e.g., *United Steelworkers v. Warrior & Gulf Navigation Co.*, 363 U.S. 574 (1960) ("[a]n

* Paper presented at the ABA 1990 Annual Meeting, Chicago, Illinois, August 5–8, 1990. Michael F. Hoellering is General Counsel of the American Arbitration Association. Vicki M. Young, Editor of Court Decisions, American Arbitration Association, assisted in the preparation of this paper.

order to arbitrate . . . should not be denied unless it may be said with positive assurance that the arbitration clause is not susceptible of an interpretation that covers the asserted dispute. Doubts should be resolved in favor of coverage.'' 363 U.S. at 582–83.). This presumption of arbitrability under a broad clause still prevails.

In 1983, the Court stated that the effect of section 2 of the Federal Arbitration Act (FAA), 9 U.S.C. § 1 *et seq.*, on arbitrability ''is to create a body of federal substantive law of arbitrability, applicable to any arbitration agreement within the coverage of the Act'' and that ''any doubts concerning the scope of arbitrable issues should be resolved in favor of arbitration. . . .'' *Moses H. Cone Memorial Hosp. v. Mercury Constr. Corp.*, 460 U.S. 1, 23–25 (1983). Application of this presumption in an international setting is illustrated by *Ledee v. Ceramiche Ragno*, 684 F.2d 184 (1st Cir. 1982), wherein the court identified four preliminary questions in the adjudication of arbitrability issues: whether there is an agreement in writing to arbitrate the subject of the dispute; whether the agreement provides for arbitration in the territory of a contracting state to the United Nations Convention on the Recognition and Enforcement of Foreign Arbitral Awards (U.N. Convention) (21 U.S.T. 2517, T.I.A.S. No. 6997, 330 U.N.T.S. 4739; implementing legislation is codified at 9 U.S.C. § 201 *et seq.*); whether the agreement arises out of a commercial relationship; and whether the commercial relationship has some reasonable relation with the foreign state.

Who Decides Question of Arbitrability?

Under *AT&T Technologies, Inc. v. Communications Workers of America*, 475 U.S. 643, 106 S. Ct. 1415 (1986), it is the court, not the arbitrator, that determines in the first instance whether a dispute is arbitrable.

AT&T and the Communications Workers of America (CWA) entered into a collective bargaining agreement that provided for arbitration of disputes, except those specifically excluded by other provisions of the contract. A dispute over layoffs arose that turned on whether AT&T had an exclusive right to lay off workers under the agreement. CWA grieved the matter, but AT&T refused to submit the grievance to arbitration, contending that the question was not arbitrable under the contract. The trial court, determining that the union's interpretation of the contract was ''arguable,'' ruled that the question of arbitrability was for the arbitrator and ordered arbitration to proceed. The order was affirmed on appeal to the Seventh Circuit, but was reversed by the United States Supreme Court.

The Court, relying on and reaffirming its position in the Steelworkers' Trilogy—*Steelworkers v. American Manufacturing Co.*, 363 U.S. 564; *Steelworkers v. Warrior & Gulf Navigation Co.*, 363 U.S. 574; *Steelworkers v.*

Enterprise Wheel & Car Corp., 363 U.S. 593 (1960)—ruled that arbitrability is unquestionably a matter for judicial determination:

> It is the court's duty to interpret the agreement and to determine whether the parties intended to arbitrate grievances concerning layoffs predicated on a "lack of work" determined by the Company. If the court determines that the agreement so provides, then it is for the arbitrator to determine the relative agreement. It was for the court, not the arbitrator, to decide in the first instance whether the dispute was to be resolved through arbitration. [106 S. Ct. at 1420.]

It thus remanded the case for a determination of arbitrability.

Note that in cases administered under the rules of the American Arbitration Association (AAA), the ruling does not require the AAA to suspend its administration in the face of a nonarbitrability claim asserted by a party. The ruling merely requires the court to decide the issue when raised in a judicial proceeding, and leaves undisturbed the authority of arbitrators to determine arbitrability issues when they are presented to them.

Securities Claims

The most notable domestic ruling in the area of arbitrability is the 1987 decision of the U.S. Supreme Court in *Shearson/American Express, Inc. v. McMahon*, 482 U.S. 220, 107 S. Ct. 2332 (1987), wherein it held that agreements to arbitrate future disputes raising statutory claims, such as those under the Securities Exchange Act of 1934 (Exchange Act) and the Racketeer Influenced and Corrupt Organizations Act (RICO), are enforceable under the FAA absent clear expression of congressional intent to the contrary. The decision represents both a significant departure from the Court's decision in *Wilko v. Swan*, 346 U.S. 427 (1953), and extends to domestic transactions the rule of *Mitsubishi v. Soler Chrysler-Plymouth, Inc.*, 473 U.S. 614 (1985).

Eugene and Julia McMahon entered into a customer agreement with Shearson/American Express, Inc., providing for arbitration of disputes. The McMahons subsequently filed a complaint against Shearson, alleging fraud in violation of section 10(b) of the Exchange Act, 15 U.S.C. § 78j(b); Securities Exchange Commission (SEC) rule 10b-5, 17 C.F.R. § 240.10b-5; and RICO, 18 U.S.C. § 1961 *et seq*. Shearson moved to compel arbitration of all claims pursuant to the customer agreement. The Second Circuit held that the Exchange Act and RICO claims were not arbitrable, relying on *Wilko* and *American Safety Equipment Corp. v. McGuire*, 391 F.2d 821 (2d Cir. 1968). The Supreme Court granted *certiorari* to resolve the conflict among the circuits regarding the arbitrability of section 10(b) and RICO claims. The AAA filed an *amicus curiae* brief with the Court in support of Shearson. In an opinion rendered June 8, 1987, the Court reversed, holding unanimously that the RICO claims were arbitrable and, with a 5 to 4 majority, that the McMahons' claims under the Exchange Act were arbitrable.

The Court began its inquiry with the FAA, finding that the FAA "mandates enforcement of agreements to arbitrate statutory claims." 107 S. Ct. at 2337. Explaining that its mandate "may be overridden by a contrary congressional command," the Court then determined that Congress had not created an exception to the FAA for either section 10(b) or RICO claims. *Id.* It first addressed the federal securities claims, concluding that Congress did not intend section 29(a) of the Exchange Act to bar enforcement of predispute arbitration agreements. Interpreting *Wilko* in light of *Scherk v. Alberto-Culver Co.*, 417 U.S. 506 (1974), the Court stated: "*Scherk* supports our understanding that *Wilko* must be read as barring waiver of a judicial forum only where arbitration is inadequate to protect the substantive rights at issue." *Id.* at 2339. The Court observed that it was "difficult to reconcile *Wilko*'s mistrust of the arbitral process with this Court's subsequent decisions involving the Arbitration Act," adding that "most of the reasons given in *Wilko* have been rejected subsequently by the Court as a basis for holding claims to be nonarbitrable." *Id.* at 2340. Relying heavily on *Scherk*, the Court concluded that arbitration was a suitable means of enforcing Exchange Act rights.

Turning to the RICO claims, the Court found that there was "nothing in the text of the RICO statute that even arguably evinces congressional intent to exclude civil RICO claims from the dictates of the Arbitration Act." *Id.* at 2343–2344. The Court reasoned that much of its analysis in *Mitsubishi*, which concerned the arbitrability of antitrust disputes in the international sphere, was equally applicable in the domestic context. After addressing the McMahons' arguments against the arbitrability of RICO claims, the Court concluded that the "McMahons may effectively vindicate their RICO claim in an arbitral forum, and therefore there is no inherent conflict between arbitration and the purposes underlying section 1964(c)." *Id.* at 2345–2346.

Because the court stopped short of overruling the *Wilko* doctrine directly, the arbitrability of claims arising under the Securities Act of 1933 (1933 Act) was left open. This issue was ultimately resolved in *Rodriguez de Quijas v. Shearson Lehman Brothers, Inc.*, ___ U.S. ___, 109 S. Ct. 1917, 104 L. Ed. 2d 526 (1989).

Opelia Rodriguez de Quijas and her family brought an action for violations of various state and federal laws against Shearson/American Express. The district court ordered arbitration of all claims, except for the federal securities claims arising under section 12(c) of the 1933 Act, pursuant to an arbitration clause contained in the customer agreements.

On appeal, the Fifth Circuit ruled that the section 12(c) claims were arbitrable. 845 F.2d 1296 (5th Cir. 1988). Noting the Supreme Court's remark in *McMahon* that *Wilko* was outdated and "must be read as barring waiver of a judicial forum only where arbitration is inadequate to protect the substantive rights at issue," and noting also that *McMahon* clearly established the adequacy of arbitration to resolve securities disputes, the court ordered arbitration of the section 12(2) claim. *Id*. at 1298.

The Court granted *certiorari* and affirmed. It held that an agreement to arbitrate claims arising under the 1933 Act is enforceable, thereby overruling *Wilko*, which it deemed was incorrectly decided and inconsistent with the prevailing uniform construction of other federal statues governing arbitration agreements in business transactions.

The Court found that *Wilko* was decided at a time when there was judicial hostility to arbitration. It also noted that the *Wilko* decision was made to ensure the protection of buyers' rights, because the 1933 Act was intended to protect buyers of securities who frequently deal neither at arm's length nor on equal terms with sellers. Finding the circumstances surrounding the *Wilko* decision to be outmoded, and that it would be inconsistent to have *Wilko* exist side by side with such recent decisions as *McMahon*, the Court determined that allowing parties to resort to arbitration would further the purpose and the effect of the FAA without undermining any of the substantive rights afforded to plaintiffs under the 1933 Act.

Accordingly, the Court held enforceable a predispute agreement to arbitrate claims arising under the 1933 Act. It also found that the customary rule of the retroactive application (i.e., applying the law decided to the case at bar) was appropriate in this case.

Intellectual Property Claims

As was reported in 1984, the arbitrability of patent disputes was aided by the signing of Public Law 97-247 on August 27, 1982. Codified at 35 U.S.C. § 294, the new law specifically provided for the voluntary arbitration of a broad range of patent disputes, including questions of validity and infringement. It became effective on February 27, 1983. Under this statute, parties to a contract may voluntarily agree to arbitrate their patent disputes, both pending and future, and such agreements and awards may be enforced under the FAA. Such arbitration shall be private, and the resulting award shall be final and binding. Awards are enforceable when notice of an award is filed with the Commissioner of Patents and Trademarks. The award is binding only on the parties to the arbitration, and the parties may agree that the award will be modified if the patent that is the subject of the arbitration is subsequently determined to be invalid or unenforceable.

Congress further expanded the scope of informal resolution of intellectual property disputes when it enacted two statutes that became effective on November 8, 1984. The Patent Law Amendments Act of 1984 adds a new subsection (d) to 35 U.S.C. § 135, which provides for arbitration of patent interferences. The Semiconductor Chip Protection Act of 1984, codified at 17 U.S.C. § 901 *et seq.*, sanctions litigation of disputes over royalties payable for innocent infringement of chip-product rights unless they are resolved by voluntary negotiation, mediation, or binding arbitration.

The arbitrability of claims arising under the Copyright Act was further strengthened by *Saturday Evening Post Co. v. Rumbleseat Press, Inc.*, 816 F.2d 1191 (7th Cir. 1987), wherein the court held that federal law does not forbid arbitration of copyright validity where that validity is at issue in a contract dispute.

The Saturday Evening Post granted Rumbleseat Press a license to manufacture porcelain dolls derived from Norman Rockwell illustrations that were published in the magazine. The license agreement contained a no-contest clause prohibiting Rumbleseat from disputing the validity of Post's copyrights and providing for arbitration of disputes. A dispute arose when Rumbleseat continued making the dolls after the agreement expired. Post filed an action charging copyright violation and sought arbitration. Rumbleseat opposed arbitration. The district court ordered arbitration and subsequently confirmed an award in Post's favor.

Rumbleseat appealed, disputing the validity of Post's copyrights and arguing that copyright validity was not arbitrable. It also contended that the district court should have ordered a jury trial on the issue of arbitrability. The Seventh Circuit disagreed. Writing for the Seventh Circuit, Judge Posner reasoned that "if the arbitrability of the parties' dispute involves no questions or only legal questions, a jury trial would be pointless because its outcome could not affect the judge's decision on whether to order arbitration." *Id.* at 1196. The court rejected Rumbleseat's argument that Congress' decision to give the federal courts exclusive jurisdiction over copyright actions implicitly precluded arbitration of disputes over the validity of copyright issues that arise in the course of state actions. Judge Posner observed that there was "no reason to think that arbitrators are more likely to err in copyright cases than state or federal judges are; the Supreme Court recently rejected such an argument in holding that the arbitration of antitrust claims arising out of an international transaction was not contrary to public policy." *Id.* at 1199 (citing to *Mitsubishi*). The court explained that the question presented was not "whether the parties to a suit for copyright infringement may decide to refer the dispute to arbitration—no one doubts they may," but "whether the arbitration of a dispute arising from a copyright license must be interrupted if the licensee challenges the validity of the copyright." *Id.* It concluded that such an interruption would "toss a monkey wrench into an important means of resolving contractual disputes over intellectual property." *Id.*

The court also disagreed that a no-contest clause in a copyright licensing agreement was against public policy, stating that "the fact that we can find no antitrust case—or for that matter any other reported case—that deals with a no-contest clause in a copyright license is evidence that these clauses are not such a source of significant restraints on freedom to compete as might warrant a per se rule of illegality." *Id.* at 1201.

Bankruptcy Petitions

In the context of arbitration, the filing of a bankruptcy petition either before or during an arbitration proceeding raises the problem of conflict between two federal statutes: the FAA and the Bankruptcy Code (Code). Specifically, can arbitration proceed despite the automatic stay imposed on all proceedings at the time the bankruptcy petition is filed? In one such case, *In re Mor-Ben*, 73 Bank. 644 (Bankr. 9th Cir. 1987), the court held that in the absence of congressional intent to exclude arbitration from bankruptcy matters or a compelling circumstance seriously affecting the rights of creditors, the bankruptcy court properly ordered arbitration to proceed in London pursuant to a valid arbitration clause in an international agreement.

Mor-Ben entered into an agreement with three insurers giving Mor-Ben the authority to bind property insurance on their behalf. A dispute arose regarding Mor-Ben's entitlement to reimbursements after it filed a Chapter 11 petition. The insurers filed proofs of claim and Mor-Ben subsequently initiated adversary proceedings. The bankruptcy court stayed the adversary proceedings and compelled arbitration against Mor-Ben.

On appeal, the court determined that the evidence supported the bankruptcy court's finding that London was the most expeditious site for resolving the disputes between the parties: it was the parties' original intent to arbitrate the dispute in London, and London was the principal place of business for the majority of the parties. The court rejected the argument that conflicting policies of the Code and the FAA precluded the FAA from applying in certain instances. Instead, the court looked to the purpose of the FAA, which is to ensure judicial enforcement of agreements to arbitrate. Noting the strong national policy favoring the settlement of disputes through arbitration, especially in international commercial cases, the court concluded that absent an indication of congressional intent to exclude arbitration from bankruptcy matters or a compelling circumstance seriously affecting the rights of creditors, a valid arbitration clause in an international agreement must be enforced. Thus, it held that the bankruptcy court properly ordered the parties to proceed to arbitration in London pursuant to their agreement.

Note that while arbitration cases involving the filing of bankruptcy petitions will still need to be decided on a case-by-case basis, *In re Mor-Ben* illustrates that arbitration, as a mechanism to resolve disputes, may be entirely appropriate in spite of the presence of a filed bankruptcy petition.

International v. Domestic

A frequent issue that arises is whether a transaction is classified as domestic or international. Resolution of this question is important because of the different standards used. As a result of the Court's decision in *McMahon*, resolution of this question has been simplified. An example is *Genesco, Inc. v. T. Kakiuchi & Co., Ltd.*, 815 F.2d 840 (2d Cir. 1987).

Genesco, an American clothing manufacturer, purchased fabric from Kakiuchi-Japan and its U.S. agent, Kakiuchi-America. The sales agreement between Genesco and Kakiuchi-Japan called for arbitration of disputes in Japan. Genesco and Kakiuchi-America agreed to arbitrate disputes in the United States. Thereafter, Genesco's vice president of purchasing allegedly conspired with the Kakiuchis to purchase certain goods solely from Kakiuchi-Japan or its affiliates and to approve the purchase of overpriced, damaged, or unsuitable goods. Genesco discovered the scheme and filed an action against Kakiuchi-Japan and Kakiuchi-America claiming fraud; violations of RICO per 18 U.S.C. § 1962(a),(c) and (d) and the Robinson-Patman Act per 15 U.S.C. § 13(c); unjust enrichment; tortious interference with the contract; and unfair competition. Both Kakiuchis moved to stay the action pending arbitration pursuant to the FAA and the U.N. Convention. The district court declined to stay the proceedings because it found only two of Genesco's claims arbitrable: the common-law fraud and RICO claims against Kakiuchi-America.

On appeal, the Second Circuit reversed. It held that Genesco's unjust enrichment and unfair competition claims against both Kakiuchis were arbitrable and that Genesco's fraud, RICO, and Robinson-Patman claims against Kakiuchi-Japan were subject to arbitration as well. In finding the RICO claims against Kakiuchi-Japan arbitrable, the court stated that "nothing in RICO's text or legislative history evidences a congressional exception to the Federal Arbitration Act for RICO violations." *Id.* at 851. It reasoned that "the mandate of *Mitsubishi* applie[d] with full force" since the arbitration agreement between Genesco and Kakiuchi-Japan arose in an international context. *Id.* at 852. Genesco's RICO claim against Kakiuchi-America was found nonarbitrable, however. The fact that the goods were produced in one country and sold in another was deemed insufficient to trigger the international concerns voiced in *Mitsubishi*.

The court further reasoned that, since arbitration was called for in New York, "refusal to compel arbitration would not demonstrate disrespect for foreign arbitral institutions, nor adversely affect international comity." *Id.*

at 853. It then remanded the issue of the arbitrability of Genesco's RICO and Robinson-Patman claims against Kakiuchi-America to the district court for further proceedings in light of the Supreme Court's then anticipated decision in *McMahon*. The court affirmed the finding of nonarbitrability of the claim of tortious interference with contract, remanding it to the district court to consider whether the claim should be stayed pending arbitration of the other claims.

Termination of Contract

In a recent decision, *Apollo v. Berg*, 886 F.2d 469 (1st Cir. 1989), the court held that parties who agree to have all disputes arising out of or in connection with the distributorship agreement submitted to arbitration for resolution have agreed to submit issues of arbitrability to the arbitrator.

Apollo and Dicoscan entered into an agreement granting Dicoscan the right to distribute Apollo's computers in four Scandinavian countries. Helge Berg and Lars Arvid Skoog, Chairman and President, signed the agreement on behalf of Dicoscan. The agreement also contained an arbitration agreement providing for the arbitration of disputes under the Rules of Arbitration of the International Chamber of Commerce (ICC), a clause stating that Massachusetts law would govern, and a nonassignment provision.

Apollo terminated the agreement after several disputes arose. Thereafter, Dicoscan filed for protection under Swedish bankruptcy law. The trustee assigned Dicoscan's right to bring claims against Apollo to Berg and Skoog, who filed a complaint and a request for arbitration with the ICC. Apollo rejected arbitration on the ground that there was no agreement to arbitrate and that arbitration was precluded by the nonassignment provision. The ICC ruled that the issues should be resolved by the arbitrator and directed the parties to proceed to arbitration. Apollo filed an action in federal court seeking a stay of arbitration. The court denied the request and Apollo appealed.

The appellate court found that it had jurisdiction because the lower court's order resolved the only issue before it—Berg's and Skoog's right to compel arbitration—in its entirety. As for the arbitrability issue, the court first reviewed the lower court's opinion. It found that the lower court determined that the "parties had explicitly agreed to have the issue of arbitrability decided by the arbitrator." *Id*. at 472. On the issue of whether the agreement's nonassignment clause prevented [Berg and Skoog] from asserting [Dicoscan's] right to arbitrate, the lower court ruled that "it did not because under Massachusetts law, a general nonassignment clause will be construed as barring only the delegation of duties, not the assignment of rights." *Id*.

Agreeing with the lower court's reasoning, the appellate court declined to consider Apollo's arguments that the right to compel arbitration did not survive the termination of the agreement and that the nonassignment clause rendered the purported assignment unenforceable against Apollo. It found that the lower court was correct in finding that the parties had contracted to submit issues of arbitrability to the arbitrator. The court further stated that whether the right to compel arbitration survives the termination of the agreement and whether that right was validly assigned were issues of arbitrability relating to the continued existence and validity of the agreement which the parties had delegated to the arbitrator for resolution. In accordance with its findings, the court affirmed the lower court's order denying a permanent stay of arbitration.

Unresolved Issues—ERISA and ADEA Claims

In *Bird v. Shearson Lehman/American Express, Inc.* 871 F.2d 292 (2d Cir. 1989), a statutory claim created by the Employee Retirement Income Security Act of 1974 (ERISA) was held not subject to compulsory arbitration, despite the existence of an arbitration agreement, because violations of the ERISA statute are the exclusive province of the federal courts.

Frank L. Bird, trustee of a retirement fund, invested funds with Shearson Lehman, a securities broker. Bird signed a standard broker-customer agreement containing a broad arbitration clause. After the value of the fund dwindled, Bird filed an action against Shearson, alleging a breach of fiduciary duty under ERISA and churning of the account in violation of federal securities law. Shearson moved to stay the court action pending arbitration pursuant to the broker-customer agreement. The court ruled that the agreement was binding upon Bird only as far as his securities claims were concerned, but that he was not obligated to arbitrate his ERISA claim. Shearson appealed.

The appellate court noted that although the FAA evinces a strong national policy favoring arbitration, the FAA is still subject to a showing that Congress intended to preclude a waiver of judicial remedies. In the present case, the court determined that Congress intended that access to federal courts be nonwaivable for resolution of statutory violations of ERISA, noting that pension issues were generally arbitrable until the enactment of ERISA, which specifically provides for federal court access. The court ruled that although suits to enforce rights to benefits that are purely contractual may be submitted to arbitration, claims predicated on substantive violations of ERISA are exclusively the province of the federal courts. It concluded that "a federal judicial forum cannot be cut off to those asserting claims created as part of a comprehensive federal scheme protecting the rights of individual participants or beneficiaries of a pension plan and which fall within the exclusive jurisdiction of the federal courts." *Id.* at 298.

Also held nonarbitrable, in *Nicholson v. CPC International Inc.*, 46 FEP Cases 1019 (D.N.J. 1988), are Age Discrimination in Employment Act (ADEA) claims.

A corporate executive entered into an employment contract containing an arbitration clause. Following his termination, the executive filed a lawsuit in federal court, alleging violation of the ADEA. The employer sought to compel arbitration pursuant to the arbitration agreement.

The court, finding that the Court's opinion in *McMahon* did not require a reassessment of the district court's holding in *Steck v. Smith Barney*, 661 F. Supp. 543 (D.N.J. 1987), held that federal age discrimination claims are not subject to arbitration. The court disagreed with the employer's argument that under *McMahon*, arbitration pursuant to the agreement was warranted because the executive failed to demonstrate a congressional intent to preclude arbitration. The court adhered to its earlier determination in *Steck* that there was a "congressional intent to preclude waiver of judicial remedies under the ADEA." *Id.* at 1022.

The court also rejected two findings by the Court upon which the employer relied. First, it ruled that in an ADEA context, "there is every reason to believe that arbitrators, at least in certain instances, *cannot* follow the law. . . . [E]quitable relief is generally beyond an arbitrator's authority." *Id.* Second, the court noted that, unlike the securities industry, which can rely on the "existence and supervisory authority of the Securities and Exchange Commission," in the ADEA context "there is no regulatory authority comparable to the SEC." *Id.* at 1022–1023. It further stated that while the "Equal Employment Opportunity Commission has authority to enforce the provisions of the ADEA, . . . [its] influence and control pales in comparison to the SEC's." *Id.* at 1023.

Because the facts in this action warranted different conclusions from those of the Court in *McMahon* the district court concluded that the *McMahon* decision did not require it to depart from its holding in *Steck*. Consequently, the executive was allowed to pursue his ADEA claim in court. The employer appealed.

The appellate court agreed with the lower court's ruling and affirmed the lower court's order. 877 F.2d 221 (3d Cir. 1989). The court reasoned that the recent decision by the Court in *McMahon* and *Rodriguez de Quijas*, while espousing a policy of enforcement of arbitration agreements in commercial transactions, did not indicate the Court's intent to preclude access to a judicial forum for resolution of claims arising under the Fair Labor Standards Act (FLSA) or under title VII of the 1964 Civil Rights Act. Because the FLSA enforcement provisions continue to govern enforcement proceedings under the ADEA and the legislative history shows that "Congress made a deliberate policy choice in favor of enforcement of ADEA claims in court proceedings," the court concluded that Nicholson should not be precluded from access to a judicial forum. *Id.* at 226.

A dissenting opinion was filed, which stated that arbitration agreements covering ADEA claims must be enforced pursuant to the FAA. The dissenting opinion reasoned in part that ADEA disputes are no more complex than other types of disputes that have been held to be arbitrable and that the majority misconstrued the Court's discussion in *McMahon* of the Securities and Exchange Commission's power. In conclusion, the dissenting judge stated that the application of general contract principles to enforce an arbitration agreement that was entered into voluntarily and knowingly would not undermine the goals of the ADEA.

Contra to *Nicholson* is *Gilmer v. Interstate/Johnson Lane Corp.*, 895 F.2d 195 (4th Cir. 1990). Robert D. Gilmer was hired by Interstate/Johnson Lane as a manager of financial services. He registered as a securities representative with the New York Stock Exchange. The registration contained an arbitration clause requiring the arbitration of disputes between himself and Interstate arising out of his employment or the termination of his employment. Gilmer's employment was later terminated and he filed suit against Interstate, alleging an ADEA violation. The district court ruled that the arbitration agreement was not enforceable. The ruling was reversed on appeal.

The appellate court found that the dispute was arbitrable, reasoning that there is "no congressional intent to preclude enforcement of arbitration agreements in the ADEA's text, its legislative history, or its underlying purposes." *Id.* at 196. The court disagreed with the reasoning of the Third Circuit in *Nicholson* regarding the role of the Equal Employment Opportunity Commission, and further stated that "[w]e are reluctant to conclude that the mere fact of administrative involvement in a statutory scheme of enforcement operates as an implicit exception to the presumption of arbitral availability under the FAA." *Id.* at 198.

In addition, the court found that the fact that "arbitrators may lack the full breadth of equitable discretion possessed by courts to go beyond the relief accorded individual victims does not deny the utility of this alternative means of resolving disputes." *Id.* at 199. It concluded that there is "no reason . . . why an arbitrator of an ADEA dispute cannot award liquidated damages should he or she find a willful violation of the statute." *Id.* at 200. Moreover, as to the ability of arbitrators to decide such disputes, the court stated that "[i]n ruling that antitrust and RICO claims were not beyond the ken of arbitrators, the Supreme Court brushed aside objections that such statutory claims were too complex for arbitrators to handle ADEA disputes are, to put it mildly, no more generically complex than claims pressed under the Sherman Act and RICO.'' *Id*. at 201.

Conclusion

The recent case law in the area of arbitrability reaffirms the voluntary contractual nature of arbitration and its suitability as a means of enforcing a broad range of rights, including those created by statute. As a consequence, arbitration is now placed on an equal footing with litigation when chosen by the parties as an alternative forum. Parties to a valid arbitration agreement are no longer able to avoid or delay the process of arbitration by the mere assertion of statutory claims. Indeed, as the Supreme Court noted in *McMahon*, ''[b]y agreeing to arbitrate a statutory claim, a party does not forgo the substantive rights afforded by the statute; it only submits to their resolution in an arbitral, rather than a judicial forum.'' *Id*. at 2339. This expansion of arbitrable subject matter and of the authority of arbitrators not only strengthens and eases the way to effective arbitration; it also poses a challenge to us all to use the process responsibly so as to realize its full potential—that of providing fair, prompt, economical, and final disposition of disputes.

COMMENTARY

Alternative Dispute Resolution

Michael F. Hoellering*

With increasing frequency in recent years, extrajudicial means of dispute resolution are providing an important supplementary avenue of justice in the United States. While litigation remains the primary method of dispute resolution, alternatives to litigation are being employed with regularity to

---

* Paper presented at a meeting of the German Arbitration Institute, Nuremberg, West Germany, November, 1989. Michael F. Hoellering is General Counsel of the American Arbitration Association. Vicki M. Young, Editor of Court Decisions at the American Arbitration Association, assisted in the article's preparation.

meet the burgeoning complexities of modern day society and provide a meaningful redress of grievances. This is especially so since the public court system, overwhelmed by crushing caseloads, insufficient resources, and inefficient traditional litigation methods, simply can no longer cope with the wealth of human problems that clamor for judicial attention.

Perhaps it should be stated at the outset that I regard the term Alternative Dispute Resolution (ADR) as encompassing all litigation alternatives, whether quasijudicial in nature or aimed primarily at furthering the negotiation process, with the outcome controlled by the parties themselves rather than a neutral decision maker. This follows, in my view, from present day notions of ADR, which may be traced, first and foremost, to the business community's early efforts to encourage private voluntary arbitration; secondly, to increased experimentation in the courts with diverse settlement procedures; and, more recently, to stepped-up corporate efforts to find ways of curtailing the high costs associated with traditional litigation.

Arbitration

Of the various litigation alternatives, arbitration is by far the most widely used. The reasons why arbitration is preferred are numerous. Arbitration provides parties with the freedom to tailor the procedure to their needs and practices. It is also final: the parties agree to be bound by the result. Additional advantages are the expertise of impartial decision makers, economy, speed, and privacy. Arbitration agreements are enforceable by laws, treaties, and conventions in many nations. And, in international transactions, a properly structured arbitration agreement serves to provide a neutral forum and freedom from parochial national law concepts.[1]

The strong United States policy favoring arbitral dispute resolution is embodied in the Federal Arbitration Act[2] and the arbitration laws of the various states.[3] Judicial decisions interpreting these statutes further provide for the vigorous enforcement of arbitration agreements, for judicial assistance in aid of arbitration when necessary, and for a high degree of arbitral finality. A broad range of claims, including those created by statute such as the securities, antitrust, and fraud laws, are subject to arbitration.[4] All in all, broad autonomy in fashioning the arbitration arrangement is accorded to contracting parties, and litigation-type discovery devices are not a part of U.S. arbitration practice in the absence of special agreement by the parties.

The high volume of cases arbitrated in the United States is reflected in the statistics of the American Arbitration Association (AAA) which, in 1989, administered 56,000 cases, ranging the gamut of commercial transactions with billions of dollars in claims. About 150 of these were classified as international, involving parties from 36 different countries.

Court-Annexed Arbitration

While a large number of commercial cases are resolved each year through private arbitration, the courts themselves, in many instances, have adopted arbitration programs which litigants must utilize prior to trial. Given the mandatory nature of these programs, the decisions of the arbitrators, for constitutional reasons, are not final but are subject to appeal by any party prepared to bear the opposing party's costs if it does not obtain a judgment that is more favorable than the arbitrator's award. Court-annexed arbitration programs now operate for most civil actions with claims up to a certain amount in both state and federal courts. These limits vary from jurisdiction to jurisdiction. For example, the state programs of Florida, Michigan, Minnesota, and New Hampshire have no limit at all; California, Colorado, Connecticut, the District of Columbia, Delaware, Missouri, Mississippi, and Rhode Island have a $50,000 limit; New York has settled on $6,000; Louisiana on $2,000; and Hawaii on $150,000. The cases actually disposed of under these programs include a high number of domestic relations and matrimonial disputes, as well as contractual, minor criminal, and tort claims. Federal court-annexed arbitration programs now operate in 20 districts. Generally, they apply a limit of $100,000 in claims, but no two districts are alike in all their dimensions. Cases may be exempted from the program if complex or novel issues are involved, if legal issues predominate over factual ones, or for other good cause. After receiving an award, any party may file a written demand for a trial *de novo*. The action is then restored to the court's docket and treated as if it had not been referred to arbitration. Arbitration does not affect a party's right to a trial by jury or the position of the case on the court calendar. Experience has shown that this form of arbitration provides an effective screening mechanism which contributes to a direct settlement between the parties in many thousands of cases, with a large number of lawyers participating in the arbitration process and/or contributing their services as arbitrators.

Mediation

Perhaps the second most popular emerging ADR technique is that of commercial mediation, sometimes referred to as conciliation. The function of the mediator, most often an expert in the area of the dispute and in mediation, is to assist the parties in reaching a settlement of their dispute by direct negotiations. A mediator participates impartially in the negotiations, advising and consulting the various parties involved. In trying to help parties maximize their interests in a written agreement, the mediator may be called upon to play a number of different roles. Sometimes a mediator will simply facilitate discussions between the parties, translate industry jargon, and help the parties sort out the real issues between them as well as identify areas of agreement. Other times he or she will need to be an educator, guiding the parties toward a better understanding by illuminating technical aspects of the dispute. Often the mediator will serve as a tactful messenger conveying information gathered in separate meetings with the parties. These demands on the skills of the mediator are a direct consequence of the fact that a mediator cannot impose a solution on the parties, but can only seek to guide them to mutual agreement.

Mediation is now employed extensively by the insurance industry, which has trained staff to seek out suitable cases for ADR treatment. A number of insurance companies are now working closely with the AAA to implement mediation programs, with the AAA serving as a bridge to claimant's counsel to facilitate the submission of appropriate cases to mediation. The actual referral procedure is quite simple. An insurance carrier interested in using the ADR system will select cases, usually already pending in court, that it is willing to submit to mediation or arbitration. The carrier provides the AAA with pertinent information, such as names, addresses, and phone numbers of the plaintiff or the plaintiff's counsel. The AAA then contacts the plaintiff or its attorney and advises of the insurer's willingness to arbitrate or mediate. The choice of method of dispute resolution is left to the plaintiff. If the plaintiff elects to use ADR, a submission form is executed, and the matter is administered pursuant to the applicable AAA procedures. The construction industry, as well, is showing great receptivity to this new form of ADR.

Experience in cases mediated under AAA auspices indicates that more than 75 percent of mediated cases resulted in a settlement between the parties. Even the AAA's arbitration rules now provide a mediation option, providing the parties with an opportunity to utilize the services of specially trained mediators.[5] Various industry organizations have included a mediation step in their industry documents. The popularity of this approach is on the rise, as parties come to realize that significant savings in time and money can be achieved through mediation in the early stages of the dispute, before claims mount and the positions of the parties harden. Special AAA mediation rules for commercial and construction disputes are available to facilitate use of this ADR technique.[6]

Med-Arb

Still another technique suggested from time to time is that of mediation-arbitration. As its name implies, it is a procedure which combines in a single individual the functions of a mediator and an arbitrator. Under this approach, if parties cannot resolve the dispute, the mediator-arbitrator is authorized to meet with anyone connected with the dispute in order to investigate, inspect, or discover relevant facts; call together all interested persons or parties for negotiating sessions; engage in mediation with the parties, either separately or together; determine that unresolved issues are appropriate for arbitration; and hold evidentiary hearings, as well as issue a final and binding award on the remaining issues.

This technique, first used in the sphere of labor management relations, particularly the negotiation of collective bargaining agreements with newly recognized unions, has not been widely accepted in the commercial sphere. Given the usually confidential nature of mediation sessions and the give and take of settlement discussions, it is understandable why a party unwilling to accept a mediator's recommendations for settlement would be reluctant to submit the same issues for final decision to that same mediator. It might be otherwise where the parties have a high degree of trust and confidence in a particular individual to serve in the combined role of mediator-arbitrator.

Disputes Review Board

Still another ADR technique, initially developed to aid the resolution of disputes in underground construction and thereafter found useful on large projects, especially those likely to generate unexpected difficulties, is that of the disputes review board. First utilized on a tunneling project in Colorado which involved excavating a 48-foot-wide by 50-foot-high 8,900-foot tunnel for Interstate 70, this procedure has been implemented on about a dozen projects, disposing of a variety of claims over such matters as the interpretation of specifications, financial responsibility for portions of the work performed, and costs of delay. Under this technique a three-member board, composed of individuals with requisite yet varying industry expertise, is organized soon after award of the contract and before any disputes arise. The impartiality and qualifications of the members of the board are critical to success, and both parties should participate actively in the board's creation.

The primary role of the disputes board is to provide independent assessments of the merits of significant disputes. While board recommendations are not binding on either party, experience has shown that there is a strong incentive towards acceptance of the findings and recommendations of a board representing various disciplines and jointly established by the contracting parties. In addition to providing recommendations for settlement, the disputes board can also promote cooperation among contractor, owner, and engineer, as well as help resolve problems before they become unmanageable. However, since the board's recommendations are advisory only, the inclusion of a final arbitration step should be considered, so as to guard against costly litigation in the event of an impasse. Where a given dispute is not resolved by the board and needs to be arbitrated or litigated, the board proceedings and recommendations may, if the parties so choose, be made available as evidence in the subsequent proceeding. The overall cost of implementing a board procedure on one recent project was approximately $130,000. The experience with such boards so far has been limited yet highly favorable, suggesting that a panel of outside experts with an understanding of the technical issues can contribute to the solution of emerging disputes without the uncertainty and high costs associated with traditional litigation. Other potential benefits are the rewards of better relationships on the job, uninterrupted work, timely completion, and expedited final payment for work performed.

Mini-Trial

An ADR technique of more recent vintage is the mini-trial. First employed in 1977, this form of ADR has paved the way for the settlement of a number of high-risk controversies involving parties in both the private and public sectors. Despite its name, the mini-trial is not a trial, but a structured settlement procedure which facilitates an abbreviated, confidential, nonbinding information exchange aimed at assisting the parties in settling their dispute. A primary purpose of the mini-trial is to facilitate dialogue between the parties on the merits of the case, with the participation of high-level executives with settlement authority, during which the controversy is narrowed, collateral issues are disposed of, and a fair and equitable settlement is encouraged. It has been stated that the mini-trial is most suitable for existing and ongoing disputes between business enterprises that may or may not be contractually bound, which do not involve constitutional issues, novel questions of law, issues of credibility, or multiple parties.

The way in which a mini-trial is structured depends entirely upon the parties. Once they agree on how to proceed, they enter into a voluntary agreement which sets the guidelines to be followed. Well-drafted mini-trial agreements seek to anticipate most problems that may occur. Generally, such an agreement contemplates presentation by the attorneys for each side and any necessary expert witnesses. Top executives with settlement authority from each side are the observers, and an impartial third party may be asked to act as chairperson to moderate the presentations and ensure compliance with agreed-upon procedures.

Customarily, a mini-trial is preceded by abbreviated court-type discovery. Such issues as filing deadlines, preparation of documents, exhibits, and witness depositions are addressed in the parties' agreement. If the parties desire, administrative assistance from an arbitral institution, such as the AAA or the Zurich Chamber of Commerce, is available.[7]

Once the summary presentations of each party's best case are made in the presence of management representatives, the executives are given an opportunity to meet and attempt to reach a settlement of the dispute. If a settlement cannot be achieved, the neutral advisor may be asked to provide recommendations based upon an evaluation of the probable outcome of the case in court or arbitration. Even where the mini-trial does not produce a settlement, each party will have gained a better idea as to the strength and weaknesses of its case, thereby aiding its preparation for any subsequent proceedings. Even where only some of the issues are resolved, a benefit has been realized.

While most mini-trials take an average of two days, some are of an even shorter duration. In one recent case, the mini-trial took less than three hours and because of the particular circumstances, the parties dispensed with live testimony. They structured the mini-trial as if it were an appeal, submitting the case on depositions, briefs, and oral argument. An opinion was rendered within 30 days.

Some of the early mini-trials dealt with patent disputes, perhaps because at the time, patent validity and infringement issues were not yet arbitrable in the United States. This does not mean, however, that the technique is not applicable to a broad range of disputes. In one such proceeding, conducted by the AAA's Atlanta office, a dispute arose out of the construction of a paper manufacturing plant. The claims and counterclaims totalled $6,000,000 and included hundreds of change orders and alleged pricing errors. Shortly before arbitration was to start, the parties agreed to a mini-trial as a final good faith effort to resolve the dispute, with a former federal judge as the third-party neutral. Two days were set aside for the proceeding. The executives who took part in the proceeding neither were involved in the day-to-day management of the project nor had previously met. Each party's representative made opening statements, used charts and documents, and answered questions from the panel, which consisted of the executives and the former judge. The remainder of the two days was spent in meetings between the executives and the judge and in conferences with the parties' legal representatives. Following the conclusion of the second day, the executives agreed to continue negotiations of a settlement of the claims and counterclaims. The negotiations involved company counsel but not trial counsel. Although negotiations continued for several months, a memorandum of agreement was finally signed. The mini-trial has also proven acceptable to agencies of the United States government. The traditional reluctance of U.S. federal agencies to agree to binding arbitration by a third party is a significant factor.

While the mini-trial so far has been used largely within the United States, there is no reason why, in appropriate cases, it cannot serve equally in the international sphere. Disputes between parties from different countries are often of a high-risk, complex nature, involving questions of confidentiality, the need to maintain business relationships, and large expenditures of time and money when adversary proceedings are required. Nevertheless, there is little evidence so far that mini-trials, developed initially to overcome difficulties with traditional litigation in U.S. courts, have been utilized in a significant way in any other country. Discussions with practitioners suggest that cultural differences and the legal regimes may explain the infrequent use of such ADR techniques. Singled out also were a greater tendency on the part of European enterprises to engage routinely in settlement discussions, reduced cost incentives based on prevailing rules governing allocation of legal costs, a large proportion of litigation costs being borne by the state, easier access to the courts, and in some countries a tradition of decision making by consensus. Nevertheless, in the United States the concept of a mini-trial is well established and it would seem advantageous for European practitioners to become familiar with this new dispute resolution technique.

Court Referral

Recent changes to rule 16 of the Federal Rules of Civil Procedure gave the federal district courts greater discretion in the management of individual actions. Rule 16 (c)(7) specifically permits the parties to explore at a pretrial conference "the possibility of settlement or the use of extra-judicial procedures to resolve the dispute."

Following adoption of this rule, the U.S. District Court for the Southern District of New York, the busiest commercial court in the nation, joined with the AAA to create a vehicle through which the court can refer appropriate cases to arbitration, mediation, fact finding, or mini-trial. Designed to operate with a minimum of judicial time and effort, the program provides for the voluntary participation by the judges of the court and their retaining complete discretion in the type of cases referred. The workings of the program are quite simple. The judge evaluates the case for suitability and, if the case is deemed appropriate, issues an order compelling the parties to attend a conference at the AAA for the purpose of exploring alternative methods of dispute resolution. The parties have 30 days in which to schedule a conference. This is the only aspect of the program which is mandatory. The parties to a dispute are free to reject ADR for resolution of their case. If, after discussion with an AAA representative, they conclude that their case is suitable for ADR, they then may choose among the ADR methods listed above. Prior to the conference, counsel for the parties receive a memorandum explaining the program, as well as a brief introduction to ADR, which describes the various dispute resolution alternatives. If the parties select mediation, fact finding, arbitration, or mini-trial, they then sign a stipulation to that effect and the court is so informed. The confidentiality of the conference is protected and is not part of the information relayed to the court. The case is then suspended on the court's docket, pending completion of ADR. When completed, a final report is issued to the court by the AAA, informing the court whether ADR efforts were successful and, if so, what the outcome was. Again, the report is brief and does not breach the confidentiality of the AAA conferences. If binding arbitration is chosen, stipulation and submission agreements are signed, which remove the case entirely from the court's docket, as parties will be bound by the arbitral result.

Experience to date reflects that in about half of the cases referred by the court to the AAA for conferences, the parties have agreed that some form of ADR would be appropriate. Of such cases, about one third were submitted to binding arbitration, and two thirds to mediation. The types of issues and amounts involved were quite diverse. Cases referred to the ADR project have moved swiftly through the process. It has become clear, through experience, that it is the attitude of the parties and their counsel, rather than the type of dispute referred, that determines the likelihood of its submission to extrajudicial dispute resolution. During the five years that it has been in operation, the program has made an important and timely contribution to advancing the practice of dispute resolution alternatives within the courts.

Conclusion

In this discussion I have sought to outline briefly the more prominent alternative dispute resolution techniques currently in use in the United States. There are others beyond the scope of this discussion—the California rent-a-judge system, the summary jury trial, and negotiated rule making, to name but a few—and there is much valuable experimentation underway. This, at times, has led to a confusion of terms and the promotion of one technique at the expense of another. To fully realize the advantages of the various techniques will require an informed appreciation of their particular characteristics and suitability under given circumstances. Clearly, the newer techniques, despite their high promise and the proliferation of organizations that seek to promote them, are still in their infancy. They deserve our full support, for with 98 percent of litigated cases settled on the courthouse steps and 50 percent of arbitrated cases settled prior to an award, it makes eminent good sense to promote earlier resolutions, before positions harden and claims escalate. Equally important are continued efforts to foster the responsible use and effectiveness of arbitration. Ultimately, the benefits of the various ADR techniques, without at the same time overformalizing the dispute resolution process, will require the close cooperation of all concerned—the business community, corporate lawyers, trial lawyers, the experts that serve in a neutral capacity, the providers of ADR services, and members of the judiciary.

Notes

1. Of interest in international transactions are the provisions of the United Nations Convention on the Recognition and Enforcement of Foreign Arbitral Awards (U.N. Convention), 21 U.S.T. 2517, T.I.A.S. No. 6997, 330 U.N.T.S. 4739, which provides for the enforcement of arbitration agreements and awards. Presently, there are now 85 countries who are contracting states to the U.N. Convention, which is also known as the New York Convention. The United States implementing legislation is codified at 9 U.S.C. § 201 *et seq.*
2. 9 U.S.C. § 1 *et seq.*
3. E.g., California Civil Proc. Code, §§ 1280 *et seq.*; Connecticut Gen. Stat. Ann., §§ 52-408 *et seq.*; District of Columbia Code, title 16 §§ 16-4301 *et seq.*; Florida Stat. Ann., §§ 682.01 *et seq.*; Georgia Code, §§ 9-9-1 *et seq*; Hawaii Rev. Stat. §§ 658-1 *et seq.*; Massachusetts Ann. Laws, Chapter 251, §§ 1 *et seq.*; New York Civ. Prac. Law. §§ 7501 *et seq.*; and Texas Rev. Civ. Stat. Ann., title 10, Articles 224 *et seq.*
4. E.g., *Prima Paint Corp. v. Flood & Conklin Mfg. Co.*, 388 U.S. 395, 87 S. Ct. 1801, 18 L. Ed. 2d 1270 (1967); *Mitsubishi Motors Corp. v. Soler Chrysler-Plymouth, Inc.*, 473 U.S. 614, 105 S. Ct. 3346, 87 L. Ed. 2d 444 (1985); and *Shearson/American Express Inc. v. McMahon*, 482 U.S. 220, 107 S. Ct. 2332, 96 L. Ed. 2d 185 (1987).
5. E.g., American Arbitration Association's Commercial Arbitration Rules, § 10, as amended and in effect January 1, 1990.
6. American Arbitration Association's Commercial Mediation Rules, as amended and in effect October 1, 1987; American Arbitration Association's Construction Industry Mediation Rules, as amended and in effect October 1, 1987.
7. E.g., American Arbitration Association's Mini-Trial Procedures, as amended and in effect December 1, 1986.

B. FOREIGN ARBITRATION LEGISLATION AND RULES

ALGERIA

Management Contracts; Law 88-01; Law 89-01

The Middle East Executive Reports, Volume 12, No. 8, reports that Law No. 89-01 on Management Contracts was promulgated in February and published in the Official Journal the following day. The law covers only management contracts entered into between a public economic enterprise or a joint venture on the one hand and a foreign company on the other. The law contains no provision on dispute settlement. However, Law 88-01 empowers public economic enterprises to accept international arbitration clauses. While joint ventures cannot resort to arbitration to resolve internal disputes between the joint venturers, this prohibition does not apply to contracts with third parties. The article concludes that it would be possible in all cases to insert an international arbitration clause in these management contracts.

BERMUDA

Arbitration Act 1986

The Association has received the country's Arbitration Act 1986, which became operative on August 25, 1986. It repeals the Arbitration Act of 1924 and the Arbitration (Foreign Awards) Act of 1976.

Readers may be particularly interested in Part II, Conciliation, which provides that a future disputes conciliation clause is enforceable, that a clause which provides that the conciliator be the arbitrator if the conciliation fails precludes objection to that dual role, and that a settlement reached through conciliation shall be enforced as if it had been an arbitration award.

Other provisions of interest deal with bankruptcy (III 6.); consolidation (III 9.); court assistance in discovery, interrogatories, and writs of habeas corpus (III 20.); interim awards (III 22.); and interest on awards (III 28.).

Section 26, Costs, has a nonwaivable provision which follows:

> 26. (3) Any provision in an arbitration agreement to the effect that the parties or any party thereto shall in any event pay their or his own costs of the reference or award or any part thereof shall be void, and this Part shall in the case of an arbitration agreement containing any such provision, have effect as if that provision were not contained therein:
>
> Provided that nothing in this subsection shall invalidate such a provision when it is a part of an agreement to submit to arbitration a dispute which has arisen before the making of that agreement.

Enforcement of awards rendered in countries signatory to the New York Convention will be refused only upon the grounds provided by the UNCITRAL Model Law.

HONG KONG

Amendment No. 2 to Arbitration Ordinance 1989

On April 6, 1990, the Arbitration (Amendment) (No. 2) Ordinance 1989 went into force.

The Ordinance deals first with the conciliation section, which is amended by providing that an arbitrator or umpire may act as a conciliator when all parties agree in writing and until one party withdraws its consent. If the conciliation ends without a settlement the neutral, before resuming the arbitration, shall disclose to all parties as much of the confidential information that he received during the conciliation as he considers material to the arbitration proceedings. Finally, no objection may be taken to an arbitration upon the ground that the arbitrator served previously as the conciliator.

Two sections deal with the confidentiality which will attach to proceedings under the Ordinance in Hong Kong courts. First, on application of a party, the proceeding shall be heard "otherwise than in open court." And, on application of a party, the court shall give directions as to what information, if any, relating to the proceedings may be published. No publication is permitted unless all parties agree to it or the court is satisfied that the information " . . . would not reveal any matter, including the identity of any party to the proceeding, that any party reasonably wishes to remain confidential." Where the court considers the judgment to be of "major legal interest," it may direct the publication in law reports and professional publications unless a party "reasonably wishes to conceal any matter, including the fact that he was a party." In that event, the court shall "conceal" that material in the report or direct that no report shall be published until a period, not to exceed ten years, has elapsed.

"For the avoidance of doubt," the law explicitly declares that sections 44, 45, and 47 of the Legal Practitioners Ordinance (Cap. 159) do not apply to arbitration proceedings, except where the services are performed in connection with court proceedings. Section 50 of the Practitioners Ordinance (which provides that no costs in respect of anything done by an unqualified person acting as a solicitor shall be recoverable in any action, suit, or matter) shall not apply to the recovery of costs directed by an arbitration award.

The Ordinance also repeals Section 23 A(4) dealing with the determination of a preliminary point of law by the court.

The Ordinance also provides that where an award is rendered by a Judge-Arbitrator or a Judge-Umpire he may also grant leave to enforce it.

The balance of the statute (the Fifth Schedule) is given over to the full-text reproduction of the UNCITRAL Model Law on International Commercial Arbitration. However, section 2(c)(IV), which is reproduced in the Fifth Schedule, mistakenly reads: "the UNCITRAL Model Law means the Model Law on International Trade Law . . . ".

PEOPLE'S REPUBLIC OF CHINA

Patent Disputes Procedures of the Shanghai Municipality

A. The Baker & McKenzie *Pacific Basin Legal Developments Bulletin*, October, 1989, features a report on Shanghai's patent dispute measures.

Joseph T. Simone writes that "The Provisional Measures of the Shanghai Municipality for Handling Patent Disputes was recently enacted." The measures, which are similar to those issued in Beijing in 1988, focus primarily on arbitration procedures. The writer summarizes the significant provisions as follows:

- Patent holders or other interested parties to infringement disputes must apply for arbitration within two years from the date that the party knew or should have known of the infringing activities. Other disputes involving patents must be submitted to arbitration within one year.
- The Shanghai Patent Bureau must decide whether to handle a patent arbitration within ten days after receipt of an application.
- Arbitration committee members may not have a personal interest in the

disputes and have the right to inspect files and relevant evidentiary material retained by other departments.

- Respondents who fail to respond to an arbitration notice may be subject to a default judgment.
- If, in the course of a patent infringement arbitration, a party seeks to invalidate a patent, the arbitration will be adjourned until the Patent Review Committee of the Shanghai Patent Bureau makes a determination on the patent's validity.

B. In the January *Bulletin*, Mr. Simone reports that China International Economic and Trade Arbitration Commission (CIETAC) established a new panel of arbitrators in August, 1989. While most of the members of the panel are P.R.C. citizens, a few foreign lawyers and technical experts have also been appointed. Among the foreign lawyers appointed to the panel is Michael J. Moser, a partner of Baker & McKenzie resident in Hong Kong, and two other Americans.

C. In 1989, members of the Shenzhen Commission visited the offices of the American Arbitration Association and gave us the new rules of the Commission and a list of its arbitrators.

The Commission was established four years ago to provide service to traders and investors from foreign countries, particularly Hong Kong and Macao. Since its establishment it has handled some 170 arbitrations including joint ventures, contractual joint ventures, processing of materials, construction, transfer of technology, leasing, and credit. Parties involved in these cases came from many parts of China and from the United States, Japan, Australia, Singapore, and Thailand as well as Hong Kong and Macao.

The current list of arbitrators includes 39 individuals who are named but whose nationality and residence are not provided. They are characterized as having expertise in, for example, "Industrial Property Law, Licensing" or "Private International Law" or "International Trade Law, Contract Law, Corporate Law, Arbitration." The rules and the list of arbitrators may be viewed by committee members at the AAA's Eastman Arbitration Library in New York.

D. The AAA has recently received the cooperation agreement between the China Council for the Promotion of International Trade Beijing Conciliation Centre and the Beijing-Hamburg Conciliation Centre concluded in May, 1987. It provides for conciliation of disputes between citizens of the two countries in accordance with the UNCITRAL Conciliation Rules. The text of the cooperation agreement and rules appear in Appendix D.

E. The People's Republic of China became a signatory of the International Centre for Settlement of Investment Disputes (ICSID) Convention on February 9, 1990. The Convention was signed in Washington on behalf of China by its ambassador to the United States.

The ICSID Convention, which entered into force in 1966, provides a system for the conciliations and arbitration of disputes between government and foreign investors and establishes the ICSID to administer cases brought under the Convention. The Convention was sponsored by the World Bank. Ninety-one of the 99 signatory countries have thus far ratified the Convention and become ICSID members.

At the signing, Mr. Ibrahim Shihata, the Vice President and General Counsel of the World Bank and Secretary-General of ICSID, noted that China had succeeded in the late '80s in attracting more foreign investment than any other developing country and was a founding member of ICSID's sister institution, the Multilateral Investment Guarantee Agency (MIGA).

HUNGARY

Rules of Procedure of the Court of Arbitration

The Hungarian Chamber of Commerce updated and revised the Rules of Procedure of its Court of Arbitration effective September 1, 1989.

Salient features of the Rules include:

Any person, whether a Hungarian national or foreigner, can be appointed an arbitrator who declares in writing to the Arbitration Court that he undertakes to perform the arbitrator's activity according to the present Rules of Procedure; is independent and unprejudiced and declares these facts in writing to the Arbitration Court; and commands the necessary level of legal, economic, and other knowledge to enable him to resolve disputes under the jurisdiction of the Arbitration Court.

The Arbitration Court compiles a roll of arbitrators and makes it public. Entries into the roll take place pursuant to the Statutes of the Hungarian Chamber of Commerce. The roll is drawn up for five years and shall include at least 25 and at most 150 persons. The roll may include Hungarian and foreign nationals alike and shall contain the given and family name of each arbitrator, his profession, qualifications, degree title, and language knowledge. Those requirements apply to both a presiding and a sole arbitrator.

A foreigner is eligible to be appointed presiding arbitrator if this is specified by the parties in the agreement to submit a legal dispute to arbitration.

In an arbitration based on an international convention, the foreign party may appoint a foreign national or a Hungarian national not included in the roll of arbitrators to act as an arbitrator only if the same right applies to the Hungarian party in the country of the foreign party. In an arbitration based on an international convention, the Hungarian party may appoint an arbitrator only from among Hungarians listed in the roll of arbitrators, and the presiding arbitrator or sole arbitrator may likewise be appointed only from among these persons.

In discharging their duties, the arbitrators shall be independent and unbiased and not represent either party; they must not accept instructions and shall retain in strict confidence, even after the completion of the proceedings, the circumstances they have addressed while discharging their duties.

There shall be either a tribunal of three arbitrators or a sole arbitrator. The constitution of the tribunal or the appointment of the sole arbitrator shall be determined according to the present Rules of Procedure. The functions of a three-member panel are identical with those of a sole arbitrator.

In the agreement to submit a dispute to arbitration, the parties may agree on the language of the hearings. Failing such agreement, the language of the hearings is the language of the contract, and, in the case of disputes arising from relations not covered by contract, it is the language of correspondence between the parties. If the language of the hearings cannot be identified or if the foreign party or parties are represented by a Hungarian lawyer or legal adviser, the language of the hearings will be Hungarian. The language of the record of the hearings and that of the decisions made in the course of the proceedings will be the language of the hearings. If the jurisdiction of the Arbitration Court is based on an international convention, the language of the hearings is Hungarian. With the consent of the parties the Arbitration Court may conduct the proceedings in another language. Upon the request and at the expense of the party ignorant of the language of the hearings, the Arbitration Court shall provide a suitable interpreter if the request is received by the Arbitration Court at least 14 days before the commencement of the hearings.

The Arbitration Court shall apply the law stipulated by the parties. The stipulation to a given legal system is to be understood to be a stipulation that refers directly to material law and not to the conflict law norms of the given state. Failing a stipulation by the parties, the Arbitration Court shall apply the law which it considers to be applicable according to the rules of Hungarian private international law. The Arbitration Court may render a decision on the basis of equity (ex aequo et bono) or as a friendly intermediator (amiable compositeur) only if it has been expressly authorized to do so by the parties. The Arbitration Court must make its award in compliance with the contract terms and in consideration of applicable trade customs.

Whoever has a legal interest in the outcome of the proceedings may interplead in the case in support of the party having the same interest. A request to interplead shall be submitted to the Arbitration Court at least 15 days before the day of the first hearing in the language of the hearing and in a number of copies enabling each party to be provided with one copy and the Arbitration Court with four copies. The admissibility of an interpleading shall be announced by the Arbitration Court. An interpleading can be admitted only where all parties consent.

Where no arbitration proceedings have yet been instituted, the Arbitration Court may conduct conciliatory proceedings between the parties even if the parties have not concluded an agreement to submit a dispute to arbitration. The conciliation procedure may be commenced by either party. The request shall be forwarded by the Arbitration Court to the other party, asking him to declare within 30 days whether he is ready to participate in the conciliation. If the other party does not participate in the conciliation, it shall be considered to have failed. If the parties agree, the President or Executive President of the Arbitration Court shall appoint a conciliator from the roll of arbitrators. The conciliator shall examine the documents submitted by the parties, invite the parties to an oral hearing, and propose a settlement of the dispute.

If an agreement is reached between the parties, it shall be entered in the record and signed by the parties and conciliator. Upon the request of all parties, the President or the Executive President of the Arbitration Court shall appoint the conciliator as sole arbitrator. In such cases the agreement shall be included in an arbitral award. If the conclusion of an agreement is impossible, the proceedings shall be ordered terminated. The proposal and declarations made by the parties in the course of the conciliatory proceedings shall not be binding in any arbitration which may follow the conciliation. Such declarations shall not be referred to by the parties in the course of an arbitration. Unless the parties agree, the conciliator cannot serve in the case as an arbitrator and cannot be the representative of, or advisor to, either party. The expenses of the conciliation shall be determined by the Secretariat as one fourth of the amount in the list of costs in the present Rules of Procedure. At the institution of the conciliation proceedings the parties shall each pay in advance 50 percent of the costs.

Administrative Rules Changes

The ICC recently announced the developments which follow:

1. The name of the ICC court was changed, effective June, 1989, to the ICC International Court of Arbitration.
   (a) *Court statistics:* In 1988, 304 requests were filed, an increase from 1987. The 1989 caseload should experience a slight increase. It is clear there is a growing demand for arbitration, and there is growing competition between ad hoc and institutional arbitration.
   (b) *American involvement with the court:* In 1988, U.S. parties comprised 84 of the 304 cases filed, the second greatest group after the French. However, people still do not come to the U.S. unless an American party is involved. The main block is the U.S. discovery system. When U.S. arbitrators are chosen, they are generally co-arbitrators in cases involving U.S. parties. In order to increase participation by American arbitrators, the Secretariat would be interested in receiving the names of American attorneys who have civil law training, so that these persons can be proposed in cases not involving American parties.

       Of the 15 cases placed in the U.S. in 1988, 50 percent were in New York City. Since 80 percent of cases name a place, there is a need to convince parties that the U.S. is a good site in which to hold arbitrations.
   (c) *Arbitration fees:* A working group on arbitrators' fees has been formed. It is chaired by David McGovern, Partner, Shearman & Sterling, and a member of the court. Three hundred questionnaires were sent to arbitrators and parties. The results showed the Swiss arbitrators were the most unhappy and that in the U.S. there is not a great degree of unhappiness. The final report should be available at the beginning of the year.
2. *Changes in administration of cases:* The old policy was to publish sanitized versions of awards because it is important as an example. There were various problems with the old system, and a new policy has been announced:
   1. No partial awards will be published before the case is entirely finished.
   2. Business-related elements not tied to the case will appear in the published award.
   3. In the past arbitrators sent draft of awards to the parties before advising the court. That practice is now absolutely forbidden.

Commercial Arbitration Rules of the Japan Commercial Arbitration Association

The American Arbitration Association has received the Commercial Arbitration Rules of the Japan Commercial Arbitration Association as amended and in effect May 24, 1989. Some salient provisions of the rules are noted below:

- "A party may be represented by a lawyer or such other person as shall be recognized to be justified in taking procedure under these Rules."
- The request for arbitration must include "the purpose of the request for arbitration and the reason for the request and the method of proof."
- When a request for arbitration is made by an agent, his power of attorney must be included in the filing papers.
- "No person not actually residing in Japan at the time of appointment shall, except in case [sic] where the parties have agreed otherwise, be an arbitrator."
- Where the parties have not agreed on the number of arbitrators, there shall be one unless a party requests three arbitrators and the AAA finds this request to be "appropriate."
- The tribunal shall postpone a hearing on the request of a party when it finds that postponement is "unavoidable."
- The tribunal shall not request any witness to be sworn.
- At the hearing the case administrator will take minutes of the proceedings and, upon the order of the tribunal or a petition from a party, a stenographic record.
- The award must bear the signature and the seal of each arbitrator unless the parties have agreed that reasons for the award are not necessary or where the award incorporates a settlement upon agreed terms.
- The award shall be written in Japanese. Upon the request of a party the award shall also be written in English and both versions shall be authentic. Duplicate awards shall also be issued when one arbitrator is a non-Japanese national. However, when a discrepancy in interpretation arises between the two versions, the interpretation of the Japanese language version shall prevail.
- The award will not be served upon the parties until all fees, expenses, and arbitrator compensation have been paid in full.
- The tribunal may, when a party fails to abide by its award, take "necessary measures in respect of such party."

SWITZERLAND

International Arbitration Rules of Zurich Chamber of Commerce

The Chamber has issued updated rules for international arbitrations which were effective January 1, 1989. Selected features of the rules include: recommended arbitration clauses in which the parties waive all challenges to the award pursuant to the 1988 Swiss arbitration law; the appointment of a single arbitrator for cases of less than SFr. 1,000,000 unless the parties have agreed otherwise; limited provisions for consolidation in whole or in part of multiparty or third party cases; an administrative procedure where an arbitrator contests a challenge to his service; and provisions for removal or replacement of an arbitrator after which the arbitration continues from where it halted.

C. RECENT DEVELOPMENTS

* * * * *

The United Nations Convention on the Recognition and Enforcement of Foreign Arbitral Awards

As of April 1, 1990, 81 states are parties to the convention. In 1989, Algeria, Antigua and Barbuda, Argentina, Kenya, and Lesotho ratified or acceded to the convention.

Except for Kenya, which took only the reciprocity reservation, the 1989 signatory countries took both the reciprocity and commercial reservations.

Argentina added to its instrument of ratification the following language:

> The Convention will be interpreted in accordance with the principles and clauses of the national Constitution in force or those resulting from modifications made by virtue of the Constitution.

France has withdrawn the reservation it made at the time of its ratification of the New York Convention on the Recognition and Enforcement of Foreign Arbitral Awards to apply the Convention only to those differences which are considered as commercial under French law.

The withdrawal was made by the permanent French delegation to the United Nations and was received by the General Secretary on November 27, 1989, the date on which it became effective.

The decision of the French government was embodied in Decree No. 90-170 of February 16, 1990, and in a letter from the French Ministry of Foreign Affairs of November 17, 1989, both published in the French *Journal Officiel* on February 23, 1990.

* * * * *

Agreement on the Reciprocal Encouragement and Protection of Investments Between Australia and the People's Republic of China

The Winter, 1990, issue of *News from ICSID* reports on Agreement on the Reciprocal Encouragement and Protection of Investments entered into between Australia and China on July 11, 1988. The Agreement, the first of its kind to be concluded by Australia, came into force on the date of its signature. It includes an informal dispute resolution mechanism which provides first for consultations and negotiations. If after three months the dispute has not been resolved, either party may:

> 2. (a) in accordance with the law of the Contracting Party which has admitted the investment, initiate proceedings before its competent judicial or administrative bodies; and (b) where the parties agree or where the dispute relates to the amount of compensation payable under Article VIII [concerning expropriation and nationalization], submit the dispute to an Arbitral Tribunal.
> 3. The action referred to in paragraph 2 of this Article shall be without prejudice to the right of the parties to seek assistance with regard to the dispute from any competent government agency of the Contracting Party which has admitted the investment.
> 4. In the event that both the People's Republic of China and Australia become party to the 1965 Convention on the Settlement of Investment Disputes Between States and Nationals of Other States, a dispute may be submitted to the International Centre for the Settlement of Investment Disputes for resolution in accordance with the terms on which the Contracting Party which has admitted the investment is a party to the Convention.

(Australia has announced that it will ratify the ICSID Convention.)

* * * * *

Japan Commercial Arbitration Association Report

In September, 1989, the Japan Commercial Arbitration Association (JCAA) issued a development report on the types of alternative dispute resolution it administers together with caseload data. The JCAA offers, as alternative dispute resolution modes, arbitration, conciliation, and mediation.

The basic services connected with arbitration under the JCAA arbitration rules are the receipt and transmittal of documents, organization of the arbitration tribunal, appointment of the sole arbitrator or any number of arbitrators when parties fail to appoint them, hearing rooms, stenographers, preparation of records, and deposit of the awards with the courts. In 1988, seventeen arbitration cases were administered. Four cases were filed during 1988. The 1988 cases were classified as follows: eight foreign trade (sales & purchase) including distributorship, four licensing, one designing supply and installment of equipment, one joint venture, and three trade between foreign countries.

The origins of the parties involved in the 17 cases, and the number of cases in which they were involved, are: Japan, 15 (five as claimant, ten as respondent); U.S.A., nine (four as claimant, five as respondent); Switzerland, three; Hong Kong, two; Argentina, one; Kuwait, one; West Germany, one; Holland, one; Israel, one.

Two hundred twenty-two mediation cases were filed in 1988. Almost all involved complaints brought by foreign companies against their Japanese counterparts when their contracts did not include an arbitration clause or when the amount involved was rather small, notwithstanding an arbitration clause in the contract. The JCAA treats these matters as mediations. The staff of the JCAA acts as mediator and tries to induce settlement between the parties through written communications. Since there is no legally binding background to mediation, settlement is not always effected.

Compared with mediation, conciliation is rarely used to settle international trade disputes in Japan. One of the main reasons is that although face-to-face negotiations between the parties with the intervention of a conciliator play an important role in conciliation, such face-to-face negotiation is not always available in international disputes because of the distance between the parties. Another reason is that while conciliation needs a previous agreement between the parties as arbitration does, a conciliation agreement is not usually contained in their contracts and, once a dispute has arisen, it is difficult for the parties to agree to conciliation.

In addition to the dispute resolution services, the JCAA offers consultation services to its member companies. This service includes providing information on international arbitration, providing guidance on dispute resolution, and drafting international commercial contracts with arbitration clauses. In 1988, more than 2,000 such consultations were conducted.

* * * * *

Multilateral Investment Guarantee Agency (MIGA)

MIGA is an international development organization created under World Bank sponsorship to encourage increased private direct investment in the developing world. It insures investments against certain political risks in the host country and offers tactical assistance and policy guidance to them. The agency was created under a Capital Convention which, to date, has 73 signatory states, of which 54 have ratified the Convention.

International Legal Materials, September 8, 1989, published the standard contract of guarantee. It provides that disputes between MIGA and an insured are to be resolved by arbitration in accordance with Article 3 of the General Conditions, the text of which follows:

Article 3. Dispute Resolution and Applicable Law

3.1 Any dispute between the Guarantee Holder and MIGA arising out of or in connection with the Contract (other than disputes regarding the determination of the Reference Rate of Exchange under Article 16) shall be settled by arbitration in accordance with the Arbitration Rules.

3.2 No award may require MIGA to pay to the Guarantee Holder more than the Amount of Guarantee, plus interest under Article 23, and the cost of the arbitral proceeding.

3.3 The award of the Arbitral Tribunal shall be final and binding on the parties and enforceable in any court of competent jurisdiction. The parties shall carry out the award without delay.

3.4 Subject to Section 3.5, the Arbitral Tribunal shall apply the Contract and the Convention and, to the extent that issues in dispute are not covered by the Contract or the Convention, general principles of law.

3.5 All provisions of the contract shall be presumed to be consistent with the Convention and the Operational Regulations. Such presumption may not be challenged by either MIGA or the Guarantee Holder.

* * * * *

Cooperation Agreement Between the British Columbia International Commercial Arbitration Centre and the American Arbitration Association

The AAA and the British Columbia International Commercial Arbitration Centre detailed their working relationship in March with the issuance of an agreement which supplements their prior cooperation agreement.

Under its terms both agencies stipulate to the services to be provided when an arbitration or mediation is conducted under B.C. Centre rules in the United States and when an arbitration or mediation is conducted under the AAA rules in the area served by the B.C. Centre.

The agreement also provides for the appointment of a joint committee to resolve locale disputes which are not cognizable under the procedures which govern the mediation or arbitration.

4

Legislation Dealing with Dispute Resolution

A. COMMERCIAL LEGISLATION

FEDERAL

FINANCIAL INSTITUTIONS REFORM, RECOVERY AND ENFORCEMENT ACT OF 1989

Effective August 9, 1989, H.R. 1278 was enacted into law as Public Law 101-73, 103 Stat. 183, to address the "Savings and Loan" emergency.

Title II of the law enables the Federal Deposit Insurance Corporation to contain, manage, and resolve failed savings associations. Section 212 (a) 103 Stat. at 222 (to be codified at 12 U.S.C. 1821 (d) (7) (B)) "Other Review Procedures" provides that:

(i) In General.—The Corporation shall also establish such alternative dispute resolution processes as may be appropriate for the resolution of claims.

(ii) Criteria.—In establishing alternative dispute resolution processes, the Corporation shall strive for procedures which are expeditious, fair, independent, and low cost.

(iii) Voluntary Binding or Nonbinding Procedures.—The Corporation may establish both binding and nonbinding processes, which may be conducted by any government or private party, but all the parties, including the claimant and the Corporation, must agree to the use of the process in a particular case.

(iv) Consideration of Incentives.—The Corporation shall seek to develop incentives for claimants to participate in the alternative dispute resolution process.

* * * * *

AMERICANS WITH DISABILITIES ACT

On July 26 President Bush signed into law the Americans with Disabilities Act of 1990 (S.933). The statute will, in timed stages, ultimately affect all private employers of 15 or more workers and all places of public accommodation and service. The Equal Employment Opportunity Commission is designated as the enforcement agency for the law and must issue implementing regulations by July 26, 1991.

Section 513 of Title V provides as follows:

> Where appropriate and to the extent authorized by law, the use of alternative means of dispute resolution, including settlement negotiations, conciliation, facilitation, mediation, factfinding, minitrials, and arbitration, is encouraged to resolve disputes arising under this Act.

The Joint Explanatory Statement of the Committee of Conference provides the following interpretation of section 513:

> . . . It is the intent of the conferees that the use of these alternative dispute resolution procedures is completely voluntary. Under no condition would an arbitration clause in a collective bargaining agreement or employment contract prevent an individual from pursuing their rights under the ADA. The conferees adopt by reference the statement of the House Judiciary Report regarding this provision.

* * * * *

CLEAN AIR ACT

The federal Clean Air Act, implemented by the United States Environmental Protection Agency, requires motor vehicle manufacturers to repair without charge to a customer a vehicle which fails emission tests and is covered by the required emission warranty. If the repair requires replacement of an EPA certified aftermarket part, the vehicle manufacturer may claim reimbursement for its reasonable repair costs from the aftermarket manufacturer. When these claims cannot be resolved by discussions, they must be arbitrated under AAA auspices and pursuant to the rules in Appendix II, pp. 32593–32596, of the August 8, 1989, Federal Register.

The full text of the rules follows:

20. The existing Appendix to Subpart V is designated as Appendix I and the heading is revised to read as follows:

Appendix I to Subpart V—

Recommended Test Procedures and Test Criteria and Recommended Durability Procedures to Demonstrate Compliance with Emission Critical Parameters

21. Appendix II is added to Subpart V to read as follows:

Appendix II—Arbitration Rules

Part A—Pre-Hearing

SECTION 1: INITIATION OF ARBITRATION

Either party may commence an arbitration under these rules by filing at any regional office of the American Arbitration Association (the AAA) three copies of a written submission to arbitrate under these rules, signed by either party. It shall contain a statement of the matter in dispute, the amount of money involved, the remedy sought, and the hearing locale requested, together with the appropriate administrative fee as provided in the Administrative Fee Schedule of the AAA in effect at the time the arbitration is filed. The filing party shall notify the MOD Director in writing within 14 days of when it files for arbitration and provide the MOD Director with the date of receipt of the bill by the part manufacturer.

Unless the AAA in its discretion determines otherwise and no party disagrees, the Expedited Procedures (as described in Part E of these Rules) shall be applied in any case where no disclosed claim or counterclaim exceeds $25,000, exclusive of interest and arbitration costs. Parties may also agree to the Expedited Procedures in cases involving claims in excess of $25,000.

All other cases, including those involving claims not in excess of $25,000 where either party so desires, shall be administered in accordance with Parts A through D of these Rules.

SECTION 2: QUALIFICATION OF ARBITRATOR

Any arbitrator appointed pursuant to these Rules shall be neutral, subject to disqualification for the reasons specified in Section 6. If the parties specifically so agree in writing, the arbitrator shall not be subject to disqualification for said reasons.

The term "arbitrator" in these rules refers to the arbitration panel, whether composed of one or more arbitrators.

SECTION 3: DIRECT APPOINTMENT BY MUTUAL AGREEMENT OF PARTIES

The involved manufacturers should select a mutually-agreeable arbitrator through which they will resolve their dispute. This step should be completed within 90 days from the date of receipt of the warranty claim bill by the part manufacturer.

SECTION 4: APPOINTMENT FROM PANEL

If the parties have not appointed an arbitrator and have not provided any other method of appointment, the arbitrator shall be appointed in the following manner: 90 days from the date of receipt of the warranty claim bill by the part manufacturer, the AAA shall submit simultaneously to each party to the dispute an identical list of names of persons chosen from the National Panel of Commercial Arbitrators, established and maintained by the AAA.

Each party to the dispute shall have ten days from the mailing date in which to cross off any names objected to, number the remaining names in order of preference, and return the list to the AAA. If a party does not return the list within the time specified, all persons named therein shall be deemed acceptable. From among the persons who have been approved on both lists, and in accordance with the designated order of mutual preference, the AAA shall invite the acceptance of an arbitrator to serve. If the parties fail to agree on any of the persons named, or if acceptable arbitrators are unable to act, or if for any other reason the appointment cannot be made from the submitted lists, the AAA shall have the power to make the appointment from among other members of the panel without the submission of additional lists.

SECTION 5: NUMBER OF ARBITRATORS;
NOTICE TO ARBITRATOR OF APPOINTMENT

The dispute shall be heard and determined by one arbitrator, unless the AAA in its discretion, directs that a greater number of arbitrators be appointed.

Notice of the appointment of the arbitrator shall be mailed to the arbitrator by the AAA, together with a copy of these rules, and the signed acceptance of the arbitrator shall be filed with the AAA prior to the opening of the first hearing.

SECTION 6: DISCLOSURE AND CHALLENGE PROCEDURE

Any person appointed as an arbitrator shall disclose to the AAA any circumstance likely to affect impartiality, including any bias or any financial or personal interest in the result of the arbitration or any past or present relationship with the parties or their representatives. Upon receipt of such information from the arbitrator or another source, the AAA shall communicate the information to the parties and, if it deems it appropriate to do so, to the arbitrator and others. Upon objection of a party to the continued service of an arbitrator, the AAA shall determine whether the arbitrator should be disqualified and shall inform the parties of its decision, which shall be conclusive.

SECTION 7: VACANCIES

If for any reason an arbitrator should be unable to perform the duties of the office, the AAA may, on proof satisfactory to it, declare the office vacant. Vacancies shall be filled in accordance with the applicable provisions of these rules.

In the event of a vacancy in a panel of arbitrators after the hearings have commenced, the remaining arbitrator or arbitrators may continue with the hearing and determination of the controversy, unless the parties agree otherwise.

SECTION 8: INTERPRETATION AND APPLICATION OF RULES

The arbitrator shall interpret and apply these rules insofar as they relate to the arbitrator's powers and duties. When there is more than one arbitrator and a difference arises among them concerning the meaning or application of these rules, it shall be decided by a majority vote. If that is unobtainable, either an arbitrator or a party may refer the question to the AAA for final decision. All other rules shall be interpreted and applied by the AAA.

SECTION 9: ADMINISTRATIVE CONFERENCE AND PRELIMINARY HEARING

At the request of any party or at the discretion of the AAA, an administrative conference with the AAA and the parties and/or their representatives will be scheduled in appropriate cases to expedite the arbitration proceedings.

In large or complex cases, at the request of any party or at the discretion of the arbitrator or the AAA, a preliminary hearing with the parties and/or their representatives and the arbitrator may be scheduled by the arbitrator to specify the issues to be resolved, stipulate to uncontested facts, and to consider any other matters that will expedite the arbitration proceedings. Consistent with the expedited nature of arbitration, the arbitrator may, at the preliminary hearing, establish (i) the extent of and the schedule for the production of relevant documents and other information, (ii) the identification of any witnesses to be called, and (iii) a schedule for further hearings to resolve the dispute.

SECTION 10: FIXING OF LOCALE

The parties may mutually agree on the locale where the arbitration is to be held. If any party requests that the hearing be held in a specific locale and the other party files no objection thereto within ten days after notice of the request has been mailed to it by the AAA, the locale shall be the one requested. If a party objects to the locale requested by the other party, the AAA shall have the power to determine the locale and its decision shall be final and binding.

Part B—The Hearing

SECTION 1: DATE, TIME, AND PLACE OF HEARING

The arbitrator shall set the date, time, and place for each hearing. The AAA shall mail to each party notice thereof at least ten days in advance, unless the parties by mutual agreement waive such notice or modify the terms thereof.

SECTION 2: REPRESENTATION

Any party may be represented by counsel or other authorized representative. A party intending to be so represented shall notify the other party and the AAA of the name and address of the representative at least three days prior to the date set for the hearing at which that person is first to appear. When such a representative initiates an arbitration or responds for a party, notice is deemed to have been given.

SECTION 3: ATTENDANCE AT HEARINGS

The arbitrator shall maintain the privacy of the hearings unless the law provides to the contrary. Representatives of the MOD director and any persons having a direct interest in the arbitration are entitled to attend hearings. The arbitrator shall otherwise have the power to require the exclusion of any witness, other than a party or other essential person, during the testimony of any other witness. It shall be discretionary with the arbitrator to determine the propriety of the attendance of any other person.

SECTION 4: OATHS

Before proceeding with the first hearing, each arbitrator may take an oath of office and, if required by law, shall do so. The arbitrator may require witnesses to testify under oath administered by any duly qualified person and, if it is required by law or requested by any party, shall do so.

SECTION 5: MAJORITY DECISION

All decisions of the arbitrators must be by a majority. The award must also be made by a majority.

SECTION 6: ORDER OF PROCEEDINGS AND COMMUNICATION WITH ARBITRATOR

A hearing shall be opened by the filing of the oath of the arbitrator, where required; by the recording of the date, time, and place of the hearing, and the presence of the arbitrator, the parties and their representatives, if any; and by the receipt by the arbitrator of the statement of the claim and the answering statement, if any.

The arbitrator may, at the beginning of the hearing, ask for statements clarifying the issues involved. In some cases, part or all of the above will have been accomplished at the preliminary hearing conducted by the arbitrator pursuant to Part A Section 9 of these Rules.

The complaining party shall then present evidence to support its claim. The defending party shall then present evidence supporting its defense. Witnesses for each party shall submit to questions or other examination. The arbitrator has the discretion to vary this procedure but shall afford a full and equal opportunity to all parties for the presentation of any material and relevant evidence.

Exhibits, when offered by either party, may be received in evidence by the arbitrator.

The names and addresses of all witnesses and a description of the exhibits in the order received shall be made a part of the record.

There shall be no direct communication between the parties and an arbitrator other than at oral hearing, unless the parties and the arbitrator agree otherwise. Any other oral or written communication from the parties to the neutral arbitrator shall be directed to the AAA for transmittal to the arbitrator.

SECTION 7: EVIDENCE

The parties may offer such evidence as is relevant and material to the dispute and shall produce such evidence as the arbitrator may deem necessary to an understanding and determination of the dispute. An arbitrator or other person authorized by law to subpoena witnesses or documents may do so upon the request of any party or independently.

The arbitrator shall be the judge of the relevance and materiality of the evidence offered, and conformity to legal rules of evidence shall not be necessary. All evidence shall be taken in the presence of all of the arbitrators and all of the parties, except where any of the parties is absent, in default, or has waived the right to be present.

SECTION 8: EVIDENCE BY AFFIDAVIT AND POST-HEARING FILING OF DOCUMENTS OR OTHER EVIDENCE

The arbitrator may receive and consider the evidence of witnesses by affidavit, but shall give it only such weight as the arbitrator deems it entitled to after consideration of any objection made to its admission.

If the parties agree or the arbitrator directs that documents or other evidence be submitted to the arbitrator after the hearing, the documents or other evidence shall be filed with the AAA for transmission to the arbitrator. All parties shall be afforded an opportunity to examine such documents or other evidence.

SECTION 9: CLOSING OF HEARING

The arbitrator shall specifically inquire of all parties whether they have any further proofs to offer or witnesses to be heard. Upon receiving negative replies or if satisfied that the record is complete, the arbitrator shall declare the hearing closed and a minute thereof shall be recorded. If briefs are to be filed, the hearing shall be declared closed as of the final date set by the arbitrator for the receipt of briefs. If documents are to be filed as provided for in Part B Section 9 and the date set for their receipt is later than that set for the receipt of briefs, the later date shall be the date of closing the hearing. The time limit within which the arbitrator is required to make the award shall commence to run, in the absence of other agreements by the parties, upon the closing of the hearing.

SECTION 10: REOPENING OF HEARING

The hearing may be reopened on the arbitrator's initiative, or upon application of a party, at any time before the award is made. The arbitrator may reopen the hearing and shall have 30 days from the closing of the reopened hearing within which to make an award.

SECTION 11: WAIVER OF ORAL HEARING

The parties may provide, by written agreement, for the waiver of oral hearings.

SECTION 12: WAIVER OF RULES

Any party who proceeds with the arbitration after knowledge that any provision or requirement of these rules has not been complied with and who fails to state an objection thereto in writing, shall be deemed to have waived the right to object.

SECTION 13: EXTENSIONS OF TIME

The parties may modify any period of time by mutual agreement. The AAA or the arbitrator may for good cause extend any period of time established by these rules, except the time for making the award. The AAA shall notify the parties of any extension.

SECTION 14: SERVING OF NOTICE

Each party shall be deemed to have consented that any papers, notices, or process necessary or proper for the initiation or continuation of an arbitration under these rules; for any court action in connection therewith; or for the entry of judgment on any award made under these rules may be served on a party by mail addressed to the party or its representative at the last known address or by personal service, inside or outside the state where the arbitration is to be held, provided that reasonable opportunity to be heard with regard thereto has been granted to the party.

The AAA and the parties may also use facsimile transmission, telex, telegram, or other written forms of electronic communication to give the notices required by these rules.

Part C—Award and Decision

SECTION 1: TIME OF AWARD

The award shall be made promptly by the arbitrator and, unless otherwise agreed by the parties or specified by law, no later than 30 days from the date of closing the hearing, or, if oral hearings have been waived, from the date of the AAA's transmittal of the final statements and proofs to the arbitrator.

SECTION 2: FORM OF AWARD

The award shall be in writing and shall be signed by the arbitrator, or if a panel is utilized, a majority of the arbitrators. It shall be accompanied by a written decision which sets forth the reasons for the award. Both the award and the decision shall be filed by the arbitrator with the MOD Director.

SECTION 3: SCOPE OF AWARD

The arbitrator may grant to the vehicle manufacturer any repair expenses that he or she deems to be just and equitable.

SECTION 4: AWARD UPON SETTLEMENT

If the parties settle their dispute during the course of the arbitration, the arbitrator may set forth the terms of the agreed settlement in an award. Such an award is referred to as a consent award. The consent award shall be filed by the arbitrator with the MOD Director.

SECTION 5: DELIVERY OF AWARD TO PARTIES

Parties shall accept as legal delivery of the award the placing of the award, or a true copy thereof in the mail addressed to a party or its representative at the last known address, personal service of the award, or the filing of the award in any other manner that is permitted by law.

SECTION 6: RELEASE OF DOCUMENTS FOR JUDICIAL PROCEEDINGS

The AAA shall, upon the written request of a party, furnish to the party, at its expense, certified copies of any papers in the AAA's possession that may be required in judicial proceedings relating to the arbitration.

Part D—Fees and Expenses

SECTION 1: ADMINISTRATIVE FEE

The AAA shall be compensated for the cost of providing administrative services according to the AAA Administrative Fee Schedule and the AAA Refund Schedule. The Schedules in effect at the time the demand for arbitration or submission agreement is received shall be applicable.

The administrative fee shall be advanced by the initiating party or parties, subject to final allocation at the end of the case.

When a claim or counterclaim is withdrawn or settled, the refund shall be made in accordance with the Refund Schedule. The AAA may, in the event of extreme hardship on the part of any party, defer or reduce the administrative fee.

SECTION 2: EXPENSES

The loser of the arbitration is liable for all arbitration expenses unless determined otherwise by the arbitrator.

SECTION 3: ARBITRATOR'S FEE

An arrangement for the compensation of an arbitrator shall be made through discussions by the parties with the AAA and not directly between the parties and the arbitrator. The terms of compensation of arbitrators on a panel shall be identical.

SECTION 4: DEPOSITS

The AAA may require the parties to deposit in advance of any hearings such sums of money as it deems necessary to defray the expense of the arbitration, including the arbitrator's fee, if any, and shall render an accounting to the parties and return any unexpended balance at the conclusion of the case.

Part E—Expedited Procedures

SECTION 1: NOTICE BY TELEPHONE

The parties shall accept all notices from the AAA by telephone. Such notices by the AAA shall subsequently be confirmed in writing to the parties. Should there be a failure to confirm in writing any notice hereunder, the proceeding shall nonetheless be valid if notice has, in fact, been given by telephone.

SECTION 2: APPOINTMENT AND QUALIFICATIONS OF ARBITRATOR

The AAA shall submit simultaneously to each party an identical list of five proposed arbitrators drawn from the National Panel of Commercial Arbitrators, from which one arbitrator shall be appointed.

Each party may strike two names from the list on a preemptory basis. The list is returnable to the AAA within seven days from the date of the AAA's mailing of the list to the parties.

If for any reason the appointment of an arbitrator cannot be made from the list, the AAA may make the appointment from among other members of the panel without the submission of additional lists.

The parties will be given notice by the AAA by telephone of the appointment of the arbitrator, who shall be subject to disqualification for the reasons specified in Part A, Section 6. The parties shall notify the AAA, by telephone, within seven days of any objection to the arbitrator appointed. Any objection by a party to the arbitrator shall be confirmed in writing to the AAA with a copy to the other party or parties.

SECTION 3: DATE, TIME, AND PLACE OF HEARING

The arbitrator shall set the date, time, and place of the hearing. The AAA will notify the parties by telephone, at least seven days in advance of the hearing date. Formal Notice of Hearing will be sent by the AAA to the parties and the MOD Director.

SECTION 4: THE HEARING

Generally, the hearing shall be completed within one day, unless the dispute is resolved by the submission of documents. The arbitrator, for good cause shown, may schedule an additional hearing to be held within seven days.

SECTION 5: TIME OF AWARD

Unless otherwise agreed by the parties, the award shall be rendered not later than 14 days from the date of the closing of the hearing.

SECTION 6: APPLICABILITY OF RULES

Unless explicitly contradicted by the provisions of this part, provisions of other parts of the Rules apply to proceedings conducted under this part.

* * * * *

ADMINISTRATIVE CONFERENCE

The Administrative Conference of the United States has established a roster of neutrals who may be called upon to resolve disputes arising out of federal administrative programs. The full text of the final rules follows:

List of Subjects in 5 CFR Part 316

Administrative practice and procedure, Claims, Intergovernmental relations.

Dated: September 6, 1989.
William J. Olmstead,
Executive Director.

Part 316 is added to title 1, chapter III, to read as follows:

PART 316—ROSTER OF DISPUTE RESOLUTION NEUTRALS

Subpart A—Conference Roster; Responsibilities

Sec.
316.100 Scope and purpose.
316.101 Definitions.
316.102 Administrative responsibilities.

Subpart B—Roster; Registration and Removal

316.200 The roster.
316.201 Adherence to standards.
316.202 Status of neutrals.
316.203 Registration.
316.204 Rights of persons listed on the roster.
316.205 Removal.

Subpart C—Procedures for Obtaining Names of Neutrals

316.300 Request.
316.301 Submissions of names and neutrals.
316.302 Conflict of interest; complaints.

Authority: Pub. L. 88-499, 78 Stat. 615, 5 U.S.C. 571 through 575; 31 U.S.C. 9701.

SUBPART A—CONFERENCE ROSTER; RESPONSIBILITIES

§ 316.100 Scope and purpose

These rules are issued pursuant to the Administrative Conference Act, 5 U.S.C. 571-575, providing authority to arrange for interchange among Federal administrative agencies of information potentially useful in improving administrative procedure, and to assist agencies to carry out regulatory activities and other Federal responsibilities expeditiously in the public interest. This part applies to all neutrals listed or seeking to be listed on the Roster, and to all persons or parties seeking to obtain from the Conference the names of neutrals listed on the Roster in connection with disputes involving federal administrative programs and, within the Conference's discretion, other disputes.

§ 316.101 Definitions

(a) "*Administrative program*" means any program administered by a federal agency and includes a federal function which involves protection of the public interest and the determination of rights, privileges, and obligations of private persons through rulemaking, adjudication, licensing, or investigation, as such terms are used in section 551 of title 5, U.S. Code.
(b) "*Chairman*" means the Chairman of the Administrative Conference of the United States or his designee.
(c) "*Dispute*" means any question material to a decision concerning an administrative program, or, within the Conference's discretion, any other decision about which persons who would be substantially affected by the decision or the agency disagree.
(d) "*Neutral*" means an individual who or organization which serves as a conciliator, facilitator, mediator, fact-finder, trainer, special master, or arbitrator, or otherwise functions specifically to aid the parties in resolving a dispute or portions thereof.
(e) "*Party*" means
  (1) For proceedings with designated parties, the same as in section 551(3) of title 5, U.S. Code;
  (2) For proceedings without designated parties, a person who will be significantly affected by the decision and who participates in the proceeding; and
  (3) The authorized representative of any agency charged with decisionmaking authority.
(f) "*Roster*" means a list maintained by the Chairman of persons qualified to provide services as neutrals in disputes.

§ 316.102 Administrative responsibilities

The Chairman may establish and maintain a Roster of persons to serve as neutrals in assisting parties in resolving disputes involving administrative programs and, within his discretion, other disputes. The Chairman shall have final responsibility for creation and maintenance of the Roster. The

Chairman may review the status of all persons whose continued eligibility for listing on the Roster has been questioned and make determinations about such eligibility according to the criteria set forth in § 316.205(a).

SUBPART B—ROSTER; REGISTRATION AND REMOVAL

§ 316.200 The roster

(a) The Roster shall consist of a listing of persons who provide all information required by the neutral registration form, and whose names have not been removed from the Roster in accordance with § 316.205(b).

(b) Neither the Chairman nor the Conference will warrant the accuracy of the information furnished by persons listed on the Roster.

§ 316.201 Adherence to standards

Persons listed on the Roster shall have committed in writing to comply with all provisions of part 316 and subsequent amendments hereto as from time to time may be issued by the Conference.

§ 316.202 Status of neutrals

Persons listed on the Roster are not employees of the Conference or Federal Government by virtue of their listing.

§ 316.203 Registration

(a) Persons wishing to be listed on the Roster will obtain and complete a current neutral registration form and have it notarized or otherwise attested.

(b) Upon receipt of a completed registration form, the Chairman will review the form to assure that all required information has been provided. The Chairman reserves the right to review and to verify data submitted, but any such attempts to verify submitted data will not constitute a warranty of accuracy. A prospective registrant shall be notified promptly in writing of a decision that an application is accepted, incomplete, or inaccurate. The Conference may require persons wishing to be listed to provide additional information from time to time. All decisions by the Chairman about whether a registration form is sufficiently complete and accurate are final.

(c) At least once every two years, a person listed on the Roster will either (1) submit a new registration form, or (2) send the Chairman a short letter verifying the continuing accuracy of the person's current listing.
(d) Persons wishing to be listed on the Roster must agree that the Chairman may provide the names, addresses, and telephone numbers of parties in cases handled, including all cases to which the neutral was referred as a result of listing on the Roster. They shall also certify that all data supplied are accurate and agree to abide by ethical standards that may be promulgated by the Society of Professionals in Dispute Resolution and such other standards as may be applicable to them.
(e) The Chairman reserves the right to charge fees for obtaining or renewing listing or for using the Roster.

§ 316.204 Rights of persons listed on the Roster

(a) No person shall have any right to be listed, to remain listed, nor to be referred or selected for any dispute.
(b) A person listed on the Roster may request placement on inactive status, return to active status, or removal from the Roster.
(c) Neutrals may request revision of data supplied on the neutral evaluation form, or any summaries thereof.

§ 316.205 Removal

(a) Any person may be removed from the Roster by the Chairman whenever the neutral:
  (1) Is found to have submitted materially false data in connection with registration on the Roster;
  (2) Fails or refuses to provide information required to obtain or maintain registration or to make reasonable and prompt reports, as required by Conference procedures;
  (3) Fails to disclose any information required by section 302(a);
  (4) Has been the subject of complaints of significant unethical or illegal behavior by parties who use the neutral's services as a result of referral from the Roster and the Chairman after appropriate inquiry finds just cause for removal; or
  (5) Is found by the Chairman to have improperly disclosed any record or communication arising from a proceeding without the parties' consent unless such record or communication is properly ordered to be disclosed under the agency's applicable procedural rule or by a Court of competent jurisdiction.
(b) Prior to removal under subsection (a), the Chairman shall offer the neutral 45 days in which to submit arguments and evidence relevant to the decision. Any decision to remove a neutral's name from the Roster shall be accompanied by a brief statement of reasons.

SUBPART C—PROCEDURE FOR OBTAINING NAMES OF NEUTRALS

§ 316.300 Request

Any party or parties to a dispute may file with the Chairman a written request for a list of neutrals. Telephone requests may be accepted at the Chairman's discretion. A request for the names of neutrals shall contain a brief statement of the nature of the dispute and the names, addresses, and telephone numbers of all parties to the dispute. A request form has been prepared for parties' use. Requests should be addressed to: Manager of Roster Services, Office of the Chairman, Administrative Conference of the United States, 2120 L Street NW, Suite 500, Washington, D.C. 20037. The initiating party shall also file a copy of the request with every other party to the dispute. Neither the request for, nor the furnishing of, a list of names constitutes a determination that an agreement to mediate or enter into any other dispute resolution procedure exists, nor does such action constitute any finding about the obligations of the parties.

§ 316.301 Submission of names of neutrals

(a) Upon receipt of a request for names involving a Federal administrative program, the Chairman shall ordinarily send the requester approximately the requested number of names of listed neutrals who appear to be qualified and a biographical statement for each name so provided. The Chairman may at his discretion respond to requests regarding other disputes, and may establish procedures or guidance for the purpose of providing the parties with a list of names of neutrals. If the parties cannot agree on a neutral after the receipt of these names, the Chairman may, on the request of the parties and at his discretion, select an individual either named or not named in the list sent to the parties.

(b) The Chairman reserves the right to decline to submit names if the request is unduly burdensome or otherwise impracticable.

(c) If jointly requested by all parties, the Chairman may furnish a second, or third, list of names to the parties. Requests for further lists in that dispute will not be honored.

(d) The parties shall notify the Chairman of their selection of a neutral and of the identity of the neutral selected, or of the decision not to use the services of a neutral whose name was furnished by the Conference.

§ 316.302 Conflict of interest; complaints

(a) Any person listed on the Roster who is contacted by a party to a dispute as a result of that listing must disclose to all parties to that dispute, prior to beginning dispute resolution efforts, the following interests or relationships:

(1) Any existing or past financial, business, professional, family, social, or other relationships with any of the parties to the dispute, their employees, or their attorneys;

(2) Previous or current involvement in the dispute at hand;

(3) Past or prospective employment, including employment as a neutral in previous disputes, by any of the parties;

(4) Past or present receipt of a significant portion of the neutral's general operating funds or grants to the neutral or the organization by which the neutral is employed from one or more of the parties to the dispute; or

(5) Any other circumstances likely to create a presumption of bias or the appearance of bias.

All scheduling conflicts which may prevent prompt meetings shall also be disclosed. Upon receipt of such information which results in the disqualification of a neutral either by the Chairman or upon the request of any party, the Chairman may supply to the requesting party one or more additional names from the Roster.

(b) The Chairman may inquire into complaints alleging violations of legal or ethical standards by a neutral in a case handled pursuant to Roster listing. If such allegations are confirmed, the Chairman may remove the neutral's name from the Roster and retain the complaint in the neutral's file. The Chairman retains the right to notify legal or other authorities if there is reason to believe illegal or unethical activity has occurred.

* * * * *

U.S. TAX COURT RULE 124

Effective July 1, 1990, U.S. Tax Court Rule 124 offers parties to pending cases at issue and before trial the option of jointly submitting any contested factual issue to binding arbitration.

The full text of the rule follows:

Rule 124. Voluntary Binding Arbitration

(a) **Availability**: The parties may move that any factual issue in controversy be resolved through voluntary binding arbitration. Such a motion may be made at any time after a case is at issue and before trial. Upon the filing of such a motion, the Chief Judge will assign the case to a Judge or Special Trial Judge for disposition of the motion and supervision of any subsequent arbitration.

(b) **Procedure**: (1) Stipulation Required: The parties shall attach to any motion filed under paragraph (a) a stipulation executed by each party or counsel for each party. Such stipulation shall include the matters specified in subparagraph (2).

(2) **Content of Stipulation**: The stipulation required by subparagrah (1) shall include the following:

(A) a statement of the issues to be resolved by the arbitrator;

(B) an agreement by the parties to be bound by the findings of the arbitrator in respect of the issues to be resolved;

(C) the identity of the arbitrator or the procedure to be used to select the arbitrator;

(D) the manner in which payment of the arbitrator's compensation and expenses, as well as any related fees and costs, is to be allocated among the parties;

(E) a prohibition against ex parte communication with the arbitrator; and

(F) such other matters as the parties deem to be appropriate.

(3) **Order by Court**: The arbitrator will be appointed by order of the Court, which order may contain such directions to the arbitrator and to the parties as the Judge or Special Trial Judge considers to be appropriate.

(4) **Report by Parties**: The parties shall promptly report to the Court the findings made by the arbitrator and shall attach to their report any written report or summary that the arbitrator may have prepared.

STATE

Alaska

SENATE BILL 522

In June the state enacted House Committee Substitute for Senate Bill No. 522, which requires the Alaska Judicial Council to establish and evaluate a pilot child visitation mediation project in one judicial district. The program enables persons having either custody or rights of visitation to a minor child to resolve child visitation disputes by voluntary agreement.

The law, effective July 1, 1990, and repealed February 1, 1992, provides that any party to a valid visitation order may request mediation by the council. The council will appoint a mediator who shall invite appropriate parties to a mandatory orientation session on mediation. Thereafter, any party may withdraw from the mediation.

The mediation conferences are confidential, and the mediator may not submit recommendations to resolve the dispute to a court.

* * * * *

California

CODE OF CIVIL PROCEDURE

In 1989 the state extended its judicial arbitration program to include motor vehicle collision cases in municipal courts. S.B. 167 amends section 1141.11 of the Code of Civil Procedure to provide that all civil actions pending on or after July 1, 1990, in a municipal court which has adopted judicial arbitration and involving a claim against a single defendant for damages resulting from a motor vehicle collision, other than those heard in small claims court, shall be submitted to judicial arbitration. A court-appointed arbitrator will hear the case within 120 days of the filing of the defendant's answer to the complaint.

WORKERS' COMPENSATION LAW

A workers' compensation reform plan enacted by the California legislature in September 1989 (AB276) includes a system of arbitration for certain issues and voluntary arbitration for all others. The state's program is the largest in the nation. [Editor's note: for more information, *see* Lerner, "State Legislation and Regulation Affecting Arbitration," *infra*.]

CENTER FOR INTERNATIONAL COMMERCIAL ARBITRATION

The Center for International Commercial Arbitration has moved its offices from Los Angeles to the World Trade Center in Long Beach and issued revised rules in December 1989 for conciliations and arbitrations under its auspices.

The arbitration rules are a modified version of the UNCITRAL Arbitration Rules. The center's modifications include the following:

- a detailed set of conciliation procedures which may be instituted by any party, and which will proceed upon full agreement of all other parties
- a prohibition against any discovery not authorized by the UNCITRAL Rules or otherwise agreed by the parties (for the purpose of alleviating concerns that arbitration in the U.S. will entail U.S. discovery procedures)
- a prohibition against the appointment of an arbitrator from a country of one of the parties to the dispute, unless otherwise agreed
- express clarification that the parties' choice of law for the determination of their disputes refers to the substantive law of the state, and not to its conflict of laws or procedural rules
- strictly enforced time limits for the issuance of the award following the arbitral hearing to provide an expeditious resolution
- provisions that the presiding arbitrator may make the award if there is no majority decision by the expiration of time for the making of an award (for the purpose of avoiding deadlock)
- provisions allowing the use of videotaped testimony at a hearing
- authorization under California law for legal fees awarded as costs as contemplated by the UNCITRAL Rules

The full text of the rules may be reviewed at the Association's Eastman Arbitration Library in New York.

* * * * *

Colorado

COURT-ANNEXED ARBITRATION

In 1987, the state began a pilot program of court-annexed arbitration in selected judicial districts pursuant to Section 13-22-402 *et seq.*, Colorado Revised Statutes, 1987 Repl. Vol. The law was reported in *Arbitration & the Law, 1987–1988*.

On May 14, 1990, that law was amended by H.B. 90-1067 to provide an extension of the law to July 1, 1991; to exclude specified equitable causes of action from the law; to permit parties to pay arbitrators more than the amounts in the fee guidelines as long as each arbitrator is paid the same fee; to provide that arbitrators may extend the date of hearing up to 130 days from the date that the case was at issue in extraordinary circumstances and upon good cause shown when the parties agree; to mandate that where a claimant does not better its position at the trial de novo by more than 10 percent, it shall pay attorney and arbitrator fees up to $1,500.

* * * * *

Florida

HB3429

In June, the state revised its securities law with respect to arbitration of customer-broker/dealer disputes.

HB3429 amends Sec. 517.122 F.S., first enacted in 1987, which provided that broker-dealers "may" offer AAA arbitration as an option to an industry forum. The new law, effective October 1, 1990, requires that an aggrieved customer be offered an independent nonindustry arbitration forum such as the American Arbitration Association as well as an industry forum. The full text of the newly amended section follows:

> 517.122 Arbitration—Any agreement to provide services that are covered by this chapter, entered into after October 1, 1990, by a person required to register under this chapter, for arbitration of disputes arising under the agreement shall provide to an aggrieved party the option of having arbitration before and pursuant to the rules of the American Arbitration Association or other independent nonindustry arbitration forum as well as any industry forum.

* * * * *

Georgia

MOTOR VEHICLE WARRANTY RIGHTS ACT

By enacting H.B. 1555 (SUB), "The Motor Vehicle Warranty Rights Act," Georgia joined the ranks of those states which have enacted so-called second generation lemon auto laws. The new statute amends Chapter 1 of Title 10 of the Official Code of Georgia Annotated by adding a new article 28.

The dispute resolution provisions of the law go into effect on January 1, 1991. That part of the statute which imposes a fee of $3 to be collected by a new motor vehicle dealer from a consumer upon a sale or lease of a new motor vehicle is effective July 1, 1990. The fee, less $1 for the dealer, will fund the new program.

Unlike most of the newer lemon auto laws, a "consumer," as defined in the new law, includes not only a purchaser of a motor vehicle for personal, family, or household purposes but also those sole proprietorships, partnerships, or corporations which own or lease no more than three motor vehicles and have 10 or fewer employees and a net after-tax income of

$100,000 per year or less for federal income tax purposes. "Consumer" also includes any person or entity regularly engaged in leasing new motor vehicles to consumers.

The new law empowers the state official responsible for implementing the statute to establish and operate an arbitration panel or panels under any of the following procedures: by contracting with a private or public entity to conduct arbitrations, by appointing private citizens to serve on a panel or panels, or by hiring temporary or permanent employees to serve on the panel or panels. Each panelist must have a degree from an "American Bar Association Accredited School of Law or . . . at least two years experience in professional arbitration." Each dispute must be heard by a panel of three arbitrators.

If a manufacturer has established an informal dispute resolution settlement mechanism which is operated in accordance with the rules promulgated under this article and has been certified by the state, it must first be utilized by a consumer before the dispute may be submitted to the new motor vehicle arbitration panel. A consumer must utilize both mechanisms before filing a lawsuit to benefit from the provisions of the law.

A consumer has 30 days to accept or reject the award of the panel. Upon receipt of notice of the consumer's decision, the manufacturer has 40 calendar days to comply with the award or request a trial *de novo* of the dispute in superior court. If, at the end of that period, the manufacturer has neither complied with the award nor filed its appeal, the state agency may impose a fine of up to $1000 per day until compliance is achieved or until a maximum of double the value of the vehicle or $100,000, whichever is less, accrues.

* * * * *

Maryland

MARYLAND INTERNATIONAL COMMERCIAL ARBITRATION ACT

In early May the state enacted the Maryland International Commercial Arbitration Act (H.B. 528). (The citation is Subtitle 2B to Title 3 of the Court and Judicial Proceedings Article, Annotated Code of Maryland.) It is effective July 1, 1990. A commentary on the law prepared by Frances J. Gorman of Semmes, Bowen & Semmes in Baltimore is excerpted below.

> Florida, Georgia, Hawaii, California, and Connecticut [ed.: and Texas] have adopted international commercial arbitration statutes which, in

> [his] opinion, have not taken the best course. They have adopted statutes which set different rules in their states for international commercial arbitration—different from their domestic arbitration statutes and different from United States federal law. These statutes, therefore, increase the potential for more disputes to end up in court. They do not make the law uniform; instead, these other state statutes make the law more diverse and less certain.

The following sections of the law should be noted:

Section 6 (3-2B-06) authorizes a Maryland arbitration panel hearing an international commercial arbitration to order, on the request of a party, "any other" party to post preaward security when there is good cause to require it or when the party required to post it resides in a country that has not ratified and adopted the 1958 New York Convention and does not have sufficient assets in the United States to satisfy the amount of the claim.

Section 7 (3-2B-07) permits a Maryland court to intervene in an arbitration "to correct any proceedings in conflict with the public policy of the State of Maryland" notwithstanding section 3 (3-2B-03) which provides that "in all matters relating to the process and enforcement of international commercial arbitration and awards" the laws of Maryland shall be the arbitration statutes and laws of the United States.

This section also contains, according to Mr. Gorman, a provision which is contrary to the Federal Arbitration Act in that a Maryland court, without a jury, will make any determination called for under the law. While this is consistent with existing Maryland law governing domestic arbitration, the federal statute permits a jury determination of the question of whether an arbitration agreement was made and under what conditions.

The full text of the law appears as follows:

HOUSE OF DELEGATES

01r1655 No. 528 D2

By: **Delegates Masters, Hergenroeder, Perkins, Montague, Poole, Maloney, and Ehrlich**

Introduced and read first time: January 24, 1990
Assigned to: Judiciary

Committee Report: Favorable with amendments
House action: Adopted
Read second time: March 6, 1990

EXPLANATION: CAPITALS INDICATE MATTER ADDED TO EXISTING LAW.
[Brackets] indicate matter deleted from existing law.
Underlining indicates amendments to bill.
~~Strike out~~ indicates matter stricken from the bill by amendment or deleted from the law by amendment.

CHAPTER______

AN ACT concerning

International Commercial Arbitration

FOR the purpose of enacting the Maryland International Commercial Arbitration Act; defining certain terms; specifying the purpose of this Act; establishing the governing law under certain circumstances; authorizing the circuit courts to enforce agreements and orders under this Act; establishing certain requirements for venue; permitting a party to request preaward security under certain circumstances; providing for intervention by the courts of this State under certain circumstances; establishing procedures for appeals; and generally relating to international commercial arbitration.

BY adding to
Article–Courts and Judicial Proceedings
Section 3–2B–01 through 3–2B–09 to be under the new subtitle "Subtitle 2B. International Commercial Arbitration"
Annotated Code of Maryland
(1989 Replacement Volume)

SECTION 1. BE IT ENACTED BY THE GENERAL ASSEMBLY OF MARYLAND, That the Laws of Maryland read as follows:

Article—Courts and Judicial Proceedings

SUBTITLE 2B. INTERNATIONAL COMMERCIAL ARBITRATION

3–2B–01.

(A) IN THIS SUBTITLE, THE FOLLOWING TERMS HAVE THE MEANINGS INDICATED.

(B) (1) "INTERNATIONAL COMMERCIAL ARBITRATION" MEANS AN ARBITRATION IN WHICH:

(I) ~~AT LEAST 1 OF THE PARTIES TO THE ARBITRATION AGREEMENT HAS A PLACE OF BUSINESS~~ THE RELEVANT PLACE OF BUSINESS OF AT LEAST 1 OF THE PARTIES TO THE AGREEMENT IS IN A COUNTRY OTHER THAN THE UNITED STATES; OR

(II) IF NONE OF THE PARTIES HAS A RELEVANT PLACE OF BUSINESS IN A COUNTRY OTHER THAN THE UNITED STATES, THE RELATIONSHIP BETWEEN ANY OF THE PARTIES TO AN ARBITRATION AGREEMENT INVOLVES PROPERTY LOCATED ABROAD, ENVISAGES PERFORMANCE OR ENFORCEMENT ABROAD, OR HAS SOME OTHER REASONABLE RELATION WITH 1 OR MORE FOREIGN COUNTRIES.

(2) (I) IF A PARTY HAS MORE THAN 1 PLACE OF BUSINESS, THE RELEVANT PLACE OF BUSINESS SHALL BE ~~THAT WHICH~~ THE PLACE OF BUSINESS:

1. THAT HAS THE CLOSEST RELATIONSHIP TO THE ARBITRATION AGREEMENT; OR

2. DESIGNATED BY THE AGREEMENT OF THE PARTIES.

(II) IF A PARTY DOES NOT HAVE A PLACE OF BUSINESS, THE PARTY'S HABITUAL RESIDENCE SHALL BE DEEMED THE PLACE OF BUSINESS.

(C) "ARBITRAL TRIBUNAL" MEANS A SOLE ARBITRATOR OR A PANEL OF ARBITRATORS.

3-2B-02.

THE PURPOSE OF THIS SUBTITLE IS TO:

(1) PROMOTE INTERNATIONAL COMMERCIAL ARBITRATION IN THIS STATE;

(2) ENFORCE ARBITRATION AGREEMENTS BY PARTIES IN INTERNATIONAL COMMERCIAL TRANSACTIONS;

(3) FACILITATE THE PROMPT AND EFFICIENT RESOLUTION BY ARBITRATION OF DISPUTES IN INTERNATIONAL COMMERCIAL AGREEMENTS AND TRANSACTIONS; AND

(4) PROMOTE UNIFORMITY IN THE LAW OF INTERNATIONAL COMMERCIAL ARBITRATION IN THE UNITED STATES.

3-2B-03.

(A) IN ALL MATTERS RELATING TO THE PROCESS AND ENFORCEMENT OF INTERNATIONAL COMMERCIAL ARBITRATION AND AWARDS, THE LAWS OF MARYLAND SHALL BE THE ARBITRATION STATUTES AND LAWS OF THE UNITED STATES ~~DEALING WITH ARBITRATION~~.

(B) THIS SUBTITLE SHALL BE INTERPRETED AND CONSTRUED AS TO PROMOTE UNIFORMITY IN THE LAW OF INTERNATIONAL COMMERCIAL ARBITRATION IN THE UNITED STATES.

3-2B-04.

THE CIRCUIT COURTS OF THIS STATE SHALL HAVE JURISDICTION:

(1) TO ENFORCE AGREEMENTS AND ORDERS PROVIDING FOR INTERNATIONAL COMMERCIAL ARBITRATION;

(2) TO ENTER JUDGMENTS ON ARBITRATION AWARDS; AND

(3) TO RECOGNIZE AND ENFORCE IN ACCORDANCE WITH THIS SUBTITLE ARBITRATION AWARDS RENDERED IN FOREIGN COUNTRIES.

3-2B-05.

(A) ANY ~~PETITION~~ COMPLAINT FILED IN CIRCUIT COURT WITH RESPECT TO INTERNATIONAL COMMERCIAL ARBITRATION SHALL BE FILED WITH THE COURT IN THE COUNTY:

(1) AS PROVIDED BY THE AGREEMENT; OR

(2) WHERE THE ARBITRATION HEARING WAS HELD.

(B) IF THE AGREEMENT DOES NOT PROVIDE FOR A COUNTY IN WHICH A ~~PETITION~~ COMPLAINT SHALL BE FILED OR IF THE HEARING HAS NOT BEEN HELD, THE ~~PETITION~~ COMPLAINT SHALL BE FILED WITH THE COURT IN THE COUNTY WHERE:

(1) THE ADVERSE PARTY RESIDES;

(2) HAS A PLACE OF BUSINESS OR OWNS REAL PROPERTY; OR

(3) IF THE PARTY HAS NEITHER A RESIDENCE NOR A PLACE OF BUSINESS OR PROPERTY IN THE STATE, IN BALTIMORE CITY.

3-2B-06.

(A) ~~NOTWITHSTANDING ANY OTHER PROVISION OF THIS SUBTITLE, AND~~ UNLESS THE ARBITRATION AGREEMENT PROVIDES OTHERWISE, THE ARBITRAL TRIBUNAL IN AN INTERNATIONAL COMMERCIAL ARBITRATION IN THIS STATE MAY, AT THE REQUEST OF A PARTY AND AFTER AN OPPORTUNITY FOR ANY OTHER PARTY TO THE ARBITRATION AGREEMENT TO BE HEARD, ORDER ANY PARTY TO POST SECURITY OR COUNTERSECURITY IN A FORM SATISFACTORY TO THE ARBITRAL TRIBUNAL IN AN AMOUNT NOT TO EXCEED THE AMOUNT OF THAT PARTY'S CLAIM, CROSS-CLAIM, OR COUNTER-CLAIM (EXCLUDING ATTORNEYS' FEES) IF:

(1) THE PARTY TO BE REQUIRED TO POST SECURITY OR COUNTERSECURITY RESIDES IN A COUNTRY THAT HAS NOT RATIFIED AND ADOPTED THE UNITED NATIONS CONVENTION ON THE RECOGNITION AND ENFORCEMENT OF FOREIGN ARBITRAL AWARD AND DOES NOT HAVE SUFFICIENT ASSETS IN THE UNITED STATES TO SATISFY THE AMOUNT OF THE CLAIM OR COUNTERCLAIM; OR

(2) THE ARBITRAL TRIBUNAL OTHERWISE DETERMINES THAT THERE IS ~~JUST~~ GOOD CAUSE TO REQUIRE SECURITY OR COUNTERSECURITY.

(B) (1) ON ~~PETITION~~ MOTION OF A PARTY TO A CIRCUIT COURT TO VACATE OR MODIFY AN ORDER FOR SECURITY OR COUNTERSECURITY, A HEARING SHALL BE HELD PROMPTLY.

(2) UNLESS THE PARTY REQUIRED TO POST SECURITY OR COUNTERSECURITY ESTABLISHES THAT AN ORDER FOR SECURITY OR COUNTERSECURITY IS AN ABUSE OF DISCRETION BY THE ARBITRAL TRIBUNAL, THE COURTS OF THIS STATE SHALL ENFORCE ORDERS FOR SECURITY OR COUNTERSECURITY.

3–2B–07.

(A) IN AN INTERNATIONAL COMMERCIAL ARBITRATION PROCEEDING IN THIS STATE, A COURT OF THIS STATE MAY NOT INTERVENE EXCEPT:

(1) IF PERMITTED BY THIS SUBTITLE AND THE STATUTES AND ~~LAW~~ LAWS INCORPORATED BY THIS SUBTITLE; OR

(2) IF THE PROCEEDING IS IN CONFLICT WITH THE PUBLIC POLICY OF THIS STATE.

(B) NOTWITHSTANDING ANY OTHER PROVISION OF LAW, THE COURT SHALL MAKE ANY DETERMINATION PROVIDED FOR IN THIS SUBTITLE WITHOUT A JURY.

3–2B–08.

(A) A PARTY TO AN ACTION INVOLVING INTERNATIONAL COMMERCIAL ARBITRATION MAY APPEAL:

(1) AN ORDER:

(I) REFUSING A STAY OF ANY COURT ACTION INVOLVING A MATTER REFERABLE TO ARBITRATION;

(II) DENYING A ~~PETITION~~ MOTION TO ORDER ARBITRATION TO PROCEED;

(III) DENYING APPLICATION TO COMPEL ARBITRATION;

(IV) CONFIRMING OR DENYING CONFIRMATION OF AN AWARD OR PARTIAL AWARD; OR

(V) MODIFYING, CORRECTING, OR VACATING AN AWARD;

(2) AN INTERLOCUTORY ORDER GRANTING, CONTINUING, OR MODIFYING AN INJUNCTION AGAINST ARBITRATION; OR

(3) A FINAL DECISION WITH RESPECT TO AN ARBITRATION THAT IS SUBJECT TO THIS SUBTITLE.

(B) AN APPEAL FROM THE CIRCUIT COURT IN AN ACTION INVOLVING INTERNATIONAL COMMERCIAL ARBITRATION MAY NOT BE TAKEN FROM AN INTERLOCUTORY ORDER:

(1) GRANTING A STAY OF ANY COURT ACTION INVOLVING A MATTER REFERABLE TO ARBITRATION;

(2) DIRECTING ARBITRATION TO PROCEED;

(3) COMPELLING ARBITRATION; OR

(4) REFUSING TO ENJOIN AN ARBITRATION.

3-2B-09.

THIS SUBTITLE MAY BE CITED AS THE MARYLAND INTERNATIONAL COMMERCIAL ARBITRATION ACT.

SECTION 2. AND BE IT FURTHER ENACTED, That this Act shall take effect July 1, 1990.

Approved:

_______________________________ Governor.

_______________________________ Speaker of the House of Delegates.

_______________________________ President of the Senate.

MONTGOMERY COUNTY

The County Council has enacted a law, effective January 1, 1991, which among other matters, requires parties to a dispute (other than over a valid assessment) which involves a common ownership community and an owner or member to chose mediation or an administrative hearing to resolve it. Any issue unresolved after a mediation must be sent to hearing under the auspices and pursuant to the rules of a new agency established by the law, the Commission on Common Ownership Communities.

An appeal may be taken from a decision of an administrative hearing only on the following grounds: inconsistent with applicable law; not supported by substantial evidence on the record; or arbitrary and capricious, considering all facts before the hearing panel.

The law also provides that a mediation settlement is as binding as a contract and enforceable as such.

The law may be cited as Ch. 33, Laws of Mont. Co., FY 90.

* * * * *

Minnesota

H.R. 2478

In 1990 the state legislature enacted a Taxpayers' Bill of Rights in Article 1 of H.R. 2478. Section 22 of the new law requires the Commissioner of Revenue to "study the cost, feasibility and means of implementation of . . . an arbitration procedure for resolving disputes between taxpayers and the department of revenue without court litigation. . . . The Commissioner shall report the results of the study to the legislature by January 7, 1991."

* * * * *

New Jersey

P.L. 1989, CHAPTER 277

In January, 1990, the state enacted three separate laws: one for the practice of architecture, one for the practice of engineering, and a third, the "Building Design Service Act," which establishes a Joint Committee of Architects and Engineers to deal with jurisdictional disputes between the two design professions. (P.L. 1989, Chapter 277.)

The Joint Committee is to be housed in the Division of Consumer Affairs in the Department of Law and Public Safety. It will consist of five members: two shall be architect members of the State Board of Architects, two shall be engineer members of the State Board of Professional Engineers and Land Surveyors, and the fifth shall be appointed by the governor.

The gubernatorial appointment shall be a New Jersey resident with experience as an arbitrator and shall not be a licensed architect, professional engineer, certified landscape architect, or member of a closely allied profession. The governor's appointee shall serve for a five-year term and for no more than two consecutive terms.

The Joint Committee is authorized to issue declaratory rulings which determine a building or structure's primary use group classification as a basis for professional jurisdiction. It will also hear complaints, allegations, or charges stemming from the law. The rulings are subject to judicial review in the Appellate Division of Superior Court.

* * * * *

New York

EXECUTIVE LAW

This pioneering 1989 law amends section 297(4)(a) of the Executive Law by adding new section 297(4)(a)(2), which directs the Commissioner of Human Rights to establish, in cooperation with the New York State Human Rights Advisory Committee, a voluntary arbitration procedure within the State Division of Human Rights. The Division is directed to notify the complainant and respondent of the availability of arbitration at the time of the finding of probable cause, and to provide a full description of the arbitration procedures and rights and responsibilities of the complainant and respondent during the arbitration process. This should occur prior to their signing an arbitration agreement and should include an explanation of the right of appeal and an estimate of the costs that may be incurred. To insure the selection of qualified arbitrators, the American Arbitration Association is designated to administer the arbitration program. The election to pursue a claim by arbitration divests the Division of Human Rights of jurisdiction.

A Human Rights Arbitration Advisory Committee is to be established to assist and advise the Commissioner on the design and implementation of the program.

The legislation sunsets on June 30, 1994.

CHAPTER 30, LAWS OF 1990

In 1989, the state raised the monetary threshold for arbitrations conducted in the New York City Civil Court from $6,000 to $10,000 exclusive of costs and interest. The new Ch. 30, Laws of 1990, also provides that these arbitrations shall be heard and determined by "a panel" of arbitrators.

S. 3460

A. 5374

1989–1990 Regular Sessions

SENATE-ASSEMBLY

March 7, 1989

EXPLANATION—Matter in *italics* (underscored) is new; matter in brackets [ ] is old law to be omitted.

IN SENATE—Introduced by Sen. VELELLA—read twice and ordered printed, and when printed to be committed to the Committee on Judiciary

IN ASSEMBLY—Introduced by M. of A. KAUFMAN—read once and referred to the Committee on Judiciary

AN ACT to amend the New York city civil court act and the civil practice law and rules, in relation to raising the monetary threshold in the civil court of the city of New York for referral to the alternative method of dispute resolution by arbitration program established by the chief administrator of the courts

The People of the State of New York, represented in Senate and Assembly, do enact as follows:

Section 1. Subdivision (c) of section 206 of the New York city civil court act, as added by chapter 523 of the laws of 1965, is amended to read as follows:

(c) Arbitration distinct from CPLR article 75. The rules may provide systems of arbitration and conciliation of claims within the court's jurisdiction without reference to CPLR article 75. *Where the chief administrator of the courts has provided by rule for an alternative method of dispute resolution by arbitration and has established by order this arbitration program in any county in this court, applicable in each such county to civil actions for a sum of money only, except those commenced in small claims parts and not subsequently transferred to a regular part of court, that on or after the effective date of such order are noticed for trial or commenced in this court, all such actions shall be heard and decided by a panel of arbitrators where the recovery sought for each cause of action is ten thousand dollars or less, exclusive of costs and interest.*

§ 2. Rule 3405 of the civil practice law and rules, as added by chapter 156 of the laws of 1978, is amended to read as follows:

Rule 3405. Arbitration of certain claims. The chief judge of the court of appeals may promulgate rules for the arbitration of claims for the recovery of a sum of money not exceeding six thousand dollars, exclusive of interest, pending in any court or courts *except the civil court of the city of New York, and not exceeding ten thousand dollars, exclusive of interest, pending in the civil court of the city of New York*. Such rules must permit a jury trial de novo upon demand by any party following the determination of the arbitrators and may require the demander to pay the cost of arbitration; and shall also provide for all procedures necessary to initiate, conduct and determine the arbitration. A judgment may be entered upon the arbitration award. The rules shall further provide for the recruitment and qualifications of the arbitrators and for their compensation. All expenses for compensation, reimbursement and administration under this rule shall be a state charge to be paid out of funds appropriated to the administrative office for the courts for that purpose.

§ 3. This act shall take effect on the sixtieth day after it shall have become a law and the new monetary threshold of ten thousand dollars established in subdivision (c) of section 206 of the New York city civil court act as amended by section one hereof shall apply only to such actions as are noticed for trial or commenced on or after the effective date of this act.

* * * * *

Texas

WORKERS' COMPENSATION ACT

Texas has joined California in offering claimants and insurers a system to resolve workers' compensation by providing options of alternative dispute resolution.

On December 12, 1989, a special session of the Texas legislature enacted a new Workers' Compensation Act. The law, S.B. 1, provides, in Article 6, for "benefit review conferences, contested case hearing, arbitration and appeals within the agency" related to workers' compensation claims.

The new law became effective January 1, 1990. The arbitration provisions in Chapter C are effective January 1, 1992. The Workers' Compensation Commission will adopt rules for arbitration and mediation.

Upon agreement of parties, and after the first step in the process has been taken, binding arbitration may be selected as an alternative to administrative hearings. The Commission will maintain regional lists of arbitrators who shall be its employees, although private arbitrators may also be used when a special need is shown. Arbitrators must be members of the National Academy of Arbitrators, and "be included on an approved list of the American Arbitration Association or the Federal Mediation and Conciliation Service" or meet qualifications established by the Commission. An arbitrator must be approved by at least two Commission members representing employers and at least two Commission members representing wage earners. Arbitrators' performance will be reviewed annually.

The law further provides for the education and training in mediation for benefit review officers, Commission employees who will be responsible for guiding parties through the new system. They will assist parties in the procedures and conduct benefit review conferences, which are the first steps in the claims process.

If unresolved issues remain after benefit review conference, the parties may mutually agree to arbitration. Arbitration may be used only "to resolve disputed benefit issues and is an alternative to a contested case hearing." The arbitration is "binding and irrevocable on all parties for the resolution for all disputes arising out of the claims that are under the jurisdiction of the Commission."

The arbitration procedures permit each party one strike from a list of panelists—replacement nominees may not be struck—and only one adjournment of hearing.

The award is a final, binding order of the Commission and may be vacated only upon a court's finding that the award was procured by corruption, fraud, or misrepresentation; the award was arbitrary and capricious; or the award was outside the jurisdiction of the Commission. If the award is vacated, the case is to be remanded to the Commission for another arbitration.

COMMENTARY

Judicial Improvement and Access to Justice Act*

Robert Coulson

The Judicial Improvement and Access to Justice Act, recently adopted by Congress, contains 10 titles. This article will discuss the four titles that concern arbitration and that express congressional support for its use.

Title I created a Federal Courts Study Committee, charged with developing a long-range plan for the federal judiciary, including how best to use alternative methods of dispute resolution. This committee is already at work. Among the matters being considered are the appropriate role for judges and magistrates in the settlement of civil suits, the creation of court administered mediation and arbitration programs and the relationship between judges and private neutrals who serve under mediation, rent-a-judge, arbitration, or referee programs.

A difficult task indeed! Federal trial judges have independent views on the subject. Most judges strongly support the use of alternative dispute resolution; a few have responded to ADR with as much enthusiasm as they have towards a skunk in their basement. Most judges take pride in being able to persuade attorneys to settle; some are reluctant to engage in settlement discussions. Most judges like arbitration; a minority remain skeptical. The Federal Arbitration Act was supposed to erase any remaining hostility toward arbitration, but a few federal judges still resent the idea that arbitrators can decide disputes without having to give reasons. Nevertheless, as the federal courts recognize the need to expedite the process, ADR will become even more necessary.

Two Different Functions

Even definitions can be a source of controversy. The American Arbitration Association provides training in ADR to many state judges and retired judges. It is not unusual for judges to view "mediation" as an opportunity to tell the parties how to settle, or to define "arbitration" as a Solomonic technique for helping the parties to reach a mutual compromise. These perceptions are at odds with reality. Private sector mediators expect the parties to hammer out their own settlement. A mediator does not "tell" the parties how to settle. Arbitrators, in contrast, are expected to consider the

---

* Copyright 1989. The New York Law Publishing Co. Reprinted with permission of the *New York Law Journal* (June 8, 1989). Robert Coulson is President of the American Arbitration Association.

evidence and the arguments, then decide the case. Mediation is compromise. Arbitration is decision.

The committee will have to decide whether ADR should be provided by the courts or obtained from agencies in the private sector. Court-administered arbitration programs can be mandatory, but their determinations cannot be legally binding. Parties have a right to their day in court, so they must be given the right to a trial de novo. Private arbitration is based upon contract, but the awards can be binding. Which is preferable? Why not give the parties a choice? Free choice is the hallmark of a democratic society.

In addition to providing ADR under the auspices of the courts, as has been done through court-annexed arbitration, summary jury trials, and the like, courts can order counsel to consider ADR under private auspices. The Southern District of New York has carried out a pilot program under which individual judges order the trial attorneys to confer with the AAA as to whether particular ADR processes might help resolve their dispute. Similar programs are being considered in other jurisdictions.

If the Federal Courts Study Committee recommends private ADR, other questions arise. Should federal districts certify a pool of mediators and arbitrators? Or should each federal trial judge be free to select mediators directly or to obtain them from an appropriate referral agency?

Judges need to be informed about those choices. The relevant facts in business litigation have become increasingly complex and technical, frequently beyond the intellectual capacity of a juror or even the normal expertise of a trial judge. To bring a higher level of expertise to the decision-making process, significant changes could be made in court procedures. Among the options are the appointment of expert lay adjudicators, greater use of impartial experts, or the creation and use of superjuries. A trial judge may not have access to such people. Here again, the AAA, which maintains a large national panel of experts, can be helpful.

Types of Disputes

To reduce the calendar of the federal courts, the Study Committee must also identify types of disputes that can be relegated to the state courts. Many federal judges would like to eliminate jurisdiction over diversity cases.

Title II of the act, entitled Diversity Reform, takes a step in that direction. At present, a party can remove civil cases from state courts when the amount in controversy is more than $10,000. Title II would increase that figure to $50,000, relieving federal trial courts of many relatively minor commercial matters. The act also provides that insurance carriers are deemed to be citizens of the state in which their insured is a citizen.

To the extent that large numbers of claims must now remain in state court, Title II will have a favorable impact upon the use of arbitration clauses. Corporations are reluctant to defend themselves in state courts, particularly in the claimant's jurisdiction. A corporation can designate a more hospitable locale by using an arbitration clause, specifying that the Federal Arbitration Act will apply, to avoid the possibility that a state court might apply state arbitration law under the doctrine recently established by the U.S. Supreme Court in *Volt Information Sciences, Inc. v. Board of Trustees of Leland Stanford Junior University*, No. 87-1318 (March 6, 1989), *The Arb. Journal*, Vol. 44, No. 2, p. 47 (1989).

Title IX of the act doubles the number of districts authorized to create court-annexed arbitration systems by court rule, from 10 to 20. Since civil cases under $50,000 and claims against insurance carriers will now be retained in state courts, the extension of court-annexed arbitration to more federal courts will have less impact.

Court-annexed systems in the federal courts make arbitration mandatory for certain types of cases, but the arbitration awards are not binding. Courts can refer actions to arbitration whenever the parties consent, and they can require such referral when the relief sought consists only of money damages, not in excess of $100,000, exclusive of interest and costs.

Among the actions not to be referred to arbitrators are claims based on alleged violation of a constitutional right or where the case involves complex or novel legal issues. The existing 10 federal arbitration programs have resolved large numbers of cases. Some cases may have been removed from state courts, on the basis of diversity. Now, those cases will remain in state courts.

Court-annexed arbitration encourages settlement by requiring parties to submit their dispute to a panel of lawyers, who are authorized to render an award. A party who is not satisfied by the amount of the award can demand a trial de novo. In practice, many cases are settled long before they would have been decided by litigation.

Title X of the act contains an amendment to the Federal Arbitration Act, Title 9, United States Code, adding a new section 15 providing that an appeal may be taken from an order refusing to stay an action pending arbitration; denying a petition to order arbitration; confirming or denying confirmation of an award; correcting, modifying, or vacating an award or any final decision with respect to an arbitration, but that no appeal may be taken from orders compelling arbitration or granting a stay of litigation, pending arbitration. This is a positive development. According to Richard Medalie, this amendment establishes order in an area of federal practice that has been marked by uncertainty, based on outmoded distinctions between actions at law and suits in equity. *The New Appeals Amendment: A Step Forward for Arbitration*, Richard J. Medalie, *The Arb. Journal*, Vol. 44, No. 2 (1989). Appellate courts may not review orders enforcing arbitration but must allow an appeal when trial courts stand in the way of arbitration.

This confirms the decision in *Gulfstream Aerospace Corp. v. Mayacamas Corp.*, 108 S. Ct. 1133 (1988), which barred appeals from the granting or denial of motions to compel arbitration except with the permission of the court.

Under this section, a party who unsuccessfully opposes arbitration has to proceed to an award and then either move to vacate or oppose the other side's motion to confirm the award. This should reduce the burden of unnecessary preliminary litigation.

At least one circuit has already used the new provision. In *Delmay v. Paine Webber, Inc.* (11th Cir. March 8, 1989), the court reinstated an appeal of an order denying arbitration, noting the "broad national concerns in the proper functioning of the judicial process and in the pursuit of alternate dispute resolution techniques."

Overall, the Judicial Improvement and Access to Justice Act shows the continuing support by Congress of arbitration as a primary dispute resolution technique. This is consistent with the positive attitude of the federal courts. In a recent Supreme Court decision, *Rodriguez de Quijas v. Shearson/American Express*, __U.S.__, 109 S. Ct. 1917 (1989), the U.S. Supreme Court reasserted its commitment towards the enforcement of agreements to arbitrate. That decision overturned *Wilko v. Swan*, 346 U.S. 427 (1953).

> To the extent that *Wilko* rested in a suspicion of arbitration as a method of weakening the protections afforded in the substantive law to would-be complainants, it has fallen far out of step with our current strong endorsement of the federal statutes favoring this method of resolving disputes [109 S. Ct. at 1920].

Four Justices dissented, but only because the *Wilko* doctrine had not been revoked by Congress. In his dissenting opinion, Justice Stevens noted the "valid policy and textual arguments on both sides regarding the interrelation of federal securities and arbitration Acts." There is no indication that the dissenting justices do not continue to favor the liberal use of arbitration.

State Legislation Affecting Arbitration Law*

Richard E. Lerner

One of the most interesting developments in state lawmaking in this area over the past three years has been a trend among individual states to enact

---

* Richard E. Lerner is Associate General Counsel of the American Arbitration Association.

legislation regulating international commercial arbitrations conducted within their borders. The Florida International Arbitration Act, passed in 1986, was followed in 1988 by similar laws in California, Georgia, and Hawaii and this year in Connecticut and Texas. This trend may well have been inspired by the issuance in 1985 by the United Nations Commission on International Trade Law (UNCITRAL) of a Model Law on International Commercial Arbitration. (The full text of each law discussed here is available on request from the author.)

The Model Law is one of three contributions of UNCITRAL to the development of a fair and efficient process of resolving disputes in international commercial transactions. One of the goals of the Model Law is to foster an acceptable worldwide uniform set of procedures and, to that end, experts representing all regions of the world and all legal and economic systems were involved in its formulation.

The Model Law, approved by the UN General Assembly, was intended for enactment by sovereign states, but six American states have not let that deter them from passing their own international arbitration laws, some of them versions close to the Model Law. While it may, at first, seem unusual for states to legislate on international matters that are the province of the federal government, it is evident from the statements of purpose of these laws that they derive, in part, from a desire to promote arbitrations within the state and to provide an environment conducive to international business and trade. Statutory provisions for resolution of disputes between domestic and foreign business, it is believed, will help to achieve that end.

Use of the Model Law

In some of the states where international commercial arbitration laws were recently enacted, legislators used the Model Law as a ready source of the content of their own statutes. Some observers question whether a law intended for adoption by independent nations can be effectively adopted by American states.

For example, Connecticut's international arbitration law is an almost verbatim copy of the UNCITRAL Model Law. Indeed, section 37 of that state statute reads, "This act may be cited as the UNCITRAL Model Law on International Commercial Arbitration." California and Texas also patterned their recent arbitration laws after the Model Law, but less closely than did Connecticut. A major departure from the Model Law is the inclusion of a chapter on conciliation in the California and Texas statutes to encourage that mode of dispute resolution. The conciliation provisions cover the essential aspects in a detailed manner, and here California seems to have set the pattern for other states. Notably absent from the California and Texas statutes are the provisions on Recourse Against Award and

Recognition and Enforcement of Awards found in the Model Law. Otherwise, except for some added provisions in the state laws regarding interim measures of protection and grounds for challenging the arbitrator, the three versions are very similar.

The Model Law and its American derivatives base the scope of their application on place of business. Parties subject to these international arbitration laws must have their place of business in different states, with all of the United States considered one state. As an alternative criterion of eligibility, both parties can have their places of business in the same state, but the arbitration site specified in the arbitration agreement or the obligation of the commercial relationship must be located in another state.

Florida, Georgia, and Hawaii, on the other hand, focus on residence of the parties to determine the reach of their international arbitration laws. If none of the parties resides outside the United States, these international arbitration laws are still applicable where the dispute involves property outside the U.S. or arises from a contract to be performed abroad.

The Florida law is not a carbon copy of the Model Law. However, it is equally detailed and covers many of the same points in its own sequence. An important provision relates to awards made in foreign currency. These must be stated by the court in equivalent U.S. currency when confirming an award.

Latitude in Hawaii

The international arbitration law enacted by Hawaii vests extensive authority to administer arbitration proceedings in centers, defined as independent nonprofit educational corporations, established mainly for that purpose. A center is given wide latitude to carry out its functions, including the right to establish arbitration tribunals that can determine the relevance of evidence, subpoena witnesses, make awards, and obtain court assistance. Parties to an arbitration administered by a center are free to select the rules that will govern their case. When a party does not reside in a country that is a signatory to the New York (UN) Convention, it may be required to post a bond to assure enforcement of an award. This requirement may have an inhibiting effect on the siting of arbitrations in Hawaii. The Hawaii law does not offer new approaches to the arbitral process; its uniqueness lies in the empowerment of centers to oversee arbitration.

The Georgia law includes provisions on the language to be used in the arbitration, use of expert testimony, and the role of the courts, but it is much less comprehensive than the UNCITRAL Model Law. Like the latter, the Georgia statute states that an award is binding provided that "it is not contrary to the public policy of [the] state with respect to international transactions." In all likelihood, that Georgia public policy has yet to be formulated.

Jurisdiction

By contrast with the state laws on international arbitration enacted to date, the Federal Arbitration Act, Chapter 2 of title 9 U.S.C. is comprised of only eight short sections. Its major provisions set forth the conditions under which international commercial disputes may be subject to its reach, establish which courts have proper jurisdiction, and establish their role in compelling arbitration and in confirming awards. It does not detail the various aspects of international commercial arbitration included in the Model Law. Rather, the federal statute provides that all proceedings are subject to the laws and treaties of the United States.

Because of the efficacy of the Federal Arbitration Act, the continued support of the federal courts, including the U.S. Supreme Court, and American arbitration practice, some U.S. attorneys have concluded that the most efficient and effective mode of international commercial arbitration would be that administered by the AAA, conducted under AAA or the UNCITRAL Arbitration Rules, and subject to federal arbitration law. They base their findings on considerations of speed, neutrality, reasonable costs, and the availability of benign and limited, but effective, judicial support that may be more important than particular rules.

The future of the United States as a site for international commercial arbitrations depends, in part, on the parties and their attorneys' perceptions of the legal regime of arbitration. While New York City remains the most favored American locale for such proceedings, the intent of the states that have enacted their laws on international commercial arbitration has been to induce parties to arbitrate within their borders. The success of such efforts cannot, of course, be assessed at present.

Summaries of some new state laws of interest to the bar follow.

Connecticut

As noted above, effective October 1, Connecticut joins the ranks of other states that enacted laws affecting international commercial arbitration. The statute, embodied in House Bill 7413, which became Public Act 89-179, is entitled the UNCITRAL Model Law on International Commercial Arbitration.

Features of the new law that will be of interest to American attorneys include section 26, which permits arbitrators to appoint experts on specific issues unless the parties have agreed otherwise; section 32, which requires arbitrators to order an end to the arbitration when its continuation has "become unnecessary or impossible"; and section 33, which deals with postaward matters, frequent references to the prominent role of Connecticut law and public policy.

Florida

Effective January 1, 1988, committee substitute for House Bill No. 379 authorized and structured a state court-annexed program of mediation and binding and nonbinding arbitration. Pursuant to rules to be issued by the Supreme Court, any civil action or a part of it, pending in a circuit or county court, may be referred to an Alternate Dispute Resolution (ADR) process.

When a party demands a trial de novo after a nonbinding arbitration and the result is "not more favorable" than the award, it shall be assessed the arbitration and court costs and other reasonable costs of the other party including an attorney's fee, investigation expenses, and expenses for expert or other testimony evidence incurred after the arbitration unless a court finds that such assessment would create a substantial economic handicap or would not be in the interest of justice.

The provisions for court-annexed "voluntary arbitration" are applicable to all "civil disputes" not involving a constitutional issue when the parties submit. Unlike other similar statutes, the Florida Evidence Code applies to these arbitrations, and appeal is limited to a review on the record in which the "harmless error doctrine shall apply." No further judicial review is permitted unless a constitutional issue is raised.

Hawaii

On June 7, 1988, the state enacted H.B. No. 2003, which adds a new section to the Hawaii Revised Statutes. The law, effective on passage, is entitled the Hawaii International Arbitration, Mediation and Conciliation Act.

The statute encourages the formation of private nonprofit dispute-resolution centers to administer cases under their rules or any others upon which the parties may agree.

Effective September 7, 1988, the state amended sections of its lemon auto law by enacting H.B. 2037. The new law requires, among other matters, that manufacturers, their agents, distributors, or authorized dealers advise consumers of a state-certified arbitration program and requires the Director of the Department of Commerce and Consumer Affairs to establish such a program that may be implemented by a nongovernmental agency.

The association was appointed the program administrator for a one-year term. Awards issued under the program are neither final nor binding, but financial disincentives are provided for parties who demand a trial de novo but do not "improve their position" after trial by at least "25 percent."

Louisiana

In July, 1988, Louisiana enacted H.B. No. 1554, which restructured a term of arbitration clauses in automobile manufacturer-dealer sales and service agreements. The law, which enacted R.S. 32:1256.1, requires that Lousiana be the venue of an arbitration under such agreements and that the arbitration shall not be inconsistent with Louisiana law.

Montana

In 1989, Montana amended its general arbitration law (§ 27-5-114, MCA *et seq.*) by enacting two laws: S.B.79 and S.B.363.

S.B.79, which adds subsection (3) to section 27-5-114, reads as follows:

> A written agreement between members of a trade or professional organization to submit to arbitration any controversies arising between members of the trade or professional organization after the agreement is made is valid and enforceable except upon such grounds as exist at law or in equity for the revocation of a contract.

S.B.363 revokes subsection 2(c) of section 27-5-114, which excluded from the reach of the law

> any contract by an individual for the acquisition of real or personal property, services, or money or credit where the total consideration to be paid or furnished by the individual is $35,000 or less . . .

New York

New York moved in a pioneering direction in 1988 in S.9207/A.11980, which adds new article 15-A to the Executive Law. This act established the Governor's Office of Minority and Women's Business Development to ensure that "a fair share" of state contracts are awarded to "minority and women-owned businesses," for contracts with state agencies effective on or after September 1, 1988. The act further requires the office to maintain a list of businesses certified as minority- and women-owned. Disputes over noncompliance with the act are initially referred to the director of the office for resolutions. If the director cannot resolve the complaint within 30 days, the act provides that it will be referred to the American Arbitration Association. The act specifies the dispute resolution procedures to be followed and that the award will be final pursuant to Article 75 C.P.L.R.

In August, 1988, the state amended its lemon auto law, subdivision 1 of general business law section 198-A by enacting L. 1988 Ch. 489. It authorizes a court to award reasonable attorneys' fees to a prevailing consumer in an action arising out of an arbitration under the state's alternative arbitration mechanisms. The mechanism is administered for the state Department of Law by the American Arbitration Association.

This month, the state again amended the lemon auto law to include used cars. A subdivision of section 198-B of the general business law provides, effective January 1, 1990, that all used car dealers who sell three or more such cars annually must provide to the purchaser a written warranty that permits him to seek a refund through the dealer's ADR mechanism or the state-approved alternative.

Vermont

In 1988, Vermont passed S. 319, which amended 16 V.S.A. 2941 *et seq.*, the law respecting the public education of handicapped children. Section 2959 of the new law, effective July 1, 1989, provides that subject to rules of the state Board of Education the Commissioner of Education shall offer mediation to parents, handicapped children, and districts and agencies involved in special education disputes.

Washington

In 1989, the state of Washington enacted H.B. 1103, which amends RCW 19.118.021 *et seq.*, the lemon auto law.

Highlights of the new law include permitting the arbitrator to levy sanctions against a party or to continue the arbitration to allow for failure to comply with a subpoena; allowing the board 45 calendar days from receipt to hold a hearing with the option to continue for 10 days and retaining the 60-day maximum to issue a decision; and allowing the refund to consumers of costs and attorney fees but only when a manufacturer was also represented.

State Legislation and Regulations Affecting Arbitration*

Richard E. Lerner

The flexibility of arbitration and other alternate dispute resolution mechanisms is amply demonstrated by the new laws and implementing regulations discussed below. Running the gamut from workers' compensation systems to human rights complaints to HMO subscriber grievances, these enactments show that new contexts in which informal dispute processes are utilized continue to appear.

While it is premature to identify the use of mediation and arbitration in workers' compensation claims procedures as a trend, it is not too early to bring the California and Texas statutes as well as the Connecticut program to the attention of the bar.

California

A workers' compensation reform plan enacted by the California legislature in September, 1989 (AB276) includes a system of arbitration for certain issues and voluntary arbitration for all others. The state's program is the largest in the nation. However, the arbitration provisions may be invoked only when the claimant is represented by counsel.

Under section 44 of the law, effective January 1, 1991, arbitration is mandated to resolve three categories of disputes. First, issues regarding the existence and the scope of insurance coverage. Second, contributions to awards by several defendants who are jointly and severally liable and must work out proportional shares of an award. And third, permanent disability claims that involve either a 15 percent or less disability and the presiding judge is unable to set a hearing within 110 calendar days from the date of application, or a disability of 20 percent or less and a scheduling minimum of 150 calendar days. The permanent disability sections are effective January 1, 1991, and sunset on January 1, 1994.

Voluntary use of arbitration may cover any controverted workers' compensation issue.

The parties to a dispute submitted to arbitration initially mutually select a panelist from a list of available arbitrators. If the parties cannot agree, either may request the workers' compensation judge to submit a list of five

---

* Copyright 1990. The New York Law Publishing Company. Reprinted with permission of the *New York Law Journal* (March 22, 1990). Richard E. Lerner is Associate General Counsel of the American Arbitration Association.

arbitrators selected at random from the panel. Of the five persons on a list submitted to the parties, no more than three defense attorneys or applicant's attorneys are allowed, and no more than two may be retired workers' compensation judges or appeals board members. Each party may strike two names and may also petition the presiding judge to remove a name from the list. The judge then chooses another eligible name to be placed on the list.

Lists of persons who are eligible and interested in serving as arbitrators will be maintained by workers' compensation judges at each district office. Qualified compensation arbitrators must be "active members of the California State Bar Association and certified specialists in workers' compensation, retired workers' compensation judges or appeals board members."

Claimants must be represented by counsel before opting for arbitration of their claim. Although the Department of Industrial Relations does not officially advise unrepresented employees to seek counsel and thus become eligible for arbitration, employees will be informally advised by the department staff who initially guide applicants through the claims procedure. Claimants must proceed directly to a judge's consultation, which would likely include a suggestion to secure counsel. A list of state certified workers' compensation specialists will be provided to interested claimants, as it is now.

Under the new law arbitrators have the statutory and regulatory duties and responsibilities of a workers' compensation judge, with two exceptions: arbitrators have no power to order disabled employees to be examined by a qualified medical evaluator, and arbitrators do not have the power to impose penalties for contempt of court.

In employer-employee disputes, all costs of the arbitration proceeding, including the arbitrator's compensation, are paid by the employer. For all other disputes, payment of costs of the arbitration proceeding varies: for arbitration of any dispute between an employer and an insurer, or an employee or former employee and a lien claimant, payment is shared equally by the parties. Where there is no dispute as to the injury causing an employee death, the dependents must pay costs in accordance with their proportionate share of death benefits.

If parties cannot agree upon a date, time, or place for arbitration proceedings, the arbitrator schedules them. Arbitration proceedings are to be commenced not less than 30 or more than 60 days from the date an arbitrator is selected, unless the parties agree otherwise.

Ten days before the arbitration, each party must submit to the arbitrator, and serve on the opposing party, all documentary evidence on which that party intends to rely. The arbitrator's findings and award are due to the parties within 30 days of submission of the case for decision. The arbitrator's decision shall have the same force and effect as if rendered by a workers' compensation judge. If an arbitrator fails to issue a decision within

30 days after hearing, the arbitrator's fee is forfeited and the submission order and all stipulations shall be vacated.

Arbitration awards are appealable.

Texas

Texas has joined California in offering claimants and insurers a system to resolve workers' compensation claims by providing options of alternative dispute resolution.

On December 12, 1989, a special session of the Texas legislature enacted a new Workers' Compensation Act. The law, S.B.1. in Article 6, provides for "benefit review conferences, contested case hearings, arbitration, and appeals within the agency" related to workers' compensation claims.

The new law became effective January 1, 1990. The arbitration provisions in Chapter C are effective January 1, 1992. The Workers' Compensation Commission will adopt rules for arbitration and mediation.

Upon agreement of parties, and after the first step in the process has been taken, binding arbitration may be selected as an alternative to administrative hearings. The Commission will maintain regional lists of arbitrators who shall be its employees, although private arbitrators may also be used when a special need is shown. Arbitrators must be members of the National Academy of Arbitrators, and "be included on an approved list of the American Arbitration Association or the Federal Mediation and Conciliation Service" or meet qualifications established by the commission. An arbitrator must be approved by at least two commission members representing employers and at least two commission members representing wage earners. Arbitrators' performance will be reviewed annually.

The law further provides for the education and training in mediation for benefit review officers: commission employees who will be responsible for guiding parties through the new system. They assist parties in the procedures and conduct benefit review conferences, which are the first step in the claims process.

If unresolved issues remain after a benefit review conference, the parties may mutually agree to arbitration. Arbitration may be used only "to resolve disputed benefit issues, and is an alternative to a contested case hearing." The arbitration is "binding and irrevocable on all parties for the resolution for all disputes arising out of the claims that are under the jurisdiction of the Commission."

The arbitration procedures permit each party one strike from a list of panelists; replacement nominees may not be struck. And only one adjournment of hearing may be granted to a party.

The award is a final, binding order of the commission and may be vacated only upon a court's finding that the award was procured by corruption, fraud, or misrepresentation, the award is arbitrary and capricious, or the award was outside the jurisdiction of the commission. If the award is vacated, the case is to be remanded to the commission for another arbitration.

Connecticut

Claimants and insurers in Connecticut facing extensive delays in resolving workers' compensation claims now have the option of resolving their cases in an alternative dispute resolution forum.

The American Arbitration Association's (AAA) Connecticut Workers' Compensation ADR Referral Program, effective October, 1989, was developed in consultation with the Connecticut Workers' Compensation Commission, insurance companies, and members of the defense and plaintiff's bar. The program offers parties a choice of arbitration, mediation, and a new process combining mediation and fact-finding, to facilitate prompt, fair, and cost-effective settlements.

The program is not limited to specific issues. Rather, the AAA will be guided by the parties' agreement on a case-by-case basis. As an example, a provisional list prepared by a participating insurer includes the following issues: occupational disease or repetitive trauma claims involving multiple carriers and/or multiple employers; multiple injuries involving more than one carrier or employer resulting in an issue of apportionment; Second Injury Fund cases, specifically involving relief under sections 31–49; disposition of a workers' compensation lien in tort cases where the employer or carrier is being asked to compromise or waive its lien; discharge or discrimination cases pursuant to alleged violations of section 31-290A; and cases in which, while the duty to compensate has been accepted, issues of causal relation or the extent of disability have arisen.

Prior to this program workers' compensation claims were heard solely by officers of the commission; in many cases, parties had to reschedule hearings several times before obtaining closure. The commission is empowered under the new program to permit parties to bring their cases before an AAA neutral. Employees are usually represented by counsel when opting for an ADR decision.

Attorneys with extensive experience in workers' compensation law are selected by the AAA to serve as arbitrators and mediators in the new program. Upon submission of a claim to the commission's alternate dispute resolution procedures, parties will receive a list of panelists, with a biographical profile of each member, from which the neutral will be selected. Neutrals are selected by mutual agreement of the parties; if they cannot agree on a neutral, the AAA will suggest additional names.

Neutrals do not have the broad and final powers of the commission members. The neutral must facilitate a settlement either through mediation or arbitration, which is then submitted to the commission for final approval.

In addition to mediation or arbitration, the program introduces a new dispute resolution procedure. In mediation-fact-finding, or "med-fac," the mediator of a case that has reached an impasse may issue a report that evaluates the parties' positions and recommends a solution. Parties may agree to use this report in any subsequent ADR or court proceeding.

The program's goal is to schedule a hearing within 30 days after a neutral has been selected. The AAA charges a fee of $150 per party for submission of a claim to ADR. The neutral's per diem fee is shared equally by the parties.

Minnesota

In September, 1989 the State Department of Health adopted regulations relating to HMO's Quality Assurance processes (Part 4685.1700). The regulations include requirements for HMO internal complaint systems, which mandate several stages and culminate in arbitration under the auspices of the American Arbitration Association.

The first stage in the complaint process calls for continuing communications between the complainant and HMO staff after the filing of a written complaint. Within 30 days thereafter, a written decision must issue. If the decision is partially or wholly adverse to the complainant, three options are available. A written reconsideration or internal hearing, arbitration, or appeal to the Health Commissioner.

If arbitration is selected, it must be conducted under the AAA Minnesota Health Maintenance Organization Arbitration Rules, which are incorporated by reference in the regulation.

Copies of the rules are available without charge from the writer.

New York

This pioneering 1989 law amends section 297(4)(a) of the Executive Law by adding new section 297(a)(2), which directs the Commissioner of Human Rights to establish, in cooperation with a new New York State Human Rights Advisory Committee, a voluntary arbitration procedure within the State Division of Human Rights. The Division is directed to notify the complainant and respondent of the availability of arbitration at the time of the finding of probable cause, and to provide them with a full description of the arbitration procedures and the rights and responsibilities of the complainant and respondent during the arbitration process. The notification should occur prior to their signing an arbitration agreement and should include an explanation of the right of appeal and an estimate of the costs that may be incurred. To ensure the selection of qualified arbitrators, the American Arbitration Association is designated to administer the arbitration program. The election to pursue a claim in arbitration divests the Division of jurisdiction.

The law sunsets on June 30, 1994.

Oregon

In 1989, the state amended its general arbitration law, ORS33.210, to provide that disputes relating to title to real estate are arbitrable. The only nonarbitral matter that remains is a dispute over the terms or conditions of employment under collective contracts between employers and employees and associations of employees.

The AAA's Office of General Counsel is often asked to serve as a technical resource in the drafting of laws and regulations dealing with arbitration and other dispute resolution processes. Those services are available to *New York Law Journal* readers on request.

5

New Rules

International Arbitration Rules of the World Arbitration Institute

A current project of the World Arbitration Institute, a program of the American Arbitration Association, is the development of new international arbitration rules designed to facilitate administered arbitration of international commercial disputes. A copy of the third draft of such rules, which continue to evolve, follows.

Introduction

The world business community needs a comprehensive international system to facilitate arbitration of disputes arising in the global marketplace. Supportive laws are already in place. The New York Convention of 1958 has been widely adopted, providing a favorable legislative climate for the use of arbitration in international commercial contracts. Arbitration clauses are enforced. International commercial arbitration awards are recognized by national courts in most parts of the world, even more than foreign court judgments.

Arbitration agencies and institutes have been established in many countries. These organizations administer international cases, and have entered into cooperative arrangements with each other and with the American Arbitration Association.

To encourage greater use of such services, these Arbitration Rules of the World Arbitration Institute have been developed. By providing for arbitration under these Rules, parties can avoid the uncertainty of having to petition a local court to resolve procedural impasses.

These Rules are intended to provide effective arbitration services to world business through the use of administered arbitration, utilizing a network of professional administrative agencies in various countries.

Parties can arbitrate future disputes under these Rules by inserting the following clause in their contracts:

"Any controversy or claim arising out of or relating to this contract shall be determined by arbitration in accordance with the International Arbitration Rules of the World Arbitration Institute and judgment upon the award rendered by the arbitrator(s) may be entered in any court having jurisdiction thereof."

It is recommended that parties agree in advance whether to use one or three arbitrators, that they designate the country in which they wish to arbitrate, and that they specify the language of the proceedings.

When a dispute arises, parties are encouraged to request a conference, in person or by telephone, with the World Arbitration Institute, or its designated representative, to discuss an appropriate method for the selection of mutually agreeable arbitrators and any other matters that might facilitate the efficient arbitration of the dispute.

Under these Rules, the parties are free to adopt any mutually agreeable procedure for appointing their arbitrators. If the parties are unable to agree on such a procedure, the World Arbitration Institute, after consulting with them, will appoint the arbitrators.

Prior to arbitrating, parties may wish to consider the possibility of mediation. This too can be discussed with the World Arbitration Institute, which is prepared to arrange for mediation services anywhere in the world.

Further information about these Rules can be secured from the World Arbitration Institute at 140 West 51st Street, New York, New York 10020-1203; (212) 484-4000.

International Arbitration Rules of the World Arbitration Institute

Article 1

1. Where parties have agreed in writing to arbitrate disputes under these International Arbitration Rules, the arbitration shall take place in accordance with their provisions, as in effect at the date of filing, subject to whatever modifications the parties may adopt in writing.
2. These Rules govern the arbitration, except that where any such Rule is

in conflict with any provision of the applicable law from which the parties cannot deviate, that provision shall prevail.

3. These Rules specify the duties and responsibilities of the administrator, the World Arbitration Institute. The administrator may provide support services through facilities of a network of administrative agencies in various countries.

I. COMMENCING THE ARBITRATION

Notice of Arbitration and Statement of Claim

Article 2

1. The party initiating arbitration ("claimant") shall give written notice of arbitration to the administrator and to the parties against whom a claim is being made ("respondents").
2. Arbitral proceedings shall be deemed to commence on the date on which the notice of arbitration is received by the administrator.
3. The notice of arbitration shall include the following:
   (a) a demand that the dispute be referred to arbitration;
   (b) the names and addresses of the parties;
   (c) a reference to the arbitration clause or agreement that is invoked;
   (d) a reference to any contract out of or in relation to which the dispute arises;
   (e) an initial description of the claim;
   (f) the relief or remedy sought; and may include proposals as to the number of arbitrators, the country in which the arbitration should take place and the language of the proceedings, if the parties have not previously agreed thereon.

Upon receipt of such notice, the administrator will communicate with all parties, acknowledging the initiation of the arbitration.

Statement of Defense

Article 3

1. Within thirty days after the date of filing, a respondent shall file a statement of defense in writing with the claimant and any other parties, and with the administrator for transmittal to the tribunal when appointed. A respondent shall respond to the administrator, the claimant and other parties within thirty days as to any proposals the

claimant may have made as to the number of arbitrators, the place of arbitration or the language of the proceedings.

2. A respondent may make counterclaims or assert set-offs as to any claim covered by the agreement to arbitrate, to which the claimant shall reply within thirty days.
3. If no defense to a claim is filed, it will be assumed that the claim is denied.

Amendments to Claims

Article 4

During the arbitral proceedings, any party may amend or supplement its claim or defense, unless the tribunal considers it inappropriate to allow such amendment because of the party's delay in making it or prejudice to the other parties or any other circumstances. A claim may not be amended if the amendment would fall outside the scope of the arbitration agreement.

II. THE TRIBUNAL

Number of Arbitrators

Article 5

If the parties have not agreed on the number of arbitrators, one arbitrator shall be appointed unless the administrator, in its discretion, determines that three arbitrators should be appointed.

Appointment of Arbitrators

Article 6

1. The parties may mutually agree upon any procedure for appointing arbitrators and shall inform the administrator as to such procedure.
2. The parties may mutually agree on the designation of arbitrators, with or without the assistance of the administrator. When such designations are made, the parties shall notify the administrator so that notice of the appointment can be communicated to the arbitrators, together with a copy of these Rules.
3. If within thirty days of the filing of the claims and counterclaims the parties have not reached agreement on the method for selecting ar-

bitrators, or if a party has failed to designate an arbitrator which it has agreed to designate, the administrator, in its discretion and at the request of any party, shall make the appointments.

4. In making such appointments, the administrator, after consulting with the parties, will endeavor to select knowledgeable and impartial arbitrators. At the request of either party, consideration will be given to the appointment of arbitrators who are nationals from a country other than that of any of the parties.

Challenge of Arbitrators

Article 7

Prior to accepting appointment, a prospective arbitrator shall disclose to the administrator any circumstance likely to give rise to justifiable doubts as to the arbitrator's impartiality or independence. Once appointed, an arbitrator shall disclose any additional such information to the parties and to the administrator. Upon receipt of such information from any source, the administrator shall communicate it to the parties and, if appropriate, to the arbitrator.

Article 8

1. A party may challenge any arbitrator whenever circumstances exist that give rise to justifiable doubts as to the arbitrator's impartiality or independence.
2. A party wishing to challenge an arbitrator shall send notice of the challenge to the administrator within fifteen days after being notified of the appointment of the challenged arbitrator, or within fifteen days after the circumstances giving rise to the challenge became known to that party.
3. The challenge shall be in writing and shall state the reasons for the challenge.
4. When an arbitrator has been challenged by one party, the other parties may agree to the acceptance of the challenge. The challenged arbitrator may also withdraw from office. In neither case does this imply acceptance of the validity of the grounds for the challenge.

Article 9

1. If the other parties do not agree to the challenge or the challenged arbitrator does not withdraw, the decision on the challenge shall be made by the administrator in its sole discretion.

2. If the administrator sustains the challenge, a substitute arbitrator shall be appointed pursuant to the provisions of Article 6.

Replacement of an Arbitrator

Article 10

1. If an arbitrator shall be unable or unwilling to perform the duties of the office, the administrator may, on proof satisfactory to it, declare the office vacant. A substitute arbitrator shall be appointed pursuant to the provisions of Article 6.

Article 11

If a vacancy occurs on a tribunal after the proceedings have commenced, the remaining arbitrators may determine whether it is appropriate to continue with the arbitration.

III. GENERAL CONDITIONS

Representation

Article 12

Any party may be represented by counsel or other authorized representative. The names, addresses and telephone numbers of such persons shall be communicated in writing to the other parties and to the administrator. Once the tribunal has been established, the representatives may communicate in writing directly with the tribunal, with copies to the administrator and other parties.

Place of Arbitration

Article 13

1. If the parties disagree as to the country and place where arbitration is to be held, the country and place shall be determined by the administrator. If the parties have agreed on the country, but not upon a place within the country, that place shall be determined by the administrator, subject to the discretion of the tribunal to vary the place at any stage of the proceeding. If the place of the proceedings has not been agreed

upon by the parties or determined by the administrator, the tribunal will make that determination. All such determinations shall be made having regard for the contentions of the parties and the circumstances of the arbitration.

2. The tribunal may hold conferences or hear witnesses or inspect property or documents at any place it deems appropriate. The parties shall be given sufficient written notice to enable them to be present at any such proceedings.

Language

Article 14

If the parties have not agreed on the language of the arbitration, the administrator shall determine the language or languages to be used in the proceedings, having regard for the contentions of the parties and the circumstances of the arbitration. The tribunal may order that any documents delivered in their original language, shall be accompanied by a translation into such language or languages.

Pleas as to Jurisdiction

Article 15

1. The tribunal may rule on its own jurisdiction, including any objections with respect to the existence or validity of the arbitration agreement.
2. The tribunal may determine the existence or validity of the contract which is the subject of an arbitration clause. Such an arbitration clause shall be treated as an agreement independent of the other terms of the contract.
3. Objections to the arbitrability of a claim or counterclaim must be raised no later than the statement of defense as to that claim.

Article 16

1. The tribunal may conduct the arbitration in whatever manner it considers appropriate, having the widest discretion allowed under the applicable law to ensure a just and expeditious determination of the dispute, provided that each party is given a fair opportunity to present its case.
2. Documents or information supplied to the tribunal by one party shall at the same time be communicated by that party to the other parties.

Further Written Statements

Article 17

The tribunal may decide whether any written statements, in addition to statements of claims and the statements of defense, shall be required from the parties or may be presented by them, and shall fix the periods of time for filing such statements.

Periods of Time

Article 18

The periods of time fixed by the tribunal for the communication of written statements should not exceed thirty days. However, the tribunal may extend such time limits if it considers such an extension justified.

Notices

Article 19

Any notices or process necessary or proper for the initiation or continuation of an arbitration under these Rules may be served on a party by registered mail addressed to the party or its representative at the last known address or by personal service. Facsimile transmission, telex, telegram, or other written forms of electronic communication may be used to give any such notices required by these Rules.

Evidence and Hearings

Article 20

1. The tribunal may order a party to deliver to the tribunal and to the other parties a summary of the documents and other evidence which that party intends to present in support of its claim, counterclaim or defense.
2. At any time during the proceedings, the tribunal may order parties to produce such other documents, exhibits or other evidence as it deems necessary or appropriate.

Article 21

1. The tribunal shall give the parties thirty days' advance notice of the date, time, and place of any oral hearings to be held.

2. At least fifteen days before the hearing, each party shall give the tribunal and the other parties the names and addresses of any witnesses it intends to present and the subject of their testimony.
3. At the request of the tribunal or pursuant to mutual agreement, the parties shall make arrangements for the interpretation of oral testimony or for a record of the hearing.
4. Hearings are private unless the parties agree otherwise or the law provides to the contrary. The tribunal may require any witness or witnesses to retire during the testimony of other witnesses. The tribunal may determine the manner in which witnesses are examined.
5. Evidence of witnesses may also be presented in the form of written statements signed by them.
6. The admissibility, relevance, materiality, and weight of the evidence offered by any party shall be determined by the tribunal.

Interim Measures of Protection

Article 22

1. At the request of any party, the tribunal may take whatever interim measures it deems necessary in respect of the subject-matter of the dispute, including measures for the conservation of the goods which are the subject-matter in dispute, such as ordering their deposit with a third person or the sale of perishable goods.
2. Such interim measures may be taken in the form of an interim award and the tribunal may require security for the costs of such measures.
3. A request for interim measures addressed by a party to a judicial authority shall not be deemed a waiver of the right to arbitrate.

Experts

Article 23

1. The tribunal may appoint one or more independent experts to report to it, in writing, on specific issues designated by the tribunal. Unless agreed otherwise, the costs for same shall be borne equally by the parties.
2. The parties shall provide such an expert with any relevant information or produce for inspection any relevant documents or goods that the expert may require. Any dispute between a party and the expert as to the relevance of the requested information or goods shall be referred to the tribunal for decision.
3. Upon receipt of an expert's report, the tribunal shall send a copy of

the report to all parties, who shall be given an opportunity to express, in writing, their opinion on the report. A party may examine any document on which the expert has relied in such a report.

4. At the request of any party, the parties shall be given an opportunity to question the expert at a hearing.

Default

Article 24

1. If a party, duly notified under these Rules, fails to appear at a hearing, the tribunal may proceed with the arbitration.
2. If a party, duly invited to produce evidence, fails to do so within the time established by the tribunal, the tribunal may make the award on the evidence before it.

Closure of Hearing

Article 25

1. After asking the parties if they have any further testimony or evidentiary submissions and, if satisfied that the case is complete, the tribunal may declare the proceedings closed.
2. If it considers it necessary, on its own motion or upon application of a party, the tribunal may reopen the proceedings at any time before the award is made.

Waiver of Rules

Article 26

A party who knows that any provision of the Rules has not been complied with, but proceeds with the arbitration without promptly stating an objection in writing thereto, shall be deemed to have waived the right to object.

Decisions

Article 27

1. When there are three arbitrators, any award or decision of the arbitral tribunal shall be made by a majority of the arbitrators.

2. When the parties or the tribunal so authorize, decisions on questions of procedure may be made by the presiding arbitrator.

Form and Effect of the Award

Article 28

1. Awards shall be made in writing, promptly by the tribunal, and shall be final and binding on the parties. The parties undertake to carry out any such award without delay.
2. The tribunal shall state the reasons upon which the award is based, unless the parties have agreed that no reasons need be given.
3. An award signed by a majority of the arbitrators shall be sufficient. The award shall contain the date and the place where the award was made. The award shall be deemed to have been made at that place.
4. An award may be made public only with the consent of all parties or as required by law.
5. Copies of the award shall be communicated to the parties by the administrator.
6. If the arbitration law of the country where the award is made requires the award to be filed or registered, the administrator shall comply with such requirement.
7. In addition to making a final award, the tribunal may make interim, interlocutory, or partial orders or awards.

Applicable Laws

Article 29

The tribunal shall apply the laws designated by the parties as applicable to the dispute. Failing such a designation by the parties, the tribunal shall apply such law or rules of law as it determines to be appropriate.

Settlement or Other Reasons for Termination

Article 30

1. If the parties settle the dispute before the award is made, the tribunal shall terminate the arbitration and, if requested by all parties, record the settlement in the form of an award on agreed terms. The tribunal is not obliged to give reasons for such an award.

2. If the continuation of the proceedings becomes unnecessary or impossible for any other reason, the tribunal may inform the parties of its intention to terminate the proceedings. The tribunal may thereafter issue an order terminating the arbitration.

Interpretation or Correction of the Award

Article 31

1. Within fifteen days after the receipt of an award, any party, with notice to the other parties, may request the tribunal to interpret the award or correct any clerical, typographical, or computation errors.
2. If the tribunal considers such a request justified, after considering the contentions of the parties, it shall comply with such a request within thirty days after the request.

Costs

Article 32

The tribunal shall fix the costs of arbitration in its award. The tribunal may apportion such costs among the parties if it determines that such apportionment is reasonable, taking into account the circumstances of the case. Such costs may include:

(a) the fees and expenses of the arbitrators;
(b) the costs of experts and of other evidence required by the tribunal;
(c) the fees and expenses of the administrator;
(d) the reasonable costs for legal representation of the successful party.

Compensation of Arbitrators

Article 33

Arbitrators shall be compensated based upon their amount of service, taking into account the size and complexity of the case. An appropriate daily or hourly rate, based on such considerations, will be arranged by the administrator with the parties and the arbitrators prior to the commencement of the arbitration. If the parties fail to agree on the terms of compensation, an appropriate rate shall be established by the administrator and communicated in writing to the parties.

Deposit of Costs

Article 34

1. When claims are filed, the administrator may request the filing party to deposit appropriate amounts, as an advance for the costs referred to in Article 32, paragraphs (a), (b), and (c).
2. During the course of the arbitral proceedings, the tribunal may request supplementary deposits from the parties.
3. If the deposits requested are not paid in full within thirty days after the receipt of the request, the administrator shall so inform the parties, in order that one or the other of them may make the required payment. If such payments are not made, the tribunal may order the suspension or termination of the proceedings.
4. After the award has been made, the administrator shall render an accounting to the parties of the deposits received and return any unexpended balance to the parties.

Confidentiality

Article 35

Confidential information disclosed during the proceedings by the parties or by witnesses shall not be divulged by an arbitrator. All records, reports, and other documents received by the tribunal shall be deemed confidential.

Exclusion of Liability

Article 36

Neither the members of the tribunal nor the administrator shall be liable to any party for any act or omission in connection with any arbitration conducted under these Rules.

Interpretation of Rules

Article 37

The tribunal shall interpret and apply these Rules insofar as they relate to its powers and duties. All other rules shall be interpreted and applied by the administrator.

GENERAL INDEX

TABLE OF CASES

STATUTORY AND JURISDICTIONAL INDEX

FEDERAL

STATE

IONAL

RULES

OTHER

TABLE OF CASES

STATUTORY AND JURISDICTIONAL INDEX

FEDERAL

STATE

INTERNATIONAL

RULES

OTHER